GuitarPlayer
Presents

CARLOS SANTANA

GuitarPlayer
Presents

CARLOS
SANTANA

· ·

Edited by Michael Molenda

Backbeat
Books

An Imprint of Hal Leonard Corporation
New York

Portions of this book are adapted from articles that originally appeared in *Guitar Player* magazine, 1970–2008.

Published in cooperation with Music Player Network,
New Bay Media, LLC, and *Guitar Player* magazine.
Guitar Player magazine is a registered trademark of
New Bay Media, LLC.

Published in 2010 by Backbeat Books
An Imprint of Hal Leonard Corporation
7777 West Bluemound Road
Milwaukee, WI 53213

Trade Book Division Editorial Offices
19 West 21st Street, New York, NY 10010

Printed in the United States of America

Book design by Damien Castaneda

Library of Congress Cataloging-in-Publication Data is
available upon request.

ISBN 978-0-87930-976-3

www.backbeatbooks.com

CONTENTS

PREFACE

The commercial music business can be a cesspool of vicious ambition, broken dreams, dashed hopes, rampant unfaithfulness, and outright dishonesty. It can destroy hearts and minds, and it can toss fragile artists into an emotional morass so far removed from a Norman Rockwell view of life that many never recover. Drugs. Alcohol. Divorce. Death. Isolation. Rehab. You've read all the sordid stories, and witnessed the destruction on reality television and episodes of VH1's *Behind the Music*. Dante's *Inferno* has nothing on the music biz.

And yet, through four decades of cultural tumult and renewal—in a career that spans from Woodstock to Warped Tours, Vietnam to Iraq, Reaganomics to the treachery of Bernie Madoff, print media to Twitter, and beyond—Carlos Santana has wielded his guitar like a lightsaber of bliss. Every note he frees from his strings is bathed in joy, spirituality, and passion, and he plays for *you*. He avoids ego, embraces the Divine, and allows his heart, rather than his head, to direct his fingers, his tone, and his soaring melodicism. He is also an exuberant seeker of knowledge who finds beauty in all music, from Miles Davis and John Coltrane, to the Beatles and the Beach Boys, to Green Day and Mastodon.

This cheerful open-mindedness has not been without risk. Some people have viewed Santana's spiritualism, his sojourn as a disciple of Sri Chinmoy, and his gentle evangelical bent as too much heavenly woo-woo when all they want to hear is the man play his guitar. But Santana has always been authentic—even to the point of admitting that Frank Zappa may have addressed the phrase "Shut Up and Play Your Guitar" to him—and he has never shied away from expressing who he is as a musician and as a planetary citizen. This is a very successful and reasonably contented man who has also fallen, failed, and faced despair, and those experiences remain a part of his every bend, trill, lick, riff, and melodic run. In this way, Santana is as much a bluesman as a pop star, although—to use his own words—he "paints with a different brush."

In this book, you'll absorb many of the elements that make Carlos Santana a legendary guitarist—well, at least the bits that can be set down on ink and paper. Through his many *Guitar Player* interviews, you'll get exhaustive insights into what drives his creativity, where he derives the foundation of his musicality, what tools he uses to get his transcendent tone, and much more. The *Guitar Player* lessons—crafted by master transcriptionists Jesse Gress and Andy Ellis—reveal explicit "physical" keys to Santana's melodic and harmonic approaches.

Santana has been a longtime friend of *Guitar Player*. On many occasions, he has publicly stated that it's one of his favorite publications. The magazine itself has often been blessed with incredible writers who hold vast knowledge and enthusiasm for guitarcraft, and this volume collects unabridged Santana interviews from 1970 to 2008 by some of the best: Fred Stuckey, Michael Brooks, Dan Forte, Jas Obrecht, James Rotondi, Andy Ellis, Jesse Gress, Darrin Fox, and Gary Brawer.

As you'll (hopefully) see, the intense collaboration between a magnificent artist who trusts his interviewers, and talented authors who voraciously dig into the mysteries of tone, technique, and creativity delivers an extraordinary degree of depth and musical intimacy. It's like standing behind a magician and seeing the architecture of magic. Enjoy!

Michael Molenda
Editor in Chief, *Guitar Player*

Many thanks to all the writers and editors who have made Guitar Player *the preeminent publication for obsessed guitarists since 1967. I also want to salute my mom, my family, my friends, and Cheryl Doll—all of whom help "keep the music in me" (apologies to Kiki Dee).*

INTERVIEWS

1.

"MUSIC IS LOPSIDED IF YOU JUST PLAY FOR YOURSELF"

by Fred Stuckey, June 1970

One phenomenon of contemporary music is the incredible speed with which rock groups can climb out of obscurity and into multimillion-dollar success stories. The best example I can think of is the recent emergence of a San Francisco band bearing the last name of a guitar player bred in the backstreets of Tijuana, a tawdry border town between California and Mexico.

Santana's first album, surprisingly entitled *Santana*, has sold somewhere in excess of a million copies and is still selling. How many musicians can claim a platinum record for their first effort? Not many.

Unlike most rock bands, Santana's hit tune "Evil Ways" is being played on both AM and FM radio, on both Top-40 and underground radio. Santana has caught the attention of the "bubble gum," commercial rock audiences as well as the sophisticates of rock among underground audiences. The musical qualities unique to Santana are elusive and not easily identifiable. But the band has something that most everybody can get into.

Getting to Carlos Santana, the band's leader and lead-guitar player, was a hassle. I had to wind through a maze of promoters, booking agents, managers, secretaries, and friends. I finally talked with Carlos at the band's rehearsal studio in the exclusive Pacific Heights district of San Francisco. The location of the studio in that high-rent neighborhood didn't fit with my preconception of the band's character. I remembered Santana as the group of brown, black, and white street musicians playing to Fillmore West audiences with the exuberance and abandon of America's hip youth. After the difficulty of getting to the band, I was expecting arrogant and jiving rock "stars."

Carlos Santana is well-spoken and hospitable. He is preoccupied with the band's music, and would rather play it than talk about it. Like most rock musicians, he approaches music from an emotional rather than an academic level. He said: "The most spectacular things I play are when I'm not programmed to play a certain thing, but when I'm free to play what I feel."

At 22, Carlos is successful, but he doesn't think much about it. He has no pretentions about being the most polished and professional of guitar players. But he is serious about what he does, and he plays hard. On stage, he writhes and grimaces to the music, hunching his shoulders and rolling his head from side to side. As he nods back and forth, his long, bushy black hair fans the air.

Carlos recently switched to a 1962 Gibson SG guitar. About the guitar and strings he said in slightly broken English: "I take my guitar to this cat who treats guitars just like you treat a woman. He uses an instrument that takes measurements in millimeters to adjust the strings the way I like it. I like my strings to lie up from the fretboard—you know, not too close. A little while ago, I switched to Ernie Ball Super Slinky strings. I found out that with those strings you can bend notes without breaking your fingers. On my other guitar, I use Gretsch strings. They're harder, and they produce more bass."

Rhythm is the cornerstone of Santana's sound. Incorporating Latin and Afro percussion instruments into the overall sound, Carlos added Mike Carabello on congas, Jose Chepito Areas on Timbales, and Mike Shrieve on drums. Powerful and complex rhythms frame the solos of Carlos on guitar and Gregg Rolie on organ. Dave Brown carries the bass lines.

I asked Carlos about his Mexican origins and Santana's heavy reliance on rhythm. "When I was a kid I listened to Latin music, but I really wasn't all that turned on by it. I dug more rock and roll and blues—you know, Chicago blues. Latin music, if you know how to control it and keep from overstating it—and can keep from letting it get boring—can make rock music very exciting. It's a part of what we play. In our music there's a lot of Latin and Afro rhythms going on. Some rhythms, like 6/8 time, we use to lead us into Afro rhythms. The timbales and conga players put down those rhythms as the bottom of the sound."

Listening to the tempo, Carlos bends and punches his guitar notes to complement the time scheme, and to build the music into crescendos and climaxes. He lends continuity to the rising and falling quality of Santana's tunes by repeating riffs at strategic points. Good examples of the way Carlos uses note patterns to signal breaks in the rhythm are the tracks "Waiting" and "Jingo" on the *Santana* album.

"The most spectacular things I play are when I'm not programmed to play a certain thing, but when I'm free to play what I feel."

Carlos talked about his picking technique. "The way I pick depends on what chops I'm doing in any particular song. On some chops, you can play like an acoustic guitar with the palm of your hand resting on the bridge. On some funky things, you can't rest your hand on anything—particularly on rhythm or chord things. I use a triangular, elastic nylon pick. They don't bend, and they'll last you forever if you don't lose them."

At key points, Carlos holds single notes through chord changes and shifts in tempo. He gets a sustaining, distorted sound out of his guitar. He said: "It feels really good to hold a note for days, to control the feedback on just one beam of power. Sometimes, the way you can hold a note depends on how you set the Tone and Volume controls on the guitar and amp—I use Fender amplifiers—and that depends on the size of the hall. To get a sustained or distorted sound, I don't necessarily use a fuzz tone. I can get that same sound with a broken speaker in an amp, and it sounds better."

Basing his solo riffs around the blues scale, Carlos owes his early influences to American music.

"I first started playing the old Top-40 stuff—the old rhythm and blues tunes like 'Blue Moon.' Then I got into B. B. King. I used to play on Revolution Street in Tijuana. Some of the brothers used to come down from San Diego, and we would play blues stuff in small clubs down there.

"In Mexico, I played the violin for six years. I worked through some heavy music books with songs like 'Poet and Peasant' in them—really intricate classical stuff. Playing the violin taught me how to hold notes when somebody else is playing, when to play and when not to play— what to play and what not to play. Right now, I want to learn more about music so I can contribute more of me to it."

Carlos was part of the early San Francisco underground rock scene. He guested as lead guitarist on a blues track on the *Adventures* album recorded live at the Fillmore West by Mike Bloomfield and Al Kooper. We talked about the fading distinction between commercial and under-ground rock. I asked Carlos how he felt about having a Top-40 hit.

"You know, I met the other guys in the band on the streets in San Francisco. We were just jamming around. In those days, we were playing what a lot of people are playing now—hard rock and blues and Cream-style things. About Top-40 stuff, I want to give and take with music. If I just play for myself and people don't relate to me, then I'm not saying what I want to say. Music is lopsided if you just play for yourself. You've got to play what people want to hear, too."

No question that Santana plays what rock audiences want to hear.

Still preoccupied with the day's rehearsing and staring off across the room, Carlos told me how Santana comes up with material.

"When we put together a tune, somebody comes in with an idea, and we all work on it. We don't play from charts. All of us contribute to put-ting a song together, and somehow we feel closer that way. When every-body can play the notes and feelings that are his, then everybody feels happier about them when we play them onstage. The notes and feelings have to be your own. The chops you play that you have created come across as being warmer than the notes that somebody tells you to play. Like on a song, when I feel that the whole thing is solid, and the rhythm is there, and everyone is relating to everyone else, then I can take off. When I solo, I do the most spectacular things when I'm not thinking about what I'm playing. When I'm feeling it is when it's good. For any musician the moments of gold are when you just sit back and think, 'Wow, how did I do that?'"

For an album recorded and mixed in the studio, *Santana* is not without flaws, particularly in regard to balance. On the "Savor" track, the organ solo is buried by the percussion instruments, and on the "Persuasion" track, the vocal could be louder. At times, the length of instrumental breaks stretches to the thin point of the soloing capabilities of the musicians. But, all in all, *Santana* is an exciting album.

As we were talking, Carlos plugged in his SG and started to play a slow tempo, *C*-minor blues. I sat down at the organ, and the organist sat down at the drums. The rest of Santana drifted into the studio one at a time and picked up their instruments. Moments later, Carlos was swaying back and forth, his eyes squinted closed and shoulders hunched. He traded 12-bar solos with us, one for one, until it was time to get back to business.

2.

"I AM THE STRING, AND THE SUPREME IS THE MUSICIAN"

. . . .

by Michael Brooks, November 1974

In the aftermath of his highly successful union with Mahavishnu John McLaughlin on Columbia's *Love Devotion Surrender*, Carlos Santana, lead guitarist with the group Santana, is still in an evolutionary process. In 1973, he performed 312 concerts, and recently finished an album with Alice Coltrane [at press time, tentatively titled *Illuminations*], feeling he was "compelled to do it by the Supreme."

Yes, Carlos is still deeply involved with his, and John McLaughlin's, guru, Sri Chinmoy. He is also producing music with "high spiritual content," and foresees no change from his present path.

The following interview with Carlos Santana was an effort to gain a better understanding of how his guitar and guitar playing blends or contrasts with his spiritual life.

Now that you have given yourself to the Supreme, do you find your music at a higher improvisational level?

Sometimes—especially when I truly humble myself. But, a lot of times, what I hear, and what the Supreme hears are two different things. Sometimes, when I listen to musical passages which come out of me—when I open my eyes—I find that I am concentrating too much on the music, and it makes it sound without feeling. Sometimes, I find myself still living in the illusion that I've got to do it the way I hear it. But when I do that, it doesn't come out right—it sounds too thought out. You know, you can tell when somebody makes a speech from his heart—it's just spontaneous—and you can tell when someone has been studying up, just through his words and tone. The most natural thing on earth is your heart—your soul—because it rarely goes out of tune with God. What goes out of tune is your mind and your body.

How do you relate your spiritual life to your guitar?

I am the string, and the Supreme is the musician.

But when you have humbled yourself to the Supreme, and he is playing through you, do you ever find a point where the Supreme's music is just not happening?

Sometimes, but when that happens, it's because my mind is still in the way. I said before that I'm the string, and that's all I am, because I go out of tune just like a string goes out of tune. By that I mean that I am not totally consistent yet. I've got a long way to go before I can be in any kind of environment and still keep that oneness with the Supreme, so I don't start swearing and trying to be stupidly proud. But when I'm really in tune with the Supreme, my guru, and my instrument, forget it, man, because it's totally beyond anything—and that's where I want to be. I just want to be in service to the Supreme. It's getting to where I don't even expect to understand a song until after I've played it and heard it back. I hear a sound and I go for it, but I know that if I hear exactly how it sounds while I'm playing it, it's not going to be that good, because then my mind is controlling it. It's like sometimes I'm not aware I can do some of these things on my guitar, because, in reality, I'm not doing them, they are being done through me—which is one of the highest places anyone can reach.

Many of our readers want to know what equipment you used on _Caravanserai?_

I used a new 1971 Gibson Les Paul with a cherry sunburst finish and a beefed-up Fender Twin Reverb for most of it. For strings, I used a mixed set with the trebles of .009, .011, and .015 from a Gibson Lights set. Then, for the bass strings, I used Ernie Ball strings, gauged .024, .036, and .042.

Do you change strings frequently?

At least every two concerts. If the concerts are long, then I change after each show. For studio work, I like to put new ones on just about every other day. Usually, I can tell by just looking at them if they need changing, because the color is different, and that's when they begin to slip and become harder to tune.

Have you switched instruments since the album with John?

"I AM THE STRING, AND THE SUPREME IS THE MUSICIAN"

Oh, I just flipped over this Gibson L6-S. It's not like I'm endorsing it, but that axe is beautiful. It's got more accessible frets, and the pickups are just incredible. With the controls, I can make it sound like a Stratocaster, a Telecaster, an SG, or a Les Paul. I get them all. It has a very fast fingerboard, and it's clean sounding.

Have you used the Gibson L6-S in the studio yet?

Yeah, I used it on the album I recently did with Alice Coltrane.

What are you presently using for an amp?

It's called a Mesa/Boogie amplifier. I'm going to turn Mahavishnu onto it, and it'll just flip him right out. There's nothing like it on the market. It gives you three volume controls. The first one on the left I crank up to 7, and then I put the Master Volume control on half, and I can play like in a hotel, but it's screaming. But if I want to play at a place like the Berkeley Community Theatre or a bigger hall, I just turn the master up to 5, and I can project. If I want to play Winterland or someplace bigger, I just turn it up to 7.

You have gained a notable reputation for your sustain. Have you ever used sustain devices of any sort?

I never use sustain devices at all. I just do it the old-fashioned way—get close to the amplifier.

Do you have to search out the optimum position of your guitar and amp for each sound setup, or do you have it pretty much down now?

Well, I still have to move back and forth until I can find just the right kind of sustain. Sometimes, I hear all these other overtones coming in, maybe out of tune, you know. So I have to keep moving around until I get it, because I don't know how to use those gadgets and stuff like that. I mean, I know there are products in the stores which you can use to get good sustain, but they all sound over-electrified to me. I like the pure sustain without speakers cracking and without overloading the amp.

As far as your guitar setting for sustain, do you find it better with full-on bass?

Well, for me, I use full midrange. Like, I don't know exactly what I do for sustain, and it has taken me some time to get it, but I hear the sound in my head, and I know what it sounds like, and I go for it. You just have to keep moving around and experiment with different settings, because each instrument is a little different, and so is each amp.

To what do you specifically attribute your fine sustain?

Carlos Santana rocking a Les Paul during a 1970s-era concert. (PHOTOFEST)

"I AM THE STRING, AND THE SUPREME IS THE MUSICIAN"

It's all in the pickups, man, the super-hum-bucking pickups. The sustain you get from those you wouldn't believe.

Were you satisfied with the outcome of *Love Devotion Surrender*?

Well, personally I think it would be a waste of time to do another album, just because I didn't think it was truly happening 100 percent on that record, you know, with the people playing. If we do another, I want to be more part of the rest of the people. Last time, John chose half, and I chose half, and like it wasn't happening after a while. We weren't

"My thing is to try to open hearts and minds to observe a deeper awareness— to real music, to divine music, to a real purpose in life."

really playing together. At times it was, but we really had to struggle to get it together. No matter who I'm playing with, I like to feel it's more than a gig. It's like John says, "It's a mission, a divine mission," and that's how I like to treat concerts. Like, anyone can make money, man. I could be a dishwasher if I wanted to make money, but my thing is to try to open hearts and minds to observe a deeper awareness—to real music, to divine music, to a real purpose in life. By this way, I can better myself, and we're all trying to do that.

In your guitar playing, how does the technical element relate to the spiritual element?

They both have to go hand-in-hand. It's like going back to Leonardo da Vinci. For him to reflect all his artwork, he had to get his chops out before he could try to reflect all that perfection the Supreme gave him. On the album with Mahavishnu, all our spirituality, in order to manifest itself, had to come out as high and as deep as da Vinci, but we rehearsed maybe a month at the most. But, really, it's all in the conviction that you do it with. It's like all those people calling Mahavishnu's and my album "far-out" and "outer-space," but to me it is like an offering of flowers to God. It is the Supreme, your highest self. But I know this music has nothing to do with "far-out" or "outer-space." You see, when you humble yourself to the Supreme, you wake up in the morning, and what happens is that I am the instrument, and the guitar is just the guitar. I just don't wear the pin, and say I'm into spirituality. I live the part, and I've *got* to live the part, because anybody can tell when it's not sincere. And the same goes for music. If you don't have the conviction, or if you aren't feeling your music, you can tell, and I can tell. That's why I really laugh when I see all these albums sold like "King of the Guitar." There's only one king, man, and that's the Supreme. And when he plays through you, according to your capacity, it's like music from beyond, and that's what I'm hungry for.

Do you find yourself playing a lot more, now that you have given yourself to the Supreme? Playing not only with a totally different perspective, but also playing more in hours per day?

Yeah. Like if I'm not practicing my guitar and my technique, I'm reading certain types of books which make me constantly aware of how much conviction, surrender, devotion I have to have so that I don't go out of tune. So when I play, all those doubts and wrong notes don't come into the picture, because really there's no such thing as wrong notes, you know. I'm finding that because my ears are so trained to play in a certain vein, I'm having to break out of certain playing habits. It's like when you're a kid, and you have a car, and people tell you a car won't go up a wall, it should just stay on the road. But that's a bunch of baloney. On the technical side, I thoroughly agree with the advice, otherwise you could kill yourself. But when you're a kid, and you just get a car, you start taking all those chances. That's the same with music, man. It's like Miles Davis taking all those chances and ending up by training a lot of people to hear different things—like all those chords Miles was doing with his band. You can hear them on commercials now. So kids are getting educated, and people are growing, but they don't even know at what rate they are growing.

When did you grow into the awareness of that jazz/Indian-flavored music as being your highest point. Was it through Mahavishnu?

Right. He brought some cassettes over the first time he came to my house. At that time, Indian music was like an ocean too big to cross. Like when you're a kid, and somebody puts you on to symphony music, and it just turns you right off. It's too deep. Some music just goes right over you, and you start yawning. And it was sort of like that, you know. John Coltrane's music used to do that to me. It's so heavy, it's like eating a big meal. But, after a while, I got hungry for it. You see, I was going to all these clubs and getting tired of hearing all this mediocrity. People just playing for the money, and not playing it because they were living it, or being it. But now, I'm really hungry, and I guess my ears expect a lot more—no matter what kind of music it is. I really expect that sincerity—that conviction. Between John, and now Indian music, I can sincerely say that they're molding me to be what I have been trying to be for a long time. It's like "they're molding me" is a way to say it, but really what I mean is that my spiritual master, guru Sri Chinmoy, John, and Alice Coltrane are all taking me home, man. They're taking me home to the place I've been away from for so long—and home is one with God. I can totally be myself, and not what my mind wants me to be or what the system wants me to be, because they are different things. What God wants me to be is it for me. And I can't delay because everything else is just an illusion. And I can tell in the music if it's being played from the heart. Then—and only then—is it coming from God.

When you find this perfection—or get very close to this perfection—do you feel it's your obligation to spread it?

Sure. That's why it takes sheer conviction to do what I'm doing. Like my parents, friends, and some other people expect me to portray the role of yesterday. Like some tell me, "Man, I really liked the way you used to play all your songs." And I say, "Well, why don't you go to all those clubs where they are playing music like I used to do." You know, I've got to move on. And I'm not moving on to impress anybody—that's not the thing for me. For me, it's just like the more I can be of service to humanity. Like in a concert—if I can inspire one more brother or sister to start getting himself together as far as praying or meditating or just humbling himself to the Supreme, then I'm making far more progress than anybody else. Because that person's energy will be conducted to the right channel—to the right time and place. And we can end this disillusionment, this frustration, this destruction, and all this ignorance.

Do you feel your spiritual path will always be involved with the guitar and music?

For right now, it all seems to be music. I have a tremendous amount of freedom still. We all do. I don't have the freedom that I used to have, though, because then I didn't have as much awareness. By that I mean that if you are not aware, like of a strong conviction, or even the universal laws—the Ten Commandments—and they haven't hit you as something to obey, then you can do anything you want. But once they start touching you, once they have soaked into your heart, you can't get away with it as much, because the Supreme is right there making it all come back.

3.

"IT TOOK ME A WHILE TO REALIZE THAT YOUR INDIVIDUALITY IS A VERY BEAUTIFUL GIFT"

. . . .

by Dan Forte, June 1978

Tenor saxophonist John Coltrane, one of modern jazz's true innovators, once said, "We are always searching. I think that now we are at the point of finding." Devadip Carlos Santana, like Coltrane, is a searcher—or, as he puts it, a seeker. The similarities between the two artists don't stop there. As with Coltrane's music, Santana's music has reflected the spiritual lifestyle he has chosen. Like Coltrane, he is an innovator, and, above all, an individual voice on his instrument, the guitar.

John Coltrane was a major inspiration for Carlos, so the parallels are no doubt more than coincidence. The title tune of the Santana band's seventh album, *Welcome*, was a Coltrane composition. The guitarist collaborated with the saxophonist's widow, pianist/harpist Turiya Alice Coltrane, on the album *Illuminations*. At one stage, Devadip would even sleep with a tape of Coltrane music playing all night long.

But Santana was wise enough to know that there could only be one John Coltrane, and he listened to the music for inspiration—not to cop lines or even stylistic modes. Carlos Santana is such an individualist that it's difficult to hear direct traces of the musicians he cites as influences, except on rare occasions. He will talk for hours about his deep love for the blues, rattling off an endless list of favorite performers of the genre. Yet in his ten albums with the Santana band and his various solo projects, he has never recorded a blues tune—at least not in standard blues form. The blues, like the other factors that make up Santana's sound, is reflected as a feeling—not as notes or rhythms.

To this day, the name Santana brings to mind a picture of a battery of Latin percussionists behind their leader, who leans backwards, eyes clenched shut in concentration, as he squeezes the notes from his guitar. The Santana band was the first group to successfully blend Latin and Afro rhythms with rock music. Originally known as the Santana Blues Band—later shortened to its leader's surname—the group built a strong following at Bill Graham's Fillmore Auditorium in San Francisco, eventually headlining shows with the likes of Taj Mahal, the Youngbloods, and Melanie before they had even recorded. The young band received national acclaim thanks to the Woodstock festival in 1969, the same year their first LP, *Santana*, debuted. *Santana* produced two hit singles in "Jingo" and "Evil Ways," and turned platinum within a year—an achievement few groups of that period could claim.

More hit albums and singles followed—"Oye Como Va," "Black Magic Woman/Gypsy Queen," "No One To Depend On"—despite numerous personnel changes in the group. The Santana band's direction changed as did its guitarist/leader's ideals. Guitarist Neal Schon and singer/keyboardist Gregg Rolie left to form Journey following the group's first major departure from Latin rock, *Caravanserai*. The album, the band's fourth, revealed the jazzier influences that had been absorbing much of Carlos Santana's energies. Artists such as Coltrane, Charles Lloyd, McCoy Tyner, Thelonious Monk, Miles Davis (whom Santana calls "the Muhammad Ali of music"), and the group Weather Report provided the inspiration that had previously come from B. B. King, Jimmy Reed, and others.

What Carlos was searching for, musically and personally, he found in Sri Chinmoy, his spiritual guru. Santana was introduced to Sri Chinmoy by electrifying guitarist Mahavishnu John McLaughlin. The two artists joined forces on *Love Devotion Surrender* in 1973, which was as much a religious statement as it was a musical one. Though McLaughlin has since dropped the Mahavishnu title and is no longer a follower of the guru, Devadip (Santana's spiritual name) has stuck close to Chinmoy's teachings.

"IT TOOK ME A WHILE TO REALIZE THAT YOUR INDIVIDUALITY IS A VERY BEAUTIFUL GIFT"

But the more Santana's music began to mirror the tranquility and inner peace Devadip had found, the less it sounded like the energetic, feverish group that had insured "street music's" inclusion in the list of psychedelic San Francisco rock outfits. Carlos began to realize that the concert-opening moments of silent meditation—and the extended improvisational excursions—were alienating some of his old fans. People wanted to move and dance.

While on tour with McLaughlin in 1973, Santana dropped by a Seattle beer bar to jam with one of his early, pre-guru inspirations, Elvin Bishop. The ex-Butterfield Blues Band guitarist's brand of ham-and-eggs rock and blues—and the crowd's involvement with it—brought Carlos to the realization that "the highest form of spirituality is joy. If you don't have that, man, then I don't care for spirituality."

Along with the two longest-surviving members of the Santana band—keyboardist Tom Coster and percussionist Ndugu Leon Chancler—Devadip took a retrospective look at the group's history, and sought to reignite the spark that had separated Santana from other rock bands in the first place. The result of their research appeared in the 1976 LP *Amigos*, and articles immediately proclaimed the "return" of Santana. The year 1977 produced two more albums on basically the same track—*Festival* and the double-album *Moonflower*—and Santana's international popularity is now probably as high as ever.

Along with the increased recognition of the band, Carlos Santana's guitar skills have finally received the notice they deserve, and his position in the elite of rock guitarists is secure to say the least. Last year's *Moonflower* was voted Best Record of the Year in the first annual Bay Area Music Awards, sponsored by San Francisco's *BAM* magazine, and, in the same poll, readers chose Carlos Best Guitarist. In last year's *Guitar Player* Readers' Poll, he placed high in both the Rock and Overall categories.

Whether or not one chooses to use adjectives such as "best" when describing Carlos' abilities on guitar, the 30-year-old instrumentalist must surely rate as one of the most distinctive and emotional players around today, regardless of style. And whether or not one wishes to believe in the spiritual path Devadip has chosen to follow, one thing is obvious—it works for him. And Santana and his music will no doubt survive long after other artists are either dried up or burned out.

When you were growing up, did your father play in mariachi bands? Did he teach you things?

Yes. I started playing the violin first. I was playing Beethoven's "Minuet in *G*" and "Poet and Peasant Overture" by Von Suppé—you know, classical songs. But I hated the violin. I just hated the sound of it, and the smell of it. And, to me, anything I played on the violin sounded like Jack Benny when he was fooling around [*laughs*]. I know he could really play well, but when he was joking around, that's what I sounded like at my best. I couldn't get into it. Later, I saw this band in Tijuana, where I grew up, and they were totally imitating B. B. King, Ray Charles, Bobby Bland, and Little Richard. They were from Tijuana, and when I heard them playing, I said, "Oh, man! This is the stuff I want to get into." I was about 11 or so, and it was the first blues I'd heard. And then Javier Batiz, the guitar player, took me to his house, and we got to be friends. He had a very beautiful sound, and you could tell that he lived with records by B. B. King, Ray Charles, and Little Richard. That's what knocked me out. I'd see my sister screaming over Elvis Presley, and even though I was a kid, I had the attitude that it was just a fad. But I never felt empathy with Mexican music. Not that I hated it—I just couldn't relate to it. I usually equated Mexican music with drunk Mexicans having a brawl, and overemphasizing the macho trips, so I really couldn't get into it. I grew up with that environment. I could get into the blues more. It was more natural to me.

When you moved to San Francisco, did you eventually get into the white blues movement that was happening at that time?

Paul Butterfield? Yeah, he was the one who started the whole thing for a lot of people. See, when I came to America, my American friends would be listening to the Dave Clark Five and the Beach Boys, and I couldn't stand that. I'd say, "Why are you into these guys? They aren't even saying nothing, man. Listen to Ray Charles and Bobby Bland." And they'd say, "That stuff is old." And all of a sudden, two things hit me: One was seeing Paul Butterfield and Muddy Waters, and the other was Cream's first record [*Fresh Cream*]. It just totally turned me around. I said, "How can these guys play blues like that?" That's when I started

"IT TOOK ME A WHILE TO REALIZE THAT YOUR INDIVIDUALITY IS A VERY BEAUTIFUL GIFT"

to play hooky from Mission High and started hanging out on Mission Street. Stan Marcum, who subsequently became my first manager, took me to Winterland to see Paul Butterfield and Muddy Waters when Muddy had Little Walter on harp. Man, I was knocked out for weeks. I was in a daze. I don't know how many dishes I broke working as a dishwasher after that. I couldn't believe what blues could do to people. See, I wasn't getting loaded at the time, so when I went to Winterland, I was totally aware of my surroundings. It wasn't like when people get loaded and become so overly aware that they [*whistles*]—they're everywhere at the same time, so they miss something. But I could see people's eyes and faces and the way they were reacting when the band was playing the blues. I could see that the group was feeding these people, and they were feeding me. It was one of the most fantastic concerts I've ever been to.

Did that lead you to search out records by older bluesmen?

Yeah, yeah. I got into Little Milton and all those people. I think the blues is about the most beautiful contribution that the black man has given to the United States, because anybody can claim them. If you're in high school, you can feel the blues, because most people who are in high school don't know where to go. You ask them, "What do you want to be when you grow up?" "I don't know." And that in itself is a burden, and that can give you a certain amount of the downers, you know, the blues. So when you listen to James Cotton or Little Walter or Junior Wells, you totally feel like they know, and they've been through what you're going through. Being from the West, that's the most universal music. Maybe if you're from India, you can't relate to it, but being from the West, that's the most universal music we have.

Did the original Santana Blues Band play blues standards?

We did songs by B. B. King, Ray Charles—like "Woke Up This Morning" and "Mary Ann"—and we would do our own versions of the first two Butterfield albums. We even did "East-West." And that's when I eventually started getting into drugs. I always saw so many people around me taking drugs, but the only thing I remember that would stop me from trying it was that I would practice with the band for a long time to get some numbers down pat, and we'd really be burning. Then we'd take a break, and they'd all go smoke some weed, come back, and forget the changes. Because weed can make you trip up, you know. And I hated that. I said, "Man, that's not the way we rehearsed it." But, once, somebody left the house and left a joint in the ashtray for me, and I had *Sergeant Pepper* or *Revolver* by the Beatles on the turntable. So I thought I'd see what it was about. It does make you aware of other things, other possibilities. But it's like tennis shoes. If you wear size eight, why put on size six? You already went through that three years ago, and it doesn't fit anymore. That's how I feel about drugs now—they just don't fit me. But if I hadn't ever taken drugs I'd probably be kind of square and more prejudiced. I don't think I would have been as open to things like [jazz flautist] Charles Lloyd and [saxophonist] John Handy. It can make you receptive and sensitive to a certain level, right? The Beatles, Cream, and the Yardbirds were all doing it, so you say, "Gee, maybe there's something to it." It did play a role. Plus, when I was a kid in Tijuana, I'd see everybody smoking pot, but I wouldn't do it.

Playing American blues music in Tijuana, did you relate more to the Mexican people or the Americans?

All the musicians that I hung around with had this beautiful pride in being hip to all the black musicians who'd come down from America to cop drugs. They'd come down to this club where I worked, and that's how I became aware of that music. They were singing the latest songs by Ray Charles and Bobby Bland, and we'd have to learn them. So I wasn't really into a Mexican atmosphere—I was more into a black man's atmosphere. Like I said, it took me a while to relate to the Beach Boys and the Beatles because of that. So I don't think I relate as much to Mexican music and Mexican people as I do to the low-income Americans. A lot of white people played over there, too, and when they played the blues you could tell that they were greatly influenced by Jerry Lee Lewis.

How old were you when you came to San Francisco?

It was 1962, so I must have been 12 or 13. It was a drag, because they put me back into junior high, because I couldn't speak English. I had to learn to adapt to a whole other way of thinking and being around kids, because I thought I was a man of the world—working and playing in this nightclub in Tijuana, watching ladies strip. We'd play for an hour, and

"IT TOOK ME A WHILE TO REALIZE THAT YOUR INDIVIDUALITY IS A VERY BEAUTIFUL GIFT"

then they'd strip for an hour, then we'd play. To me, I was a grown-up, so when I came here I had to live the life of a young adolescent all over again, and I couldn't relate. But, fortunately, I did find some musicians who helped me make the transition much faster.

Were you on your own, working for a living as a kid in Tijuana?

In Tijuana, I was working for a living. I wasn't going to school anymore. And when I came here, that was a burden, because I had to go back to school, and I hated school. I mean, I always knew I was going to be a musician even before they put me in junior high. So I couldn't see why I had to know algebra and that sort of trip. But what was fascinating—which many Americans take for granted—is that you meet so many friends in one day of school, with the different teachers and classes. In Mexico, you have the same kids all day.

Did you want to come to America, or were you content playing in clubs in Tijuana?

I was very content there, because I was making my own money, nobody was telling me what to do, and I didn't have to be home at any special time. I was living on my own. I'd had a falling-out with my parents, and they were up here already. When you're a kid, it's like nothing is a burden.

Did the Latin influences creep into the Santana band because of the things you'd heard as a kid, or did an outside musician bring that element to the band?

[*Long pause.*] It took me a long time, just now, to remember when the congas came in. We were exclusively a blues band at first. People ask me a lot of times how the change took place, and I think the reason was that we'd go around "hippy hill" and Aquatic Park in San Francisco, and they used to have congas and wine, and that's where we got the congas in the band. And then I heard Gabor Szabo, and his album *Spellbinder* has congas on it. Somebody brought this conga player to jam with us, and he threw us into a whole different thing. Actually, we never play "Latin music"—you know, it's a crossover. I just play whatever I hear.

Did you originally plan to add a conga player, yet continue playing blues?

Yeah. Even when we had a conga player it was still the Santana Blues Band. Later we got Chepito [Areas], and he was playing congas and timbales. Then we dropped the "Blues Band" and started to play more of a crossover. And we were listening to Miles and the Jazz Crusaders. After that, it was really interesting, because even Chicago came out with congas. Actually, Harvey Mandel was probably the first guy to put congas on a rock and roll album [*Cristo Redentor*]. I saw him and Charlie Musselwhite [as the Southside Sound System] at the Avalon one time, and they played "Cristo Redentor" and "Wade in the Water," and I was knocked out. I learned a lot from them. I really admire guys like Harvey Mandel whose sound I can identify, because it takes a lot of work. Nobody can say that you are born with it. You work for it, and carve your own individuality. In fact, if people want to find out how to develop this, a good way is to get a tape recorder, and for half an hour, turn out the lights in your house and get into a room that's kind of dark, where you don't have interruptions. Then just play with a rhythm machine. After a while, it's like a deck of cards on the table, and you can begin to see the riffs that came from this guy, the riffs that came from that guy, and then the two or three riffs that are yours. Then you start concentrating on yours, and, to me, that's how you develop your own individual sound. You play a couple of notes and say, "Gee, that sounds like Eric Clapton" or "That sounds like George Benson." But then you play two or three notes, and say, "Man, that's me." Not until a couple of years ago did I consciously start doing it that way. I'd just sit down, turn everything off, get a rhythm machine, and just play and play.

Do you find much time to practice guitar these days?

Yeah, I still do it a lot—as much as I can. Mainly with the rhythm machine. I practice so that my fingers will respond to what I feel. Sometimes, I have this incredible craving just to get a music teacher to teach me chords and fancy scales that you'd find in *The Thesaurus of Scales and Melodic Patterns*. I pick up that book once in a while and play two or three lines. Sometimes it scares me, because I start playing something really significant. Then, sometimes, I start sounding like everybody else, and I don't want to sound like that. I leave that stuff to Jerry Hahn and Larry Coryell, who are really great at what they do. I admire their craft, but I prefer simplicity. It's like eating. If you don't discriminate what you eat, you get sick—you know, indigestion. You have to know what's good for you. You are digesting it by learning it. It is stored up in your memory cells. Recently, I was playing a song by

"IT TOOK ME A WHILE TO REALIZE THAT YOUR INDIVIDUALITY IS A VERY BEAUTIFUL GIFT"

Roberta Flack with Donny Hathaway, "The Closer I Get to You." That's one way I practice—I put on a record when there's nobody home, and if it hits me, my face contorts and I start crying. I feel that if I can't cry to something that is moving, I'm not going to cry onstage. I think a lot of musicians become very callous, and, after a while, they can't feel pain. That's not what music is about. Before I found Sri Chinmoy, I used to take LSD just to feel pain, when all I had to do was look inside my heart and it's all there. I think that's what saved me from real hard drugs and that self-destructive path that a lot of musicians take.

Where did you learn chords?

From my father. He taught me the basic chords. My brother Jorge has been teaching me chords, and showing me how it takes years to unlearn what some books throw at you. He has been teaching me how you hear the chord and start building other chords around it just by hearing the notes. I didn't even know this stuff until about three days ago. Jorge came to my house and showed me. I'm going to stick around my brother, because he does know a lot about chords, and I need it. I think if I'm really lacking something it's harmony and chords. I don't think I'm lacking as far as imagination or vision are concerned.

Most of your playing is single-note lines—not many chords.

Right, but I know that sometimes when Tom [Coster] is playing a solo, he yearns for somebody to throw chords at him, so he can take it to something else. I can see his point. It's to his advantage and my advantage.

Do you prefer to do concept albums rather than just collections of songs?

Yes. That's the only thing that I always deal with. Mostly, it's like a vision. Each song is a vision, rather than a musical approach. It's like painting. I don't think of what kind of stroke I'm going to give it, I just picture it, and then I know instantly what instrument, what color, to use. It's just easier for me, because I can't read music. I don't know nothing about music. Tom helps me out with the music. I give him a feeling—I hear something—and we work together, and he'll say, "What you're talking about is a *B* diminished 7th. . . ." "Oh really?" I should get into music, and I probably will this year—chords and harmony. It would make it easier. I used to think it would get in the way, because I've seen musicians who are so technical with music that they always get caught on a technique of approaching a song the same way. They're bound to a technique, whereas a child who never practiced music can get the song any variety of ways, because he's not bound to a certain approach to music. Of course, I've heard a lot of pros and cons about music. I was always put off by a lot of snobbish musicians who can read music, but, fortunately, I met a lot of good musicians who had an open attitude about it. I once heard someone putting someone else down because he couldn't read music, and it was almost like in the movie *Never On Sunday*, where the mandolin player was feeling so down. They told him he wasn't a musician, because he couldn't read music. Then somebody told him, "Birds don't read music." So, in a way, it's an excuse, and I know that I should learn it and really make an effort to understand more about music, so I don't have to stutter as much. But I always feel I have enough spontaneity and enough vision not to be bound by, "Gee, I have to start with a *C♯*."

Have you ever felt hindered by your lack of formal training when you're playing with someone like Stanley Clarke or Chick Corea?

We can play together easily. As soon as I close my eyes, it's like where you're sitting right now—you can just take for granted that you're sitting. But when you close your eyes and feel the chair holding you, and you start feeling your surroundings, then it makes it easier, because you remove your mind out of the way. To me, the heart is always in tune with the time and the melody. But if you start to think about, "I wonder what key he is playing in," then you can't even tune your guitar, because you spend so much time calculating and fabricating and criticizing, that by the time you get to the song, they've finished already. But if you just feel, it's the most natural thing to do. If you just feel, you can create. I think music training would help me from the point of writing my own songs a little bit faster. Sometimes, it does take me longer, because what I hear I have to search for in different positions until I find it, instead of saying, "I think what I hear is a *D*-something."

Do you mainly write songs by trial and error?

Yeah, I just hear something, and I have to look for it. A lot of times, I don't have to look for it—I just find it. Other times, what I'm finding is—since I'm getting away from three-chord progressions or *G* minor to *D*

"IT TOOK ME A WHILE TO REALIZE THAT YOUR INDIVIDUALITY IS A VERY BEAUTIFUL GIFT"

major kinds of things—you have to use so many chords. And it's just natural to be a product of what you hear sometimes in your environment, like Stevie Wonder. I'm hearing more harmony, so it takes me a little bit longer now.

When you hear an idea for a song in your head, is it usually a melody or a set of changes or a rhythmic motif or what?

It's a cry. It's a crying melody. That's mostly what I hear, and then I have to find the chords. Sometimes, it's the other way around, and one chord could almost make up for three melodies. But, sometimes, the melody is so clear, you want to find three passing chords for that melody.

Your guitar solos seem to stay pretty close to the melody of the song itself, as opposed to players like, say, Al Di Meola or John McLaughlin, who use a lot of scalar things. Are you thinking of the song's basic theme throughout your solo?

Yes. To me, the heart of the song is the melody. And I approach the melody from a singer's point of view—a simple singer, not a singer who scats a lot like George Benson. If you'll notice, a lot of guitar players riff like horn players. And I don't really like guitar players like that. Not that I dislike them with a passion, but it doesn't appeal to me—it's boring. I think more like the layman kind of person singing [*sings*], "Lovely Rita meter maid . . . ." You don't care what chords are underneath—it's the basic feeling of the song that gets you immediately. I listen to the radio a lot, so I don't think like "deedleedoodah" and that sort of thing. And I figure, why do it like that when there are so many thousands of cats who can do it a zillion times better? That's what they are, and I just get into what I am now. It's like your signature. This is a very valid point for me now. Some people may think it's negative, but I think it's positive, because I am aware that out of thousands and thousands of guitar players, there are only, like, 30 who you can listen to and know who they are. The rest all sound the same—at least that's what I think. And it took me a while to realize that that's a very beautiful gift—your own individuality—even if you only know three notes, man, if you are able to play those well, and know who you are. I don't think I was aware of my sound until three or four years ago. Even when I did that album with Mahavishnu [*Love Devotion Surrender*]—after a while it was, "Gee, who's playing what?" It even took me a while to figure out who was doing what, because we were playing so many notes that, after a while, the sound was all the same. Then I started hearing a certain amount of chops, and I said, "That's Mahavishnu." Then I'd hear three notes and say, "Well, that's me." I think it goes back to when I was listening to Johnny Mathis and Dionne Warwick and playing behind the melody, rather than doing what the trumpets and horns or somebody else was playing. I really didn't listen that much to bebop. I missed that era. I was into all these blues people like Jimmy Reed who only play three notes, but they grab you. As far as I'm concerned, the point of music is to tell stories with a melody. All that stuff about playing notes, to me, is just like watching some cat pick up weights. After a while, who wants to see somebody flex their muscles?

Your guitar playing is extremely vocal-like in tone and phrasing, yet you've never been the lead singer of the Santana band. Do you try to compensate for that in your playing?

Right. I think that's exactly it. I sing through the guitar. The main theme is always haunting melodies.

Your sets in concerts are almost like concept albums in that there are very few breaks between songs, and the transitions from mood to mood are very subtle.

Yes, it's the mood. I learned that from Miles. He goes through an hour-and-a-half, and it's like showing you a whole desk of beautiful jewels and just looking at them without breaking the continuity. Like, "Okay, I'm going outside to put a dime in the parking meter." You just sit there, and, all of a sudden, it hits you like that. I think mostly I learned that from Miles—to put everything so that it's constantly transcending itself. You try to make it peak and resolve. Sometimes, we feel like we do have to pause and let the people, like, gulp it in and digest it for a while. But I like to go from song to song to song. It's more fun.

Is *Lotus* [Santana's triple-set import] ever going to be released in the United States?

I don't think so, because they want to condense it into one or two records, and that would destroy the whole thing. That was all one concert, you know. We recorded that in 1973, in Japan. We were playing close to four hours in those days. But you can only play for so long like that. It's like giving people too much food, instead of giving them a nice portion so they don't start yawning and falling asleep. But we don't like to break, because then you lose momentum. Whereas, if you're already sweating you're getting into it. Once you stop, you don't want to start again.

When you were listening to Miles Davis and John Coltrane, was there any particular band or period in their careers that you especially liked?

Well, I identify with their music and them so much—not what they're about, but what's inside them. Not the personality. I don't identify with a part of the personality at all. But the creative and spontaneous musician, I totally identify with him and everything that he does. Sometimes, I wake up and start listening to Miles' quintet when he had [drummer] Tony Williams [along with bassist Ron Carter, keyboardist Herbie Hancock, and saxophonist Wayne Shorter], and I can just go through the day. Other times, I can listen to it, and I don't get as much out of it as I would from, say, when he had [percussionist] Ntume and [bassist] Michael Henderson. It depends on what kind of mood I'm in. I love all of it, and I can relate to all of it. The only period that I really can't get into still is the old, real cool jazz and bebop with [alto saxophonist] Charlie Parker. It still takes me a while to get into that. I put it on, and it's like being a little kid and somebody puts on Guy Lombardo. When you're a kid, you don't want to hear nothing like that. You want to hear Mickey Mouse, or maybe Chuck Berry. So with this kind of music, I don't think it's really over my head—I just don't think it's my style. I try to listen to it as much as I can, but, after a while, I can't relate to it. I can listen to [pianist] Thelonious Monk more than that, but in some of the other stuff there's too many riffs for my taste. But then I'm not a bebopper.

What about Miles' later period, beginning with, say, *Bitches Brew*?

I can relate to it, because being into airports and being into New York streets, I could see where that comes from, and I begin to love it, because I've been there. I've been through all that. It's like someone flashing you a year of New York in 25 minutes, and they pick the best outrageous scenes and put them to music. Miles is an incredible storyteller of outrageous, funny things.

Have you ever met him?

Yes, I've met him a couple of times. We've done a few concerts together. I begged Bill Graham to put us on the same bill. We did a couple of concerts at the Fillmore when he had Chick Corea and Keith Jarrett, and I couldn't believe the audience's response.

Did you ever have occasion to jam with him?

No. One time, he invited me to play in this club, and, like a fool, I said no. He kept pressuring me to go get my guitar. I kept looking him straight in the eye, and I was so insecure about my playing at the time—I think because of the dope. If I had been aware of what I'm aware of now, I would have said "sure." I should have trusted my ears to know what to play and what not to play. But, at the time, I was so paranoid. But that feeling was valid, because most rock and roll musicians that I know get paranoid when they see a jazz musician. You feel like those guys are older brothers. It's like being a kid, and your brother tries to get you to swim on the deeper side of the pool, and you don't know how to swim that well [*laughs*].

Is there anyone today who you'd be afraid to jam with?

When I have a good meditation, it would be pretty hard for anyone to intimidate me, or for my own mind to intimidate me, because then I'm in my heart. If I was in my mind, anyone could scare me. When I close my eyes, I completely identify with Joe Zawinul and Chick Corea and Herbie Hancock and Wayne Shorter and people like that. No, I don't think I would be intimidated if I felt at one with myself. I was really surprised when they told me that George Benson had chosen me to play with him on TV on *The Midnight Special*. I was really honored. In fact, I was overjoyed when I did talk to him, because I found out that success has changed him so much for the better. He's become more aware that people are listening to him. A lot of jazz musicians play in small clubs, and they couldn't give a heck who's listening to them. They just play, and they play incredible stuff. But, to me, the first duty is to make people relate and have a good time. It's like a mirror—you start feeding off each other. One time I saw George, and he was playing a little more to himself than to the people, and to me that's disrespect, because the people paid, and they feed you. I don't care what anybody says, if you want to be a musician, it takes two hands. One is to feed yourself, and one is to feed the people. But the last time I saw George Benson he was so incredibly receptive to the people. He had become warmer. It was really nice.

When you two played "Breezin'" together on TV it seemed to come off especially well because your styles are so different, yet complementary.

"IT TOOK ME A WHILE TO REALIZE THAT YOUR INDIVIDUALITY IS A VERY BEAUTIFUL GIFT"

Yeah. One time, I saw another guy who was incredible. I couldn't believe he could play like he was playing when he jammed with George Benson. It was Glen Campbell. I said, "Wait a minute!" But it's interesting to never underestimate any musician, because everybody has a heart, and when they become one with the heart, man, they can scare you. They can just play two or three notes and say so much. Jamming with George was very significant to me because he was very courteous to me. Some jazz players try to make you uncomfortable. They have the attitude that rock and roll guitar players—"What do they know?" George made me feel very comfortable, and that's what you have to do with musicians to bring out the best in them—make them comfortable. I think George has become aware that there's something extremely valid in the Beatles and the Beach Boys and Chuck Berry. It's just as valid as Charlie Parker and John Coltrane, only in a different way. God flows through everybody and everything, and that's what you have to realize. I think that's the best thing that crossovers are doing to people—making them aware that, "Okay, far out. Nobody can play jazz the way you can, but try to get into a straight B. B. King shuffle and swing it like B. B. swings it." You're going to have a hard time, unless you're open to that kind of music.

Have you ever seen or gotten into any guitar battles onstage?

I don't like that kind of pressure. I used to hang around the Fillmore and see a bunch of guitar players come up to B. B. King like they were gunslingers. You could see in their eyes that they wanted to burn him. And B. B. would just come out with some Django Reinhardt or Charlie Christian licks, and then after that play some B. B. King. I'd just laugh at the looks on those other guys' faces. When I went on tour with Mahavishnu, we did about 12 concerts together, and for about the first six, I think I was really intimidated by him. After that, I started seeing how people were waiting for me—like, they'd had enough of him. And I said, "Well, maybe I do have a position where I'll say something and they'll listen." I was intimidated until I saw people being moved by what I was playing. After a while, we gave some concerts together with acoustic guitars, and it's like anything. If you remove your mind, you can give someone a good run for their money, and you can even scare yourself, You just have to go inside yourself. If you spend your whole time thinking about what you're going to say, it's gone. You don't have time when you're onstage—you have to just go within and hear and feel and play. One time, B. B. invited me to play with him and Bobby Bland at Winterland. I was backstage, and, all of a sudden, he announced me, and they put the light on me. I walked out there with my eyes about this big, and he put his guitar, Lucille, in my hands, so I started playing. Growing up listening to those two, I felt like they were my fathers. I started playing, and B. B. and Bobby were singing, and old Bobby came over and put his arm around me. I have a picture of it, and I'm standing there with my mouth hanging open. I felt like a three-year-old kid next to those guys. To me, it was really significant, because they're almost like the forefathers of the blues. The blues is such a familiar part of me. I guess it is for most Americans, too. The first time Santana played in Chicago, believe it or not, the show was Led Zeppelin, us, and Albert King in the afternoon, and then B. B. King, us, and Albert King that night. I was sandwiched between B. B. and Albert, and I said, "Great. As long as I don't play no B. B. King or Albert King licks, I'm going to be cool." And I just played what I had from the Santana band, and, in fact, it was good, because playing this kind of almost Latin music in between two blues players was a perfect contrast. It went over very well.

What was it like the time you jammed with McLaughlin and Eric Clapton in Michigan?

That was a great one, man. See, Mahavishnu has this thing where you know when he's totally into his heart, because he gets into this little dance. And no matter where time goes, he is like the equator on earth— he holds it together. And he started playing all this stuff and dancing, and Eric yelled and took his solo, and then he passed it to me. Then I passed it to Mahavishnu, and we started trading around. Alphonse Mouzon was on drums, too. It was incredibly fun. It was a beautiful combination, really. One cat just elaborates on a ceiling kind of level— Mahavishnu, right?—and the other cat just plays two or three notes, man, with simple, hard power. And I'm somewhere in between. Eric Clapton is one of my favorite human beings of all time.

Did the collaboration with John McLaughlin come about because you were both involved with Sri Chinmoy?

"IT TOOK ME A WHILE TO REALIZE THAT YOUR INDIVIDUALITY IS A VERY BEAUTIFUL GIFT"

I was a seeker, and I still am a seeker. Even music is secondary to me—as much as I love it. Mahavishnu called me and said they wanted to know if we could do this album together, and he also wanted to know if I was interested in coming to see Sri Chinmoy. He felt that I was aspiring or crying for another kind of awareness, because, at that time, I had already made a commitment to close the book on drugs and booze and that kind of stuff. I just felt that it was like being in the same classroom and seeing the same people. I had to move on. Then I started reading books about India and about spiritual masters, and it inspired me to work harder. Some people call it ambition, but I call it inspiration. When you have that, it's like having a different kind of energy—pure energy—a different kind of fuel. Sometimes, it's totally in this center of creativity, and it just flows through you, and, all of a sudden, you don't have to worry about who's going to like or dislike it. When it's over, you feel just like a bee. You don't know why you did it, but, all of a sudden, you've accumulated all this honey. So that's what brought us together. We had the same cry for the same purpose. But I did learn so much from him. He's an incredible musician. Of course, you always find the number one guitar player that you never heard before—someone who's probably never been recorded—but since I don't know him yet, Mahavishnu, George Benson, and Pat Martino are probably my favorite guitar players.

That seems odd, since their very technical guitar styles are almost the antithesis of your melodic style.

Well, I don't listen to them as much anymore—that's why I can say they're my favorites. The people who I listen to a lot are my favorites in another kind of way, because they're so close to me. I put them in another category. The people that I'm really close to, I don't even consider them to be guitarists. I consider them to be more like painters. But Mahavishnu and George Benson and Pat Martino are definitely guitar players. B. B. King doesn't seem like a guitarist to me—he seems to cry and play the blues and that kind of stuff. So when I hear him play, I don't even hear a guitar—I just hear this cry. If I was really into guitar players, I would say Django Reinhardt was really a "guitar player." He had both—he could cry with the melody, and then scare you to death with a couple of runs. He had everything. When we were first playing in

Haight-Ashbury at the Straight Theater, this friend of the band brought me this album by him and said, "This is who you should listen to, because you remind me of him." And I listened, and was totally blown out. He could play runs like a horn player, a piano player, or a guitar player, and then play some sweet melodies. And then when they told me he only had two good fingers, I really flipped.

Do you think the LP with Mahavishnu worked musically?

Yes, but our intentions weren't to bring any music together. Our purpose was to make people who are on the edge—like we were—of pursuing a different awareness, seeking a different goal, become aware. That was our purpose—the core of it. It wasn't really a commercial or musical piece.

How much do you think the music of Santana has changed over the years?

Well, it changed, because in the beginning I was flowing with [keyboardist] Gregg Rolie and everyone who was affiliated with the Santana band, so we were all a collaboration. We'd write everything together. We'd all put our two cents in. Later on, I found myself writing more alone, and it just took a different kind of route and purpose. I don't think it changed what I'm about drastically, because what I was always about—even when I wasn't aware of spiritual values—was that I really wanted to have people dancing and enjoying themselves. Forget about the rent and all the other problems and just have a good time. I feel like that's my primary motivation—to inspire people. If they want to dance, fine. But the other way that it did drastically change was that—instead of the Beatles and Jimi Hendrix—I got more into John Coltrane and Miles Davis and Mahavishnu and Weather Report. It's like what you eat is what you are after a while. It has to affect what you play. But it's like everything—you try something, and then you go back to what's natural to you. And with all that music around you, why not listen to it and see how somebody else reaches a song? But now, I'm back into dealing with what's more natural to me, instead of struggling in different kinds of music. I mean, it's still a struggle to get into my own sound and own individuality that God gave me. You always transcend yourself no matter what you play. But, at that time, I was struggling a little more, because it took me hours and hours. I would even sleep with a tape

"IT TOOK ME A WHILE TO REALIZE THAT YOUR INDIVIDUALITY IS A VERY BEAUTIFUL GIFT"

recorder on. I bought a tape recorder that would play both sides continuously, and I'd listen to John Coltrane all the time, because I couldn't understand the later albums. They were so hectic. Then, all of a sudden, it wasn't hectic at all. It was so sweet. It's like everything. You have to condition your mind to see that there's crying children in it, the love and compassion of a mother in the notes. The most significant thing that I learned in my whole life about music is the consciousness of it. It's like if you go to a bar where Elvin Bishop is playing, there's a certain consciousness he puts out. It's almost like being in a barn where there are chickens and pigs, and it's a very beautiful, happy atmosphere—very down-to-earth. Whereas if you go to a church or, say, to India, every music has its own consciousness. Music becomes like an empty glass, and whatever you put inside is the consciousness. If you play country and western or Brazilian samba or whatever, that's just the shell. It's how you feel—what you put inside the music—that's really significant.

"I forget that I'm maybe a significant figure in the world of music, and I become like a child who doesn't know anything except that I'm crying for spiritual values."

Around the time of the *Amigos* album a lot of articles came out stating that you'd "come back home" to the kind of music the Santana band had started out playing. Was that a conscious decision, or had you just absorbed different influences?

It was both. At the time that Jeff Beck came out with *Blow by Blow*, I was seeing the last of the musicians who got into the Mahavishnu thing, and I said, "Man, I'm ready to move on to something else." Why should I keep listening to John Coltrane and trying to play like that? So I went to New York and started listening to Latin music again, and I started listening through a lot of people's ears—how they listened to the first three Santana albums. I started learning something about myself. Even Earth, Wind & Fire and a lot of people gained something from the

Santana band's approach to music. So if they were willing to even say in an interview that they learned something from us, I figured, "Well, what the heck am I doing looking for something else? Maybe I already got something within myself—my own individuality." That's when I started getting into the room with the tape recorder and separating my playing from all the other musicians. Then I started realizing that I like Latin music and the Beatles and Eric Clapton, and that I shouldn't live in a world of nothing but Thelonious Monk and Art Tatum. Some might think that's a whole galaxy in itself, and it is. They're all great, but why limit yourself to a certain standard?

Did you notice the music affecting the audience in a different way?

We went for a year without a vocalist, and we were just playing as avant-garde as we were ever gonna get—like some things on *Lotus*. But, after a while, I started seeing people yawning, wondering when we were going to play something they could tap their feet to. You know, it was going a little bit over the ceiling, so I said, "Wait a minute. Maybe I should try to make a bridge and not be so drastic." Although I was having fun at the time, it's no fun if you're alone. At least for me, it ain't fun if you're trying to play basketball and all the other guys are on the other side of the court, and you're over here with the ball [*laughs*]. So Tom Coster and Ndugu [Leon Chancler] did a little bit of research on the band, and picked up what people sort of liked about the old band, and they started arranging songs like that. But I don't think that until the last album, *Moonflower*, has everything felt more natural to us. We don't have to go back to the first three albums to write like that anymore. We just get together, and it starts happening.

With a song like "Europa," which is very emotional, is it hard to play that night after night and still feel it as deeply as you did when you wrote it?

It's not as hard as it used to be, because I learned a trick to it, a way to condition the mind. I used to listen to B. B. King and say, "Wow, it took me forever to learn that riff, and I still don't have it down pat the way B. B. hits it." Then, after I saw him play, I could see that he'd make a certain face, and then hit the note. Every time he made the face like that, he'd hit the note. And I figured that he would go back somewhere in time to a certain place or somewhere inside himself and then hit the note. So that's what I do now. I forget that I'm maybe a significant figure in the world of music, and I become like a child who doesn't know anything except that I'm crying for spiritual values. I don't have to fabricate any grandeur trip or anything. It's like I'm very, very natural—which is what a spiritual master does. I think of Sri Chinmoy, and it makes it easier. I don't have to think, "Jesus, Al Di Meola is out in the audience," or any of that kind of stuff—all that pressure. I just feel like I'm playing for my guru, and instead of all those people around it's just one person, my spiritual master. I keep a picture of him next to the monitor.

Your father Jose plays violin?

Yes, and he sings Mexican folk songs. My father is like mariachi-type music. I'm doing this solo album called *Oneness: Silver Dream, Golden Reality*, and my father is going to be on it, and my wife, my brother Jorge, Narada Michael Walden, and my father-in-law, Saunders King. You know, I think it was in *Guitar Player*, they asked B. B. King to name his favorite guitar players, and one he mentioned was my father-in-law, Saunders King. He plays tremendous R&B guitar. I can pick up where Wes Montgomery and Kenny Burrell heard things from him. His sound is very big, fat, Rolls-Royce classy—not just fast chops. In fact, he doesn't play that much. He plays a couple of lines and then rests. But it's what he says. We played together at the Old Waldorf [in San Francisco]. He opened for us. It was an incredible experience. That's going to be a very interesting album, because it covers such a range of music with people who are very close to me. Like, I want to mix my father's Mexican music with Cuban music—you know, with mariachis and all the strings and then bongos and congas, too. And my father-in-law sings so sweet. I can't even think of anybody who he sounds like. It almost sounds like a high, soulful combination of Eddie Kendricks, Nat King Cole, and Billy Eckstein. It's very unique.

What kind of gut-string guitar do you play?

It's a Yamaha. I just endorsed them, and I'm really happy I did, because they go out of their way to make good instruments. The reason I left Gibson was because I feel like they're like McDonald's now. They just wrap a hamburger and throw it at you. There's nothing individual about it. Whereas Yamaha, to me, is more like my wife at Thanksgiving.

She spends a whole day in the kitchen just to knock you out with the food. She puts effort and time and love behind it, and you can feel it. People might think I'm crazy, but you can feel it when you pick up that guitar. You know whether or not somebody put something of himself into it with his hands. And Yamaha has that in their pianos and guitars. They're ambitious. They want quality.

Was your Yamaha electric built to your specifications?

Yeah. It's almost shaped like a Yamaha SG body, but it's really fat like a Les Paul. It has more frets, and for sustain I asked them to put a big chunk of metal like a grand piano right where the tailpiece is. You hit it, and it's like hitting an acoustic grand piano—it really resonates. When Yamaha first approached me, the guitar felt like a toy. You couldn't believe it—it was really light. You couldn't get nothing out of it. The frets were really thin. It just didn't feel like a guitar. It was like something you'd get in a hock shop—really cheap. So I sat down with them, and said, "Look, I can't play the guitar, man. I hope you won't be offended, but I just can't play it. But if you make it more solid, and put more wood on it . . ." Now, I think they make them like that for a lot of people.

Does the guitar weigh a lot?

It weighs a lot, although it's not too heavy. It's just heavy enough for you. When you hit the note, you don't have to use all those gadgets to sustain. In fact, I never use sustain pedals, and it really sustains better. Gadgets always make you sound like you're frying hamburgers through the amp. You have to find a kind of guitar that resonates.

There's some really nice acoustic work on *Amigos*. When did you get interested in that?

Well, my father had an acoustic nylon-string around the house, and that's how I learned Mexican folk songs. I noticed that when you play with the thumb, it gives it that sound synonymous with classical, or Spanish. There's a certain way of playing it. I don't know how to use my fingers—I use a pick on my thumb—but I heard enough Spanish music in my life, and I know what it sounds like, and I know how you can make it very emotional. If you've been to a Greek restaurant and seen those guys dancing, you know the emotional buildup. This is the same thing. I met Paco de Lucia in Spain, and I really got the chance to see

"IT TOOK ME A WHILE TO REALIZE THAT YOUR INDIVIDUALITY IS A VERY BEAUTIFUL GIFT"

what a real Spanish guitar player can do. It's such a beautiful art. I like him, because he's crossover, too. I'm probably going to get a lot of letters from people, but some guitarists put me to sleep. I have to have something that's close to me personally—what I'm into—and he is very close to me. He reminds me of Gabor Szabo. I like Gabor a lot—he's very expressive. The thing I like about Gabor is that he's a spellbinding kind of man. The way he stands is like a mongoose—it charms the snake and hypnotizes it until he gets it. Gabor does the same onstage with his music and his presence. He catches the groove, and you forget where the floor is and where the drink is, and he just engulfs you and drenches you with his presence. And Paco de Lucia has this, too. He starts playing, and you forget that you have arms and legs—you just become his feelings.

When did you start using the Mesa/Boogie amp?

My brother Jorge turned me on to that. I was in New York, and I was really unhappy with my Fender Twins. It gave me headaches just to try to sustain. When Leo Fender left the company, he took something with him, because almost overnight I couldn't get sustain from the new Fenders. Jorge came over and said, "You got to try this amp." And it really looked like the Tubes' amplifiers. It had a snakeskin kind of cover—really cheesy looking [laughs]. But, man, it sustained like crazy and was pure. So I never gave it back to Jorge [laughs]. I left him on the road without it—but I think he had another one. After a while I met Randy Smith [of Mesa Engineering] and I endorsed them. I'm sure that we started something, because Mahavishnu and Chick Corea and George Harrison and Elton John and everybody are playing them. The beautiful thing about it is it has three volume controls.

How do the controls work?

Well, if you want to practice really fast like Allan Holdsworth plays, you can still have that edge like you're bowing a violin—sustaining like that. Or you can play soft enough where the guy next door won't even hear you. By putting the first knob on the left on 10, and then the master on 1, you sustain like crazy, and it's about as loud as I'm talking right now. Or you can put the master a little louder and bring the other ones down, and you can play at the Berkeley Community Theater. But I never play with any of them above 7 1/2.

The Rapture: Santana channels his muse at San Francisco's Fillmore Auditorium, 1970. (©20TH CENTURY FOX / PHOTOFEST)

"IT TOOK ME A WHILE TO REALIZE THAT YOUR INDIVIDUALITY IS A VERY BEAUTIFUL GIFT"

Not even onstage?

No, all three volumes are at 7 1/2, and that is really loud, and I don't even have them put me through my monitors.

What other controls are on the Mesa/Boogie?

Treble and Bass, and it has another one called Gain, which I put on 7 1/2 or 8. And it has a reverb and this Presence button that you turn on, and then pull the three volumes, and you get even more edge on it. I don't use that unless I'm going to play something really 1960s psychedelic. I don't like too much fuzz, but it's there if you want it. It also has a graphic equalizer, but I don't use that much. I use it in the studio, but not onstage.

What are your tone settings?

The Treble is at 7 1/2, and Bass is, like, 1 or 2. I don't like too much bass. Fred Meyers [Santana's sound man] did something where I'm playing through six 10s just by flipping a switch. Then I flip the switch, and I go back into the Boogie output. But the Boogie with one 12 is enough. When I play through the six 10s, that's when I play rhythm—it's clean and naturally gives you a lot of bass. I don't know how the Mesa/Boogie came about, but I remember going to Randy at Prune Music in Mill Valley, California, and saying, "Man, I wish somebody would come out with a volume that I could sustain at any kind of level." And he said, "Man, you're dreaming," or something. Then, all of a sudden, he had three volume controls. He's a very remarkable man, and I think he beat a lot of people to the punch. A lot of people still wouldn't think of that.

What type of strings are you using?

I use Yamaha strings—generally .008, .011, .014, .024, .032, and .042.

It's surprising that you get such a full-bodied sound with such a light setup.

Well, it depends on how high you put the bridge, too. The lower you bring it down, the more you can bend the lighter strings. But if it's higher, then it's more comfortable for me. Mine's not too high, but not too low. Sometimes, I feel kind of lazy, and I don't feel like really bending, so then I go to the acoustic guitar and start building myself up all over again.

Have you been using the Yamaha electric on your albums?

I've used it ever since *Amigos*. They made me another one—a beautiful green one—and it's better for ballads, because the pickups are original

Yamahas. I always change the pickups—that's the only thing that I change from Yamaha—but, this time, I kept them on. On the other Yamaha, I had Larry Cragg put in new pickups that he rewires, and the response is incredible. Larry knows what I want and what I need, and he goes for it. He really knows me, but I don't think he's ever listened that much to our albums. I've just been to his shop [Prune Music] so many times.

Do you still use the Gibson L6-S that you were using before the Yamaha?

Well, Yamaha came out with a guitar called a Super Combinator, and the body looks like a takeoff on a Stratocaster, but it has all those phases that the L6-S has. It sounds like a Telecaster, or like a Strat with the switch between the pickup positions. That's why I liked the L6-S—because it was a Gibson, but it sounded almost like a Strat. But I've got to tell you the truth: That guitar was like a General Motors car. Within two months, man, something would always go out. I found myself almost bleeding to sustain a note, and I know it wasn't all the amp's fault.

Before the L6-S you were playing a Les Paul, right?

Yes. It was a 1968 or '69 model. Neal [Schon] and I got them at the same time, but his got stolen. It's a very good guitar.

Have you ever played Fenders?

I play Fenders in the studio. Onstage I don't, because to sustain I have to play almost twice as loud on a Fender. See, I don't beef them up. I don't do anything to the pickups. And for sustain, Gibson humbuckers have always been hotter, from the get-go. On the other guitars, you have to have gadgets to sustain, or you have to play even louder, and I'm not ready to make the jump. But in the studio I use Fenders a lot. I played a Stratocaster on "She's Not There" [*Moonflower*].

Ever play hollowbody or semi-hollowbody electrics?

Yeah, I played a Gibson Byrdland on *Amigos* for chord work. But they might have mixed me out [*laughs*]. You know, it's incredible, because each guitar makes you play totally different. You don't even have to try, and the Strat will throw you into a different way of playing, like Montrose—really raunchy. But every time I play the Byrdland, I find myself playing more like Kenny Burrell. I was into him for a long time. When you play the Byrdland, you want to use the thumb more to get that beautiful tone. It's really solid for playing jazz guitar.

"IT TOOK ME A WHILE TO REALIZE THAT YOUR INDIVIDUALITY IS A VERY BEAUTIFUL GIFT"

What's in the rest of your guitar collection?

I have most of the ones Gibson put out, Yamahas, most of the old Fenders. Don Wehr [of Don Wehr's Music City, San Francisco] called me, because he had a real old Stratocaster in very good condition, and that's the one I play a lot when I record. But the rest just occupy space. Mostly, I just play the Yamaha now. A friend of mine, Linda Manzer, built me a guitar that has a great tone. Just recently, I got a new white Gibson SG with three pickups, because I wanted to get a tremolo. And it's mainly because I was listening so much to Allan Holdsworth, and I know that's what he uses. He's one of my favorite new players. I'd like to record one song with that kind of sound. Of course, I can't think or play like him. Certain notes and bends he does are extremely unique.

"Each guitar makes you play totally different. You don't even have to try, and the Strat will throw you into a different way of playing."

You've mentioned several artists as being crossovers, which is somewhat controversial, as some jazz purists no doubt resent a rocker like Jeff Beck winning this year's Playboy poll as Best Jazz Guitarist. In fact, the term "jazz" has been used by some to describe your playing.

And I'm not, right. I don't know why they classify certain artists like they do, but I'm not bothered by it, because I know that, first and foremost I'm an instrument myself trying to play something back to you. I don't consider myself a guitar player as much as I am a seeker who wants to manifest his vision through that particular instrument. I consider a guitar player somebody who sounds like a guitar player. In this day and age, it's hard to tell who's not a crossover, except Keith Jarrett. Even McCoy Tyner sounds like a crossover, although he plays acoustic piano. But the variety of songs he does—with strings or people singing—is a positive crossover. I don't consider "crossover" to be a negative term. Some players have used it just to make more bread, and their heart isn't in it, and that's prostitution. But somebody who is making an honest attempt to master another kind of music his own way is a positive crossover. I think the only one, to my ears, who day or night doesn't sound like a crossover is Keith Jarrett. But, to me, it's a challenge to learn everything on earth. One time, I felt like it was my duty to be a pioneer, but that kind of stuff I leave to someone else now. I don't care to be a pioneer, except for my own heart. But, consciously, I wouldn't make it a commitment to put that kind of pressure on myself. I just play whatever is comfortable without offending or belittling my instrument or my own integrity.

You said earlier that you don't play Latin music.

I mean strictly Latin music. If you listen to real Latin music, we don't sound like that.

What would you consider real Latin music?

Real Latin music is Tito Puente, people from Puerto Rico, people from Cuba, and some in Venezuela. Everyone else is a conglomeration. They hear something that sounds like Latin music, and they adapt it to their own style—like Gato Barbieri and myself. Which is a healthy thing. Like Blood, Sweat & Tears did on their second album with jazz and Latin things. Even Steve Winwood and Traffic put out some Latin things on *Mister Fantasy*. But it's not a real Latin sound—it's Latin *colored*. By me saying this, I feel that I really cleared the air to a lot of people—Latin people and any other kind of people. I don't want to be labeled like that, because I don't play like that. You know, if I wanted to play blues, it takes a long time to play the blues and really be known as a blues player.

Even though your original band was called the Santana Blues Band, you've never put a straight blues tune on any of your albums.

I only use blues for feeling. I think as close as I came to playing blues on an album was a song called "Practice What You Preach" on *Borboletta*. I always wanted to do a blues, but to play blues you have to have a blues keyboard player who can play like Otis Spann—someone like Alberto Gianquinto. He used to play with B. B. King, James Cotton, and Charlie Musselwhite. That cat is a monster. You can tell that his main people are Thelonious Monk, Otis Spann, Horace Silver, and Chick Corea—those are the people he's really into. I collaborated with him on

"IT TOOK ME A WHILE TO REALIZE THAT YOUR INDIVIDUALITY IS A VERY BEAUTIFUL GIFT"

"Incident at Neshubar." I did the last part of it, and he did the 6/8 part and played piano on it. He helped us on the first two albums, because we'd never cut a record before. He said, "Look, all you have to do is take the fat out. Don't be going on and on, overstating anything—just pick the best part of the song." That's what we did. Otherwise, we would still be there [*laughs*].

Your first album didn't come out until 1969.

We were playing at least two-and-a-half years before we put out an album. That's how we got the reputation. We were headlining the Fillmore a couple of times, and we didn't even have an album out—you can ask Bill Graham. We must have been doing something right.

4.

"ERIC CLAPTON'S GUITAR IS A VOICE IN ITSELF"

. . . .

by Carlos Santana, July 1985

The first time I saw Eric Clapton was with Cream at the old Fillmore Auditorium in San Francisco. I didn't even know how they were going to sound, because *Fresh Cream* sounded so fantastic for being just three people. But they sounded *better* than the album the day that I heard them. They looked like giants—like they were on stilts or something. The music was overpowering. There were, like, three albums that came out that year—1967—that knocked everybody out: *The Doors*, *Fresh Cream*, and *East-West* by the Butterfield Blues Band.

The center of Eric Clapton's music—to me—is obviously the blues. But he has another plus—he is very lyrical. All of a sudden, his guitar is a voice in itself—or a trumpet, or an orchestra. He revolutionized a lot of things. From what I understand, even Jimi wanted to meet Eric when he first went to England.

Eric would crank it up, but he made it sound like music. A lot of other guys cranked it up, and it sounded like noise. Eric sounded celestial. I believe Cream opened the doors for a lot of bands, such as Tony Williams Lifetime, Jimi Hendrix, Led Zeppelin, and a lot of other people.

Eric and I toured together in 1975, and we got to spend time talking about things that we both love—blues players and things that inspired us. Boy, I learned from personal experience that Jimmy Page, Jeff Beck, and Eric Clapton—you can't back those guys against the wall. They have incredible arsenals of stuff. For example, we did a show at Nassau

Coliseum in New York where John McLaughlin jammed with us. Clapton waited for John to say his thing, and for me to say my thing, and then he came out with a switch-blade, man. You know, he doesn't play fast, but like my conga player Armando Peraza says, "He gets inside the note."

A lot of other guys cranked it up, and it sounded like noise. Eric sounded celestial.

I think it would be great to hear Eric in another setting—like with Brasil '77 or Jimmy Cliff—because what he has, he can't lose anymore. That identity will never be lost, but it would be interesting to hear it in a different setting.

The last time we really spent time together was when Eric did the ARMS show in San Francisco. He hung out at my house, and I took him to Village Music in Mill Valley, and he bought a bunch of blues records. He gave me a tape with three or four songs that are not on his new album [*Behind the Sun*], and they're killer. One is called "Jailbreak," and another is "Heaven's Just One Step Away"—which is an incredible single, with reggae and stuff in it. I don't know why they didn't put those cuts out—they're happening!

5.

"THE MOST IMPORTANT THING IS TO LEARN THE ESSENCE OF THE SONG"

. . . .

by Jas Obrecht, November 1988

The three-record *Viva Santana!* celebrates the career of Carlos Santana, presenting a mixture of earlier releases and previously unheard tracks dating back to 1968. To take the show on the road, Carlos reassembled his late-'60s lineup for the first time in nearly two decades. After two weeks of intensive rehearsals with keyboardist Gregg Rolie, drummer Michael Shrieve, and percussionist Chepito Areas, Carlos called on the eve of the tour to offer his views on the fine art of rehearsing.

How can musicians make the most of rehearsal time?

I think people spend a lot of wasted time on getting sounds together. They work for hours on their sound, and that stuff is never-ending, anyway. They MIDI to this and do that, and then when you tell them to play, they don't know the song. They should just rehearse with a plain, simple keyboard, one guitar, one conga, and just learn the songs. I tell people—and I don't care who they are—that it's important for them to spend more time knowing the changes, what the breaks are, and the transitions. When they go home, they can learn to MIDI and get their sound together, but the best way to utilize rehearsal time is to memorize dynamics, intensity, nuances, and things like that. I like to make sure that people know these in their dreams, so it becomes a very natural extension of transitions.

How do you teach them the songs?

*Santana onstage in the '80s—the same era in which he forged
a lasting relationship with PRS Guitars.* (© ROSS BARNATT / RETNA LTD.)

"THE MOST IMPORTANT THING IS TO LEARN THE ESSENCE OF THE SONG"

To me, the song is primarily the groove, which is the heart. If you have an incredible groove, who cares about the intro and the bridge and the end and the verses and the chorus? That's what I like the best about Talking Heads' *Remain in Light*. Those songs don't sound like songs—they sound like straight-ahead grooves. For new songs, I try to break it down so that people don't get too much cholesterol from either melody or rhythm. I try to balance it out, so that there's valleys and mountains, and it's not too frenetic. It's just like making love—there has to be tension and release, tension and release.

The main thing I teach people is the groove—you know, "This is how it goes." Let me hear what the drummer and bass player are doing, and then I bring in the congas. A lot of people can be a little bit too clever for you. They disguise what they don't know by just playing a lot. I say, "No, no, no. When I want you to play, really play it. But what I want you to really do is hold the groove." Wayne Shorter and I were talking about this. We want to lay a groove down that Wynton Marsalis to the guy with the green mohawk hair can get off on, because then we will hit everything in between.

"As soon as you leave your house, you're at the mercy of all kinds of things. So I don't like to over-rehearse, but I like to rehearse enough so that everybody feels totally free and natural, and then we can improvise."

What percent of rehearsal time should be spent actually playing music?

From the morning when you walk in until you leave. I feel like a fish in water, man, when the music is right, and that's what I try to go for in rehearsals. I can't stand it when people have to stop the groove a lot—it kills me.

How long is your typical rehearsal?

Usually from 1:00 to like 6:00 or 8:00. We take breaks to go eat and to discuss how things feel to people, whether somebody needs coaching, or if they need to know the breakdown on the song, how come the song works like this—that kind of stuff. I like to rehearse the band from eight to 12 days. Then, when we go onstage, we can just walk through it, even if the monitors suck or whatever. As soon as you leave your house, you're at the mercy of all kinds of things. So I don't like to over-rehearse, but I like to rehearse enough so that everybody feels totally free and natural, and then we can improvise. I always give the analogy that to rehearse is to know the corners, so you can always get home right. Once you know how to get home right, then you can take another route.

Do you typically update the songs at each rehearsal?

Yeah. With a lot of the songs, we have to. There are different musicians, and everybody plays differently. Nobody plays a shuffle, or even just a straight-ahead Jimmy Reed riff the same. The only people who play the way Jimmy Reed played it is Jimmy Reed and Philip Upchurch. The rest of us, we try to take some essence from it, but we're not going to play exactly like it. Ain't no way.

Should rehearsals follow the pattern of the show?

No, because rehearsal is only a schematic. It's a column of vertebrae. Once you get it, then you put the spirit on it. I try to put spirit anywhere—rehearsals and everything. To me, the most beautiful thing about rehearsing is when I can catch myself and the other guys in the band literally drooling. You know, when they get into the solo, you look up, and these people have gobs of saliva flowing from their mouth. You go, "Yeah! Yeah!" They're so blissed out and opiated with their own thing that they know the rehearsal was good for them. If they get lost, it's a good way to get lost—not in confusion, but imbued with the spirit.

What's the best attitude to bring to rehearsal?

The best attitude is to know that music should always be boiling—like boiling water. Whether it's soft or loud or fast or slow, it should always be intense. A lot of people play half-hearted when they play softly. They should never do that, because the spirit of the song goes out. The main thing is to not lose that intensity, and also to learn to project—not loud in volume, but to project.

Is it important to work with people you get along with?

"THE MOST IMPORTANT THING IS TO LEARN THE ESSENCE OF THE SONG"

Yeah. I'm professional enough that I can work with people that I don't get along with, but, first and foremost, music is harmony. If you only work with a person onstage—and offstage you can't stand his guts—there's no point, because all that stuff is going to come out onstage also. Some people are really good at masking their feelings. I'm not that way, so for me it's best to work with people who have respect for everybody in the band. Whether I'm onstage or offstage, I just don't want to be a psychiatrist or a cop or a nurse or a babysitter for anybody. I like people who can play the music and get along in the restaurant, too, and still complement life. That's what music is all about—to complement life.

How does it feel to be back with your old bandmates?

It feels great, because now after 20 years, there's a lot of mutual respect and admiration. They don't have to fight me like they used to, to be in charge of the band. I usually don't impose authority on anybody. I try to create the best possible setting so that every musician can express himself and bring the best out of the music and the other musicians. I believe that Gregg and Michael are comfortable with me now, and whenever they want to say something, I'm not going to stop them or block them. I'll say yea or nay, according to where they are. I go by people's eyes. I'll say, "Yeah, you're right. Let's do it that way," or "Whoa. Let's think about it overnight," or, "Let's play it, and see what it tells us." We have a better communication with each other now. It's not a do-or-die feel—like it used to be when we were kids. We can laugh at ourselves now.

You know, a guy came up to me in Jamaica earlier this year, and said, "Hey, man, I want you to listen to the baddest guitar player in the island." The first thing I said was, "Hey, man, do you know why the Lord created the world round? So we can *all* have center stage." That obliterates all that.

6.

"THE MUSICIANS I LOVE DIDN'T HAVE A PHD IN ANYTHING EXCEPT LIFE"

. . . .

by James Rotondi, January 1993

C arlos Santana believes in music—not just music's potential to amaze and delight, but its power to transform emotions, channel energy, and touch lives. The source of this power, the universal truth that connects Mozart to Monk, has been the subtext to the musical vision-quest Carlos began at age five, when he was first introduced to traditional mariachi music by his father, Jose Santana. Today, after 26 albums, Carlos hasn't lost touch with the humanity and generosity that inspired Eric Clapton to call him "the sweetest man I know."

If anything, Carlos' vision of the role he wants his music to play is clearer than ever. His newest release, the inspiring *Milagro*, is testimony to the strength of his convictions and the freshness and relevance of his singular guitar mastery. After 22 years with Columbia Records, Carlos recently signed with Polydor—a deal that includes the formation of Carlos' own custom record label, Guts & Grace. He remains a vital, explosive concert attraction and continues to pursue the fine art of jamming, sitting in with artists like B. B. King and Buddy Guy whenever the opportunity arises. The Santana band, featuring monster players like keyboardist Chester Thompson, bassist Benny Rietveld, and drummer Walfredo Reyes, is as strong as ever, and the accompaniment on *Milagro*'s "Saja/Right On" and "Agua Que Va Caer" supports some of Carlos' most lyrical and intuitive soloing.

Santana greets you warmly, without a trace of star affectation or suspicion. He speaks softly, with an earnest tone and a gentle sense of

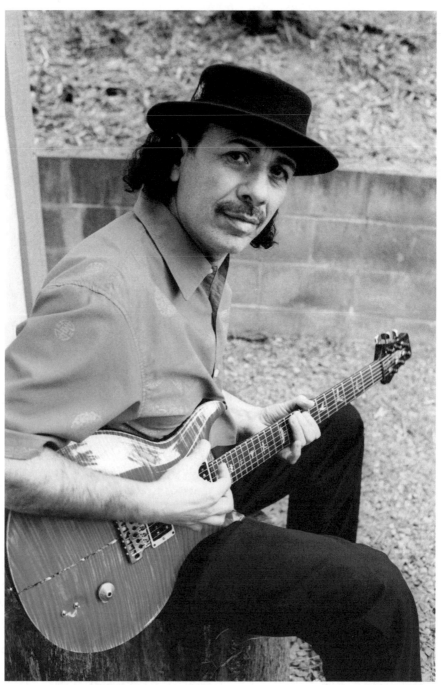

Santana with one of his custom PRS models in the '90s.

humor. The admiration he feels for seminal musicians like John Coltrane, Jimi Hendrix, Miles Davis, B. B. King, and Bob Marley verges on worship, but one senses that it's enlightened respect, not mere awe, that informs Carlos' allegiance. After three decades of performing, writing, and recording, Carlos is not fooled by flashy gestures, technical overkill, or contrived feeling. He wants the real thing, because he is aware, as few are, that the right note in the right place can quite literally change lives.

"The first rule of music: If you don't feel it, why should they?"

THE LANGUAGE OF THE HEART

"The musicians I love, like Coltrane, Miles, Jimi, and Bob Marley—they didn't have a PhD in anything except life. If you told them they were legends, they'd probably look at you like you were stupid. The most important thing is to live life and tell the truth in a language of the heart. In the movie *'Round Midnight*, there was a guy who was following Dexter Gordon, and he said to Dexter, 'The way you played those three notes changed my life forever.' B. B. did that for me, and I'm sure I've done that for someone else. That's what's important. Bill Graham was the one who told me: 'Your music is a perfect balance of spirituality and sensuality, whether you accept it or not.' I'm not trying to exploit it, but I am trying to explore it. Most of the time, when we play in Texas or the Midwest, you'll see a guy with his hands clasped like he's meditating, and next to him is a lady with her eyes like she's having an orgasm, and with her hands she's saying, 'Come on, come on.' Her body is quivering. That's part of a concert—that's what should be in there, because music does all those things. The best thing is when you strip people of their hang-ups. There's a lot of people not too far from suicide or homicide. But music has the power to touch those people before they get to that point. When you make people cry and laugh at the same time, no matter what nationality or language they speak, you disarm them, and keep them from carrying those two hitchhikers that kill people—depression and frustration. To me that's very real, man. I got a letter as soon as John Lee Hooker's *The Healer* came out [*Carlos collaborated on the title track*]. This guy said, 'My wife ran away with this other cat. Life is too painful, and I had the knife ready to cut my veins. But I had the TV on, and 'The Healer' came on. Then I started to cry, and I started to laugh. I wanted to live. So I want to thank you for the tone, the message in the song. Because you and John Lee, you're the healers.' To me, that's what music is really for. That's the first rule of music: If you don't feel it, why should they?"

STREET UNIVERSITY

"I very rarely think of what chords, or what notes, or where I put my finger. You should have learned all the technical and physical aspects of the guitar in junior high school as far as I'm concerned. I don't think musicians who can really play think of music like that. When I'm playing a solo now, most of the time I'm thinking of combing my daughter's hair before she goes to bed, and I have to do it a special way so I don't make her cry by pulling her hair. Believe me, that's what I'm thinking lately, man! Unless I'm playing with Wayne Shorter. Wayne has an incredible way of writing everything. Those are the few times that I'm a musician with a short leash. If you read music, you've got to turn it down, and get to the paper, and get to what Wayne is trying to say. There are rules you need to learn when you play with Wayne Shorter or Joe Zawinul. You have to learn really quickly what they're trying to get across, and then make it your own. But to make it your own requires street learning. You cannot learn that in Harvard or Berkeley—you have to learn from the streets. The street university is very important, man."

BULLETS PENETRATING PAPER

"When people ask me to play on their albums, I ask them to send me a tape. I'll listen to the song first without playing a solo, and then I'll just go for what I hear. I know what chord I'm in, but I don't know what note I'm going to start with. All I know is a certain sound. If I hear country western or jazz or reggae, I hear a sound. Sometimes, it sounds like a baby crying in another room in the back of your mind. Sometimes, it

"THE MUSICIANS I LOVE DIDN'T HAVE A PHD IN ANYTHING EXCEPT LIFE"

sounds like a bird, and, sometimes, it sounds like Jimi Hendrix's guitar coming at your face. Sometimes, it sounds like one of John Lee Hooker's moans. So then I try to capture that on the box. Usually, by trusting my hand, it goes right to what I heard. I think if I knew exactly what I was doing, I wouldn't have done it. A lot of times, you may hit some really ugly notes, but that's okay in the pursuit of that perfect thing. That's the whole romance of losing and finding yourself when you take a solo. You must lose yourself to find yourself. If you approach everything from an analytical point of view, the mind takes over. By the time you do your solo, it might sound great, but it's not going to penetrate. It will be like bullets that don't penetrate paper. There are a lot of guitarists with bullets that don't penetrate paper. Whereas other players—like Buddy Guy—they hit one note, and you see everybody fall out and go, 'Jesus Christ!' We've been jamming with Trey Anastasio from Phish [*who have opened many dates on Santana's current tour*]. I swear, he got so into his solo that a big ol' goo of saliva came over him and his guitar. He was drooling over himself like a baby. It was great! He looked up, and kind of cleaned up his slobber, and I said, 'Yeah, man—that's it!' That's the goal: to lose yourself to the point that Miles used to call 'a two-hour orgasm.' A spiritual orgasm onstage. That's what he'd wake up every morning for. That's a great goal in itself."

MUSIC IN BLOOM

"My time with Sri Chinmoy gave me some discipline, and an awareness of Eastern philosophy. But I look at it like my old tennis shoes from Mission High School. They don't fit me anymore. I came to him because of my fascination with John Coltrane and John McLaughlin, and I left him because of the same thing—my fascination with the spiritual side of music. I didn't go over there to join the Marines. I went because I was looking to clarify my feelings to an extent that when I play, it's as significant as a flower. Because flowers signify gratitude on Planet Earth—whether people look at them or not. When people say you should stop and smell the roses, it means that unless you identify with gratitude, you're always going to be miserable. At that time, when I got into Sri Chimnoy, everyone was dying, OD-ing left and right. So it was either the stuff they put in your veins, or fold your hands and give yourself to the Lord. I never wanted to become a casualty. I was afraid that I wasn't strong enough to shake off the same road that everybody takes, which was booze and drugs and 'I just play guitar so f**k everyone else.' Pretty soon, you see those people, like old boxers working in Las Vegas opening doors for somebody else. I didn't want to be a loser. What I like is clarity. I'm very simple. My mind is not complex like Frank Zappa or Wayne Shorter, so I always try to bring everything down to the most simple denomination, which is the heart.

"My father and I used to talk about the universal note, the universal tone. John Lee and Coltrane have that thing. Martin Luther King has that tone. I don't know why it is, but certain people are so powerful that when they speak, the soul stands at attention. That's 'Trane, Bob Marley, John Lee—just the tone. They could be talking about beans, it don't even matter. 'A Love Supreme' or 'Louie, Louie.' It doesn't matter. It's the presence they bring that makes it so strong."

SPIRITS DANCING IN THE FLESH

"There are very few musicians who can say something simple and soulful through a lot of chord changes, and not just run at the mouth. So what? I hear so many trumpet players who can play rings around Miles Davis in his last days. But two or three notes from him meant all of the chord changes, because he touched my heart. I listen to Charlie Christian a lot—and Django Reinhardt—but when it starts getting too complex and too dense and too thick with the chords, then what the f**k are you trying to say? Aren't you just trying to say, 'I love you? Whether you love me or not, I love you and the song is for you.' Isn't that what you're trying to say? Or are you trying to say, 'Dig how great I am, and I don't give a sh*t if you like it or not?' John McLaughlin, along with Pat Metheny, is one of the few musicians who can run all of it and make it sound 1992, instead of old like the '30s, '40s, and '50s. That's what I keep my ears open for: people who can run all those chord changes, yet I can still hear a child cry. I can still hear something human. Not just a typewriter. Who wants to hear a typewriter?

"I read books about how people in their 30s or 40s are just beginning

"THE MUSICIANS I LOVE DIDN'T HAVE A PHD IN ANYTHING EXCEPT LIFE"

to find out what their purpose in life is. I found that out when I was five years old, but it was reinforced when I heard B. B. King for the first time in 1966 at the Fillmore West. That's when I know I would be nothing else but that, no matter what. I'm very blessed. I'm very fortunate, because what I know I've known all my life, and that's all I want to know. I didn't want to know about algebra or George Washington's morals or wooden teeth or whatever. I couldn't wait to get out of school so I could go buy some John Lee Hooker records or Wes Montgomery records and tear them apart.

"Since Miles left and Bill Graham left, it really made me face up to the fact that time is short, and I have to get to the heart of what I'm trying to do. I learned the tools of the box when I was young. Now, it's just easier. I don't think of A, B, C when I'm talking to you. I don't think of consonants—I think of feelings. It's the same with the guitar. After a while, don't think of chords or progressions or time changes. You play what you hear. I get right to the main chorus, instead of walking around and nibbling here or there like I used to do. It gives me a lot of confidence, man, just to get to the heart of it, and get the hell out of there! [*Laughs.*] If you think, then forget it.

"What I'd like to do before I die is bring people closer to the same reality that John Coltrane and Bob Marley were trying to bring people to—no borders, one race, just one body, and we all take responsibility so nobody starves to death tomorrow morning. If you could do that with music, that's more important than becoming Hendrix or Beethoven, because you cause and affect the whole wheel of life in such a way that even though you are one person you made a difference—like Martin Luther King or Mahatma Gandhi. Then songs come like windows for people to look inside or look outside. That's why we love Jimi Hendrix. Because they're beautiful windows. When we look into them, we like what we see.

"So I'm more clear now as to why I'm doing everything. It's not just to make people happy or make them dance. It's to change things. Change myself, the people in my band, change people all around, so we can have a clearer vision about life and about ourselves, so there won't be as much disharmony in the world."

7.

"I PLAY RAINBOW MUSIC. IT'S LIKE DIAMONDS—ALL THE COLORS ARE THERE, BUT IT'S STILL CLEAR"

by Andy Ellis, August 1999

I had only one concern when making my new record," says Carlos Santana. "Would Jimi Hendrix like it if he were here? Would there be enough guitar? It's important for me to appease Jimi and Wes Montgomery because I play for them, too."

We're sitting in Santana's large rehearsal hall in San Rafael, California. Surrounded by bright wall hangings depicting his musical heroes—John Coltrane, Miles Davis, Jimi Hendrix, Charlie Parker, and Bob Marley—Santana is describing the genesis of his latest album, *Supernatural*. Featuring collaborations with an intriguing assortment of contemporary musicians, including Lauryn Hill, Wyclef Jean, Dave Matthews, Everlast, Rob Thomas of Matchbox 20, Eagle Eye Cherry, and the Dust Brothers, this release is Santana's debut on Arista Records.

"We're still finishing some tracks," Santana explains, as he cues up "Love of My Life," a song he co-wrote with Dave Matthews. "In fact, right after this interview I'm going into the studio to put some guitar on 'The Call,' which I wrote with Eric Clapton. It's time to put that one to bed."

As the punchy intro to "Love of My Life" emerges from the boom box, Santana's head bobs with the music. "You know what? There *is* enough guitar in there!"

Santana holds passionate views on a variety of subjects, and whether discussing songwriting, tone, and soloing—or such hot-button topics as spirit guides, self-validation, synchronicity, senility, and suicide—he presents his thoughts calmly, without a hint of rock-star posturing. Santana's speech is as distinctive as his playing, and he weaves his colorful tales of music and mysticism with unguarded sincerity.

Even if you don't share all of his beliefs, his ideas will get you thinking about the guitar and its role in our lives. Santana has survived more than three decades in the fickle music business without losing an iota of his enthusiasm for the 6-string and its great players. We can all learn from that.

Your new record is a remarkably collaborative effort. How did this come about?

Through meditations and dreams, I received these instructions: "We want you to hook up with people at junior high schools, high schools, and universities. We're going to get you back into radio airplay." I said, "Okay," because a lot of young people are not happy unless they are miserable. You can tell by what's happening at the schools. The vibrations of this music and the resonance in the lyrics will present these people with new options. I don't want them to feel like me or think like me—we're all individuals, and we're all unique. But with our music, we're presenting a new octave—a new menu. This menu says: "We are multi-dimensional spirits dwelling in the flesh, solely for the purpose of evolution."

You see, if you take the time to crystallize your intentions, motives, and purpose, and direct them for the highest good of life and people on the planet—behold, you get synchronicity. I'll give you an example. Working with [Arista label head] Clive Davis, we got hooked up with Lauryn Hill. She said, "Oh man, I love your music. Since I was a child, I listened to 'Samba Pa Ti'—I even wanted to put lyrics to it." So Lauryn invited me to play with her at the Grammy Awards. Playing with her was my first time there.

And what a night—she won five Grammys.

Yes, she cleaned up. Eric Clapton was in the audience, and he saw us perform. After the show, he called and said, "Look man, I heard that people at Arista were trying to contact me to play on your new record. I've

"I PLAY RAINBOW MUSIC. IT'S LIKE DIAMONDS—ALL THE COLORS ARE THERE, BUT IT'S STILL CLEAR"

been going through some serious changes in my life, and I was at a really critical point, but things are better now. Do you still hear me on your album? Is there room for me?" To hear Eric say that! I grew up listening to him, Peter Green, and Michael Bloomfield.

Then what happened?

Well, my spirits are Miles Davis and Bill Graham [*the impresario, not the evangelist*]. Even though they've left the physical world, they still come in my dreams and give me instructions. So when Eric asked if there was room for him on the record, I could hear Bill saying, "No, you schmuck, you're too late!" So I'm on the phone having a conversation with Bill and Eric at the same time. To Bill, I said, "Wait. Maybe you can talk to him like that, but I can't." And to Eric, I said, "Yeah, but you know what? I wouldn't think of dipping you into something that has already been recorded. Why don't you come over, and we'll write something from scratch?"

And that's how we started. We went through a couple of things and settled on something I had written, but never recorded. It has a Prince bass groove, but it's very swampy—you could hear John Lee Hooker or the Staple Singers playing it.

So that's synchronicity at work?

Exactly. Here's another example: Last summer, I asked an artist named Michael Rios to create a poster for us. I marked some passages in a few books and asked him to start with those ideas, and then continue with his own vision. Do you know what's really amazing? The images for lyrics that Dave Matthews, Everlast, Wyclef, Lauryn Hill, and Eagle Eye Cherry brought to the album are all in the poster! I didn't tell them to look at it or anything.

So I know there is something happening. It was like that from '69 until '73, and then it went somewhere else. Now it's happening again with this music. I'm in total awe of how fast and smooth things have been. Nobody has had a cow, nobody is bugged out—and there are a lot of producers, engineers, and artists involved with this record. They're putting their best foot forward, and all being very gracious. I keep pinching myself. I feel very incidental—I just show up, we see each other's eyes, we hear the music, and we start recording.

How do you describe your music?

I don't see myself playing black music or white music or gray music. I play rainbow music. It's like diamonds—all the colors are there, but it's still clear.

DAVE MATTHEWS
ON SONGWRITING
WITH SANTANA
BY KYLEE SWENSON

"We saw each other when we were both playing a festival in Germany," recalls Dave Matthews. "When Carlos was playing his set, he invited us to come up and play 'Exodus' by Bob Marley, and afterwards we talked about doing something together. We didn't really have a plan for what to do, just that we'd set aside five days to do it. Carlos had some music he'd been listening to that was inspirational to him, but when we got to the studio, we were just standing there with nothing but potential. As soon as he walked into the room, however, it was just joy. He threw his ideas out, and we came up with 'Love of My Life.'

"It's an incredibly simple song, which was an inspiration. He had the idea of reusing this Brahms melody, cutting it in half, repeating one part of it, and using the second half as a bridge. I'm always searching to make my life more complicated, but very often, lessons, inspirations, and moments of clarity come out of the simplest things. I think the most poignant moments in music are the most simple. Beauty doesn't always have to be complex.

"It's funny to think of the Brahms melody as it was originally. It's so different from what Carlos played—just changing the rhythm hid its origin. I love it because I can hear it so clearly, whereas if I were to play it for my mother and ask, 'Do you recognize the melody?' she probably wouldn't. He took that melody and turned it into a different piece of music. Just seeing how he put a song together opened my eyes to a different technique of writing. When I'm writing with the band—or by myself—I sort of wait for an idea and then put pieces together. But with Carlos, it's almost like he just sits down and builds something.

"Hanging out with Carlos was really enlightening. Even though he's such a heavy-weight, he's an incredibly kind man. It was very pleasant to meet someone who spoke with so much knowledge and experience. I enjoy his analogies, his mixture of the mind and the heart, his beautiful parallels. Recording with him was like being away on a retreat as opposed to going into work."

"I PLAY RAINBOW MUSIC. IT'S LIKE DIAMONDS—ALL THE COLORS ARE THERE, BUT IT'S STILL CLEAR"

What's the process when you co-write a song with, say, Dave Matthews? Do you send tapes back and forth, or do you write in the studio?

There's a story behind that one. When my father passed away two or three years ago, I didn't listen to music for four days—that's a long time for me. I was picking up my son from school, and I thought, "Okay, time to listen to some radio." I turned on a classical station, and the first thing I heard was this melody [*gently sings a slow, six-note theme*]. The melody just stayed with me. They didn't say who the composer was, but I thought it was Strauss.

I wanted to find out what this was, so I went to the classical music section at Tower Records, and said, "All I have is this melody." I sang it, and the guy goes, "Oh yeah. Brahms Concerto No. 2." They get me the CD, and that's the song! I said, "Damn, you guys are good!"

So I brought this melody to Dave Matthews in New York. I said, "I hear this with a '1999' bass." I also recited these lines:

You're the love of my life
You're the breath of my prayers
Take my hand, lead me there
With you is where I want to be

Dave sat down and—bam!—wrote the song lyrics right there on the spot, and we recorded it.

Your guitar melody swings a bit more than the Brahms theme.

If Brahms were alive today, he would swing it, too, because it's what's happening. Listen to Dave's phrasing—he sang it like Billie Holiday or Frank Sinatra—way behind the beat. It's that human thing. Only squares sing in the middle.

As always, your guitar sound is very vocal.

When you listen to vocalists like Aretha Franklin and Dionne Warwick, you learn to phrase differently. For a long time, I wouldn't listen to guitar players—Joe Pass, Pat Martino, Jim Hall—because I felt that was another generation's music. I felt my music was blues and rock. But now, I'm discovering all this music by Jim Hall, Kenny Burrell, and Wes Montgomery, and it's like, "Oh, this guy is burning just as hard, but with a different fire."

I'm able to check out all the guitar players, take what I need, and still make those notes like Miles—you know, when you hit that note, you don't want to breathe until you finish with it. You go [*exhales*]. Miles, Peter Green—there are very few people who make you hold your breath until that note is ended. You literally feel like you've got a colic in your stomach. You get goosebumps. I love musicians who make you want to cry and laugh at the same time. When they go for it, you go with them, and you don't come back until they come back. [*Laughs.*] There are not that many players who can consistently do that. Potentially, we all should be doing it.

Were you listening to any particular musicians while working on this album?

I was listening to Peter Green, John Coltrane, and Miles Davis.

What were you listening for?

Peter Green for his legato tones. I mean, the first four or five years of Peter Green, because lately he plays more like Pat Martino. Staccato notes—John Coltrane. And from Miles, you get the alchemy of making 50,000 notes into five. But with those five, you shake the world. That was Miles' supreme gift. He could play two or three notes and, man or woman, you'd just go, "Oh, my God." Listen to *Sketches of Spain*. Play your guitar and try to keep up with the notes, the way he holds them, the breath of it. That's the voice of angels, man.

You see, great music comes not from thinking, but from pure emotion. As the Grateful Dead people say, "It's when the music plays you." You make the best music when you're not conscious of doing it. I've been saying these things since the beginning. I remember getting in trouble with Frank Zappa—I'm pretty sure he coined the phrase, "Shut up and play your guitar" for people like me, because we talk a lot! But I am passionate about turning on massive amounts of kids, and pulling them out of that miserable state. I want to turn them over. You don't have to be Jimi Hendrix or Charlie Parker—you can get it done in your own way. God made the world round so we can all have center stage. Everybody is important, as long as you're doing it from your heart. Frustration and depression lead to homicide and genocide, but inspiration and vision lead to a spiritual orgasm.

Can you describe this?

It's where you're constantly happy, and you don't have to feel weird when people say, "Man, what are you laughing about?" I'm laughing because I know the secret of life. And the secret of life is that I have validated my existence. I know that I am worth more than my house, my bank account, or any physical thing. When I hit that note—if I hit it correctly—I'm just as important as Jimi Hendrix, Eric Clapton, or anybody. Because when I hit that note, I hit the umbilical cord of anybody who is listening.

"When you feel that the world is not appreciating your genius, you're already setting yourself up to be a victim."

When you hit a note like that, people say, "What kind of guitar is that? What kind of speakers are you using? What kind of strings?" No, man. It's not all that—it's the *note*. Now, when you explain this to kids, they say, "Really? I can do that too?" Sure. We can teach you how to put five things into one note. [*To illustrate, Santana holds out the karate edge of his hand, and then rotates it to reveal his palm and five fingers.*] These are the ingredients for being a complete communicator: Soul, heart, mind, body, cojones. One note.

I validated my existence before I got out of high school. People would ask, "What are you going to do when you leave school?" I'd say, "I'm going to play with Michael Bloomfield and B. B. King." They thought I was crazy! I'd say, "Why are you laughing?" They'd say, "Man, you're tripping." "No, *you're* tripping because you don't know what you want to do. I know what I want to do, and I know who I'm going to be doing it with. And I'm going to play with those people."

Once you learn to validate your existence, you have the wind in your sails—where do you want to go?—and you can never commit suicide. I would say that as great as Danny Gatton was, he never took the time to validate his existence. When you feel that the world is not appreciating your genius, you're already setting yourself up to be a victim. There are a lot of musicians like that: "My manager ripped me off. My record company ripped me off. I'm going to eat beans, but I'm not going to play what they want me to play."

Which albums inspire you?

Tell everybody to hear *Spellbinder* by Gabor Szabo. That is a must for anybody who plays guitar. He's the person who I credit with pulling me out of B. B. King. B. B. had us in a headlock—Michael Bloomfield, Peter Green—we were all under his spell. Gabor played like a Gypsy, but different from Paco de Lucia. I first heard Gabor with [drummer] Chico Hamilton. The band had no piano player. It was just congas, timbales, and drums with Gabor and [bassist] Ron Carter. It sounded unbelievable.

So *Spellbinder* is one of those "Holy Grail" recordings?

Exactly. Also "The Supernatural" by Peter Green, Bola Sete's *At the Monterey Jazz Festival*, and Wes Montgomery's *Goin' Out of My Head*. Unplug the phone, sit down with these, and you're in for a real surprise.

If someone was searching for essential Santana, which of your records would you recommend?

For pure songs, *Abraxas*. For pure guitar, I would say *Caravanserai*. Neal Schon and I played really well on that album. At the time, the

SUPERNATURAL GEAR

BY ANDY ELLIS

According to renowned guitar tech René Martinez, Santana recorded *Supernatural* using Paul Reed Smith guitars strung with D'Addario nickel strings, gauged .009–.042. "The PRS pickups are specially wound for Carlos," details Martinez. "There's a Dragon humbucker in the bridge position and a Santana model humbucker in the neck position. Carlos also played a stock '57 sunburst Strat with a maple neck. For amps, he used a '70s Marshall 100-watt head and 4x12 cab, a '65 blackface Fender Twin, and a Mesa/Boogie combo loaded with a single 12" Altec. The Boogie has been with Carlos a long time. All these amps are in good condition, and they sound great.

"We placed the mics to reproduce the overall sound we heard in the studio and to capture the authentic amp tone," continues Martinez. "Carlos played through all three amps simultaneously. This way we were able to blend tones for each song. There never is a 'right' setting. You have to get into a studio and tweak the sounds for that particular room. For effects, Carlos kept it simple, relying on a wah, spring reverb from the Twin and Boogie, and a reissue Ibanez TS-9 Tube Screamer."

"I PLAY RAINBOW MUSIC. IT'S LIKE DIAMONDS—ALL THE COLORS ARE THERE, BUT IT'S STILL CLEAR"

Allman Brothers had two guitar players. I remember Miles was really upset with me because I had another guitarist, but I told him, "I think Neal is a great guitar player, and that's what I hear right now." I believe it worked. Later, Neal went to do his thing with Journey, and because I still craved to play with another guitarist, I played with John McLaughlin.

Once I got that craving out of the way, I wanted to learn why I was so fascinated with Coltrane and that "sky-church music," as Jimi called it. So I got together with [pianist and harpist] Alice Coltrane, and I found out why she writes, and how she writes those celestial strings. It's important for guitarists to listen to her and [tenor saxophonist] Pharoah Sanders.

How do you write songs? Do you keep a tape recorder running to document your ideas?

All the time. I play for two or three hours and keep flipping tapes. I mark them, and then come in the next day and listen to them. After a half an hour, I might say, "Ooh—right there. Let me transfer this." I keep another tape recorder filled with little nuggets of all that rambling. That's what I present to Eric or Dave Matthews.

So it's a two-stage process—first you capture inspiration, then later you organize those magic moments so you can play them for people.

Right. That's what I've been doing since I can remember. It works for me. Late at night, if I want to check in with my internal Internet, I load the tape recorder, get some nice tones, and play. And sometimes it's okay to watch TV with the sound off. Maybe you're playing music to a car chase, and the next day you go, "What was I thinking?" Well, you were watching TV and putting music to it.

I'd be remiss if I didn't ask you about tone and how you got it on this record.

I'm very honored to be working with René Martinez, who worked with Stevie Ray Vaughan. René can play the hell out of the Segovia guitar. I should be his roadie! He told me everything that Stevie Ray went through to get his tone on tape. Amps all over the place—in the kitchen, bathroom, halls, and everything. Everybody has to find out what works for them.

What works for you?

Well, I bring my amps and microphones to every studio, because I found out that when you position certain microphones in a certain way, the room doesn't matter after a while. I have one microphone placed at the amplifier and another one positioned farther back so you can hear [claps] the ghost sound. You can't get that with knobs. They just give you an emulation.

As you recorded *Supernatural* in several different studios, was it difficult to get a consistent tone?

Sometimes, I would say, "Look man, you're giving me a snapshot of me. Imagine I'm a singer—you're only giving me head tones, nose tones, and throat tones. I want the chest tones and belly tones—even toe tones! Give me the whole thing. That's why I've got a Marshall." The technician might say, "I don't know what you mean." I'd say, "You want to know what I mean? Open the damn door." As soon as he'd open the studio door, I'd say, "Hear that sound coming in? I want that in the speakers. I don't want to sound compressed and chopped. I don't sound like that." Sometimes, I'll help place the microphones, and now I even bring my own engineer, Jim Gaines.

The only thing that I have is my tone. That's like my face. Your tone is your fingerprint and your personality. Don't mess with that. Otherwise, you can get anyone from L.A. who just does it with pedals and sounds like a beer commercial. That's okay for them, but I learned by listening to T-Bone Walker and Peter Green, so I have a tone.

You mentioned Marshalls. What amps did you use for this record?

I used Marshalls, Boogies, and Twins. I went through my six Marshalls and got rid of the ones that weren't consistent. Some you plug in and it's glorious. Some you have to babysit and change diapers and change tubes. I found the ones that are happening in the studio or a coliseum or anywhere, and I kept those. We mark them—these speakers go with this head. That way, you're not shooting in the dark. You know exactly what you're going for when you're recording.

Are you still playing your signature PRS?

Still the PRS, although with Eric, we both played Strats because I wanted to keep it even. It's such a pretty tone. Because of René, I finally played through a Tube Screamer. In the past, I always said, "I'll never use those things because I want to sound like me." I would just mark the floor in the places where my guitar sustains. When I'm onstage, there are marks for

"I PLAY RAINBOW MUSIC. IT'S LIKE DIAMONDS—ALL THE COLORS ARE THERE, BUT IT'S STILL CLEAR"

this song, marks for that song . . .

Do you mark the studio floor, too?

Oh yes. At first, I told René that I didn't want to play a Strat, because to make it sustain, I'd have to play so loud that I didn't know if I could have babies! So he goes, "You don't have to play that loud. Try this Tube Screamer." So we plug it in, and—bam!—it sustains right through a Twin or a Marshall. You can still talk, but you're sustaining furiously. I said, "Oh, I shouldn't have been so bullheaded. I'm so stubborn." And he says, "You didn't know. Stevie used pedals to sustain." I went, "No kidding? I thought he was just loud."

"The only thing that I have is my tone. That's like my face. Your tone is your fingerprint and your personality. Don't mess with that."

It has been a real education working with René. In fact, the entire process of making this album is new to me. Even though I've been recording since '67, all of a sudden, I'm thrown into a whole new way of doing things. I really like it—it's fresh and very challenging.

Any advice for fellow guitarists?

The last thing I want to say is that whether you play blues, bluegrass, or jazz—whatever—realize that when you get older, you either get senile or become gracious. There's no in-between.

You become senile when you think the world shortchanged you, or everybody wakes up to screw you. You become gracious when you realize that you have something the world needs, and people are happy to see you when you come into the room. Your wrinkles either show that you're nasty, cranky, and senile, or that you're always smiling.

That's why I hang around with Wayne Shorter, John Lee Hooker, Herbie Hancock—people who have passion. I've never seen them bored. I'm like a kid—I'm 51 years old, but I still feel like 17. I got the recent

Guitar Player at my house yesterday, and I sat down and read it. It's the only magazine I read from beginning to end, nonstop. Most magazines are very biased into one octave. Your magazine covers women and men, the gifted and the beginners, brilliant and crazy garage bands—all of it—and I relate to that. Whether you've got a green mohawk or a suit and a tie, it's still the same: Are you saying something valid? Are you contributing, bringing new flowers that we haven't seen in the garden?

I'm looking at the new guitars and new amplifiers like a painter discovering new brushes or mediums. That fascination with instruments and sound and texture hasn't gone yet. It's really fun.

SANTANA'S SETUP
BY GARY BRAWER

If you see Carlos Santana perform, you are sure to notice this Santana model PRS. This guitar—which he feels sounds and plays better than his other instruments—features a highly flamed maple top on a mahogany body with a mahogany neck and Brazilian rosewood fingerboard. The Gibson-esque 24$1/2$" scale, 11$1/2$" radius, and slightly larger-than-stock PRS .105" x .050" jumbo frets all add up to easy bending.

Santana's tech, René Martinez, likes to keep the stock PRS tremolo floating off the body because he feels it stays in tune better for dive-bombing. The neck is kept perfectly straight, and the string height at the 12th fret is $5/64$" on the bass side and $4/64$" on the treble side. The PRS Santana model neck pickup and the PRS Dragon II bridge pickup both have chrome covers. The bridge pickup is custom wound for a sweeter high end—as well as optimum feedback and sustain. The bridge pickup sits $3/32$" from the strings, while the stock neck pickup is at $1/16$". The volume and tone pots are 500k, and the volume pot sports a 181pf capacitor to preserve high end as Santana backs down his level. The unique switching consists of two 2-way mini-toggles, which perform as follows:

- Both switches up—neck pickup
- Both switches down—bridge pickup
- One up and one down—both pickups

Santana uses D'Addario nickel strings, gauged .009–.042. Martinez adds that the bottom line for his boss is simple: "The guitar must sustain and have great tone

8.

"YOU'RE WORKING IN A FIELD OF MYSTICAL RESONANCE, SOUND, AND VIBRATION"

. . . .

by Andy Ellis, January 2003

The astounding success of Carlos Santana's *Supernatural*—which has sold more than 24 million copies since its June '99 release, and earned eight Grammy Awards (including Album of the Year)—has made fans wonder what the soft-spoken guitarist could possibly do for an encore. With his latest record, *Shaman* [Arista], Santana proves that his fiery licks and singing tones are, in fact, hotter and more vocal than ever, and that his collaborative instincts remain strong. Once again, he has teamed up with a small army of musicians, singers, and writers, including Macy Gray, Seal, Ozomatli, Nickelback's Chad Kroeger, Michelle Branch, P.O.D, Marc Anthony, Dido, Wyclef Jean, and, most surprising, opera singer Plácido Domingo.

While the teamwork is strong, the real action lies in the wall-to-wall guitar that alternately moans, wails, and rips through the 16 tracks. Ripe and tubular—and often accompanied by the audible thump of a beleaguered 4x12 cabinet—Santana's notes seem to spring effortlessly from his trusty signature PRS.

As always, the 55-year-old icon answers questions with a compelling mix of allusion and candor, and even if you take issue with some of his observations, they'll make you stop and think. Above all, his enthusiasm for guitar will make you smile, and his latest amplifier discovery will have you scouring basements, attics, and classified ads for one of ampdom's rarest beasts.

Like its predecessor, *Shaman* is a cooperative effort. Did you try to approach this project differently from *Supernatural*?

I'll use Wayne Shorter's beautiful words: "It was completely new and totally familiar." As before, I used six strings and an amplifier to find my way into the music. But I also took some advice from [Arista label head] Clive Davis. He said, "The dimensions of *Supernatural* make it so that many people want to play with you now. But I think we should concentrate on the songs. They're more important than the people at the moment. Once you find the right songs, then we can see who would be best suited to play them."

Like my brother Ry Cooder, I'm learning to navigate different routes. Before it was Hammond organ, congas, guitar, and, finally, songs. Now it's the opposite—it's songs and then guitar, Hammond, and congas. But I still don't think in terms of numbers and commercial success. I think of opportunities and possibilities. Working with Dido, Macy Gray, and Michelle Branch—and all these new people—I feel the same energy that I felt when I first heard Michael Bloomfield, B. B. King, or Son House. So I ask myself, how do I express this intensity of emotion and spirit without imposing on the song? The goal is to complement, and also to give some spiritual information.

As you know, the only magazine I read cover to cover is *Guitar Player*. I say this because you cover everything—woman or man, super fast or super slow, deep or shallow. You're not exclusively jazz or country or heavy metal. In this way, I feel really honored and grateful to participate in *Shaman*, because when you go from P.O.D. to Plácido Domingo, it's like your magazine—it's pretty vast.

What do you look for in a song?

I'd better be able to live with it for the next 10 or 20 years! When we were selecting songs for *Shaman*, I heard several that just weren't me. One was by Diane Warren, who has written humongous hits for Aerosmith and so many others. This song, with all respect, was probably written for John Cougar Mellencamp, and it was too far for me to reach. A song has to make it into the galaxy of Santana. If it doesn't, I don't care if it's a number one hit—I won't play it.

Throughout the album, your tone is remarkably clean and articulate, yet fat and sustaining. On "Amore (Sexo)," for example, did you use a dual amp setup to get that elusive mix of detail and girth?

"YOU'RE WORKING IN A FIELD OF MYSTICAL RESONANCE, SOUND, AND VIBRATION"

No. Early this year, I discovered a phenomenal amplifier made by Alexander Dumble. I'd heard that Stevie Ray used Dumble amplifiers, but I thought, "Sure, whatever. He has great tone anyway." As soon as I tried it, however, I heard Robben Ford and Larry Carlton in the sound. That's how I got hooked for life.

What draws you to a Dumble?

They're touch sensitive. Caress a note, and it goes soft. If you have mean intentions, and hit a note a certain way, the amp screams, and you get those seven overtones on one note. You know those supernatural sounds we always look for in Peter Green or Michael Bloomfield? They're right there.

Dumbles are rare. Where did you find one?

A gentleman named David Workman—a musician in the San Francisco area—lent me his. He said, "I want you to try this amp, but under no circumstances can you buy it. I won't sell it for any price, but you can use it in the studio and on the road." From there, I made the personal communication with Alexander Dumble, and that was it. I went from not knowing about Dumble amps to having four.

Has the Dumble changed how you work in the studio?

Sometimes, it used to take days just to get a tone. Even with the incredible [engineer] Jim Gaines, I was getting frustrated because my sound wouldn't happen in certain rooms. It's really depressing when you're ready to play, but you listen to the playback, and it sounds so horrible it hurts your teeth. I'd go home and think, "Maybe it's me. Maybe I can't play anymore."

The beautiful thing is that with the Dumble, I just plug in and play. I don't have to go through hours of placing microphones. We used the same setup at the Hit Factory in New York as we did here in California. Same microphone, same position. Bam!—there it is. You don't have to wrestle a wet bear just to get a tone.

Can you compare the Dumble to the amps you've used in the past?

Since '72, I've played through a Boogie amp with one 12" Altec speaker. With the Boogie, I have to turn the volume past seven-and-a-half to get the beautiful, warm tones. If I play under that, it sounds really wimpy and thin and annoying. Playing the Boogie is like being inside a light beam. If you stand in front of it, it's really loud, but if you move two feet to the left, you don't hear it.

With the Dumble, you can play at any volume—like at Sweetwater [a tiny club in Mill Valley, California] or the Berkeley Community Theatre or the Oakland Coliseum—and get all those overtones. With other amps, you have to open them up really loud to get the richness. Bring them down, and it's like a big balloon that's not inflated. Dumble? No, he's got balloons at any size you want.

And you're also using a bigger cabinet.

Yes, a 4x12. We found this gentleman who makes speakers with hemp cones [these are Tone Tubby alnico speakers made by A Brown Soun in San Rafael, California]. When I told this to Dumble, he cracked up. "Oh, I know who that is." They all know each other, these amp guys.

It's remarkable that you can draw so many timbral colors from one amp, from the bright, squawky leads in "Game of Love," to the sweet Peter Green bends in "Sideways," to the thick cello tones in "One of These Days."

Ah, you're listening. "Game of Love" was the last track I did with the Boogie before I found the Dumble. The rest of the album is all Dumble. People think that I'm crazy, but, one day, my Boogie amp got really jealous of the Dumble and broke down. "Hey, you've been playing me for 30 years. Why are you playing that other one?" I was like, "Shut up. Let's just work together." I got the Boogie fixed, and the amps made peace. Onstage, I use the Boogie and Dumble together.

Why?

Like a singer, you want to get belly tones, chest tones, throat tones, nasal tones, and head tones from your guitar. With its 12" Altec, the Boogie is a soprano. It gives me throat tones, nasal tones, and head tones, but not chest or belly tones. But now because I use four 12s with the Dumble head, I get the Pavarotti and Plácido Domingo belly tones.

Several songs on _Shaman_ feature beautiful nylon-string guitar. Did you play those parts?

Yes. I used an Alvarez and recorded it with a combination of a direct signal and a mic. I love acoustic nylon tones. With all due respect to my brothers Paco de Lucia and Ottmar Liebert, the best acoustic nylon tones I hear are from B-Tribe. They do their own version of Concierto de

"YOU'RE WORKING IN A FIELD OF MYSTICAL RESONANCE, SOUND, AND VIBRATION"

Aranjuez, and they do a theme from the movie *Once Upon a Time in the West*. The way they hit the nylon strings is really mystical. Some musicians, man, you hear the note almost before they hit it. Jimi, Coltrane, and Charlie Parker were like that. Some conga players too—they raise their hand and before they hit the skin, you hear ta-duk.

What do you listen for in others' music?

You know "People are Strange," the Doors' song? Sometimes, you walk around, and it's this weird day and people look like old potatoes or apples. Their features are so exaggerated—even if you're straight. But then you hear a certain kind of music, and it makes everything beautiful. You remind yourself on a molecular level that there's goodness in everyone. Beauty, elegance, excellence, grace, and dignity—they're more important than what key you're in, or what chord or what scale you're playing. These qualities transcend what you learn in music school.

How do you translate these qualities into music?

You have to learn how to articulate emotion. When I first heard Jimi Hendrix, I thought, "My God, this guy has a different kind of brush." His was much thicker than everyone else's. They were using tiny little brushes and doing watercolors, while he was painting galactic scenes in CinemaScope. We're working in a field of mystical resonance, sound, and vibration. That's what makes people cry, laugh, and feel their hair stand up.

You play with many young musicians. Do they understand what you're talking about now?

I'm not judging anybody—it's just an observation at this point—but I can tell people's intentions, motives, and purpose from their eyes. I went to see Derek Trucks at the Fillmore, and I could tell that he's looking for the same things I am. I like Jonny Lang, because he puts so much pain and energy into his playing. Yet I see other musicians—I won't mention their names because I don't want to hurt their feelings—who act like they're posing in front of the mirror. They cop a tone in order to get something else. They're not going for the pure joy of creating a glorious sound like Otis Rush, B. B. King, or Buddy Guy.

Years ago you told *GP* readers that to find your sound, you'd play guitar for hours, alone in candlelight. Do you still explore the fretboard this way?

Oh yeah—every night when I'm not on the road. My family is on the school timetable, so after they go to bed, I play until 2:00 in the morning. I play with everybody I love, from John Coltrane to Wes Montgomery.

So you jam with their records?

Yes. When the inspiration runs dry, or I get stuck with too much cosmic music, I go back to John Lee Hooker, Jimmy Reed, or Lightnin' Hopkins. From those roots, I find my way back to Coltrane. Or I turn them off and just lose myself—and find myself—in the music. I'm not technically proficient, so I run a video camera while I play. That way, if I want to go back to a tone, I can see where that note is and what guitar and amp I used. When I view a tape two days later, it's like watching somebody peel an artichoke. You're peeling Peter Green, Bola Sete, George Benson,

SHAMAN SPELL

When guitar tech René Martinez (who worked with Stevie Ray Vaughan for five years) decided to take time off from his gig with Santana, Ed Adair was drafted as the new gear guru. "The day I came onboard," says Adair, "René told me, 'Here, I'm handing you the keys to the Cadillac.' He was right—this is the best ride."

According to Adair, Santana brings four signature Paul Reed Smith guitars on the road—including the original prototype—and strings his namesake PRS models with D'Addario lights, gauged .009–.042. Onstage, Santana plays through two amps: his faithful '72 Mesa Boogie Mk I combo (loaded with a 417 Altec 12") and a 100-watt Dumble head. The Dumble powers a Marshall 4x12 with stock Celestions, and a straight-front 4x12 made by A Brown Soun of San Rafael, California. The Brown Soun cab is loaded with alnico Tone Tubby 12s sporting hemp-paper cones.

"The Brown Soun cab is rather compact, so we use the Marshall to kick out extra bottom," reveals Adair.

For his lively Spanish tones, Santana flatpicks Alvarez classical guitars with factory undersaddle transducers, and, for wah sounds, he uses an ancient Mu-Tron III pedal. Santana wires his rig with Belden 1192A cable.

Royer ribbon mics are a recent addition to Santana's studio rig.

"The combination of the Dumble amp, the hemp speakers, and this new mic means I don't have to look for tone anymore," says Santana. "You just plug in and go 'mamma mia'—even if you're not Italian."

"YOU'RE WORKING IN A FIELD OF MYSTICAL RESONANCE, SOUND, AND VIBRATION"

John McLaughlin, Buddy Guy, and, all of a sudden, three notes right at the core are just you. And in those three notes—the way they were placed in time and space and feeling—you have the seed of a song.

I'm not tripping about Carlos. I'm tripping about what is that melody, and what is that mood? Because those moods are what penetrate people deeply. It's like cracking a walnut—you have to get past the shell to get into the heart of it. You can only do that by playing nonstop for an hour-and-a-half or two hours.

Can you tell us about recording with Plácido Domingo? An operatic tenor and a thumping 4x12 cab make a unique blend.

I wanted to transmute opera, symphony, Afro-Cuban beats, and blues into something new. I'm really grateful for Plácido's spirit. Many opera singers don't want to sing in English—only Italian, Spanish, or German. When I asked him if he'd have a problem singing in English, he said, "Of course not." He's 60 years old, but when he hit that microphone from ten feet away, he sounded like two Marshall amplifiers. And he hit those notes at 3:00 in the morning after doing two concerts with a sore throat.

The dictionary defines a shaman as someone who uses magic to heal, or reveal the hidden. How does this relate to your music?

Absoluteness and totality—that's the message of *Shaman*. If you want to start healing yourself, you have to start feeling, because nothing is real to you unless you feel it. There's something about bending a string that gets inside your vitals—your cojones—and works its way to your brain. The next thing you know, you feel like you're worth more than what's in your wallet or bank account. Sometimes people get so intellectual, cute, and clever with music that only they understand it. To me, music shouldn't be such a mystery. It should be something that all humans can say, "Wow, I feel it—you're touching me in a place I haven't been touched before."

As guitarists, we all want to learn how to get so inside the note that time and space disappear. It comes like an orgasm. When you have an orgasm, you don't know if you're Irish, Mexican, Apache, Japanese, Hebrew, or Palestinian. You're in the fullness of a complete Niagara Falls of absolute totality. And that's where I try to take people with my guitar.

9.

"THERE ARE A LOT OF TONES WITHIN MYSELF THAT I CAN FORM SIMPLY BY LOOKING INWARD"

. . . .

by Darrin Fox, June 2005

I'm proof that a musician can coexist with everyone from Wayne Shorter and Kirk Hammett to Plácido Domingo and P.O.D.," exclaims Carlos Santana, as he reclines in his San Rafael, California, headquarters. "I'll even play with Kenny G., Billy Joel, or Elton John if the song is right."

If that previous quote doesn't confirm that Santana is sticking with the star-infused collaborations that have garnered him tons of mainstream cheese, two smash albums (*Supernatural* and *Shaman*), and an attic's worth of Grammys, well, consider Carlos jamming with Antonio Banderas on the 2005 Academy Awards telecast.

"I thought the whole experience was going to be a lot weirder than it actually was," says Santana. "But after you play Woodstock on acid, nothing's a big deal anymore!"

With the same peaceful strength that stands behind every note he plays, Santana makes it clear that he doesn't care what people think of his star-struck pop collaborations—the latest of which is *All That I Am*.

"I'm not going to have the opportunity to play with Herbie Hancock, and then worry about the weird expectations people put on me, and not work with a talented songwriter like Rob Thomas," he exclaims. "I don't care what people say about Santana playing corporate rock, and I never have. It's like, 'Whatever, man, I'm going to go hang out with Buddy Guy and John Lee Hooker [*laughs*].'" And I've got news for all of those intellectual snobs and brainiacs: You try and write a song like Green Day, and get it on the radio and connect with people. Even John Coltrane connected with larger audiences with 'My Favorite Things'—a pop song. No matter what you're playing, it all comes down to one basic thing: Can you connect with the people—whether it's a three-year old, a 17-year-old, or a 50-year-old? What's the point of speaking an elite musical language that only you can understand?"

It's tough to argue with that—especially when Santana is far more than "just" a popular artist. Sure, his guitar solos are on nearly every radio station across the land, but he has also been an adored and respected collaborator with the likes of John Lee Hooker, Wayne Shorter, and John McLaughlin. And his current workload includes several decidedly non-pop-star projects, such as finishing some tracks with blues legend Buddy Guy, readying the release of the *Santana/Shorter at Montreux* DVD (a performance at 1988's Montreux Jazz Festival), and wrapping up an all-instrumental Santana album. If the preview I heard is any indication, the instrumental record will delight fans of Santana's pure 6-string magic with everything from thoughtful nylon-string workouts ("Gabor") to heavy Latin-rock numbers ("Nomad").

"At this stage of my life, all is one in my eyes," he says. "I don't have to be just the 'Latin rock guy.' If I have the chance, I want to be able to play the Grand Ole Opry, or in the middle of Africa. Look, it's not like I want to be liked by everybody, but who wouldn't want to reach as many people's hearts as they can?"

There aren't many rock guitarists who keep company with people such as Wayne Shorter, John McLaughlin, and John Lee Hooker. Why do you think these players are so accepting of you?

Well, I remember Wynton Marsalis saying that I shouldn't even be on the same stage with Wayne Shorter because I was playing rock music. But Wayne's response was beautiful. He said, "Wynton, you could put children from different parts of the world in the same sandbox, and even

"THERE ARE A LOT OF TONES WITHIN MYSELF THAT I CAN FORM SIMPLY BY LOOKING INWARD"

though they won't speak the same language, they're still going to play with the same bucket and the same shovel."

But, first and foremost, I think people like Wayne and John Lee read my intentions. They saw it in my eyes that I wasn't there to steal from them or disrespect their music. I'm there to learn from them and honor the music. And that attitude gave me a first-class ticket with those guys.

What's your first reaction when you hear guitarists who have been influenced by your approach to tone and phrasing, such as Los Lonely Boys' Henry Garza or Orianthi?

I cheer so loud, man. It feels good, because for a long time I wasn't sure if people thought of me as an influential guitar player. As a matter of fact, it wasn't until Prince told me that I was a major influence on his playing that I realized maybe I had left a mark with my guitar.

When you recorded *Shaman*, you were over the moon about discovering Dumble amplifiers. Did you have any tonal discoveries on the new albums?

What I'm learning more and more is that there are a lot of tones within myself that I can form simply by looking inward. Sure, Dumbles are incredible amps. But Alexander Dumble himself would tell you that Larry Carlton, Robben Ford, Eric Johnson, and myself have our own fingerprints with or without a Dumble amplifier. I can tell you every little piece of gear I've ever used, and you're still not going to sound like me. Your sound as an individual comes from sitting and playing for one, two, or three hours nonstop. It's where you get into this zone, and something takes over where the music truly plays you, and your mind is free of insecurities. The muscle memory and mechanics will handle themselves at a certain point, and you can get down to the matter of true expression that goes straight to the instrument from your heart. You have to reach inside yourself. There's absolutely no substitute for locking yourself away and not coming out until you have your own sound.

Do you think guitar magazines perpetuate gear lust too much?

Guitar mags have a valid role. They turn people on to the gear that's out there, and help them understand that certain gear sounds a certain way. For example, a Strat is going to sound the way it sounds simply because of its construction. That hasn't changed since Ritchie Valens and Buddy Holly. And with a certain amp, your tone is going to be a certain way.

But people should try to go deeper into the instrument, and transcend its actual construction. To do that, you have to make ugly faces, pucker up your butt, and get to that note. You need to put different levels of brutal freakin' force behind your playing. The next thing you know, you start getting into the territory that Stevie Ray Vaughan and Jeff Beck inhabit. Let's face it, Stevie made some pretty ugly faces. And, hopefully, so do I. Anybody who goes for the note makes that face. It's like having an orgasm. I don't know anybody who looks nice when they have an

ALL THAT GEAR

"For the most part, Carlos' setup has stayed the same," says René Martinez, who, along with Ed Adair, watches after Santana's tonal arsenal. "His main guitar is a stock, green PRS Santana model which he has used consistently for the past year. From his guitar, the signal goes to a switcher box that allows Carlos to choose between two Dumble Overdrive Reverbs and a mid-'70s Mesa/Boogie Mark I head. The Boogie and one Dumble are dialed in with a fair amount of overdrive for sustain, whereas I try to dial in the other Dumble for a cleaner tone. All of the amplifiers are ready to go when Carlos steps onstage, and it's up to him to decide what he wants to hear. Sometimes, he'll only use the Boogie for most of the night, or he'll use all three amps at once. The only effects Carlos uses are a Dunlop 535Q wah and a delay pedal." (Martinez was reluctant to divulge the brand of delay, as Santana is always changing it, but word is he's currently stomping on a T-Rex Replica at rehearsals.)

As for speaker cabs, the Mesa/Boogie Mark I runs into a 1x12 cabinet loaded with a JBL E120 that has been outfitted with a hemp cone for its slightly mellower tone and added durability. The first Dumble Overdrive Special powers two Marshall 4x12 slant cabinets. One is loaded with Celestion Vintage 30s, and the other sports two Vintage 30s and two Celestion G12M-25 greenbacks. The second Dumble drives an A Brown Soun 4x12 open-back cabinet loaded with Tone Tubby 12s.

"Carlos records with this exact stage setup," says Adair, who assisted Santana at Berkeley's Fantasy Studios while the guitarist was recording his two new records. "The only difference being, instead of a delay pedal, we'll use an old 1/4" Studer tape machine or a Lexicon PCM-80 for about 350ms of delay. Carlos tracks everything in the control room, and we typically use Royer ribbon mics on the 4x12s, and a Neumann on the Mesa/Boogie 1x12."

orgasm. And if you're not having an orgasm, then you're not all the way into it like you're supposed to be.

Is there a guitarist who best typifies overcoming an instrument's construction?

Jimi did it. He willed a Strat to do what he wanted it to do. Back then, Strats sounded like the Beach Boys and Jan and Dean and Dick Dale. Not until Jimi came along did the Stratocaster get away from the surf sound. Why do you think Jimi said, "You'll never hear surf music again"? It's not that his music is better or worse than surf, it's just that Jimi wanted a Strat to sound like Mt. St. Helens, so he made it happen.

"The three Bs— Butterfield, Bloomfield, and Bishop were scary, man! They opened up the entire spectrum."

At a certain point, it becomes a question of dedication.

Exactly. Take John Coltrane. He played nonstop—even to the point of going to the kitchen and playing when other guys were soloing on the bandstand! That's supreme dedication. If you go for supreme dedication, you get a bonus—the big tone. But for people who have that kind of dedication, it's almost like they aren't allowed to have quality tender time with other people, or their kids. I don't want that. I don't need that. I'd rather drive my daughter to school. As much as I love music, it's what I do, it's not who I am.

Did you ever start going the route of supreme dedication at the expense of personal relationships?

Sure. But once I had children, I knew I couldn't b.s. myself. My son and two daughters are more important than anything. I'd rather go back to washing dishes in the Mission district than play music and not take care of them.

Can you point to an album of yours as a watershed moment in your development as a player?

There were two: *Caravanserai* [1972] and *Welcome* [1973]. At that time, I felt my whole existence being pulled toward John Coltrane. I remember going to the record company and telling them, "I know what you want, but I can't give it to you because I don't hear it." I knew I would pay the price by not selling a ton of records, but I didn't care.

You've said that you practice with John Coltrane records, but that you don't play or sound like Coltrane. What specifically are you listening for that can be applied to your own style?

I'm trying to get to that tone that's not merely a result of what gear I'm using. When I listen to Coltrane, I hear children playing and birds singing. I'm not romanticizing—that is actually what I hear. It wasn't always that way. His music used to sound like the equivalent of someone opening a fire hydrant. But because I'm open, I began to understand what he was going for. It's the same thing Jimi Hendrix strove toward—tones that serve to remind us that we're multi-dimensional spirits, not just blacks or whites, Jews or Mexicans. That's small stuff.

Are there any guitarists who you go to for that kind of inspiration?

I still find myself going back to my John Lee Hooker and Jimmy Reed albums. I just read a Branford Marsalis interview where he said that he noticed his tone improved when he started listening to more John Lee Hooker and Son House. Something about their music compels you to look at the bigger picture of tone—not just a guitar or an amplifier. You'd be surprised how much time I spend with the Paul Butterfield Blues Band's *East-West*, too. That album was a major groundbreaker. The three Bs—Butterfield, Bloomfield, and Bishop were scary, man! They opened up the entire spectrum.

How much do you feel a person's life experiences add to their depth as a player?

Well, there's the saying, "To get to it, you gotta go through it." But the flip side of that was Miles Davis, who said, "My dad is rich. My mom is good looking. I've never suffered, nor do I intend to suffer. But, man, I can play some blues." So he broke that stereotype. It's funny—I remember John Lee Hooker telling me that a lot of people play the blues, but if they don't wear those silky pimp socks, he doesn't believe them [*laughs*]. As for me, I knew when I saw B. B. King for the first time, I had to leave my mom and move out with no one to wash my clothes and cook for me. It wasn't that I was looking to suffer. I just knew that I had to go out and get some real, first-hand life experience in order to create.

"THERE ARE A LOT OF TONES WITHIN MYSELF THAT I CAN FORM SIMPLY BY LOOKING INWARD"

Do you ever look at your fabulous success and think about the players you came up with—say Elvin Bishop or Harvey Mandel or Mike Bloomfield—and ask, "Why me?"

Of course. I remember standing onstage accepting a Grammy from Bob Dylan and Lauryn Hill, and I swear, guys like Tommy Castro and Otis Rush were going through my mind, and all I could think about was, "Why me?" And then, all of a sudden, I hear this voice that says, "Because of your heart." See, my heart wants to wake people up to their full potential. And to realize that potential in yourself, your heart must dictate to your brain. It should never be the other way around. If your brain dictates to your heart, then you're just shucking and jiving. No person or thing is going to validate you more than your own heart. So which one do you want to hang with?

10.

"EGO ONLY HAS ONE AGENDA—TO CREATE DEATH, DESTRUCTION, AND FAILURE"

. . . .

by Michael Molenda, December 2008

In addition to being a great friend to *Guitar Player* over the years, Carlos Santana has endeavored to fire up the magazine's creative juices by hipping the staff to noteworthy under-the-radar guitarists, as well as sending us mix CDs full of music that has inspired him. Every few months, I'll receive a little package from his San Rafael, California, offices bearing something delightful, inspirational, or out-and-out humbling. It's kind of a one-way relationship, however, as Santana is so in tune with what's going on in every musical universe that it seems hopeless I would ever come across an artist, style, or technique that would surprise him. (I don't think my quest for the perfectly distorted punk-rock *A* chord qualifies as a "discovery of note.") Furthermore, his adventurous and inquisitive spirit leads him to consider much more about what it means to be a guitarist than one's choice of a favored style and the gear needed to construct a suitable tone.

So it wasn't really a surprise when Santana artfully dodged a discussion of his gear and tonal evolution in the wake of his new, dual-CD compilation, *Multi-Dimensional Warrior*—a handpicked collection of vocal songs and instrumentals spanning nearly four decades of the guitarist's prodigious musical output.

"I'd like to talk about intangibles," he said when first contacted about this cover story. "I haven't changed my gear all that much since the last

Guitar Player story [June '05], and I'd like to get beyond those physical things and think about the roles of the heart and mind in making music."

Santana was so excited about the concept that he proceeded to suggest several more article ideas, a few twists on the typical guitar book and lesson DVDs, and, I think, even a live-concert event. (It was a bit hard to keep up with the snappy tempo of his well-considered proposals.) And, trust me, when Carlos Santana is that thrilled about a subject, you go with it. So what follows is a bit of a different *Guitar Player* article, but one that is no less instructive or valuable than a treatise on tone and technique. Few artists in these pages have attempted to detail the messy and often inexplicable engines of imagination, inspiration, and creation. (The last time was likely Bill Nelson's "Chasing the Muse" feature in the March '04 issue.) By necessity, the discussion tends to leave the world of the pragmatic, and sails into areas that can be uncomfortable for many players—God, spirituality, openness, self-assessment, self-awareness, ego, habit, ambition, and the potential evil of comfort zones. But if a player seeks to truly jettison stylistic mimicry, and fight like a cornered jackal to develop a unique and personal musical fingerprint, then studying the creative ramifications of intangibles is an essential part of the mission. In this quest, you couldn't have a better guide and confidant than Carlos Santana.

What directed your selection of the songs on *Multi-Dimensional Warrior*?

What happened was that I had just come home from Hawaii, where I realized how Bob Marley's music was made. It's all from the islands and the clouds and the waves. It's very calm and peaceful and pure, and you can just focus on nothing—which is very difficult for the ego to do, because the ego has "ifs" and "buts" firing off all the time. And while I was not thinking about anything, I heard a voice say, "Carlos, go to your cassettes, records, and CDs, and compile a letter to your fans." I found myself drawn to music that didn't get heard anywhere near as much as *Abraxas* or *Supernatural*, as well as the desire to turn people on to freedom and the light within themselves—like Bob Marley and John Coltrane. Everything just came so naturally that it was like composing a love letter.

"EGO ONLY HAS ONE AGENDA—TO CREATE DEATH, DESTRUCTION, AND FAILURE"

Some musicians might consider a "letter to their fans" to be a greatest hits package, but as you consciously avoided that approach, what does this collection represent for you?

Thank you for asking that. There's a part of me that loves learning from musicians such as John Lee Hooker, Jimmy Reed, B. B. King, and Miles Davis. But there's also a part of me that wants to invest—like Desmond Tutu or the Dalai Lama or Harry Belafonte—in the healing of the common man. So it's not enough for me to play music, learn from all these guys, and be recognized worldwide. I also want to serve—to be of service. We are capable of creating miracles ourselves, and the greatest miracle is to create a masterpiece of joy out of your life with no excuses. This is what led to the combination of songs on *Multi-Dimensional Warrior*—I wanted people to taste their own triumph through this music. In fact, I was amazed how many times the word "light" appears in all the songs with lyrics.

So I'm assuming the album title isn't just a clever turn of phrase?

Oh, no [*laughs*]. When people have asked me to define "multi-dimensional," I say that it's not being stuck or stuck up. When you start thinking that you're superior or inferior—that's being stuck. Your fear has betrayed you. Being free is seeing the beauty of you in everybody else. You say, "I can see myself in this guy and that guy. I want to phrase like Otis Redding and Nat King Cole and Wes Montgomery." You see the connections between what you do and what all the musicians before you have done, and between what every musician is doing right now. So I'm grateful that your magazine is here, because you remind people that we're all in it together. *Guitar Player* is multi-dimensional.

Could you elaborate on what you mean by saying "your fear has betrayed you"?

Fear only has one agenda—to negate your beauty and your truth. Ego only has one agenda—to create death, destruction, and failure. That's the only function of the ego. We should compliment it, because at least it's predictable. E-g-o stands for "Etch God Out." But even an atheist can understand the need for wonderment. You don't have to believe in God. God believes in you. God could not care less if you call him Buddha, Allah, Jesus, or Krishna. The best part of you—that's what God is, and it is in all of us. It's called the spark of the divine.

Rays of Light: Santana soloing at Fiddler's Green Amphitheater in Denver, Colorado, September 13, 2008. (© SCOTT D. SMITH / RETNA LTD.)

"EGO ONLY HAS ONE AGENDA—TO CREATE DEATH, DESTRUCTION, AND FAILURE"

Do you remember that scene in *2001: A Space Odyssey* where the astronaut was being bombarded with all these colors? It's like some type of Coltrane solo, or Jimi when he's feeding back. That's what we call the stream of consciousness—which is actually the state of grace, because all is one and one is all. The mind is not equipped to understand that, because the mind likes to compartmentalize. The heart just takes it all in.

But how does a musician transcend compartmentalization? In many ways, we are driven to embrace specific styles such as rock or jazz or blues—which are large compartments—and then there are mini compartments such as scales, chords, and riffs.

The thing I focus on—whether I'm playing with Kirk Hammett or John McLaughlin—is going straight to the heart. I go to mine first, because if I don't feel it, you're not going to feel it. I take a deep breath, and I remind myself that before I give it to you, I have to give it to myself. I have to receive it. It doesn't matter if I drink a shot of tequila, or half a glass of wine, or if I smoke a toke, or if I'm totally straight and just drinking water—none of that is going to get in my way. We are talking about intangibles now. The intangible is that thing you put your finger in, and it's wet and it gives you chills. It's half of the equation. It's not just the amplifier or the string. It's not Fender. It's not Gibson. It's not your technique, or Dorian scales, or even chords. When I am open to the intangibles, I can play with Buddy Guy and hold my own, because Buddy Guy is a hurricane, and if you're not playing from your heart, he will wash you out.

Although musicians talk about it a lot, I think the role of the heart in actual creative performance remains a huge mystery. A guitarist can more clearly understand technique. He or she can say, "Buddy Guy is over there, and I've practiced this blues scale forever. I can fly over the notes, add a few tricks, and not give any ground. I'm going to burn."

That's not going to help you. I've seen Buddy destroy a couple of musicians. I won't say their names, because I don't want to hurt their feelings. But they were playing a gazillion notes per second, while he was holding one note, and he looked like a man who was on top of the Grand Canyon wielding a lightning bolt that sounded like Jimi Hendrix. He's holding that one note, and he's grinning at these guys playing a bunch of little notes that sound like mosquitoes stuck in a screen door. That's not going to hurt him. But he'll hurt you with one note that transcends the blues, and all the equipment he's using. That's heart, and Buddy Guy has an incredible heart.

Well, once again, that's fabulous for Buddy Guy, but how can someone who has been taught to trust the rewards of practicing gestures best understand the implications of following their heart?

Everyone has a heart, of course, so it typically comes down to how much you are willing to let it come out. How fast can you get to your heart and not let anything get in the way—children, the rent, the set list, taxes, nothing? How fast can you get to that place in your heart where you don't even have to think about what to play, because the notes will play themselves? Those are the best notes. Listen, carrying a melody is very difficult for a musician, because in order to carry a melody, you have to let go. A lot of people carry chords and speed. Let them go. Let go of everything you have learned, and, in return, receive the thing that will be channeled through you. Don't the best articles you've written just appear? And you go, "Wow, I don't even know how I put those words together!" This is the center of it. Musicians hear 1,000 voices saying they're not good enough—that they're just lucky, that they always play out of tune or their tone sucks, that they never get it right. John Lennon once said he hated everything he did, because he could have done it better. That's the ego. All those voices are the ego in disguise giving you guilt, shame, judgment, condemnation, and fear that you're never going to be good enough. Then you have one voice that is very quiet, but it's louder and clearer than the other voices. This voice says, "Pick up the guitar. Here it comes." And out comes a song that's like Jeff Beck playing "People Get Ready" [sings the main melody]. Bam! Your freaking hair stands up, you've got tears coming out of your eyes, and you don't even know why. These are the things that drive me to go inside my heart, and going there is the only thing that is worth attaining for me. When I'm there, the heart will lead me to play a melody that makes families put all their sh*t aside, and just see how beautiful their families are. That's what is really beautiful about music—it brings you into harmony. The other stuff you can learn by repetition, like a hamster. With willingness, you can truly learn why people adore Jimi Hendrix.

"EGO ONLY HAS ONE AGENDA—TO CREATE DEATH, DESTRUCTION, AND FAILURE"

Can you be a bit more specific about the role of willingness?

Let's look at it this way—what is this intangible world that Jimi Hendrix and Beethoven dipped into? You can call it hocus- pocus or whatever, but this world exists. How often are you willing to dip into it? Do you dip into it at all? Do you ever have those moments where you're playing by yourself, and you think you've been at it for 30 minutes, but you suddenly realize you've got sweat and saliva all over your guitar because you've been at it for more than two hours? I think this is the next step for *Guitar Player* magazine. You should invite people to go beyond the mechanics of the physical brain and the fingers, and go to that place where—like one of my favorite bands, the Doors—we can all open the doors to perception. When you hear Robby Krieger's creepy minor-major blues thing at the beginning of "The End," it's like Dracula giving you a hug, but you don't mind it. I love music that makes me feel like I'm seven years old, going to the movies for the first time and experiencing Panavision. That's why we love Jimi Hendrix—he assaults all of our senses. His music has a wide circumference. Hendrix is another name for a bridge to the unknown, because what he was playing, even he couldn't reproduce sometimes. He couldn't quantize it—as much as he might have tried to get back there by taking seven tabs of acid and a little bit of wine and some coke. Sometimes, it's nothing—just the willingness. The willingness to take a deep breath and take what was given to you. It's inside you, as John Lee Hooker said, and it has to come out. But maybe you won't let it out, because you want to analyze it before it comes out. Don't analyze it. Leave that for other people. Just take a deep breath, stop what you're thinking, and let go. Let God light you up, and let it come out. Then you can get rid of all the sh*t you know, and play things that sound like singing water.

Intangibles and willingness are, by definition, far more mysterious than pragmatic results—such as mastering a difficult melodic run. The poet William Blake was a visionary who spoke to angels, Jackson Pollack was a drunk, and Jimi Hendrix took drugs. Those are just three examples of artists swimming in pure creative inspiration. While I'd never advocate the abuse of alcohol or pharmaceuticals, is there some trigger needed to launch a musician beyond the concrete and into the unknown?

I don't need to take acid or mescaline to trip anymore, but I learned enough from that stuff to realize what Einstein meant when he said, "Imagination is more important than knowledge." Your imagination is your best equipment, and you cannot learn it or earn it—it was given to you. Take it. It's yours. You don't have to go down to the crossroads, and wait for a black cat or the full moon. You don't have to sell yourself to the devil. What for? You have God's love, and what can be better than that? Whether you're Yngwie Malmsteen or Steve Vai or Joe Satriani or John Scofield, you just need to shut everything off and utilize the main television—your imagination.

You see, the ultimate destination for guitar players is to create heaven and wonderment for both themselves and the listeners. If you're not doing that, you're just shucking and jiving. But if you can let go and trust God, then you can change yourself, and then you can change me, and we can change everybody. What is deep inside of you is something that might make Buddy Guy turn around and say, "Hmmm—that's interesting." And then everyone else starts saying, "Damn, did you hear this new cat? He has a very fertile imagination."

Here's another way of looking at it. I loved the debate in your letters column [September '08] commenting on Al Di Meola and Kenny Neal [who were both profiled in the July '08 GP] talking separately about whether it's better to express yourself with one note or one million notes. But let's suppose that you can express a million things with one note. Let's consider for a moment that it's not wishful thinking, or a lazy man's way of justifying not practicing. How would you go about doing it? Is it the amplifier? Is it your technique? Is it the guitar? Do you need sympathetic strings like Ravi Shankar? Or can you use your imagination to see a note as a crystal that you put next to the sun, and that crystal then reflects the whole spectrum of the rainbow. Now, you can play for half an hour in each color! Your imagination is what makes this possible. You just have to invite your imagination into your creative process.

Now, let me comment a little bit on the pragmatic or tangible aspects of playing guitar that you've been mentioning. To me, getting all the scales and gear together is like practicing in a mirror while sucking in your cheeks. You're posing. Don't let the scales and the speed and the knowledge of chords and gear get in the way of that note that's going to

"EGO ONLY HAS ONE AGENDA—TO CREATE DEATH, DESTRUCTION, AND FAILURE"

disarm other people's egos and make every hair on their body stand up. Then they get to a place where they say to you, "You know, Michael, that note touched me in a place I've never been touched before." All of a sudden, your playing is not about comparing or competing. You go to a place where you become like what Derek Trucks is to me—a minister. In your ministry, you utilize music to take people back to where they have always been, and to where they have never been. You want to play a note that's so beautiful that the audience goes [*makes gasping noise*], and they can't breathe out until you finish your phrase.

Do you know Sonny Sharrock? He could shred like a tornado—like the Tasmanian Devil—and then create melodies out of all that madness. When people smoke cigars while they're playing cards, and the smoke goes to the ceiling and creates something beautiful—that's Sonny Sharrock. He is the person I wish was still alive more than any other musician, because I think he was in between Jimi Hendrix and Coltrane more than anybody.

Actually, Sharrock taught me about savvy repetition. I forgot the name of his song, but I played it constantly because it held onto a theme seemingly forever, but it was never boring. In fact, it was quite beguiling, and I drove myself nuts trying to deconstruct what Sonny was doing to make something that should have been mind-numbingly tedious so evocative and musical.

It's a good thing you brought that up, because I think people need to understand that there's a difference between repetition and a spell. A spell is another word for wonderment. No matter who you are, that's what you long to get into. Otherwise, you're going to get bored with your sh*t. But you will never be bored with your wonderment. Wonderment has nothing to do with scales or repetition or amplifiers. It has to do with your own being, and what's inside your heart. Your mind will just be like, "Okay, I can't quantize this or understand it, so I'll just shut up and be quiet." Behold—that's wonderment.

You know, being from San Francisco, like you, we have something over the rest of this nation. I don't consider San Franciscans inferior or superior, but we do have an edge because we dare to think outside the box—musically, politically, aesthetically, and philosophically. We get accused of—"Oh yeah, that reminds me of the cows and the cheese. You know how the California people are." But, the fact is, we invest time and energy pursuing the intangible. That's the vortex we're talking about—that state of grace where you go beyond what you know and the equipment you're using. You get into that place where everybody in your band is looking at you, and they're going, "Damn! What the hell was that?"

Here's a recent example of what I'm talking about. I played a benefit concert last year for Angela Bofill with [drummer] Narada Michael Walden and [keyboardist] Chester Thompson at Grace Cathedral in San Francisco, and, as I was waiting for my solo, a voice said to me, "Carlos, this is the Grace Cathedral, and people are used to hearing 'Ave Maria,' but I want you to go to this Sonny Sharrock/Coltrane place and bug out. You're going to show people and yourself that the halo and the horns are cool. Go for it." But, just then, I looked at Chester and he was gone. His eyes were closed, and he was giving it his all. I looked at Narada, and he was gone, too. He looked like a cross-eyed lion. And I realized, "Man, they're there already. I have to go to another place. Can I do it?" So I changed my stance, and I went for it. I said, "I'm going for it, and if I get a freaking heart attack, then I die. I don't care." A month later, people who saw the concert were still telling me, "You created this vortex between heaven and earth that I know wasn't of this planet." I said, "I know exactly when I went for it, and I'm glad you picked up on it." You see, people intuitively applaud your pursuance—not necessarily the attainment. For example, you can perform a perfect solo, and the people might say, "Eh, whatever," because maybe you were 99 percent perfect, but you were an asshole about reaching that final one percent of perfection. You weren't open and giving, and your ego was too involved, so people will only remember that you were an asshole. The true beauty is in the pursuance, so I'd recommend looking at that one percent "shortfall" as the sacrifice you had to make in order for the other notes to be perfect. It's funny, Wayne Shorter once said, "I like mistakes. Sometimes, big ones—like scars."

That's interesting. I just interviewed Alvin Lee from Ten Years After about how the British Invasion players took American blues and revved it up into the blues-rock hybrid. He said that, back then, they didn't really have a lot of influences to relate to, and that many of the blues solos they heard were far from perfect. There were

"EGO ONLY HAS ONE AGENDA—TO CREATE DEATH, DESTRUCTION, AND FAILURE"

tons of mistakes. So what he and his peers got from the original blues guitarists was their energy and passion—which is why he said he still cranks up his amp and goes for feel over precision to this day. The whole thing about striving for so-called "perfect" rock solos came later.

Here's where we crystallize this statement—for you, for me, and for everybody. Perfect perfection exists in the heart, not in the mind. Perfect perfection is—I just learned this word, man, and I want to share it with you—"unalterable." It means something that you can't add to, because it's already perfect. People say, "What's that?" The sun. The sun has never said to the earth, "You owe me," so it's unalterable. The Mona Lisa is unalterable. You can't add anything to it, or subtract anything from it. The eyes of a brand new baby are unalterable. Within those eyes is pure innocence, and they are incapable of disappointing you. I think it's good news to understand that perfect perfection does exist, but there are certain things musicians need to identify in order for them to play music that uplifts, transforms, and moves people beyond show business—beyond "look what I can do"—and to a place where people drop their guard and go, "Wow!"

A lot of people practice everything meticulously, and they go onstage and play it meticulously exactly the same way. Now, this can be incredible, but, after a while, it's like watching something through plexiglass—you can't get to the other side. Me—I need a hug. I don't kiss the air like the kids in Los Angeles. Give me a hug. So I feel that people really need to learn how to hug that note.

How do you "hug" a note?

Well, I was recording this supreme singer once, and he said, "Carlos, I'm inside this vocal booth, and you're out there in the control room, so tell me where I am." Now, whether it's Pavarotti or Larry Graham, I always say the same thing: "You're going around the block. Get inside the sheets." That means to get a little closer to the melody. And don't make it staccato—make it legato. Legato is a hug. That's why we love Peter Green—"The Supernatural" is all legato.

So you're not down with staccato phrasing—like, say, how a horn section might place its accents?

Oh, there's also a need for staccato. It's fun. It's like skipping rocks across a lake. "Ch-ch-ch-ch-splash." Hey, can you skip it seven times?

Let's talk a bit about leading a band. When I saw you perform at the Fillmore in San Francisco last month, I was amazed at how much your band members were listening to everything going on around them. It seemed you never had to cue them— you'd change a feel, and they'd just adapt immediately, as if everyone was psychic. These moments didn't seem rehearsed or choreographed—they'd just happen. How do you ensure every player is on the same wavelength?

Thank you for saying that. My answer to your question is "trust." My band members trust me. The only things I ever rehearse are grooves. I want to make sure you put your finger in it, and you touch it with your tongue, and it's freaking divinely delicious. The tempo has to be right for a certain song. We can't fall in different places. It's just like football— there can't be no penalty flags! We all have to hit the collective "wa."

SANTANA'S LOVE LETTER

"When I started picking out songs, the process just flew, and I didn't hesitate over anything or second-guess any of my choices," says Santana of his personal selection and sequencing of the tracks on *Multi-Dimensional Warrior*. "Everything just felt right. It was like writing a love letter."

The 28-track, dual-CD release is a welcome left turn from the typical repackaging practices of many labels. For one thing, there's the obvious fact that Santana himself was intimately involved in the project—even to the point of supervising the recording of brand new parts for a few songs. He added guitars to "Spirit" and "Right Now," had Chester Thompson lay down a piano on "Let There Be Light," and directed Barbara Higbie to track harp melodies for "Praise" and "Let There Be Light."

Perhaps most importantly, however, Santana abandoned the (re)hawk-the-hits tactic in favor of presenting an uplifting and undulating soundscape of moods, vibes, and rhythmic feels from the past 30-plus years of his oeuvre. As a result, Multi-Dimensional Warrior lives up to its title, unfolding as a harmonious symphony of themes, rather than a disconnected collection of songs. It's also one of those rare occasions where we get a peek into an artist's re-evaluation of his or her music, guided and nurtured only by the experiences and wisdom they've sustained over the passing years, and uncorrupted by purely commercial considerations. Oh yeah, and the guitar playing totally rocks.

"EGO ONLY HAS ONE AGENDA—TO CREATE DEATH, DESTRUCTION, AND FAILURE"

You should do an article in *Guitar Player* on wa. What the hell is the wa? Imagine 100 women in a circle around you in the middle of a field, and they're all going, "Hey ya, nay nay , , , wa!" When you all hit the wa together—that's when music is happening. So I tell my band, "I need the wa. Let's hit the wa together. Don't overstate it, but visit it." All music, whether it's Segovia or Paco de Lucia or Hendrix, has the wa. If you don't hit the wa, your music is redundant, repetitious, and monotonous. James Brown called it "hitting on the one," and he visited the wa enough to put a collective conscious on it. A lot of bands have come from James Brown.

Do you listen for melodic clues from drummers?

Absolutely. Tony Williams, Elvin Jones, Mitch Mitchell, Ginger Baker—these are drummers who know how to be possessed, and, as a result, they can take the guitar player beyond what he can play. Drummers play melodies in the cymbals, and if you hear them—whether you're Pat Metheny or John Scofield—it's like, "Man, you played something in the cymbals that brought me to a whole other room in the house I haven't visited before."

Again, we're talking about being open and trusting yourself to finding inspiration in everything around you.

My Uncle Max used to say, "By any means necessary." So show me the brilliance. Show me the wonderment. Don't show me excuses. No ifs, no buts, no slipping, no sliding, no superiority, no inferiority. Don't let what you know get in the way. Get to that place where everyone is uplifted in spirit and revived.

Unfortunately, there's a fair amount of pressure on ambitious young musicians to clone what's successful, as many of today's besieged record labels are practicing strict "risk management." Do you feel you can embrace the spirit and still serve commerce?

The more McDonald's that are out there, the more you need a grandma who spends all day in the kitchen stirring the sauce on Thanksgiving. This is why I'm very grateful to Derek Trucks, Ben Harper, Trey Anastasio, and others like them. They are successful, and they play from their hearts. Now, there are a lot of successful posers, as well. These are the musicians I was talking about who practice in front of mirrors, and plan every note to do a certain thing. It's all calculated. But I think these people would be afraid to get onstage with Jeff Beck,

Buddy Guy, and me, because they would think they'd have to compete with Jeff Beck, Buddy Guy, and me. I don't compete or compare, man. I just wait my turn.

Can we explore that a bit? You've shared stages with a lot of amazing guitarists and other instrumentalists. How do you approach your performance when you're sharing licks with another player?

If they go up and down, I go from side to side. I'm going to bring counter motion to whatever is happening in the room. I figure the best way I can be welcome is to bring something different from what they're doing. That's what I learned from Miles Davis: Always go for the counter motion. It's a great insight. He said, "If you hear something, don't play it. Play what's around it. Play like you don't know what to play." Again, this is about letting go of what you know.

I'm still a bit of a coward. If I'm hearing *A*, *C#m*, *F#m*, *D*, I'm probably going to surrender to my comfort zone and play an *A* major scale.

Here's that word again: Trust. In order to trust, you have to be able to see something beautiful first, and then feel something beautiful. I can close my eyes, and in this very second I can be Buddy Guy, John McLaughlin, Pat Metheny, and Jeff Beck, and we're all having a ball. We don't even know we're guitar players. We're just saying, "Hey man," and each one of us is telling some marvelous stories. Buddy has some great blues stories about Muddy Waters and B. B. King and John Lee Hooker. So tell me a story with your guitar, man. If I wanted to see a screwdriver or a hammer, I'd ask you to play me scales and chords. You see what I mean? You have to learn how to tell a story. You have to learn to carry a melody. You have to learn to access the intangible at will. These things will make you a different kind of musician.

Ultimately, you should utilize music the same way you utilize your imagination. Sometimes, you can just drop something in and make people go, "Wow!" It doesn't have to be deep. For example, there's a place in our set—between "Soul Sacrifice" and the finale—where the band doesn't know what I'm going to do. I might play something raw or beautiful, or I'll throw in a Looney Tunes theme. Any direction is okay, because music doesn't have to be so boring, constrictive, and serious. Music is supposed to be fun.

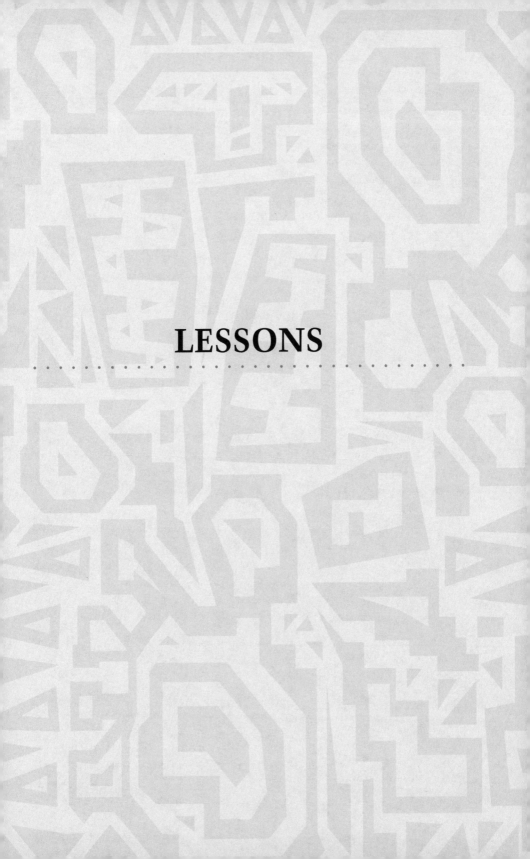

LESSONS

11.

CLASSIC CARLOS: A PORTRAIT OF DORIAN UN-GRAY

. . . .

by Jesse Gress, January 1993

Ever find yourself feeling less than inspired by the latest wave of half-baked, generic music? One sure remedy is immersion in the music of the masters. And who better personifies the ideal of the musician who is emotionally committed to every note than Carlos Santana? When Santana hit the international scene in 1969 with a sound that combined jazz, blues, rock, and Latin, no one had yet coined that notorious "f" word—"fusion."

Carlos' playing sounded totally unlike anything in rock. Abstractly speaking, many of Santana's melodic lines are constructed from the usual materials: pentatonic major and minor scales, blues scales, and diatonic modes (he particularly favors Dorian). But rhythm may be the most important aspect of Carlos' playing. If you were to remove the pitches from his melodic lines, the pure rhythms would be as much at home on a conga or timbale as on the guitar. When working out the following examples, try learning the rhythms before adding the notes. Some aspects of Carlos' playing are difficult to translate on paper. His breathy elastic rhythms often defy accurate notation by accelerating ahead of or dropping slightly behind the beat. One way to get a handle on this "bouncing ball" effect is to practice rhythms in which each successive beat is increased or decreased by evenly divided accent (see **Fig. 1**).

Fig. 1

A typical Santana solo—if there is such a thing—might contain blues-drenched call-and-response phrases, unexpected melodic twists colored with intervals outside of the pedestrian pentatonic scale, syncopated rhythm motifs, a tremolo-picked slow glissando moving to a climactic high bend, and perhaps conclude with an infinitely sustained note. (In the live Osaka version of "Europa," Carlos holds one note for 59 seconds!) And, of course, every note drips with that inexplicable something that the late music critic Ralph J. Gleason once described as the "X-factor." Though we can barely scratch the surface, here are a few of Carlos' finest.

Ex. 1 is one of Santana's most familiar early-period licks. Begin in the tenth position, making sure you milk the release of the first bend for all it's worth. Enhance the heavy Peter Green vibe with a slide into the 9th (E); also the 5th of the Vm chord (Am).

Ex. 2 begins with a two-bar call-and-response phrase featuring six-teenth-note syncopations. The phrase repeats and then concludes with a dip to the ♭7 (C), eventually returning to the tonic D via a lazy quarter-note triplet. This flurry of activity followed by a long sustained resolution is another Santana trademark.

Framed by a signature Im–IV Dorian vamp (Am–D), **Ex. 3** finds Carlos playing musical question and answer between the upper and middle registers of the fifth-position A Dorian mode. The half-step slides into the F♯s evoke Wes Montgomery and George Benson.

A combination of ascending bends peppered with dramatic rests and mixed rhythmic groupings creates a sense of urgency in the opening measure of **Ex. 4**. For the shift back to the twelfth position, play the F♯ at the end of bar 1 with your middle or ring finger so you can comfortably finger the remaining E Dorian/pentatonic minor phrase. The underlying chord progression is built from a harmonized E pentatonic minor scale.

While **Ex. 5**'s sax-like opening figure is derived from the F harmonic minor scale, you can also think of it as a C7 arpeggio played over the F Dorian vamp. Bars 2 and 3 superimpose arpeggiated E♭, and B♭, major triads, followed by a short B. B. King-ism. Next, two chromatically descending 4ths raise the tension. Barre the 16th fret with your 3rd finger and the 15th with your 2nd finger to assure a comfortable arrival at the thirteenth position for the bluesy wrap-up in bar 5.

CLASSIC CARLOS: A PORTRAIT OF DORIAN UN-GRAY

Ex. 6 exemplifies Carlos' Coltrane-infused collaborations with John McLaughlin. Santana opens with a descending F♯ pentatonic minor scale superimposed over a B Mixolydian vamp (A6–B). Note how these rhythms accelerate, as we discussed earlier. The D♯ alludes to F♯ Dorian (relative to B Mixolydian, as do the following pair of broken minor-third intervals descending in whole steps. The next minor third descends only a half-step, bringing the ♭5 into the picture for a split second before moving back to F♯ Dorian. The phrase beginning at the end of bar 4 moves from low-register, twelfth position F♯ pentatonic minor to a rapid, sixteenth-note ascent via F♯ Dorian. A tremolo-picked even gliss beginning on F# peaks with a high bend into C♯. Extremely hip: the fact that this C♯ and the notes of the closing F♯ pentatonic minor lick are the 9, ♭7, and 5 of the tonic B.

A lush IV–I progression in C (Fmaj7–Cmaj7) accompanies **Ex. 7**'s combination of seventh and eighth-position C major scale and fifth-position C major pentatonic (phrased as A pentatonic minor). The final two measures offer proof that you don't have to play a lot of notes if you've got a good sense of rhythm.

Representative of Carlos' current work, **Ex. 8** offers another lively Im-IV D Dorian vamp. Here, in tenth position, he plays a short, memorable rhythm motif, rests for three beats, then plays a perfectly executed sixteenth-note phrase that flows seamlessly into a restatement of the first motif. Note the "mirror image" sixteenth-note groupings on beats 2 and 3 of the second measure. The concluding lick leans heavily on the 6th (B), a key Dorian ingredient.

In **Ex. 9**, unison bends on the 9th kick off an F Mixolydian excursion combining Carlos' legato stylings and salsa rhythms. After the sustained bends, Santana hammers and pulls his way down the B string to first position. The extra-hot F Mixolydian conclusion contains a beautifully placed 9th (G) where one might normally expect to hear the root.

Ex. 10 shows a more recent variation of the accelerating rhythm effect, this time using pull-offs. Begin with your 2nd finger (to accommodate the fingering of the final lick) and think "bouncing ball." The unique closing lick combines twelfth position E Dorian and blues scales, and it's just one more reason why we love you, Carlos!

Ex. 6

Ex. 7

Ex. 8

Ex. 9

Ex. 10

12.

GUTS AND GRACE: EXPLORE THE TOUGH SENSUALITY OF SANTANA'S LINES

by Andy Ellis, August 1999

It's fun to deconstruct a great guitarist's characteristic phrases. Discovering something as simple as a new fingering or note sequence can alter your perspective of the fretboard and open the door to fresh sounds. Santana puts it best: "We all come from T-Bone Walker, Django Reinhardt, and Charlie Christian, and it shows in our music, man. It's like what [jazz composer] Gil Evans said, 'Take what you need, but honor it.' The kings—Otis Rush, Buddy Guy, Wes Montgomery—we honor all of them. But remember to always make it yours."

Santana's fiery fretwork on "Evil Ways," "Samba Pa Ti," "Black Magic Woman," "Oye Como Va," "Jingo," and "Everybody's Everything" (all found on *Santana—Greatest Hits*), is full of inspiring ideas. Distilled from these early classics, the lines in this lesson are ready for you to honor and make your own.

SYNCOPATION AND SLURS

Ex. 1 is clearly inspired by Peter Green. Emphasize the syncopation (on the and of beat two), and accent the anticipated *E* going into bar 2. Pick close to the bridge,

Ex. 1

using a fairly clean tone and a generous dose of reverb. The bend, release, and pull-off (bar 1, beat four) add a vocal quality to the sixteenth notes and keep them from sounding choppy. Santana played this over *Em*, but the lick also works nicely against the IV7 of an *E* blues—*A7* or *A9*.

The first two beats in **Ex. 2** contain one of Santana's favorite moves: a matching pair of triplets played across the top two strings. The whole-step bend and release keeps each triplet smooth. Notice how Examples 1 and 2 end with the identical melodic figure. However, it occurs a beat earlier in Ex. 2. Such rhythmic displacement lets you get maximum mileage from any motif.

FILLING THE CRACKS

Ex. 3 borrows several ideas from the previous two examples. Like Ex. 1, this lick starts on beat two. In a band, the bass and drums typically nail the first beat of a given measure, so to avoid competing with the low frequencies of the kick drum and bass, it makes sense to start a melodic phrase after this big downbeat. Santana is a master at working the rhythmic "cracks," and will often launch a lick on a weak beat or on the and of a strong beat.

As in Ex. 2, Santana rolls triplets—each containing a bend and release—across the top strings. This time, there are three bends—two half-step stretches, followed by a whole-step squeeze. The concluding half-step slide takes us from a *Dm* chord tone (*F*) to an *Am* chord tone (*E*). Slick.

In **Ex. 4**, Santana uses hammers and pulls to make a busy line sing instead of chatter. That opening whole-step bend—yeah, way up there at the 18th fret—is a signature Santana exclamation. For an authentic "yow," quickly slide down the string immediately after stretching into high *C*. This sounds great with some reverb. Lean into each hammered *F*—this will help you feel the syncopation.

Ex. 5a reveals Santana's jazzy side. Played over *Gm*—the IVm in a *D* minor blues—it emphasizes the 9 (*A*). This lick lies nicely on the fretboard and sounds just as cool an octave lower (**Ex. 5b**). In either case, keep beat one crisp by accenting the first A and snapping the hammer and pull.

GUTS AND GRACE: EXPLORE THE TOUGH SENSUALITY OF SANTANA'S LINES

Ex. 2

Ex. 3

Ex. 4

Ex. 5a   **Ex. 5b**

DORIAN MOVES

Next time you're playing a *G* minor blues, slip **Ex. 6** into the mix. As in the previous example, accent the first note and snap the slurs. Practice the position shift (beat two) slowly until the fingering makes sense.

In his many minor vamps, Santana often solos using the Dorian mode—one of several minor modes. Over a minor chord, you can play a Dorian line with the same root. In this example, the harmony is *Gm*, so we're in search of *G* Dorian.

Some background: The Dorian formula is 1, 2, ♭3, 4, 5, 6, ♭7. Compared to a parallel major scale, Dorian has a lowered 3 and 7. Step by step, let's work out *G* Dorian.

- Start with a *G* major scale: *G, A, B, C, D, E,* and *F♯* (1, 2, 3, 4, 5, 6, 7).
- Lowering the 3 and 7 yields *B♭* (♭3) and *F* (♭7).
- Thus *G* Dorian contains *G, A, B♭, C, D, E,* and *F* (1, 2, ♭3, 4, 5, 6, ♭7).

Ex. 6 emphasizes *E* and *B♭*—the 6 and ♭3. What's so special about these two notes? All minor modes and scales have a ♭3—it's the one note that makes them "minor." However, most minor modes and scales contain the ♭6—in this case, *E♭*—rather than the 6. By highlighting the ♭3 and 6, as in this lick, Santana accentuates the Dorian flavor.

Ex. 7, another of Santana's *G* Dorian phrases, combines the slurs from Examples 5a and 6. This two-bar figure will turn heads when you play it with conviction and a fat, squawking tone. Hit those accents in beats one, two, and three. Kenny Burrell pioneered lines like this in his blues jams with organist Jimmy Smith. Check out the soul-jazz classic *Blues Bash* (which Verve recently reissued on CD) to hear Burrell and Smith in action.

Ex. 8 features a descending *G* Dorian line on the first string. This "play along the string" technique is key to Santana's sound. In bar one, fret all the notes using your 1st finger and accent the downbeats. To play bar 2's third and fourth beats smoothly, drop a partial barre across the second and third string, simultaneously fretting *E* and *C* with your 1st finger.

OFFSET MAGIC

Santana is crafty. Unlike many rockers who stumble when soloing over major-7th chords, he knows how to make blues licks fly in jazzy settings. The secret is to offset the lick in relation to the harmony. Take **Ex. 9**, for

GUTS AND GRACE: EXPLORE THE TOUGH SENSUALITY OF SANTANA'S LINES

Ex. 6

Ex. 7

Ex. 8

Ex. 9

instance. Melodically, this is pure Cream-era Clapton—a lick right out of "Crossroads." In that context, this would be considered an A blues phrase. But Santana uses it to connect *Cmaj7* to *Fmaj7*, and it sounds fabulous. (Be sure to hear this line against the harmony—record the changes or have someone play them. It's worth the effort, because offsetting blues licks is such an important concept.)

Here's how it works: Most blues licks contain the ♭3 and are, therefore, minor. It's the contrast of a minor melody played over a I7—say, an *A* blues lick against *A7*—that gives blues its bittersweet sound. Notice that the scale and chord roots are the same.

In this example, however, Santana plays a minor lick against its relative major chord, so the roots are offset by a minor third. The formula is easy: Play your blues lick three frets below the target major 7. When you see *Dmaj7*, play a *B* blues lick. Against *Gmaj7*, play an *E* blues lick, and so on.

Ex. 10 opens with an *A* blues lick against *Fmaj7*. This time we're riding the IVmaj7 back to the Imaj7. Just as the progression resolves to *Cmaj7*, Santana pulls out another jazz trick—the chord-over-chord technique. See how he arpeggiates an *Em* triad in those last three notes? *Em* (*E, G, B*) matches the top three chords tones in *Cmaj7* (*C, E, G, B*), so this substitution makes complete musical sense. Here's the recipe: When you see a major-7th chord, arpeggiate a minor triad starting from the major 7's 3. For *Fmaj7*, arpeggiate *Am*; for *B♭maj7*, arpeggiate *Dm*. Cool.

Sustained tones play a crucial role in Santana's trademark sound, so keep that six-beat note ringing for its full value.

In **Ex. 11**, Santana reworks a country lick so it fits an *Fmaj7–Cmaj7* (IVmaj7–Imaj7) change. By itself, the figure could be a twangy honky-tonk intro in the key of *C*. Played against these major 7s, however, it sounds very smooth and uptown, proving that context is everything. Like several previous examples, this one starts on beat two.

STRING STRETCHING

The next two licks focus on Santana's bends. **Ex. 12a** is B. B. King channeled through Peter Green. Based on a series of duplicate notes on the top two strings, the line features a type of call-and-response: First, bend a whole-step to *E*; then fret *E* on the higher string. Repeat these notes to build tension that's resolved in beat four.

The quarter-bend on the and of beat four is a bit tricky: Fret both *B* and *G* with your 1st finger, hold *B* steady, and gently pull *G* toward your feet. Try this phrase with a stinging bridge-pickup tone.

GUTS AND GRACE: EXPLORE THE TOUGH SENSUALITY
OF SANTANA'S LINES

Ex. 10

Ex. 11

Ex. 12a

Ex. 12b

Ex. 12b is Jan Hammer channeled through Jeff Beck. Here, the game is to fret *E* on the first string, pre-bend E on the second string, and then drop down a whole-step. Again, we're using duplicate notes, but this time the fretted note precedes the bend. Ex. 12a is pure blues, Ex. 12b is certified fusion, and Santana uses them both.

Ex. 13

With its speech-like phrasing, **Ex. 13** is quintessential Santana. "There's cursing and praying, and all that language is part of music," he says. "A lot of my best solos remind me of when my mom used to scold me, 'Dit-doo-dup-dat-doo-doo-bah!'" Feel the rhythmic contrast between the straight eighth-notes and the following syncopations.

"Attitude is as important as notes," asserts Santana. "You learn not to be intimidated. You learn to respect and find your place—to complement. That's how I was able to survive working with John McLaughlin, because it ain't easy being with a musician like that. [*Laughs.*] When we were on the road, I thought, 'Man, what am I going to do? I should just shine his shoes.' Then I found that after he finished playing, people would go, 'Okay, we love what he says, but what do you have to say?' I may not play as many notes, or know as much as he does, but three notes—if you put them in the right place at the right time—are just as important. So when you think, 'I should hang up my guitar and be a dishwasher,' listen to your other side: 'No, you too have something they need.'"

"Don't analyze your playing. Let God light you up, and let it come out."—Carlos Santana (© JACQUES LOWE / RETNA LTD.)

13.

HOW TO PLAY LIKE CARLOS SANTANA

by Jesse Gress, November 2007

A staunch advocate of peace and universal brotherhood, Carlos Santana's guitar playing has always conveyed a similar sentiment. Okay, maybe it's hokey to claim that you can "hear" such qualities in a guitar part, but with Carlos, well, you can actually feel the love he puts into each note.

Santana is also a devotee of the Dorian mode, and he has a particular knack for combining its characteristic sweetness with nasty blues sounds, as well as a talent for manipulating it to form other modalities. Add plenty of Latin-influenced rhythmic syncopations and a sublime, sustained tone and you've got the basic recipe for Santana stew.

Check it out: The rhythms alone in **Ex. 1** create musical excitement, but a few bluesy D pentatonic minor-based intervals coupled with Santana's innate sense of call-and-response add some serious sizzle.

Ex. 1

Ex. 2's run, played over a typical Im-IV progression, brings some fluttery Dorian flavor to the blues party, while **Ex. 3** reveals how Santana substitutes *F♯* Dorian (plus a few outside tones in bar 2) to create a wailing B Mixolydian modality over a ♭VII-I "A Love Supreme"-style vamp. (This last example recalls Santana's mid-'70s, Coltrane-influenced collaborations with John McLaughlin.)

Just remember that when it comes to making these tasty musical recipes successful, it's up to you to provide the main ingredient: Heart.

Ex. 2

Ex. 3

Jack V. Huffman
1983

Winging It!

Winging It!

His own story by Jack Jefford, pioneer Alaskan aviator

Edited by
Carmen Jefford Fisher & Mark Fisher
with **Clifford Cernick**

Rand McNally & Company

Chicago · New York · San Francisco

PHOTO CREDITS: Jack Jefford's personal photographs, 10, 33, 34, 88, 89(top), 90, 92, 93(top), 94, 95, 191, 193(top), 195(top), 196(top), 275(bot.), 279(top), 280(bot.), 281, 284; University of Alaska Archives—Jack Jefford collection, 35, 36, 89(bot.), 91; National Park Service, frontispiece, 87, 93(bot.), 189, 277(bot.); Federal Aviation Administration, 190, 192(top), 193(bot.), 194(bot.), 196(bot.), 276, 277(top), 279(bot.), 280(top), 282, 283; courtesy of May Nock, 192(bot.), 278, back cover; U.S. Air Force, 194(top), 195(bot.); Fish & Wildlife Service, 274–275.

Frontispiece: Mount St. Elias.

First printing, 1981
Library of Congress Cataloging in Publication Data
Jefford, Jack.
    Winging It!
    Includes index.
    1. Jefford, Jack. 2. Air pilots—Alaska—
Biography. I. Fisher, Carmen Jefford.
II. Fisher, Mark. III. Title.
TL540.J43A37   629.13'092'4 [B]   81-5906
ISBN 0-528-81111-8   AACR2

Jack Jefford
1910–1979

Jack Jefford passed away on Sunday evening, August 12, 1979, at his home in Wasilla. He was 68 years old.

FAA employees will remember Jack as Chief Pilot for the Alaskan Region from 1940 to 1972, when he retired. He was one of the true giants of Alaskan aviation history. A "pilot's pilot," Jefford figured in scores of dramatic rescue flights, when supreme flying skill meant a life-or-death difference for victims of accident or illness in the bush. Jefford helped blaze the aerial trailways that today are flown by wide-bodied jets. Jack Jefford could fly anything, and did. When the props were still, Jack turned his hand to the cargo. He labored with the rest of the crew when the commissary materials had to move. Jack could tell a story with flair and dramatic skill. When he laughed, everyone laughed with him. An evening with Jack was an evening to be remembered. But, most of all, Jack Jefford was a kind and gentle man. He was true to his friends, always ready with a helpful hand for anyone who needed it. He was a big man, as modest as his achievements were great. His parting leaves a vast gap in Alaska's aviation fraternity. He shall be missed. As long as Alaskans fly, he shall be remembered.

Warren G. Runnerstrom
from the FAA Alaskan Region *Intercom*

Contents

HAVE PLANE
WILL TRAVEL

BRENNAN - NOV. 1960

Foreword

My father, Jack Jefford, was an excellent storyteller. Whether he was addressing a banquet or just shooting the breeze with friends, people enjoyed his ability to see humor in the things that happened to him. And quite a few things happened in the course of his career as a pilot.

Once, when we were weathered in with Dad at Teslin Lake on a flight across Canada, my husband, Mark, and I were treated to a marathon story telling session. For two days Mark and I listened and laughed, and we were actually disappointed when the storm passed. We found Dad's tales so fascinating we agreed it would be criminal not to record them for others to enjoy.

That summer Dad began telling some of his adventures to a tape recorder. Over a five-year period, he made eighteen tapes. Mark and I transcribed, organized, and edited the stories, always striving not to change Dad's conversational style. We had additional help on the editing from Cliff Cernick, Public Information Officer for the FAA's Alaskan Region. We were just a few stories away from completing the final draft at the time of Dad's sudden death in August, 1979.

This book is not a well-rounded autobiography; it's simply a collection of Dad's flying stories. It was Dad's particular wish not to dwell at any length on his family life. Nor is this story collection in any way complete. Dad was a warm-hearted, generous man, and his multitude of friends have their own "Jack Jefford stories" to tell.

We are grateful to the family and friends who offered moral support, and particularly want to thank Dorothy Revell for her careful review of each draft and for her unfailing enthusiasm. We would also like to acknowledge the assistance of the University of Alaska Archives and early suggestions and support from Charles Kiem.

It is my hope that you will enjoy these stories of Dad's as I have, perhaps even hear the chuckle in his voice as you read.

Carmen Jefford Fisher
Anchorage, Alaska
June, 1981

Winging It!

Part 1

Riding the Grub Line

1

Becoming a Pilot

I SAW MY FIRST AIRPLANE when I was six years old and felt such an incredible sense of wonder that I still remember the scene vividly.

The disassembled biplane, an old Wright Pusher, had been shipped into town on the Burlington Railroad to serve as an attraction for the 1916 county fair at Scottsbluff, Nebraska. Goggle-eyed, I watched the aircraft take shape as the double wings were attached to the fuselage. Others at the fairgrounds soon crowded around in fascination. Like me, most people in western Nebraska had never before seen an airplane.

It was unforgettable. Chain-driven propellers whipping up billowing clouds of yellow dust . . . the sturdy biplane taxiing down the alfalfa field in the bright Nebraska sunshine. . . . Then, the plane lifting free of the earth . . . circling over the gaping crowd . . . circling over me, a six-year-old boy caught from that time onward by the wonder, the excitement, the adventure of flying.

My younger brother, Bill, and I got our first taste of actual flying in California, where my family spent the winter of 1925. Diligently we saved our money until we had $10, enough to buy two tickets for a ride in an old OX Jenny based at Santa Monica's Clover Field. Ten dollars seemed like a small fortune, but we were eager to fly and more than willing to pay.

That pilot must have enjoyed kids because he gave us quite a lengthy ride. Gazing out through the flying wires as the earth's features grew smaller, feeling the wind in my face, watching the dance of the rocker arms atop the OX-5 engine—the flight was pure magic to me.

While growing up in Nebraska, both Bill and I worked with my father, a building contractor. Dad's favorite saying was, "Idle hands are the devil's workshop." Rather than aid the devil, Dad always gave Bill and me plenty to do.

One day we were pouring a basement in Ogallala. My job was to mix the cement according to the prescribed formula: toss a bucket of water into the cement mixer, add two shovels of cement, eight shovels of sand and gravel, mix well, then dump the batch into the wheelbarrow. It was heavy work—a tiring process, repeated over and over without respite.

Suddenly I heard a low drone from the sky, and the boredom vanished. Far overhead one of the early mail planes was headed west. Cement mixing was temporarily forgotten. "That guy up there is sitting down," I thought, "and flying's a hell of a lot better way of life than mixing cement!"

That was the exact moment I decided to become an aviator, as pilots were known in those days.

But how do you become an aviator in Ogallala, Nebraska, in the heart of the Depression? First you need to get a paying job. I didn't have much money, and flying lessons cost a bundle.

Bill and I found work with the Goodall Electric Manufacturing Company. Bob Goodall, a jeweler, was also an inventor whose creations included a watch-cleaning machine, a jeweler's soldering iron, and a spot welder for orthodontists. But sound systems for movie theaters comprised the largest part of Goodall's business. Bill and I worked in the machine shop assembling heads that could be attached to outmoded silent or sound-on-disk projectors, enabling them to accept the newly popular sound-on-film movies.

I started working for $18 a week. Periodic raises brought my salary to $27.50—practically every nickel of which went for flying lessons. My instructor, a character named Jack Westfall, owned an OX Travelair. For ten bucks he provided fifteen minutes of instruction. For thirty-five you'd get a whole hour, but since the shorter lessons usually ran a few minutes over, they appealed to me as the better deal.

After a few lessons, one thing began to disturb me a bit. None of Westfall's students ever soloed, though he gave them all sorts of flying time. I think he valued his Travelair to such an extent that he wasn't about to let any soloing student bust it up for him.

While taking lessons from Westfall, I met Major Carlos Reavis of Denver, who operated a modern flying school equipped with a Waco F and a Lycoming Stinson. If I could save up enough money to enroll, I knew I'd be able to solo—something Westfall wasn't likely to let happen in Ogallala.

The Depression bankruptcy of the Curtiss-Wright Flying Service, a national organization with fifty-two flying schools and overhaul shops, hastened my departure to Denver. Major Reavis told me that the company's misfortune had made available an OX Robin, one of the first cabin monoplanes, powered by a World War I surplus engine.

By hocking everything I owned and borrowing money from Goodall and all my friends, I was able to come up with the $500 to buy the Robin, number NC 377E, and with an extra $250 to pay for flying lessons.

I rented a $3-a-week room on Larimer Street in a rundown area of

Denver inhabited mostly by hookers. Though raunchy, the restaurants suited me just right. You could get breakfast for fifteen cents, lunch for thirty-five cents, and dinner for forty-five cents. The T-bone steaks served for dinner covered your plate, but they were only an eighth of an inch thick.

The honky-tonk surroundings and my tiny room with its single-window view of a drab brick wall didn't depress me in the least. I was in Denver and I was learning to fly.

On April 28, 1931, Jack Euler, my instructor at Reavis's school, declared I was ready to solo. For forty-five glorious minutes I was airborne, all by myself. Later I was checked out in my own Robin and began practicing for a private pilot's license, mastering some of the basics—landings, stalls, figure eights, and spirals. A lot of the landings were deadstick practice because the early engines, including the OX-5, weren't noted for their reliability.

On May 7, 1931, a private license was issued to one Jack Jefford by Harold Montee, Inspector with the Department of Commerce. The license allowed me to fly anywhere I wanted in the United States and to carry passengers, as long as I didn't charge them for the ride.

Bill hitchhiked to Denver so he could share my moment of triumph—the return to Ogallala in the Robin. With its kelly green fuselage and bright, berry-red wings, we called it the "Christmas Tree Robin."

I had completed my test for the private license late in the day, and with four hours of daylight remaining we spent our last nickel on gasoline and left Denver for Ogallala. As we flew east on my first cross-country flight we began encountering thunderstorms. Finally they were everywhere, and it began to rain. I had done all my flying under ideal circumstances. Now all at once my windshield was streaked with huge splattering raindrops, and visibility was decreasing. "I'd better get this bird down, or else!" I told Bill.

If you're going to select a site for a forced landing, you can't beat eastern Colorado. I picked out an alfalfa field and brought in the Robin pretty hot. This was before planes had brakes; "braking" was provided by a tail skid that dragged along the ground. To increase the braking action, you held the stick back so the skid would plough a deeper furrow. The Robin finally rolled to a stop about twenty feet from an irrigation ditch. Had I been any faster on the approach, I imagine my aviation career would have ended in the ditch with a smashed-up Robin.

In about an hour the typical Midwestern storm passed, and the weather improved. We cranked up and were able to take off from the field without incident. But then darkness began to close in, so we decided to put down on the deserted airport at Sterling, Colorado.

After taxiing up to the lone hangar and parking there for a while, we realized we were damned hungry—and neither of us had a cent. If I'm ever reincarnated, I don't want to come back as a younger brother— I always got brother Bill to do the lousy jobs. This time I talked him into walking over to a farmhouse about a half mile away to see if he could get us some food.

You hate to go begging, so I had him rehearse a little speech in which he was to say we were big-shot aviators and had left all our cash in my checkered vest, or some such yarn. But I think Bill just told the truth—we were broke and hungry. He was gone quite a while and it was pitch dark when he returned, carrying a loaf of bread and a coffee can of milk. Bread and milk never tasted so good.

Well, that night we just sat in the airplane. Both of us loved her so— she was all ours and I could fly her. Everything considered, life seemed pretty good for the Jefford brothers. The plane's limited instruments— oil pressure, water temperature, and airspeed gauges, altimeter and tachometer—all had fluorescent hands. As we periodically awakened through the night, it was a great thrill to see the numbers glowing softly on the panel.

2
The Voice from the Sky

THE PROPRIETOR of the Goodall Electric Manufacturing Company devised a spectacular new advertising gimmick he called "The Voice from the Sky." It consisted of a microphone, two powerful amplifiers energized by a wind-driven AC generator, and large horn-shaped airborne speakers. Under Bob Goodall's direction, Bill and I installed the gear on the Robin and experimented with the equipment.

In theory it was a great idea, but a few vexing problems had to be ironed out before the invention could be termed a success. For one thing, obtaining a stable voltage and AC frequency for the amplifiers was very difficult using the wind-driven generator. By careful adjustment of the generator's propeller pitch, we managed to make the system work. But I had to be very cautious in flight. If I got my airspeed a little too high, the voltage would increase and I'd blow out the amplifier tubes.

Even so, the contraption, mounted under the wings of my aircraft, worked amazingly well. Bill and I enjoyed flying around the countryside, addressing startled people on the ground in a thundering, highly amplified voice that could be heard for miles.

There was another reason I liked these flights. Goodall was paying all my expenses while we tested "The Voice from the Sky" with my Robin. In the process I was building up the 200 hours of flight time necessary to qualify for the coveted transport license—the next hurdle before becoming a professional aviator.

With only a private license, my flying activities were quite limited. All I could do was joyride and fly friends. While I could stretch the law a little and let them pay for gas, the regulations plainly stated it was illegal to haul passengers or property for hire. I was fortunate to have Goodall more or less underwriting a number of flights as I set about logging air time so I could take the transport test.

After "The Voice from the Sky" had been pretty well debugged, we took the device to Denver for a demonstration. Goodall found a prospective customer, a company that planned to fly over Denver and other cities delivering sales pitches for various stores. While Goodall was downtown conducting business with the customers, I was up over the city with Goodall's sales manager, who was broadcasting on the microphone.

Suddenly, the OX engine quit running. I knew I couldn't make it to any of Denver's three airports—Curtiss-Wright, Lowry, or Municipal—so I settled for a fairway on the nearby Park Hill golf course. As we approached the links, I asked the sales manager to broadcast to the golfers below that we were going to land. We watched as they scattered and hid behind the trees.

I was able to set the Robin down on the fairway without a scratch. We contacted the airport, and they brought us a pickup truck. After loading the tail of the Robin onto the pickup bed, we started back to the hangar. By then it was dark, so I turned on the plane's navigation lights. But our luck had run out. A woman, driving rather fast, struck the airplane, severely damaging both the plane and her car.

That night we took the Robin apart and shipped it to Colorado Springs to be rebuilt by the Alexander Aircraft Company, with Goodall footing the bill for repairs to both the airplane and the car.

As for "The Voice from the Sky," it vanished ignominiously when cities began passing ordinances against it. Too many people were looking up at the "Voice" and running into one another. I guess the authorities felt we had enough racket from the sky without deliberately making more.

A year after soloing, I accumulated the 200 hours necessary to apply for my transport license and went back to Reavis's school in Denver for advanced training prior to the actual test. Though I passed the written portion, I flunked the flight test because my spins were pretty ragged.

I couldn't fault the examiner for my failure. Harold Montee, the Department of Commerce Inspector and an excellent pilot himself, was responsible for licensing all aircraft and pilots in Colorado and Nebraska. Without a doubt, Montee was one of the finest persons I have ever known. After practicing spins, I once again made an appointment with Montee, and on March 3, 1933, earned my transport license at Sterling, Colorado.

Now I was in business!

3

Riding the Grub Line

CHARLIE BRENNAN was a one-of-a-kind cowboy I had admired during the childhood years I spent on a ranch in the Sand Hills of Nebraska. Charlie was with me in spirit on that midwinter day I left Cheyenne for Scottsbluff in my OX Robin.

The morning was cold, gray, and overcast—definitely not good weather, but seemingly flyable. Heading northeastward from Wyoming toward Nebraska, I watched the ceiling slowly descend. I kept under the cloud cover, flying closer and closer to the ground, hoping the weather might improve.

But as I continued on my way, I began encountering a few advance snowflakes. A short while later, I found myself in the middle of a heavy snow squall. In the rising wind I was flying as low as I dared, and the going had become pretty thick. I realized I'd better get on the ground, so while skimming over the prairie I started sizing up the ranches, looking for one of the better ones where I might put to use a practice I'd learned from old Charlie Brennan—a consummate artist at "riding the grub line."

The most singular thing about Charlie was his being Irish, rather unusual for a cowhand. He seemed awfully old to me then, though I suppose he wasn't much over fifty. His constant companion was Ginger, a white-footed, white-nosed bay saddle horse. Charlie had trained Ginger to be a fine cutting horse, and together they worked the ranches of westcentral Nebraska.

A veteran cowboy and disciple of the old school, Charlie hated any form of machinery, automobiles included. Although he would grudgingly tolerate a limited amount of mechanized equipment when we put up hay, Charlie much preferred the back-breaking pitchfork work of stacking the hay to the bother of tangling with mowing and raking machinery.

At his best working cattle, Charlie was considered a top hand by all the Sand Hills ranchers. An excellent roper and all-around cowboy, Charlie always walked off with top honors at rodeos and roping contests. Having worked with horses all his life, he was so bowlegged the soles of his boots wore down on their outside edges.

Spry, wiry, and robustly healthy, Charlie needed a doctor's care only once, the time he broke his leg when thrown from a horse. Other than that, Charlie's only sickness was an occasional hangover, easily remedied with his own special cure, senna tea. Charlie would generously brew it for anyone who was sick and seemed so confident of the tea's miraculous power that most of us tried a cup at one time or another.

Charlie had one trait that drove both men and women up the wall in exasperation. He very carefully and studiously avoided all romantic entanglements. He was sociable, a perfect gentleman, and loved to dance. The ladies who watched him glide effortlessly through a waltz or sashay and do-si-do at a square dance would earmark him as "just right" for the new schoolmarm. The town's matchmakers were certain he'd be a good catch; it was only a matter of getting old Charlie to settle down.

The men were bothered at seeing him so carefree and unencumbered. They felt he should have a wife, a couple of kids, a mortgage, and all the other problems they had. But Charlie wouldn't allow himself to be corralled. No schoolmarm, or any other woman for that matter, was about to put the halter on Charlie.

During the season, a topnotch cowhand could earn between $30 and $40 a month, plus room and board. Charlie was in great demand and had ranchers vying for his services. Whoever employed him felt fortunate to have such a nice guy around.

Throughout the hot summers Charlie would work tirelessly, spending hardly a penny. But everyone knew that when the season was over,

Charlie would be heading to North Platte, rip-roaring division head-quarters of the Union Pacific Railroad. There, in about four glorious days, he'd blow his entire hard-earned summer's wages on his two loves besides horses—whiskey and the sportin' women.

His fling over, Charlie would return from North Platte with a crest-fallen, hangdog look. A Catholic of sorts, he'd go to confession and attend Mass a time or two, hoping to get his sins forgiven for the days spent in North Platte.

His money gone and with no job—and there were no winter jobs—Charlie would be facing a bleak winter. It was a grim prospect in those days before the welfare state, but Charlie took it in stride, fixing to "ride the grub line."

I remember the times Charlie came riding up to our little ranch, astride Ginger, his lean face raw and peeling from the sun and wind. "Dad! Mom! Charlie's here!" I'd yell as I spotted him approaching the gate.

He always arrived shortly before lunch, looking calmly indifferent, as though he just happened to be passing through. In those days it was the unwritten law among ranchers that if someone came along before mealtime, be he friend or stranger, you always invited him to share your meal.

We all recognized Charlie as a good-natured con artist and knew he would begin the "grub line" game at lunch. "Where you headed, Char-lie?" my dad would ask.

Charlie would remain silent for a moment, allowing for proper tim-ing. "Nowhere special," he'd say. "This time of year, a man's always got a little time on his hands. No need to rush anywhere particular."

Dad would study Charlie for a while—he was playing the game too. "Look, Charlie," he'd finally say, "since you've got some time, what do you think about spending a couple days with us?"

The ritual called for Charlie never to accept too eagerly. "Don't know for sure," he'd reply, seeming to mull over the proposition. And then he'd allow maybe he *would* spend a few days with us. "Besides," he would add, "I been meaning to get even with you for the last time you beat me at cribbage." Dad warmed to the challenge. He enjoyed cards, and Charlie was an excellent player.

And we children were overjoyed when Charlie came to stay. Charlie loved kids and we loved him. He'd tell us hair-raising stories, play checkers with us, and introduce us to puzzles, riddles, and games. He never overlooked or talked down to children, the way so many adults are prone to do, and was always very good to us.

As soon as lunch was over, Charlie would bounce up and help my mother with the dishes, further securing his position. He was always the first to dump the garbage and do the heavy chores. That was another reason I was glad to see Charlie show up. He'd do a lot of the dirty jobs I usually had to do.

Charlie made himself handy wherever there was something to be done, whether it was in the house, the barn, or out in the fields. He worked hard at maintaining his welcome, trying to keep his position secure with everyone, especially us youngsters. For as long as he stayed, he was a constant delight to everybody. But he seemed to know, as if by some unseen clock, when it was time to move on.

One sad morning we'd see Charlie packing his two saddle bags with all his worldly possessions. Carefully, he would fold his suit of "Sunday" clothes into his old bedroll, along with a spare pair of boots and his Colt Peacemaker .45 revolver.

Having heard Charlie was an expert shot, I was always fascinated by his gun. Two notches were filed on the butt. "What're the notches for, Charlie?" I asked. "Shootouts?"

Charlie smiled, "No, those notches were there when I got it, Jack. Don't really much like to shoot anything unless I have to. One time I had to send an old, badly hurt horse to glory, and I've killed a few rattlesnakes. But that's about it."

Whenever Charlie left, I always felt a sense of loss. "Why do you have to go, Charlie?" I once asked.

He busied himself with the saddle and ran his hand along Ginger's mane. "It's time I was moving on, son. It's that time. . . ."

There to see him off were Mom and Dad. "Wish you could see fit to stay a couple more days," said my dad, standing beside me.

"We'd love to have you," echoed my mother.

"No, sorry I can't. I really enjoyed every bit of your fine hospitality. But now, I figure it's time for Ginger and me to be movin' on."

So Charlie would ride off—not into the sunset, but over to our neighbors, where he'd do the same thing for a couple more weeks. Charlie "rode the grub line" throughout the winter, biding his time until work opened up again in the spring.

Peering down from the snow-filled Wyoming sky, I surveyed the ranches, looking for a good place to land. Just ahead of me I spotted a nice, solidly built ranch house next to a long pasture. "There's my airport!" I thought.

I circled back and landed on the snow-swept pasture, then taxied up to a fence near the house. The aircraft's roar attracted the rancher, and he was out at the plane before the prop stopped spinning. "What's

the problem?" the tall, rawboned rancher asked, looking me over carefully, suspiciously.

"I was headed for Scottsbluff from Cheyenne when I ran into this
storm. Sorry, but it was so thick up there I just had to land."

His expression softened. "It's okay, kid. You're welcome to spend
the night here. I'll get those cattle out of the feed lot so they won't butt
into your airplane." He helped me tie down the Robin, after which I
was ready to "ride the grub line" the way old Charlie Brennan used
to do.

After supper I practiced Charlie's technique, losing no time in
bounding up to do the dishes. Then I dumped the garbage and brought
in a big load of wood. From the looks of the weather, this was not just
an overnight deal—we could easily be in for a three- or four-day blizzard. A conscientious student of Charlie Brennan's methods, I helped
feed the cattle, cleaned the barn, and did as many dirty jobs as I could
find.

Before long I began developing a solid rapport with the rancher and
his brother, both bachelors, who lived together and operated the
spread. Unlike typical bachelors, however, they kept their farmhouse
neat as a pin.

Characteristic of ranch country, there was a bunkhouse out in the
yard where they suggested I sleep. I started the bunkhouse fire, banked
it with coal, and spent a very comfortable night.

The next day the weather was considerably worse. A raging storm,
typical of Wyoming, had really set in, snowing and blowing so badly
that visibility fell to less than half a mile.

After the evening chores were done, the three of us sat around the
stove in the warm ranch house and swapped stories. The brothers
were glad to see someone with the news, and we had a good time
talking to each other.

This went on for three days, and it didn't look like the damn storm
was ever going to let up. On the evening of the fourth day, life on the
snowbound farm had begun to pall on me. "I've just gotta get out of
here in the morning," I told the ranchers.

When one of the brothers nodded, I felt my welcome had worn thin.
Like old Charlie Brennan, I knew it was time to saddle up my horse
and leave. Only in my case, time to go or not, the weather wouldn't let
me fly off in my Robin.

On the fifth day my hosts began eyeing me uneasily. A couple of
times I observed them whispering to each other. Knowing they wanted
to get rid of me, I wondered where I'd gone wrong in applying old
Charlie's techniques. At midmorning one of the brothers came up to

me, looking somewhat nervous. "Seems to us . . ." He stopped, then blurted, "It don't look to us like you're gonna be able to fly away from here for at least another day or so."

"That's right," I replied apologetically. "I'm real sorry, but there's just no way I can take off until the weather lets up."

The rancher dug the toe of his boot into a hole in the worn carpet. "Well, young feller, me and my brother are just in an awful spot here! An awful spot!"

"What do you mean?" I asked.

"Well, might as well tell you, we've got a little side enterprise . . . the short of it is—we make moonshine. Right about now, our mash is all fermented out and it's time to start distillin' it. We can't very well run you off, but yet we're not very happy to have you here while we're distillin' this whiskey. But seein' it's got to be done now, we just hope you'll never mention to anyone what you're gonna see happenin' in the next few hours."

"You don't have to worry about me, I'll never say a word!" I assured him. "I never thought much of prohibition or the revenuers—maybe I'll even take a sip or two of the stuff if you can spare me a little."

The brothers seemed pleased and started to work. They set up two portable Coleman gasoline stoves and brought out three ten-gallon copper boilers. Wooden barrels of mash had been fermenting up in the attic, reachable only through a disappearing stairway. Though their distilling equipment was stashed all over the place, I hadn't suspected a thing, in spite of the time I'd spent with them.

After they realized I wasn't likely to inform on them, the brothers began to tell me about their operation. "We make only good stuff here, good moonshine," one of them said. "We age it right and sell it to the business folks down in Cheyenne."

"It's first class!" the other brother added. "And we never sell it on the street, just to the businessmen."

I helped the brothers bucket down the mash, pouring it into the copper boilers. Lids sprouting copper coils were placed on the boilers, then sealed with a thick paste made of flour and water. When the paste dried, it made a very effective gasket, keeping the steam from pouring out around the edges.

As the vats heated, they made simmering noises to which the brothers paid careful attention. The "brewers" insisted everything be just so, and it took a long time to bring the boilers to heat. Boiling the mash too fast could produce a poisonous fusel oil.

Eventually a few pearly drops and then a thin stream of moonshine began trickling into a glass jug set on the outer end of the still. In spite of their primitive system, the pair were expert bootleggers, and there was no fusel oil.

It was very late at night before all the mash was cooked out and disposed of. The whiskey was then redistilled and poured into charred oak kegs, which were stowed in a compartment beneath the hay racks used to feed the cattle.

Cautiously, I sampled the end result of an earlier distillation, several months old. Unlike some of the other often poisonous rotgut that used to be sold by Midwest bootleggers, this liquor was as excellent as anything "bottled in bond."

Keeping old Charlie Brennan in mind, I diligently helped out in every phase of the operation, hoping to make it clear I was becoming so deeply involved that, if we were raided, I'd be tossed into the slammer right along with them.

After the booze episode I was considered one of the family. As far as the two ranchers were concerned, I could have stayed there all winter. But a few days later the weather cleared. I cranked up the Robin and took off from the pasture. As I circled, I could see the moonshiners waving goodbye.

On the way to Scottsbluff I thought once again about old Charlie Brennan and how his methods had worked for me the same way they'd worked for him. I had occasion to use his system a number of times during my flying career, and I shall always be grateful to Charlie for teaching me the art of riding the grub line.

4

Barnstorming

I WANTED TO QUIT my job at Goodall's and make aviation my full-time career. But even though I sought out ways to make my transport license pay, the opportunities were very limited. I had become used to eating regularly, and there just wasn't enough money in flying.

Charter trips were very rare. People didn't have enough money, and the aircraft were too slow. The OX Robin cruised at eighty-five miles per hour, not that much faster than an automobile. About the only ways you could make money were instructing would-be pilots and barnstorming at county fairs.

Though I had a number of students, I was pretty much like old Jack Westfall. I wasn't too keen on letting any of them solo my airplane, but I was hell for dual.

Barnstorming was a nomadic way of life. While I did not become as deeply involved as many of the oldtimers, I had a sufficient taste of it to call myself a barnstormer. My area—eastern Colorado, eastern Wyoming, and Nebraska—was hard hit by the Depression, and the only prayer of success was to pick a weekend or holiday in a place having a local fair or celebration of some sort that would attract a crowd. Then you might have a chance to make a few dollars. But during the week it was really starvation.

Barnstorming was extremely competitive. We were all at one another's throats for the few events where money could be made. Even so, it was a funny thing that if two or three—or even four of us—found ourselves together at the same show, we often did much better collectively than one of us would have done alone. Farmers seeing several airplanes flying in formation might flock out, whereas a single aircraft was no draw at all.

A lot of the locals asked to go up for a thrill ride—mostly young bucks with their girl friends. They had in mind something that would cause the girl to scream and put her arms around the guy's neck. Well, the old Civil Aeronautics Authority (CAA) was spread pretty thin and, as a rule, you could get away with nearly anything. However, Inspector Harold Montee had a way of showing up and catching pilots doing acrobatics with passengers. Steep turns, wingovers, and chandelles were relatively legal. But if you got into heavy acrobatics, you were definitely violating the law.

A pilot needed a partner on a barnstorming trip, someone to hawk tickets, take care of the gasoline, and drum up business. On several of my barnstorming trips my assistant was Harlowe Eiker, a fellow Goodall employee.

Too poor to pay for a hotel room, Harlowe and I would fly cross-country and attempt to find lodging with farmers or ranchers. After scouting a likely looking place from the air, I sometimes faked engine trouble and made an "emergency" landing. We would greet the farmer and explain our problem, and, like old Charlie Brennan, we were often invited to stay a few days. In general, the farmers were honored to put up "aviators" who had a forced landing.

During our stay, we'd help out with the chores around our host's farm. We'd also pretend to tinker with the plane. At an opportune time we'd find the problem and "fix" the airplane. Then we'd offer to take the family for their first airplane ride. The missus was always very reluctant, but we'd explain how safe it was and pick an evening when the air was smooth. Most of them seemed to enjoy it, and we provided many a family with an exciting story to tell on a long winter night. When the weekend rolled around, we were ready for another barnstorm hop.

One time, Harlowe and I had arranged for a leave of absence from Goodall's and hit the road again. We would land on fields near likely looking towns, but the people were just not in the mood to take a nice high ride over their city for a few dollars. Discouraged and broke, we pulled into Holyoke, Colorado, in the midst of the town's Fourth of July celebration. We set the plane down on a stubble field near the fairgrounds. After we landed, we noticed a guy driving by in an old Model T Ford with a pet coyote occupying the seat beside him. In talking to him, we found he was the owner of a large hot-air balloon. The city had offered him the tidy sum of $25 to make a balloon ascension, followed by a parachute jump.

The old hot-air balloon ascension was quite a sight to see. The first step was to dig a large hole and excavate a long ditch, twenty feet or more, connecting the hole to the balloon site. The ditch was covered with pieces of tin and then dirt. Then a barrel was put in the hole and stoked with kerosene to produce the heated air.

The balloonist induced five spectators to hold up the deflated balloon while it began to fill, a seemingly endless process. As the bag started to lift, more volunteers were needed. Sooty hot air pouring from the kerosene barrel soon converted the volunteers into chimney sweeps, but they were caught up in the excitement and didn't seem to mind.

While the people waited for the balloon to fill, they began buying airplane rides. I stayed in the air quite a while on the first few flights, but the rides became so popular we started cutting them shorter and shorter. By one o'clock in the afternoon, a long line was waiting to pay $2.50 for a few minutes aloft. I'd never seen anything like it.

As the huge gas bag nearby continued to expand, our business kept improving. But while flying one group of passengers around the edge of town, I observed a cloud of black smoke mushrooming above the Colorado countryside in the vicinity of the fairgrounds. Something had gone awry with the balloon—it caught fire and went up in a great puff of smoke and flame.

Though uninjured, the balloonist was crestfallen. Losing the balloon left him without his means of livelihood and deprived him of the $25 he'd hoped to receive for his ascension. The city fathers were pretty hardnosed—no parachute jump, no money.

Since we attributed most of our success to the size of the crowd attracted by the balloon, we invited the poor fellow down to our hotel, treated him to dinner, and bought him a room. We also bought food for his ravenously hungry coyote.

Harlowe and I got the best room in the hotel for ourselves. Up to this time, we'd been forced, mostly, to sleep in the airplane. In our room, Harlowe began yanking money out of all his pockets, heaping it on the middle of the bed. There were twenty-dollar bills—rare things in those days—tens, fives, and ones, and a stack of silver that must have come out of scores of piggy banks. It all added up to $450—a small fortune in our circumstances. We literally plunged down into all the money and wallowed in it. We knew then how a bank robber must feel after a big, successful heist.

Simple joyrides became rather commonplace, and barnstormers were forced to add more excitement to their acts. Brother Bill took up wing walking and parachuting to help us draw crowds on the circuit.

In those days each parachute jumper packed his own chute. Most of them liked to do it in the long hotel hallways. But Bill would just stretch his chute out on the grass. On his jumps there'd be a startling puff like smoke when the chute opened, and you'd see weeds and blades of grass come settling down.

I hated to carry Bill when he was wing walking—boy, there was not much, even on a biplane, to hang onto. Seeing the crowd would pump adrenalin into Bill's blood, and he would get pretty reckless, at least in my opinion. He liked to lean against the struts and then wave both hands at the people below.

I remember one day when he'd gotten out of the cockpit during our fly-by of the crowd. As we turned back again he started out toward the very tip of the wing. Soon he was out so far that I couldn't hold the wing up. I kept shouting at him, but he couldn't hear. With the wing down all I could do was continue the turn, losing altitude all the while. Eventually Bill got a look at my face, saw that we were in real trouble, and scrambled back to the center section.

I hauled quite a few parachute jumpers. Usually we made that the last event of the day, so we could sell as many rides as possible.

We imported one jumper for an air show at Broken Bow. He would jump from 12,000 feet with a fifty-pound sack of flour, spilling out the flour on his way down. His specialty was to delay opening the chute until he was only a thousand feet above the ground.

Whether he did it by timing or not, I don't know, but he was very emphatic that we have exactly 12,000 feet. My airplane wouldn't attain that altitude very easily, so I borrowed one that could—Dr. Foote's Stinson, powered by a Wright Whirlwind engine. We had the door off, and just the jumper and I were in the airplane. After opening one corner of the flour sack he pushed himself out backwards, and down he went. Watching the little ribbon of flour, like a white pencil line, I felt sure he would hit the ground. But at the last minute the chute opened.

The parachutist was a sad sort of guy who always remained in his hotel room until jump time. The organizers would go get him. He'd make his jump, gather his chute, and retreat to his hotel. He never hung around the air show at all.

It turned out that I had hauled him on the last successful parachute jump he ever made. Unfortunately, on his next jump, down in Kansas, he waited too long.

5
Coyote Slayer

WALT DISNEY'S MOVIES have made the coyote out to be not such a bad guy. But during the thirties in Nebraska, predatory coyotes were considered a serious problem, and any method of hunting them was widely encouraged. Although there was no bounty, their pelts sold for about $6. With a little luck, a pilot could garner a fair day's wages hunting coyotes from the air.

Game to try almost anything to earn money with my Robin, I found a willing helper, Claude Kimball, to ride shotgun. Claude and I would leave in the early morning, cruising at low horsepower until we spotted a coyote loping across the prairie. Then I'd attempt to come in low behind the animal. Occasionally, the coyote would turn and continue running in the open, although as a rule it would scoot for a place to hide.

Claude learned that coyotes are difficult to shoot from the air, since the airplane moves faster than they do. To get a hit, he had to aim behind them, exactly opposite to the way most ground-based shotgunners must lead game birds.

After making the kill we'd land, taking a few minutes to skin the animal. Then we'd store the pelt in the plane and continue hunting.

Jack Jefford (right) and his brother, Bill, in 1933 at the nose of the OX Robin with which Jack barnstormed Nebraska, eastern Colorado, and eastern Wyoming. The brothers were partners until 1937, when Jack left for Alaska.

A farmer's field was a common landing spot for the Robin during Jack's early flying days.

Jack (center) displays coyotes bagged from his Robin.

The crash of the Jeffords' Alexander Flyabout, in which Terry Hatchett lost his life after a wing fell off.

The hangar at Hastings, Nebraska, site of Jefford Bros. School of Aeronautics. In the foreground are the company truck and aircraft.

At Broken Bow, Nebraska—
Jack with the Aeronca C-3
trainer (above), which
crashed (left), fatally injur-
ing former Jefford student
Chris Hald.

Farmers welcomed us and never objected to our landing on their fields or trespassing on their property.

The Robin wasn't an ideal aircraft for coyote hunting. The wheels and struts hindered the gunman, limiting his shooting arc. As we became more proficient, we realized we could do better with a different airplane, a Curtiss-Wright Pusher whose forty-five-horsepower Szekley engine was mounted rearward of the wing.

Burning only four to five gallons of gas an hour, the Szekley engine was very economical, allowing Claude and me to do quite well with the new airplane. I'd fly the aircraft from the back cockpit to give Claude, riding in front, a clear, 180-degree shooting radius. The Pusher had the added advantage of being relatively slow. It could be throttled down to about thirty-five miles an hour—and a good coyote could run nearly that fast.

One thing the Szekley lacked was carburetor heat. On days when carburetor icing was a problem, the engine would jam with ice and quit, forcing a deadstick landing. That wasn't too serious in most of Nebraska with its numerous alfalfa and stubble fields. We'd just set her down and wait for the ice to melt out of the carburetor. Then we'd crank up and go on again. But it didn't always work that well.

The sky was overcast and appeared to have some snow in store as we started the hunt early one cold morning. Our luck was excellent; before long we had six coyote pelts. However, the engine had been giving us trouble with carburetor icing. After numerous forced landings, we were about ready to call it a day and head home.

The engine began running rough again, and I knew it wouldn't be long before we had to set the plane down and let the ice thaw. Just then we spotted a coyote. Claude pounded on the fuselage to get my attention, but I'd already spotted it myself. I shook my head to say no, thinking the engine was probably too iced up to give it a try.

Claude, however, kept pointing and I thought, "Well, six bucks is six bucks." So I took off after the coyote, flying downwind as it dashed toward a canyon. I was slowing the aircraft as much as possible to give Claude a good shot, when the engine quit. We both knew we were going to crack her up because of our downwind position in the mouth of the canyon. I'll say this about old Claude—he's cool under pressure. Even though he knew we were going to crash, he shot and killed the coyote as we flew by.

I eased the plane down as slowly as I could. It slammed into a fence, ripping off one wing and bending the fuselage. Neither of us was scratched. We'd come down near the little town of Thedford, about forty miles from home. A farmer who had seen us bust up the airplane came over and was nice enough to give us a ride home.

The next day we came back to determine what we could do to repair or salvage the Curtiss-Wright Pusher. We took it apart and hauled it to Thedford, where we looked for a place to begin the repairs. A generous blacksmith allowed us to move in with him and use his shop while we rebuilt the airplane.

We started with the wing, putting in new ribs, splicing the spar, and then re-covering it. The fuselage had to be stripped entirely. Though some of the longerons were repairable, most had to be replaced.

After re-covering the fuselage, we decided to paint the new fabric pale green. We had gotten as far as the silver base coat when the blacksmith fired up his forge. As we watched, aghast, black clouds of soot and smoke settled over the wings. We solved the problem by painting the whole thing black.

While coyote hunting by air is a way to make a buck, I've never run across any rich coyote hunters. After my experience that winter, I doubt that I ever will.

6

Crossroads

AFTER OUR SUCCESSES at barnstorming, brother Bill and I decided it might actually be feasible to make aviation a full-time career. But before taking the plunge, we needed an Airframe and Engine Mechanic's license so we could do our own maintenance and repair work. We figured the fastest way to do this would be to split the duty. Bill would go after the airframe portion, and I would work on the engine segment. Between the two of us we'd have both ratings after passing the tests and satisfying the requirement of a year's experience in each category.

I continued to work at Goodall's, studying on my own and practicing with the OX-5 engine on the Robin. The airframe half of the license was more difficult to get. Bill thought his best bet was to go to Colorado Springs as an apprentice in the old Eagle Rock Aircraft Factory owned by the J. H. Alexander Company. About the time Bill arrived in Colorado Springs, Eagle Rock went under. However, like the phoenix, a new firm sprang from the ashes—Aircraft Mechanics Incorporated—

formed by a group of the old mechanics, who convinced the creditors they could keep the corporation going.

Bill was taken under the wing of Hank Burnstein, who made sure Bill had the opportunity to work in all portions of the factory. Aircraft Mechanics continued to turn out a few Hisso Eagle Rocks and also came out with an ill-fated aircraft called the Eagle Rock Bullet. Among its several deficiencies was a tendency to plunge into an unrecoverable spin, a defect that cost more than one test pilot his life.

By the end of the year, Bill and I had received our Airframe and Engine Mechanic's license. Between the two of us, we were a full-fledged mechanic.

With Bill back, I was preparing to leave Goodall's when Bob Goodall told me he had decided to purchase a large airplane for his company—an eight-passenger Stinson with a Wasp C motor. This drastically changed my plans.

I picked up the aircraft in Omaha and began to dream the dream of most pilots of that day—getting enough flying time in a large aircraft to qualify for flying the mail. I knew that a few hundred hours at the controls of an airplane as large as the Stinson would look good in my logbook. Though passenger airlines hadn't developed to any great degree, Boeing Air Transport was enjoying an expanding business in flying the mail—and pilots for Boeing had pretty plush jobs.

The new company plane was a fine aircraft. It had two magnetos, an excellent engine, and would carry a fantastic payload. However, it burned an inordinate amount of fuel. Despite my enthusiasm about flying the airplane, its large fuel consumption discouraged Goodall, a rather frugal person, so the airplane proved quite a disappointment to him.

One day Goodall advised me that he was putting an ad in *Western Flying* magazine, offering the plane for sale. Upon hearing of this development, Bill and I decided we'd strike out on our own. But before we left Goodall's an incident occurred that marked a real crossroads in my life. It seemed inconsequential at the time, but it put me at last on a somewhat roundabout road that led, years later, to Alaska and the kind of aviation career I'd always dreamed about.

I was working in the machine shop when Goodall walked in with a yellow envelope in his hand. "Here's a telegram I just got," he said, handing it to me. It was from Hans Mirow of Northern Air Transport in Nome, Alaska. The telegram said Mirow would be stopping in Ogallala within a few days to look at the Stinson, with the possibility of his purchasing it for use in Alaska.

Less than a week later, Hans and his bride, Madeline, arrived in

Ogallala. I took an instant liking to him and was fascinated by the stories he told of flying in Alaska. I demonstrated the aircraft for Hans but it turned out he actually wanted a Fokker. I said I'd see what I could find for him while he enjoyed his honeymoon in Germany. A few weeks later, a couple of fellows from Florida bought the Stinson, and the last I heard it was hauling fresh fish to East Coast markets.

By the time Mirow returned from Germany, I'd located a really fine, reasonably priced Fokker for him. It belonged to Ray Wilson of Denver.

Again, Mirow fascinated me with his great Alaskan stories. I found myself yearning to go to Alaska where, according to Mirow, the airplane was far more appreciated than it had ever been in the Midwest. When we parted, I let him know that, although I wouldn't go to Alaska without a job, I'd be glad to come up if a suitable opening ever developed.

"I'll certainly keep you in mind, Jack," he promised.

Hans later started his own firm, Mirow Air Service. In three years he would send me a telegram with a job offer from Alaska, and I'd be flying the mail to native villages dotting the vast expanse of the awakening Territory.

7

Broken Bow

IN THE SPRING OF 1934, Bill and I made the big decision. We pulled the pin on our jobs at Goodall's. We left with mixed emotions—Bob Goodall had been very good to us. But he fully understood our motives and wished us well in our new business venture.

We settled on Broken Bow, Nebraska, as the place to establish our flying service. It was more or less off the beaten path, but the city was very supportive of our plans. Dedicating a quarter section of farm land to be their airport, the town tapped its citizens by individual subscription to erect a nice little hangar for us. Bill and I bunked in the abandoned farmhouse, which kept our living expenses to a bare minimum.

Starting our operation with great ambition, we decided to do aircraft overhaul and repair work, make charter trips, and give flight instruction. Since Nebraska was in the middle of the Dust Bowl and the Depression was at its height, money was extremely hard to come by.

Nevertheless, about ten loyal students signed up for instruction.

I used my OX Robin for charters. For student training we found an Alexander Flyabout, a small aircraft built by the Eagle Rock Factory. It was a two-place, forty-five-horsepower monoplane with a three-cylinder Szekley motor. The Szekley was one of the poorer engines. It vibrated so badly that the wing struts would oscillate in flight. And the Flyabout lacked shock absorbers on the landing gear, another disadvantage for a trainer. But it was cheap to operate and very economical on fuel.

One of my most able students was a kid by the name of Carl Nicholson, who took to flying like a duck takes to water. He bought his own airplane so he could build up time, but then he began barnstorming with it, even though he held only a private pilot's license. The CAA got wind of his activities, and before long Carl had them chasing after him. The war eventually made his antics respectable. He became an instructor for the Air Force and developed into one of the best acrobatic pilots I've ever known.

Another of my accomplished Broken Bow students was Dr. Loren Beck. He enjoyed flying and really worked at it. I believe he held the distinction of being one of the few pilots ever to do rescue work on a student permit.

One morning I received a telephone call from the Western Union office in North Platte. The manager told me that a sudden cloudburst had broken a dam on the Republican River, releasing a wall of water that had smashed downstream, ravaging several small towns.

Telegrams were piling up for residents of these towns, and it was the manager's job to get them delivered. But roads, bridges, railroad tracks, and telephone lines had been washed out, and he thought an airplane would be the only likely way to get through to the towns.

I cranked up an SM8A Stinson we had recently purchased from Wyoming Air Service, and picked up the manager and his telegrams at North Platte. McCook, Nebraska, was our first stop. Before landing, we flew down the river a ways, surveying the incredible damage caused by the wall of water. Long sections of railroad track lay upended, with broken ties and twisted rails. Bridges had collapsed. Houses floated downstream—and on some of them people were clinging to the rooftops.

We quickly got rid of the telegrams, realizing there was a more pressing need for my airplane. We patrolled up and down the river locating stranded people, many of whom were injured. Where it was possible to land, we picked them up. Otherwise, we dropped food and supplies and relayed their position to other rescue workers. Before

long, additional pilots and aircraft from all over the state began con-
verging on the area to assist in the rescue effort.

McCook remained in fair shape. They'd lost their power plant, but
the hospital had emergency power and was doing its best for the
injured. I was just leaving McCook for another flight when I looked
down to see my Robin landing and then discharging passengers! I
couldn't believe my eyes, because there was no one in Broken Bow
with a commerical license to fly it. Nonetheless, there it was.

I flew to a town downriver to ferry people to the McCook hospital
for treatment. While on the ground back at McCook, I saw the Robin
coming in again. It was Dr. Beck, carrying a load of injured passengers—even though he held only a student permit and had less than
ten hours of experience in the Robin! Brother Bill was riding along as
technical advisor. They had come to help with the rescue.

Well, I couldn't say much, because they were certainly needed. Between the two of them, they did a lot of good work. And if Inspector
Montee ever heard about it, he never said anything either. He no doubt
gave consideration to the emergency nature of the flights and let it go
at that.

I was able to leave after about four days. The Republican River had
receded to its usual small-creek size, and men with bulldozers were
putting temporary bridges across it. Gradually, the situation was getting back under control.

The Republican River experience stayed with me. I felt good about
accomplishing something positive with the airplane—something beyond thrill rides at air shows—and it couldn't have been done by any
other means.

One day we got a call from Terry Hatchett of Lamar, Colorado, who
wondered if we would re-cover his Robin for him. We agreed eagerly.
Winter was coming on, and both flight instruction and barnstorming
were slowing down.

Bill and I rented an old steam-heated store building to do the job,
though I don't believe the building owner would have let us use the
place had he known how volatile and explosive aircraft dope is. Under
the ideal working conditions in the old store, we completed an excellent re-cover job on the Robin. Then we called Terry and told him
we'd have it ready to fly in a couple of days. He said he'd grab a train
from Lamar and come to Broken Bow as soon as possible.

We towed the fuselage on its wheels to the airport and then hauled
one wing over on a flatbed truck. On the second trip, a gust of wind
caught the other wing as the two of us struggled to hold it down on

a couple of mattresses. The wing decided it was going to fly and whipped out of the truck, landing on its end in the roadside ditch, breaking the spar and collapsing half the trailing edge ribs.

Bill and I were absolutely heartsick. We had accepted the work on a contract basis, had completed it, and had called the owner to come for his airplane. Now, we'd have to put in a new spar and new ribs and redo the entire wing, losing all the time, effort, and money we'd expended so far.

Nothing in my life up to then had ever looked more grim and miserable. We were broke and had been depending on the money from the re-covering job to bail us out.

Hatchett showed up the following day. While he commiserated with us, he fully expected us to make good the repair. He stayed in Broken Bow several days, helping us strip the wing and advancing us the money for a new spar and ribs. As a businessman and former flight instructor, he more or less knew the game and was careful to see that we sent the check on to the Curtiss-Wright Company.

I'd been instructing students most of the morning when Terry walked over to see me. He operated a filling station at Lamar and said he needed to go home that weekend to take care of his monthly billings.

"Why don't you take the Flyabout?" I suggested. "You can fly down to Lamar in a few hours and come back on Monday. I'll use my Robin for students."

"That's a good idea. Thanks a lot, Jack," said Terry. He took off later in the afternoon. At six that evening I got a call from his brother, saying that Terry had been killed. A wing had come off while the plane was approaching Lamar, and the Flyabout had crashed.

I called Harold Montee, Inspector with the Commerce Department. He had already learned of the tragedy over the radio. We agreed to meet in Lamar the next morning. As owners, Bill and I would assist him in the accident investigation.

The accident site was about five miles from town. A farmer who had witnessed the crash told us the airplane had been traveling in level flight when the wing tipped backward and peeled off the fuselage. The plane turned partially over and plunged to the ground at a high rate of speed. The lone wing drifted downward like a leaf, coming to rest against a fence. It was hardly damaged.

We sawed the fittings off the airplane and discovered a defective weld, or cold weld as it was called, on the right front lift strut. The Commerce Department impounded the parts and sent them to the Bureau of Standards for analysis. Years later, the Bureau sent me a letter asking what disposition I wanted made of the parts. I told them to pitch them into the Potomac. I wanted nothing more to do with the Flyabout.

The Hatchett crash dealt a serious blow to the Jefford brothers, both financially and emotionally. Both of us had liked Terry and were appalled that he had lost his life in our airplane.

Three Broken Bow businessmen loaned us the money to buy another small trainer—a C-3 Aeronca with a thirty-six-horsepower, two-cylinder opposed engine, a fine little airplane. Its four-gallon-an-hour fuel consumption reduced operating costs to the point where we could offer dual instruction for $7 an hour and solo for $6. (In other words, I was worth a buck an hour as an instructor.)

Even so, there just weren't enough students in Broken Bow to keep us going, so I developed a circuit. I'd go to Loup, Burwell, Ord, and back to Broken Bow, spending anywhere from one to three days at each site and lining up more than forty students.

Among the students I worked through to a private license, was Chris Hald of Burwell, who bought his own Aeronca C-3. Chris was doing quite well until he cracked up his Aeronca, though the damage was slight. While I was on my rounds at Burwell, Chris asked to fly my airplane.

"Sure, Chris," I said. "Go have a shot at it." I watched him take off and fly toward the home of one of his friends. Then he began slowly circling the house. His turns got awfully damn tight for such a low altitude. And the way he was flying the plane made me apprehensive and uneasy.

With a sick feeling I watched the aircraft fall into a spin, disappearing behind a row of trees. Somehow I just knew it was a fatality but stood rooted to the spot, hoping and praying I'd see the airplane pull up. Yet I knew it was impossible. Another student and I jumped into a car and rushed to the crash site. When we got Chris out of the twisted wreckage, he was still alive. But he died shortly afterward in the Burwell hospital.

Most long-time pilots spend a certain part of their careers instructing students, but I believe you can take just so much of it. You need to be half psychologist. You worry and you stew. And finally you need to get out of the racket.

After Chris's death, I felt a strong need to get into some other field of flying. I enjoyed working with advanced students, and over the years I've enjoyed being a check pilot. But primary instruction, where you start students out from scratch—I'd had enough of it.

Our fixed-base operation at Broken Bow had been bleak and hungry at best. The continuing struggle to stay afloat under Depression conditions, plus the heavy blow delivered by two tragedies, finally compelled Bill and me to throw in the towel.

8
Flying the Weather

EVERETT HOGAN was on the telephone, calling me long-distance from Scottsbluff, Nebraska. He operated a small flying service similar to ours—students, charters, aerial photography. Like everybody else in the business, he was just one jump ahead of his creditors.

"Jack, I heard about a job you can't turn down," he said. "It's a deal that's gonna mean money every week. You'd be a fool not to take it."

Having had this bait dangled in front of me, I was curious to hear more.

"Well, it's right up your alley—sort of a scientific type of flying out of Oklahoma City. You make one high-altitude flight each day, seven days a week, for $30 a week. The flight takes only about an hour and fifteen minutes. Maybe two hours, depending on the weather."

"What kind of airplane?" I asked.

"A Monocoupe," he replied. "I got it for a fellow in Wheatland, Wyoming, who's been awarded a high-altitude observation contract from the Weather Bureau. He wanted me to fly it, but I have so many deals cooking I can't leave. Jack, you'd be a natural for the job."

I paused for a moment, wondering about his aircraft. "How high are the weather flights? Will the Monocoupe hack it?"

"The contract calls for 17,500 feet and the Monocoupe's got that beat—it's rated for 18,000."

I wasn't too sure a Monocoupe could fly that high, but who can argue with the book? "Let me think about it, Everett, and I'll call you back," I said.

After a long discussion, Bill and I decided that I should accept the job in Oklahoma while he stayed in Broken Bow to maintain our aircraft for student use. We hoped that setup would keep him eating, but it didn't work out. Bill later found a job in Big Springs, Nebraska. A fellow there needed an aircraft mechanic and some help with his farm.

I went to Scottsbluff, where Hogan introduced me to the Monocoupe's owner and my new boss, Boots Meglemere. Together Boots and I flew to Oklahoma City, arriving a few days before the contract flights were scheduled to begin on July 1, 1935, the start of the new fiscal year.

The Monocoupe, with its Velie engine, was a little jewel to fly. It seemed to me to be loaded with instrumentation, including an artificial horizon, directional gyro, and radio receiver, although today these are considered just basics. It had been re-covered recently and was in beautiful shape.

The Monocoupe required some customizing to accommodate the Weather Bureau instrument. A forerunner of the radiosonde, the aerometeorograph recorded temperature, humidity, and atmospheric pressure. The contract specified that the instrument be suspended by four shock cords inside a small steel cage fastened to a wing spar.

The weather flights were an expansion of an experimental program begun in South Dakota. The original high-altitude observations had been made using kites. A serious kite flier could place his kite higher than 20,000 feet, although it had to be done in stages. The first box kite contained the aerometeorograph. It would be flown, using a thin cable, to a height at which the weight of the cable became too great for the kite to support. Then another kite would be attached to provide more lift for the next length of cable. The end result was a string of perhaps a dozen or more kites. It was an all-day job to attain these great heights.

Oklahoma City was just one of the many airplane weather observation sites. Omaha, Cheyenne, and Salt Lake were others in my area; the rest were scattered all over the United States. Some of the flights were performed by the military. All the observations were made simultaneously at 2:30 a.m. Ninetieth Meridian Time. (Everyone but the Weather Bureau called it Central Time.)

I was flat broke upon arriving at Oklahoma City, so I asked Boots Meglemere if he could advance me a few bucks for food and lodging. "Jack, I'm broke, too," he told me. "Until some money comes through from the weather contract, I can't help you."

I registered at the old Hudgins Hotel, requesting that dinner be sent to my room and put on the tab. For the next week, I more or less existed this way on just one daily meal. Starvation seemed to be the story of my aviation career.

Shortly after midnight on the morning of July 1, we drove to the airport, rolled out the Monocoupe, and taxied to the terminal. The weather officials wanted us there at least forty-five minutes before takeoff time so they could install the aerometeorograph in the instrument cage and allow the delicate machinery to equilibrate.

The contract called for a controlled, low rate of climb, not over 300 feet per minute. Every 1,500 feet I had to fly level for one minute, then begin climbing again. As I rose to altitude, the aerometeorograph inked an interesting stair-step line on a spring-driven paper chart.

At 2:30 that morning it was still pitch black, a beautiful crystal-clear night with stars filling the heavens. From the night sky, Oklahoma City's lights formed a bright, multicolored carpet.

Things were going well until I got the Monocoupe up to nearly 12,000 feet. I adjusted the fuel mixture and put the throttle against the peg, but somewhere between 13,000 and 14,000 feet the Monocoupe reached her limit. With colder air I might possibly have coaxed a little more altitude out of her, but even though I milled around for thirty minutes or so, the aircraft simply wouldn't climb any higher. To Meglemere's and the Weather Bureau's chagrin, I could not get to 17,500 feet.

Boots couldn't accept the idea that his new Monocoupe was incapable of meeting the contract specifications. He thought the problem must have been in the engine, so at his urging I tinkered with it. He also called on various experts for advice. Their consensus was that the Monocoupe couldn't fly anywhere near 17,500 feet.

Meglemere was sick to think he'd spent a bundle for the airplane and the damn thing was useless. He didn't know what to do, but he did know that without an adequate airplane he'd soon lose the contract.

I told him about a doctor in Holyoke, Colorado, who owned a J-6 Cessna with a J-6-7 engine. Though an old aircraft, a model made even before the Airmaster, it was nonetheless an excellent plane for altitude—it loved altitude.

I telephoned the good doctor and explained our predicament. He offered to sell us the aircraft for $1,700, but we certainly didn't have the money to buy it. "Would you consider a trade for the Monocoupe?" I asked, hoping to arrange some sort of swap.

"I don't really need a Monocoupe," he replied, "but I think I can help you anyway. Since you need my Cessna so badly, I'll let you go ahead and take it right now. You can pay me when you sell the Monocoupe." Doctor Hill had given us the reprieve we needed!

I flew the Monocoupe to Holyoke and returned to Oklahoma City with the Cessna. We fabricated the instrument cage supports and, after having forfeited two flights, were ready for another go at it.

The Cessna readily passed through 17,500 feet. We couldn't afford oxygen, but I wondered how high the old girl would go. I went on up to 20,000. I began to get a little light-headed, but at least I knew we had an airplane capable of making high-altitude flights.

For a time everything was like a honeymoon. Except for a few thunderstorms, which quickly passed through, the weather was beautiful and the flights more or less uneventful. Then a weather pilot was killed in Omaha. The investigation indicated that his lack of instrument training was a principal cause. As a result, the CAA, in conjunction with the Weather Bureau, issued a ruling that all weather pilots had to pass the Airline Transport Instrument Test within thirty days.

After making a hood for the Cessna, I recruited a volunteer to act as safety pilot while I practiced instrument flight during the daytime hours. After a few weeks I got in touch with the Air Carrier Inspector and easily passed the flight test.

Looking back at those high-altitude weather operations, I wonder how I ever survived them. The plane was equipped with only a simple low-frequency receiver, no transmitter. My instruments were driven with venturis, which were subject to freezing, whereupon the gyros would slow down and become lethargic. And there was no deicing equipment on the aircraft. On days when icing was a problem, I'd have to struggle and struggle to break out of the overcast or to attain the magic number of 17,500.

Shortly after I began making these flights, and while still not too proficient on instruments, I experienced my first case of vertigo—complete disorientation. It was so frightening I have never forgotten the simple lesson it taught me—always believe your instruments.

That particular night there was a high overcast at about 6,000 feet. Normally, after entering the overcast, I'd fly straight ahead. That time I started fooling around, making turns. All at once I fell into a spiral. The airspeed indicator floated up. I was yanking back on the stick, but the airplane kept plunging at an alarming rate.

The only thing that saved me was breaking out of the overcast and seeing Oklahoma City standing ninety degrees to what I thought was the horizon. It took a while before I got reoriented and had the aircraft flying level. Then, before I had a chance to get too scared, I climbed back into the overcast. That was a most valuable lesson. Never since have I experienced vertigo in flight.

As the winter wore on, Oklahoma City's weather got worse. Northers—twenty- to thirty-knot chilling winds and 500-foot ceilings—were frequent and sometimes lasted many days at a time.

One night I broke out on top at about 9,000 feet. At that altitude I'd ordinarily see the lights of Oklahoma City through the overcast. But this night the overcast was so dense that lights couldn't penetrate.

I was continuing the climb when suddenly the radio quit, depriving me of all navigational capability. I couldn't believe it. My umbilical cord to earth was cut! Without radio, I'd be taking a hell of a chance if I tried to feel my way down through the thick, low overcast.

I wore a parachute, known as the "ticket home," and always had the option of bailing out and saving my own hide. While I debated what to do, I continued the flight on up to 17,500.

Descending back down to the surface of the overcast, I throttled the engine to minimum power and began circling. I remembered that the winds aloft were from the southwest at about twenty knots, so I flew the upwind leg a bit longer than the downwind leg, hoping to stay in the vicinity of Oklahoma City. When my fuel was about exhausted I had a big decision to make—either bail out, or descend to see if there was enough ceiling for a landing. I thought about it a long time, hating to bail out of a perfectly good aircraft, and knowing that if I did the strong northerly surface winds would make for a very unpleasant parachute jump.

Dawn arrived, and I made the decision to start down. During the descent I became very uneasy because I knew there were mountains south of Oklahoma City in the vicinity of Ardmore, to say nothing of a forest of oil derricks. I had no reason to believe the ceiling would be any higher than the 500 feet prevailing when I left Oklahoma City.

After descending below 3,000, I took a northerly heading. Oklahoma City's airport is 1,300 feet above sea level, so I knew I wasn't too far above the surface of the ground. When my altimeter showed 2,000 feet, I noticed little breaks in the clouds and saw flashes of the ground. I continued descending and finally broke out underneath.

I found myself flying amid hundreds of oil derricks. Figuring I might be up near Ponca City, I thought the wise thing to do was land alongside one of the rigs and determine my location. I spotted one that had a pretty good pasture nearby, landed, and hiked over to the rig.

A pilot always feels rather stupid asking where he is. However, I was so thankful to be on the ground that I felt rather humble. A roughneck was standing near the rig, and I walked up to him. "I just landed over there," I explained. "Can you tell me where I am?"

"Well, the Oklahoma City airport is over there about seven miles," the surprised worker told me, pointing eastward through the derricks. It was amazing how I'd lucked out and stayed right in my own area.

I spent a lot of time at the Oklahoma City airport that year, and it was there I ran across a world-famous aviation-minded gentleman, Will Rogers. Will just loved to fly, and I met him several times that winter when he passed through Oklahoma City as a passenger on the early Braniff flights in the Lockheed Vega.

One day I heard the tragic news that Rogers and Wiley Post had lost their lives in an air crash near Point Barrow, Alaska. Post was laid to rest in his hometown, Oklahoma City. His body lay in state at the Capitol, and on the day of his funeral, every available airplane flew by the cemetery in tribute to him and Rogers. Even I was there with the old weather ship.

Contracts for the weather flights were put out for bid each fiscal year. At the close of our first contract, Boots Meglemere again submitted a price for the Cessna and me, but unfortunately he was underbid. Once more I was out of a job. Brother Bill also happened to be free, so together we began looking for work.

9

Hastings

"BETWEEN JOBS" after my Oklahoma City flights fizzled, Bill and I weren't having much luck finding work. Hastings, Nebraska, proved to be our salvation. The city fathers decided their small municipal airport needed caretaking and installed me as airport manager. There was no salary associated with the position, but it was a good base for re-establishing a flying service. Hastings was a larger, wealthier community than Broken Bow, and in these greener pastures we felt our business might succeed.

The airstrip was on the site of an old farm—much the same setup we'd had at Broken Bow. We headquartered at the old farmhouse. The city furnished it to us rent-free and paid for the telephone and electricity.

There was a nice brick hangar at the Hastings airport. Bill and I thought we'd start a repair shop in the hangar to give us something to do when the weather was bad. The city agreed that anything we made off the hangar was ours.

One of our first repairs was on a badly neglected Stinson Trimotor, so run-down that even the tailpost had rusted out. The owner insisted he wanted the plane brought back into shape for relicensing. It was one of those situations where there's really no good place to start nor any definite place to stop. Bill and I tackled it anyway, welding in a new tailpost and making numerous other repairs. Although the aircraft's condition was marginal, we were pretty sure we'd done enough so that the federal inspector would relicense it.

A number of high school students had been hanging around our hangar, helping us work on the Stinson. In return I promised them all a plane ride to Lincoln when we were finished and ready for the inspection. I contacted Montee to see when he'd be available at Lincoln, and on the appointed day, the boys and I piled into the Stinson for the flight.

In Lincoln, Montee performed the inspection and found everything satisfactory. He endorsed the airplane and approved the new aircraft certificate. He had picked up his briefcase and was walking toward his car when he was halted in his tracks by the sound of breaking glass and a deafening explosion.

I had seen what happened. Apparently the outer flange on one of the Stinson's wheels was cracked. The rim broke, shooting a chunk of metal through a glass window in the hangar door. The inner tube immediately swelled to about four feet in diameter before bursting violently. The cloud of dust raised by the blowout enveloped the airplane, now canted awkwardly on the broken rim. Montee just shook his head and continued on to his car.

Since we couldn't fly back home to Hastings—the wheel parts would take at least a week to order—the kids and I decided to hitchhike, an art in which we were all experienced. We had no trouble getting rides from farmers, but the rides were usually short. We soon became separated and strung out all along the road from Lincoln to Hastings. The kids and I waved as we alternately passed one another from ride to ride.

Bill and I thought repair work would keep us afloat, but the unfortunate fact was that most of our customers were broke. They'd bring in an airplane. We'd work on it and get it licensed. Then they'd tell us they couldn't pay. We couldn't blame them too much—we were often in the same boat ourselves and had our own episodes with the creditors.

It's a strange thing about automobile finance companies—they like to be paid. When you're a week or two behind on your payments, you get a little reminder—they're sure it's just an oversight, but you've fallen into arrears. Next you get a tough letter. As time goes by, the letters keep getting tougher. Finally, you receive a reasonably nice letter from the Credit Manager himself. He knows you want to keep your credit rating good, and although some little problem may have occurred, he's sure your payments will be brought up to date. When you get that letter, it's the beginning of the end. The very last notice informs you that legal steps are being taken to repossess your vehicle.

That's the stage Bill and I had reached when we ran behind in making payments on our Ford pickup truck. We were desperately trying to scrounge a few bucks to get the finance people off our backs—maybe make one payment—but we hadn't been able to raise the money.

One blustery autumn day, fallen leaves were scudding across the airstrip as a car drove up to the hangar, bearing the ominous prefix 2 on its license plate. That meant the driver wasn't local; he was from Lincoln County. Bad news for the Jefford brothers.

The driver, dressed in a business suit, left his car and walked up to our hangar door. He looked like a nice guy, but he also appeared determined. "I'm from the finance company," he told us bluntly. "I've come to get the truck."

I felt like a condemned man on the scaffold. We just couldn't operate without that truck. All our appeals had been exhausted, and here we were in front of the hangman with no possibility of making a deal. But I thought I'd give it a try anyway.

We kept a pot of coffee in our little office, so I poured the man a cup and steered the conversation to flying. "Ever done any flying yourself?" I asked.

"No, I can't say that I have," he replied. A tiny ray of hope filtered down into the room.

"Well, we've got a dandy little trainer, and the wind's not really too bad. Why don't you let me take you up and see what you can do?"

He hesitated a moment, but I knew I'd aroused his interest. "By golly, I'll just try it," he finally said. Like the camel, we had our nose under the tent.

Bill and I rolled out the airplane. Our guest climbed into the left-hand seat, and I spent about an hour in the air with him. The guy proved to be a natural pilot and realized himself that he was doing well. As we taxied back to the hangar he told me, "You know, I really enjoyed it." He thought awhile. "Tell you what I'll do," he said. "You keep your truck and I'll bring the payments up to date. I'll make a point of getting out here often enough to take it out in flying lessons."

Sure enough, he showed up regularly for lessons once each week, and I saw him all the way through to his private license. Later he got a commercial license and hired on with United Airlines. Though he's undoubtedly retired by now, the last I heard he was a captain flying the Boeing 707 jets, and I'm sure he went through to the 747s.

Most commercial pilots must pass through purgatory before becoming established, and that purgatory is instructing primary students. Some pilots genuinely enjoy it and do a great job. But for the average instructor, it's more a means to an end, a way to get paid while building up time and experience. There's not a great deal of money in the work, and it's fraught with worry. No two students are ever the same.

Although I'd sworn off instructing students after my experience at Broken Bow, the passage of time gradually softened my feelings. And I needed the money to continue eating, so I began to accept students at Hastings.

The average student needs about eight hours of dual time in a trainer before the instructor has taught him all the emergency procedures and feels he's competent to solo. That's the average. Some students are ready in half that time; others are never really ready.

One of the most common student problems I had to correct was rudder control. Almost every kid in the northern United States played with small sleds like the American Flyer. The sleds were equipped with a front steering bar that warped the runners slightly for changes in direction. If you pushed your foot on the left side of the bar, the sled would turn right; if you pushed right, the sled would turn left.

An airplane's rudder controls are just the opposite, and practically all my students had rudder problems. It was so bad for some that, on a calm day, I'd run them up and down the runway at reduced power—tail lifted into the air—hoping they'd learn to keep the airplane on the right heading.

Students have a sixth sense and can usually tell the day you're going to let them go up alone. It's a big event in their lives. I think every pilot vividly recalls his solo. If a student had been shooting acceptable landings and had made about three in a row that I considered good, then I'd generally let him go.

Each instructor has his own drills, but the one I used most often went something like this: "All right, Charlie, you've been trying to kill me now for eight hours and I've had enough of it. I'm getting out and you can just do it by yourself." This brings a kind of sick laugh from the student. Then you go on to tell him that the airplane will be much lighter without you along and will respond better and climb a lot faster. That was especially true with me, because I'm six feet tall and weigh about 200 pounds.

If you happen to see an individual out along the runway, pacing around chewing on his fingernails, you know he's an instructor with a student up on a solo flight.

One of my best students in Hastings was Dr. Otto A. Kostal, who eventually went on to obtain a commercial license and an instrument rating. On his solo, I gave him the old lecture about the light airplane. He was eager to go and immediately took off. The unspoken understanding was that the student would go around the pattern a time or two, then come in for a landing. I'd congratulate him, and that was pretty much the end of it. On Dr. Kostal's solo I couldn't believe what I was seeing. He took off, turned northeast, and just kept going. The airplane dwindled to a tiny speck, then disappeared. I doubt whether any other student in the history of aviation has ever done such a thing. Their one concern is always to stay close to the airport. But not Dr. Kostal!

I walked back to the hangar, listening all the while, hoping to hear the drone of the returning airplane. Thirty minutes went by, then an hour. The aircraft had only about forty-five minutes of fuel in the tanks, so I knew it had to be down somewhere. At sunset I considered calling the sheriff, but decided to hold off a while longer.

As dusk deepened I finally heard the welcome sound of the trainer coming back. Sure enough, it was Dr. Kostal, making a downwind approach and a beautiful landing. I was relieved to see him, yet at the same time felt like chewing him out because he'd caused me such worry. I noticed grass and straw hanging on the tail skid and demanded an explanation. As it turned out, Dr. Kostal hadn't realized there would be any problem if he flew to a farm he owned about thirty miles from Hastings. He had picked out a stubble field, landed, and visited with his tenants, no doubt showing off his skill as a pilot. The field must have been all right, because he got back off and returned safely to town. I was the only one to suffer.

After getting his private license, Kostal one day flew to Lincoln, where he was caught by a passing storm and had to wait on weather. He began his return flight too late in the day and finally came dragging into Hastings after dark. Our airstrip wasn't lighted, so we hurriedly set out some lanterns for him. The Hastings *Tribune* called us to get the story—an airplane buzzing Hastings at night was something totally unheard of. My brother, Bill, who always had an answer for everything, quipped, "Oh, that's just Dr. Kostal on one of his routine night flights."

10
Kelly One and Kelly Two

IN DECEMBER OF 1936, a Western Air Express Boeing 247 disappeared on a flight from Los Angeles to Salt Lake City, carrying a full load of passengers, mail, and cargo. It had last reported over Milford, Utah, then vanished. Western immediately launched a search for the missing plane and was recruiting all available flyers to aid in the search.

News of the lost aircraft reached the Texaco distributor at Grand Island, Nebraska—a chap by the name of McIntosh—who owned a beautiful Waco biplane. He wanted to help the rescue effort by volunteering the use of his airplane, so he telephoned me in Hastings, offering to pay all my expenses if I would fly his Waco and participate in the search. I had been following the story and jumped at the chance to get involved.

I flew the Waco to Salt Lake City and checked in with Western. They filled my fuel tanks and sent me on to search headquarters at Milford. Among those gathered there were Amelia Earhart and Hollywood stunt pilot Paul Mantz, flying together in Amelia's Lockheed Electra. Also joining the search were aircraft dispatched from a number of airlines, as well as a squadron of Marine fighters.

The Waco was one of the only planes small enough to land on rural fields, so I was given the job of flying out to check reports from people living along the flight path who said they'd heard an airplane. We had our share of kooky tips and false alarms, typical of many such searches. Ham radio operators were hearing the lost aircraft on the air, mediums and fortune tellers suggested places to look, and there were countless blind leads. Even so, Western checked out every report, leaving no stone unturned.

Two of Western's senior pilots, both named Kelly, directed the search effort. We distinguished them as Kelly One and Kelly Two. After having stayed at Milford until December 31, they decided to move the search headquarters to Salt Lake City. Kelly One, flying a Boeing 40-B4, planned to lead all the other airplanes on the flight, since the weather was deteriorating rapidly and many of the pilots, including the squadron of Marines, were totally unfamiliar with that part of the country.

Kelly One's aircraft was full of Western's observers, so Kelly Two asked to ride with me. The others had been gone only briefly when I took off with Kelly Two. Unsure of the route to Salt Lake City, I decided to follow the railroad. We hadn't gone far when it began to snow heavily, and visibility was reduced to about a half mile. I was barely able to maintain sight of the railroad tracks.

The front cockpit of the three-place Waco was covered in the fashion of a small fighter. We had removed the front cockpit cover for the search, but this meant there was no windshield for Kelly Two. He would pop up and look out occasionally, then duck below the edge of the cowling.

Before long, a little town showed up below us. The town had sets of railroad tracks running in every direction. Very confused, I followed a set of tracks that turned to the left, deciding to stick with those regardless of the outcome. Kelly Two rose up out of the cockpit in the front of the Waco and looked back at me, shaking his head. I was going the wrong way, at least to his way of thinking.

I would have turned back, but it was snowing so heavily I had to wait until I could see enough terrain to make a safe 180-degree turn. All at once the weather began to improve. I pounded on the fuselage to attract Kelly's attention. He took a quick look and motioned me to proceed in the direction we were headed. Well, it was just one of those weird things. We came out near the south end of Salt Lake. In another twenty minutes we were at the airport.

We had expected to find the rest of the searchers waiting for us; but, to our surprise, they had not arrived. Western told us that all of them had been compelled to land at Tintic, a remote CAA airstrip about seventy miles south of Salt Lake. Snowdrifts on the road to the airport were so deep that the searchers were marooned there and had to spend the night in the little CAA operations building.

I was beginning to feel pretty important now, especially in the company of Kelly Two, one of Western's top pilots. I more or less followed him around like a dog. We checked into the Utah Hotel and, this being New Year's Eve and a night to celebrate, we got a bottle and proceeded to get half bombed.

In his cups, Kelly Two put in a call to the CAA station where Kelly One was stuck. As soon as he got his counterpart on the line I heard him yell, "What the hell are you guys doing down there? This *kid* from Nebraska didn't have the slightest trouble making it to Salt Lake—why aren't *you* here?"

Little did he know. It was just one of those freak happenings. My making the wrong turn had actually taken us into better weather and enabled us to get to Salt Lake City by skirting the storm.

The next day Western abandoned the search, and I returned home.

In the spring, a Utah farmer found some postmarked letters while plowing his field. He turned in the letters to the post office, where it was determined they had been aboard the missing aircraft.

The search was resumed. Since the snow had melted, it was much easier to spot the aircraft, which had crashed near the top of a mountain. Apparently the wind had blown envelopes from the ripped mail sacks down to the valley below, leading to the location of the wreckage.

Fate often deals strange hands. It wasn't long after that, on a brisk autumn day in 1937, that I received a Western Union telegram from Nome, Alaska: HAVE PILOT'S JOB FOR YOU. $300 A MONTH AND EX-PENSES. WIRE IF INTERESTED. It was signed "Hans Mirow."

Part 2

Foul-Weather Flyer

1
Nome

I DON'T KNOW what I expected, but my first glimpse of Nome was an unpleasant surprise. As the Lockheed Vega circled for a landing, I viewed the little gold rush town in all its misery. And the more I saw, the worse it looked.

Located 150 miles south of the Arctic Circle on the western coast of Alaska, the community was a study in disorder. A sorry assortment of dilapidated shacks was scattered helter-skelter over the rolling tundra. Along the shore of the gray and brooding Bering Sea stretched Nome's dreary main street, with run-down, false-fronted buildings on either side. From the air the town had a strange, deserted look—an ugly blemish on a bleak landscape that extended treeless and lonely to the horizon.

I was sure of one thing—this godforsaken "metropolis" on the Seward Peninsula was not for me. "I'm going to get the hell out of this place just as soon as I can scrape up enough money!" I vowed. Nebraska never looked so good.

My long journey to Nome had begun rather abruptly. After reading Mirow's telegram, I hastily consulted with Bill. Our backs were against the wall financially, and $300 a month sounded very tempting. Bill agreed I should accept Hans's offer.

Within forty-eight hours the Northern Pacific Railroad was carrying me out of Nebraska toward the West Coast. In Seattle I had to wait two days before boarding the Alaska Steamship Company's liner *Yukon* for the voyage north.

Southeastern Alaska's immense coastal mountains—plunging directly into the sea, usually with no hint of a beach—were somewhat overwhelming at first sight. As the ship plowed northward along the Inside Passage, the September air made me realize winter was not far off. I wasn't at all sure what I was getting into and began having second thoughts. I wondered if I'd made the right decision.

Eventually, after stops along the way at Ketchikan, Wrangell, and Petersburg, the ship arrived in Juneau. I bought a Pacific Alaska Airlines ticket to Fairbanks, where Hans was to meet me for the last leg of my trip to Nome.

But I couldn't get out of Juneau as easily as I'd planned. Bad weather prevented the arrival of the Lockheed Electra 10 that flew the Juneau-Fairbanks run, with an intermediate stop at Whitehorse, in Canada's Yukon Territory.

After three days of baggage drill—packing my bag, checking out of the hotel, and going to the airport to find that the flight had turned back to Whitehorse—I began to wonder if I was ever going to get out of Juneau. And I was running out of eating money. In desperation I asked the hotel if I could cash a counter check on my Hastings bank, neglecting to tell them my account there had been closed. Then I immediately sent an airmail letter to Nebraska, asking a friend to cover my incoming check. (Walter Hickel, ex-Governor of Alaska and former Secretary of the Interior, likes to relate how he arrived in Alaska with thirty-seven cents in his pocket. Others boast they arrived broke. Hell, I got to Alaska worse than broke—just ahead of a hot check!)

One thing that made waiting in Juneau a little easier was the friendship I struck up with Alex Holden, operator of Marine Airways. He was president, pilot, chief mechanic, and baggage boy—one of the struggling Alaskan air pioneers. Both of us were members of a closely knit fraternity, the Ancient and Secret Order of Quiet Birdmen. The QB organization was founded in New York in 1921 by veteran World War I pilots for the sole purpose of promoting good-fellowship among its members. Although the group has always shunned ceremony and publicity, through the years numerous chapters have sprung up across the country. Alex and I enjoyed shooting the breeze, and even though I was in Juneau for only a short time, we became close friends.

After repeated bad weather and frustrating dry runs, a nice day finally dawned, and Pacific Alaska's Lockheed arrived from Whitehorse with Captain Al Monsen in the left seat and Walt Hall as copilot. Seeing my QB wings, Monsen mentioned that Hall might let me sit in the copilot's seat for part of the flight. Sure enough, after the Whitehorse stop I was allowed to take over for Hall, observe their operation, and fly the bird from Whitehorse to Fairbanks. It did a lot for my ego.

I spent the night in Fairbanks, and the next day Hans arrived in his Lockheed Vega. I was his only passenger to Nome. It was difficult to see much from the back end of the Vega, but the country I could see looked awfully hostile. For someone used to the neat patchwork-quilt pattern of Midwestern farms—the orderly section lines, fences, roads, and other familiar landmarks—the vast Territory seemed remote, forbidding, and desolate.

Then we arrived over Nome, and I'm sure my jaw must have dropped. I saw enough in our pass over the city to convince me that I didn't want any part of it, and I wondered how long it would take me to earn enough money to leave.

After landing at the gravel airstrip, Mirow proudly pointed out his company's five other aircraft: the workhorse Gullwing Stinson, used mostly for local flights; a Fairchild 24; an amphibian S-39 Sikorsky; a modified Bach freighter; and a Travelair. The pride of his fleet was the Lockheed Vega we'd flown from Fairbanks.

I had arrived at a slack time for the company, so Hans suggested I just take it easy and get settled into Nome. Most of my days were spent hanging around Mirow's one-room office, swapping stories with the firm's other pilot, Jack Hermann.

Jack practiced the old tradition of trying to scare the pants off the new pilot. He unreeled numerous hair-raising tales about the incredible flying hazards of the North, the treacherous short strips, and the grisly fate that awaited a guy who crashed in the wilderness. Even though I was aware that most of what he was saying was bull, there were many moments when I wished I were back in Nebraska, where flying was far less colorful and exciting but a hell of a lot safer.

I was getting powerfully bored, just passing time in the office and going out for coffee with Hans and Jack. Occasionally Hermann would have a flight. He promised to take me along if there was ever any space aboard so that I could get acquainted with the country. Unfortunately, there was never any extra room.

One day I did get a chance to take a trip. Jack owned a Monocoupe that had been wrecked at Teller, a small native village on Port Clarence Bay, eighty miles northwest of Nome. "Now that we've got the Monocoupe patched up, how'd you like to ride over to Teller with me and fly it back?" Jack asked.

"Sure," I told him, jumping at the chance to get out of the office. When I got to Teller, I found the Monocoupe still in pretty bad shape, but I was able to get the engine started and take off for Nome. On the way back, the cowling broke loose and many of the poorly done fabric patches began blowing off. I had to nurse the bedraggled little plane back to Nome, but I really felt great. At last I was flying somewhere in Alaska by myself.

A few days later, I was the only pilot around the office. Hans was in Fairbanks and Jack was on a trip to Kotzebue. A call came through from the village of Golovin, requesting help in an emergency medical evacuation. The message was transmitted along ninety miles of primitive single-strand ground-return telephone line that had been strung on wooden tripods back during gold-rush times.

Bill Barber, Mirow's office manager, dispatcher, and body snatcher, was contacted about arranging the flight. Bill turned to me. "There's a very sick Eskimo over in Golovin who needs immediate transportation to the Nome hospital. Ever flown a Gullwing Stinson? It's all we've got left. Think you can handle the trip?"

I was already putting on my heavy jacket. "Sure, I'll leave right away." I'd never been in a Gullwing Stinson, but I'd had some experience with the older SM8A model. And to me, a Stinson was a Stinson.

As far as I was concerned, a bigger problem was my lack of familiarity with the area. I'd never been to Golovin. Harboring some misgivings, Bill took me to the airport, handed me a map of the Seward Peninsula, and told me the field was right in back of town. I fired up the Stinson and was on my way—my first official trip for the company.

I found Golovin without much trouble. The town's handful of buildings included a Bureau of Indian Affairs school, a roadhouse, and a store. But when I saw the "airstrip" in back of town I couldn't believe my eyes. It was only about 800 feet long, narrow, and crowded right up against the buildings. However, I could see some tracks, so I knew planes had been landing there. I guess I was used to the hot weather and higher altitudes of the Nebraska plains, where it took fairly good-sized strips to operate. But I'd always considered myself pretty good at short-field operation, so I brought the Stinson down slowly and managed to bring it in safely.

To my amazement, the entire village turned out to meet me on the dirt strip, quite a change from the relative obscurity accorded most pilots in Nebraska. In the bush, it was customary for nearly all the residents to meet incoming planes. Another of their customs was to write short notes to other villages right on the aircraft's fabric. Most airplanes would be covered with these scribbled messages from one village to another.

The natives crowded around as the sick Eskimo was carried over on a stretcher and placed aboard. Their expressions revealed both anxiety and a gratitude that didn't need words. The faces of those villagers stayed with me on the trip back to Nome. I was highly gratified to be performing meaningful work with the aircraft and to realize that people deeply appreciated my skills as a pilot.

Back in Nebraska the airplane was something to be used for pleasure. But here, and throughout the isolated villages of bush Alaska, the airplane could be a real lifeline, a vital link to the outside world. It could mean the difference between life and death. My thoughts of returning to Nebraska gradually faded; each new flight helped convince me to stay.

During January of my first winter in Alaska, Hans and his wife took a well-deserved vacation trip back to Germany. They left office manager Bill Barber, Jack Hermann, and me to run the company. Hans hadn't been gone more than three weeks when Jack and Bill had a fight. Jack quit and went to work for Ferguson Airways in Kotzebue, and I was left as the only flyer. In the space of a few months, I had gone from rank newcomer and cheechako to chief pilot of Mirow Air Service.

2

Working the Mines

NEWS OF GOLD DISCOVERIES on Anvil Creek and along the beaches of Nome spread to the outside world in the fall of 1899. By the following spring more than 10,000 prospectors and adventure-seekers had thronged north, hoping to share in the bonanza. The rush had passed long before I began flying for Mirow Air Service, but gold mining remained the major activity in the Nome area during my years with the company.

A few individual miners continued to work their claims. For the most part, however, they had been replaced by well-organized businesses with large-scale dredging operations. The largest of these operators was the United States Mining, Smelting, and Refining Company, owner of several mammoth electrically powered dredges. All told, there were perhaps thirty working mines scattered across the Seward Peninsula. Mirow's flights serviced the entire area, and during the summer season the mines provided our greatest source of revenue.

During the winter, the mines were closed down. Winter in Nome was a very long, drawn-out affair. Sooner or later nearly everyone contracted cabin fever—a gnawing sense of frustration brought on by the miserable cold, the nearly twenty-four-hour-a-day darkness, and the prolonged isolation.

Provisions dwindled, and fresh produce vanished. Cold-storage eggs were treated with suspicion. Common procedure was to crack them individually into a bowl. If you were lucky, two or three out of a dozen might be fit to eat. Even those few good eggs required a liberal application of Tabasco sauce to make them palatable—which is why most old-time Alaskans still use Tabasco on their eggs.

We pilots would have occasional flights to Fairbanks or Anchorage, enjoying the opportunity to meet new people and escape the Nome environment for a while. But most of the residents were stuck there, forced to sweat out the confining winter.

Each year, late in March, Nome began waking from its winter hibernation as the first few miners returned to town. They booked passage by steamship to one of Alaska's southern seacoast towns—Juneau, Cordova, Valdez, or Seward. At Mirow's we kept watch on the miners' progress and would pick them up at the first stop that had favorable weather. Those who stayed on board all the way to Seward could take the Alaska Railroad to Anchorage or Fairbanks. From those points we would ferry them to Nome and then out to the mines.

These men traveled north well in advance of the regular mining season. It was their job to open the camps and get them ready for the bulk of the workers, who arrived when the eagerly awaited first boat was able to negotiate the ice into Nome.

High excitement was generated by the arrival of the first boat in spring. Anticipation began to build when we'd get word that the boat was on its way, usually in June. If things went well, the journey would take from ten days to two weeks, depending upon weather. All the way from the Pribilof Islands to Nome, the ship would have to fight its way through pack ice dumped into the Bering Sea by the Yukon and Kuskokwim rivers. The Alaska Communication System, part of the Army Signal Corps, kept track of the boat by wireless, while the Alaska Steamship-Company's office in Nome maintained a much-studied bulletin board on which the vessel's position and estimated time of arrival were updated frequently.

A favorite pastime during those long June days in Nome, with their almost twenty-four hours of daylight, was scanning the horizon far out to sea, looking for that first glimpse of the arriving boat. First you'd see a tiny plume of smoke etched against the distant sky. Then the boat itself could be seen steaming across Norton Sound. The sighting always sparked an electric atmosphere in our little community. At last the year's isolation was ended. Old friends were returning, and the store shelves would soon be filled with the latest merchandise.

Because of the shallow water in the Nome area, the ship would anchor about a mile from the beach. Then the passengers and cargo would be lightered ashore on barges operated by the Lomen Commercial Company.

For us in the flying business, all hell broke loose when the first group arrived ashore. The men and supplies needed immediate transportation to their respective mines in the bush. I could fly up to ten people at a time in the old Bach; Wien Alaska Airlines, our chief competitor, usually flew their Ford Trimotor over from Fairbanks to cash in on the action; and sometimes even a few flyers from Anchorage would come up to take advantage of the booming demand for air service.

With the continuous daylight there was no limitation, except for total fatigue, to the amount of time we could work. As all the pilots did, I sometimes flew twenty-four or more hours at a stretch, taking only brief catnaps while my airplane was being serviced, fueled, and loaded for another trip. At times I'd get so punchy and stupid from lack of sleep that even while staring at the windsock I couldn't figure out which way the wind was blowing. Most of the trips were short— thirty minutes to an hour. That alone kept us from falling asleep at the controls.

The feverish flying pace provided an important steam valve for the city of Nome. The first boat would dump more than 500 men into our town of less than 1,000 people. There simply weren't enough hotel rooms or other facilities to accommodate the arriving crowds. If the weather was too bad for flying—and it had to be damn bad before we'd abandon the practice of scud-running the coast (skimming along the beach under the low-lying clouds until we could find a break to turn inland)—then all that the hordes of miners could do was pack the saloons.

Once the mining season began, our flying continued at an intense pace throughout the brief summer. We'd fly equipment, replacement parts, fuel, provisions. You name it, we flew it.

Every Tuesday was meat-hauling day for the mines we serviced. Almost none of them had refrigeration, so they planned on keeping their meat for only a week. We would usually use the Gullwing Stinson for these operations because its left window would roll down, conveniently enabling the pilot to pitch out the meat.

Meat was shipped in what were called "rounds"—the best part of a hindquarter, fairly uniform in weight (sixty to eighty pounds), and wrapped in burlap. We'd work out an itinerary for the delivery, packing the copilot's seat with all the items consigned to the first mine and stacking the rest in more or less consecutive order for the other camps along the route. The trips were nonstop; we didn't land again until we returned to Nome.

Our first meat drop was usually at the Gold Run, a mine in a little canyon near Teller. Standard procedure was to buzz the cookshack and wait for the cook to come running out. Then, depending on his skill and ability as "bomber," the pilot would drop the load as close as possible to the cookshack without sending it through the roof.

I became unusually proficient at the art. First, I'd get the cook's attention by buzzing low over the kitchen. Then, I'd flatten out the prop, swing around, and return for the drop. I got so I could deposit a package within about fifty feet of the cook. Staggering through the tundra with eighty pounds of meat is no easy task, so I always tried to get it as close to him as possible. If a guy were too wild with his bombing, the meat would plunge into the tundra and the cook would never find it. Legend has it that one pilot demolished an outhouse when he missed his target near the cookshack.

Eventually, after swooping over camp after camp, I'd have dropped all the meat close to me. Then I'd climb to about 3,000 feet and trim the aircraft until it was fairly stable. Leaving the controls, I'd scramble to the back end so I could pile up additional rounds of meat on the copilot's seat, where they would be handy for subsequent drops. To be good at this operation, a pilot had to be rather agile.

Weekly meat runs to the camps were followed by additional trips that required a landing and stop at each mine. We brought in other perishables, staples and canned goods that had fallen into short supply, spare parts for the dredge, perhaps acetylene or oxygen for the welder—whatever was required. And we also brought the mail. Most mines had their correspondence sent to Nome in care of our office, and we delivered it along with the other supplies.

At regular intervals the dredges were stopped and the riffles "cleaned" of accumulated gold nuggets and dust. Often we were asked to take the gold cleanups to the bank at Nome.

You could tell fairly closely how well a mine was doing from the amount of gold you hauled. The mines put their gold into buckskin leather pouches, tied the tops with string, then covered the fastening with melted wax. Each mine pressed its own special seal into the melted wax, apparently as a deterrent to pilots who might be tempted to open the pokes and extract a nugget or two. The seal had to be intact when the poke was delivered to the Miners and Merchants Bank in Nome. I've seen the assayer examine the gold and tell me the exact creek from which it came, just from the appearance of the nuggets.

The largest poke I ever hauled came from the Ungalik Syndicate mine on the east side of Norton Sound. That magnificent poke weighed almost 100 pounds avoirdupois!

3

Henry Gumm Goes South and Brother Hansen Returns Home

AT THE CLOSE OF SUMMER most of Nome's mining company operators would return south to the Lower Forty-eight. Some would leave on the last boat. Others flew with us to Fairbanks, then went on to Anchorage or Juneau to continue their homeward trip. But Henry Gumm, one of three partners in the North Star Dredging Company, decided to stay in town during the winter of 1937.

Walking home late one night from a meeting of the Pioneer's Club, Henry suffered a massive heart attack and collapsed at the side of the street, sprawling dead on the planked boardwalk. The body was discovered the next morning and taken over to Jacobs's Mortuary. Then Henry's will was located. One of his requests was that he be buried down south in his hometown—back where it was warmer, I guess.

Jacobs, the mortician, came up with an obscure territorial law (or, for all I know, it could have been one of Jacobs's own laws) requiring that a corpse be transported inside a coffin once it reached a city large enough to have a mortuary. Out in the bush you could haul a cadaver wrapped in canvas or whatever was handy. But as soon as the deceased reached a town with a mortuary, he was supposed to travel in style inside a coffin.

An attorney was appointed administrator, and he began soliciting bids for hauling Henry and his coffin to Fairbanks, the first leg of the journey south. Mirow bid. Pacific Alaska bid. And Wien bid, planning to fly their Trimotor over from Fairbanks. Our offer of $750 turned out to be the lowest, so we were given the job.

We met with Jacobs at the mortuary and measured the coffin. I was hoping it would fit inside the Lockheed, but we found that only one of our planes, Mirow's miserable old Bach, had a door large enough to accommodate it.

The Bach ranked at the very bottom of Mirow's fleet, and all his new pilots went through purgatory having to fly that old misfit. Hans had purchased the aircraft for only $750, so he didn't have a great deal to lose, and pilots were expendable in the days before people were so hot to sue one another.

The aircraft was designed to be a trimotor, but ours had been converted to single-engine operation by eliminating the two outboard power plants and replacing the center engine with a Hornet-A. Pratt and Whitney is one of the finest engine manufacturers in the world, but even the best come out with a clinker once in a while. In my opinion, the Hornet-A was one of the most rough-running, unreliable engines Pratt and Whitney ever built. It swung a long prop, but turned rather slowly at about 1,700 rpm. The vibration was something scandalous. And since the conversion created a weight and balance problem, the Hornet-A had to be stuck way out on a long motor mount.

I had seen only one other Bach in my lifetime. It was an original trimotor version owned by the Bonfels of the Denver *Post.* As a trimotor, the Bach was an outstanding performer. I'd watched it soar off the ground from Denver's mile-high airport like a homesick angel. But that Bach was a cousin far removed from its single-engine namesake at Mirow Air Service.

Instead of being on the floor, as is usual, the brakes were operated by hand on the wooden wheel, as was the throttle control. If the plane began a ground loop, you had to release the brake to gun the engine. Since the Bach had once been a trimotor, it was equipped with a lot of spare fuel-line plumbing and a hopeless confusion of valves. I was never able to figure out the fuel system, so to be on the safe side I'd always turn each and every valve to the "on" position.

The Bach had fabric wings and a fuselage composed of fabric-coated plywood over wooden ribs. Even though it was ugly, awkward, and balky, the aircraft had two redeeming features: its wide landing gear was one of the softest I've ever used, so a bumpy landing was almost impossible; and the Bach would carry a tremendous load at the respectable speed of nearly 110 miles per hour.

Nevertheless, I often wished something would happen to ground the old Bach—maybe one of the firepots we used to warm the engine could go berserk and ignite it. But the Bach seemed to live a charmed life.

For our current project of outfitting a flying hearse, the Bach was the only aircraft in our stable capable of accepting poor Henry and his coffin. But there was still one thorny problem. The skis for the Bach had been left in Fairbanks. Without skis there was nowhere to land between Nome and Fairbanks during the winter months, so the trip would have to be done nonstop. But the Bach didn't carry enough fuel to make a nonstop trip all the way between the two cities.

Ray Decker, our mechanic, solved the problem by placing a fifty-five-gallon barrel of gasoline up front near the cockpit and connecting it to a hand-operated wobble pump. He unscrewed the cap from the barrel, put in a length of hose, and sealed the opening with tape to make it more or less leakproof. Then Ray made a hole in the plane's plastic window and ran the hose out to the fuel tank.

After a two-day wait on weather, it looked as though we were all set. Dawn was still hours away as we went outside on that cold winter morning to begin firepotting and warming the old Bach. Just as a few streaks of light became visible in the east, we called the office and told them to bring out the body.

The Mirow company truck, carrying the coffin topped with a wreath of plastic flowers, arrived a few minutes later and backed up to the plane. Much to our amazement and chagrin, we discovered that we couldn't turn the coffin to get it completely into the cabin. While it would clear the door opening, as we had measured, there wasn't enough room to swing it the rest of the way into the plane.

The Bach just sat there like a sullen dog.

We studied the situation a bit, concluding that it would be possible to load the coffin if its lids were removed. So we deposited Henry's frozen remains on a couple of sawhorses we found at the hangar, tipped the coffin on edge, and easily moved it into the plane. Then we returned Henry to his coffin, refastened the lids, and tossed in the plastic flowers. After closing the door of the aircraft and pulling off the engine cover, we were ready to go. Decker, acting as copilot and flight mechanic, joined me in the cockpit, and we headed toward Fairbanks.

In retrospect, it was really a bad deal. On wheels in the middle of winter, we had absolutely no place to put down in case of emergency— and then there was the nature of our grisly load.

We encountered heavy snow squalls over the Nulato Hills but were able to work our way around to the Yukon River, picking it up near the village of Nulato. Conditions became a little more favorable after that, because we had the Yukon to follow and no more hills to cross.

Darkness began to fall as we encountered more snow squalls close to the junction of the Tanana and Yukon rivers. Normally I'd cut cross-country by Fish Lake and head directly for Fairbanks. But with the increasing snow and deepening darkness, we were forced to follow the Tanana River. Decker pumped in the last of the drum gasoline; all we could do now was sweat it out as we continued along the winding river.

Jacobs had sent a message ahead to the mortuary in Fairbanks, informing them of our approximate arrival time. After spotting the city lights and landing, we found a polished black hearse waiting for us.

The hearse must have been out there a long time, because it had drawn a large crowd of curiosity seekers. We taxied up and shut down, then met the mortician.

"Okay, let's get the coffin out of the plane and into the hearse," he said.

I hesitated, trying to figure out some way to stall until the crowd dispersed. "Well, it's just not that easy," I told him.

"What do you mean?" he asked.

"Well, we've got to take the body out of the casket. And with all these people here . . ."

"Never mind them," he said. "Let's get on with it."

So we went ahead and began the morbid task. While the onlookers gawked, we pried the lids off the coffin and reversed the process we'd gone through in Nome. However, not having the sawhorses, we just found a nice flat place to set Henry down—putting him back into his coffin after we'd angled it out of the Bach.

I hope Henry had a satisfactory journey on the rest of his trip. As for me, as I watched that black hearse drive away that night in Fairbanks, I know I was glad to be rid of my cargo.

That same winter I became involved in a similarly sad and unpleasant experience. I had landed in Nome after a flight from Fairbanks in the Lockheed Vega. Bill Barber was waiting for me when I arrived.

"Brother Hansen's sick over at the Pilgrim Hot Springs mission and needs to be brought here to the hospital."

"I'll go right away," I told Bill. After refueling the plane I took off immediately because it was getting late and the flight would take me over the Sawtooth Mountains in back of Nome.

Arriving at my destination I circled the mission, a Jesuit orphanage, and saw a sled start out toward the Pilgrim River, where I could land on the ice. The river was about half a mile from the mission, but I had barely shut off the motor before they arrived.

Brother Hansen, obviously a very sick man, was wrapped in blankets and put aboard the Vega. The flight back to Nome was uneventful, but the next day the hospital informed us that Brother Hansen had died during the night.

We decided to take his body back to the mission the next morning. That year we were using the sea ice in front of town as an airstrip; some years it would freeze quite smooth and provide a very convenient landing area. The hospital brought Brother Hansen down to the beach on a sled, and willing hands put him aboard.

The morning was beautiful, the weather was clear, and the air was smooth. The landscape reflected an almost picture-postcard peacefulness. As I flew over the mission, I saw the boys gather together and begin running down to the river strip where I would land. Father Cunningham, his cassock flapping, was right in the middle.

I opened the hatch and intercepted them before they got to the airplane, explaining the bad news to Father Cunningham. I will always remember his words. "Boys, we have a very, very sad task. Go get a sled; Brother Hansen is dead."

Rough and tough was the way of life in Nome. Rawness permeated every facet of existence. Even the funerals were something not to be believed. Most were held in a church. The police ambulance would be pressed into service as the hearse. Usually, it would get stuck in the snow on the way to the graveyard, and the six parka-clad pallbearers would have to push and shove to get the procession moving again.

A boiler would be steaming at the gravesite, where it had been used to thaw enough of the frozen ground to permit a hasty excavation. Last words would be said in the shadow of the D-8 caterpillar tractor, which had pushed out the snowdrifts and was now standing by to replace the dirt.

Most of the preparations were arranged by Jacobs, the mortician. Like any small town undertaker, Jacobs was also involved in a number of other things. In fact, he was Nome's professional photographer.

But one evening Jacobs apparently decided he'd had enough. He took a bath, manicured his nails, put on his best suit, then settled into one of his finest caskets. Using a small bore pistol, probably in order to be tidy and eliminate any gore, he put a single well-placed shot into his brain. About all that needed to be done was fold his hands and carry him to the gravesite.

Nome was full of many such stories. The makeshift and bizarre were the town's way of life.

4

To Cordova in the Vega

MANY PILOTS FEEL a special affection for certain airplanes they've flown during their career. When an aircraft has performed for you safely and dependably flight after flight, through good weather and bad, an almost tangible bond develops between man and machine. Having become intimately familiar with the aircraft through long hours spent at the controls, a pilot, they say, seems to "wear" the plane rather than fly it. Although I've worn many airplanes, my greatest love was the Lockheed Vega.

The Vega was an aircraft that was way ahead of its time. It set performance records that defied the imagination. Ours was a sister ship of Wiley Post's *Winnie Mae,* the Vega he twice flew around the world. After his globe-trotting adventures, Post collaborated with engineers from Pratt and Whitney to install a large supercharged engine and a special landing gear system that could be dropped after takeoff, relying on just a skid for the return to earth. Donning a sort of spacesuit, Post attained an altitude of over 50,000 feet, 9,000 feet higher than the normal service ceiling of modern commercial jetliners.

The Vega had a full cantilever wing and a smooth, round fuselage. Except for the landing gear and a few metal fittings, the whole ship, wings included, was constructed entirely of wood. The fuselage was formed under great pressure by inflating an enormous bladder inside a concrete mold, forcing thin wood and glue on the mold's surface into the desired shape. Then circumferential support rings were added for extra strength. I liked the rounded look of the Vega, but our competition sneeringly called it the "hollow log." That really used to burn me up—like someone calling your girl friend a hooker.

The Vega's structure was very strong in the air. The landing gear, however, was rather frail; the shock-absorbing oleo struts were just tiny little things. They were covered by fairings, ostensibly to reduce wind drag. But I always suspected the fairings might have been put there mainly for cosmetic purposes—to keep from scaring the hell out of the people flying her.

The pilot sat alone, centered in the cockpit right up front behind the engine. I've heard many arguments pro and con about being situated that close to the engine. Some pilots felt that, in the event of a crash, the engine would run interference for them; others preferred to be a little farther back toward the tail.

You entered the cockpit through an overhead hatch; thus, the pilot could board without disturbing the passengers. However, in a pinch it was possible to enter the cockpit through a little triangular access door that formed the pilot's backrest.

Passenger comfort wasn't the greatest. The Vega was crowded when carrying its maximum of six passengers, and the cabin temperature was generally too cold. But up front the pilot was always warm and cozy. During the winter I often found it embarrassing to get out of the

Vega in my shirt sleeves, while the shivering passengers looked like they'd just emerged from a deep freeze.

Mirow's Vega was a beautiful airplane, painted white with green trim. She cruised at a good 160 miles per hour, although for part of the year we had to replace her sleek wheel pants with skis, slowing the cruising speed a bit. With proper management the Vega's 150 gallons of fuel would last about seven hours, enough to enable us to fly nonstop from Nome all the way to southcentral Alaska.

In early spring the Lockheed really paid off when we used it on our flights to pick up the first groups of returning miners. I was once in Fairbanks on a trip with the Vega when I received a telegram from Mirow. He informed me that six miners destined for Nome would arrive on a boat due to dock at Cordova the following day.

I'd never been to Cordova before, but knew that out of Fairbanks I could fly the Richardson Highway to Copper Center, then follow the Copper River to Chitina. At Chitina I'd find the Copper River Railroad, constructed for the Kennecott Copper Mine (still operating in 1938, the year I made this flight). The railroad followed the river nearly to the sea, then headed over to Cordova.

Harold Gillam, a pioneer bush pilot acknowledged to be the most daring foul-weather flyer in the Territory, was also out at the Fairbanks airport preparing to leave for Cordova and meet the ship. I watched him take off about forty minutes or so before I was ready to go.

Out of Fairbanks the air was quite rough, but the overcast was nice and high. The only weather I'd been able to get was Cordova's, an unencouraging report describing rather poor conditions.

The weather began to deteriorate as I followed the gravel highway, and I grew a little concerned that Gillam might also have been forced to follow the road. He was flying a Pilgrim, and since the Vega was faster I knew I'd be gaining on him. But then the weather picked up a little and stayed reasonably nice all the way to Chitina, where I found the railbed for the last leg into Cordova.

As I proceeded southwest from Chitina, the weather worsened with each passing mile. Light fog mixed with snow limited forward visibility to less than half a mile. I finally wound up right on top of the railroad tracks in order to keep them in sight. I found myself wishing I hadn't gotten into it this far. But there was one consolation—I knew it couldn't get a whole lot worse.

And at least I was in the Vega. You couldn't find a better airplane for scud-running in bad weather. The engine cowling deflected snow and freezing mists so that there was always a narrow band of clear windshield to see through. After stabilizer had been pumped in to maintain trim, the Vega could be slowed down to a speed of about eighty miles per hour. And if it were necessary to make a quick 180-degree turn, all you had to do was pour the power to her, rack it up, and she'd just come around by herself. Right turn or left turn—both were equally easy, since you sat in the center of the cockpit.

Occasionally the weather picked up just a hair. Then it would deteriorate, becoming even worse than before. But I felt I was committed. Win, lose, or draw I was going to tough it out to Cordova.

It seemed to take forever, but eventually the tracks led me to the shore of Eyak Lake, where I landed the Vega gently on her skis. I then had to taxi perhaps a mile up the ice to reach the Cordova airport, located adjacent to the lake. As I walked over to the airport I saw Gillam unloading some passengers from his Pilgrim. He had arrived just ahead of me.

"Damn nasty weather," I said, passing by his aircraft. "A little thicker than I wanted for my first trip to Cordova." He agreed the weather was certainly ripe for improvement. Nothing else was said, but he must have been pretty impressed that I'd been able to make it into town that day. Back in Nome a few days later I received a telegram from Gillam offering me a job with his flying service. It's still one of my prized possessions.

5
Foul-Weather Flyer

McGRATH WAS THE AIR CROSSROADS of westcentral Alaska. Think of a rough rectangle drawn upon a map of the Territory, with Nome near the northwest corner, Fairbanks on the northeast, Anchorage near the southeast, and Bethel to the southwest; these four towns were our most important centers for bush aviation. Now, about where the diagonal from Bethel to Fairbanks intersects the diagonal from Nome to Anchorage you'll find McGrath, a small settlement lying alongside the Kuskokwim River. Since the community was right on the river, the fuel suppliers were able to barge in large stockpiles of aviation gasoline. Plentiful gas coupled with its central location made McGrath a good checkpoint and refueling stop for bush flyers.

During periods of bad weather when the mountain passes were closed, everyone holed up at the local hostelry, Clough's Roadhouse. In winter the entire lodge was kept warm with one huge woodstove. The homemade furnace, two hundred-gallon steel barrels joined together with a welded pipe, was one of the most efficient heating plants I've ever seen. A few daily stokings of green logs kept the roadhouse warm, even in the worst of winters.

Aircraft passengers and pilots made up about ninety percent of Dave Clough's winter business. To make life easier for us, Dave had built racks near the stove to hold our engine oil. After we landed and drained the oil, it was nice to be able to bring it in and set it on the shelf, where the oil would be kept at exactly the right temperature to be poured back into the airplane.

The dining room was located immediately off the area that would have been the lobby if the roadhouse were a hotel. The Cloughs fed everyone family-style. Moose steaks and caribou stew were the staples. In those early days, roadhouses could use any kind of wild game for meat, provided the establishments were located a certain distance away from the railroad. That prohibition prevented Anchorage and Fairbanks restaurants from serving wild game, but everyone else did.

During one week in winter, a group of us who were trying to fly through Rainy Pass to Anchorage had piled up at Clough's Roadhouse in McGrath. I was from Nome, two or three were from Bethel, and a couple of flyers were based there in McGrath. We also knew there were some pilots at Star Airlines in Anchorage who wanted to fly through the pass in the opposite direction and come over to McGrath. None of our bush planes carried radios, but Pacific Alaska Airlines had a base station in Anchorage and a radio set in McGrath. We could get radio reports of the weather at our destination, Anchorage; but, without actually looking, we never knew what kind of weather we'd find at Rainy Pass.

We pilots had our own little code of the hills. Once a day, or if conditions seemed to be improving, perhaps twice a day, one of us would bundle up, go through the painstaking task of warming his airplane, load his passengers, and give Rainy Pass a try. The distance from McGrath to the entrance of Rainy Pass is approximately fifty-five nautical miles. If the pilot didn't return within an hour and a half, we'd figure he'd made it through, and all of us would grab our engine oil and go.

I was a newcomer, and a newcomer was treated rather coolly until he proved himself. I more or less hung back, observing how the other pilots handled themselves. Day after cloudy day each took his turn checking the obscured pass, only to return in disgust. In the evenings we all sat around the big poker table at the roadhouse. That was about the extent of any organized entertainment in McGrath.

I was carrying two passengers, a woman and a small child who were headed Outside. They were even more bored than I was at having to stay in McGrath, but they were good sports. Present-day airline passengers are unbelievably pampered in comparison to the old days. Passengers of the thirties were delighted to have any form of winter transportation, regardless of a few discomforts. We would remind them that they'd better spend some time in the bathroom before take-off (that type of facility certainly wasn't in any of the airplanes) and to be sure they were dressed warmly, because the cabin heat was very, very limited. Our passengers dressed for the trail. If you were forced down, at least you wouldn't have to worry about your passengers freezing to death. Many of them packed their own sleeping bags, although we carried a spare or two in the plane. Passengers were also expected to turn to and help with the chores associated with taking care of the airplane. If you were refueling with five-gallon cans of gasoline, then they were expected to carry the gas or help put the cans up on the wing or assist in some other way. And they were all very good about it.

My turn to try Rainy Pass finally rolled around. I loaded my passengers, fired up the Vega and was on my way.

You go into the pass on the South Fork of the Kuskokwim River. There's a very prominent marker next to the river, a large hill named Egypt Mountain, so you know you're headed into the right pass.

Well, I flew by Egypt Mountain and found that the ceiling was right down to the ground. There was heavy snow and turbulence. Visibility was nil. I sniffed at it, ran in and came back out a couple of times, but it was obvious we weren't going to get through that pass with a whole skin.

As I circled away from Egypt Mountain, a bright idea occurred to me. I'd just skirt the mountains to the north until I hit the railroad and come down the tracks into Anchorage. And if the railroad passes were plugged up, I'd go on into Fairbanks. I sure must have been getting bored with life at Clough's Roadhouse!

You'd have to think twice about doing that with a Bellanca, or almost any of the other airplanes, but the Vega was so fast and had such a range that it was a very sound idea. I wondered why I hadn't thought of it sooner.

I headed northeast along the edge of the mountains. As I proceeded north, the weather grew better. In due time I arrived over the railroad at Healy, then turned right. It was a breeze to cross the mountains following the railroad through Broad and Windy passes. In a little while I was over Anchorage.

I arrived in town about the time the others were figuring I'd made it okay through Rainy Pass and were warming up their airplanes. Pacific Alaska saw me land; they radioed McGrath that I had arrived in Anchorage. The local Star Airlines pilots cranked up for McGrath, and the McGrath pilots headed for Anchorage. Of course, all of them were eventually stopped by the impenetrable pass and had to return to their respective communities.

Well, as soon as word got out that I had been the only one able to make it through Rainy Pass that day, I was immediately moved up to a class on a par with the legendary Harold Gillam. Whenever I'd run across any of the pilots who'd been waiting with me at McGrath they'd ask, "How in the hell did you ever get through Rainy Pass?"

I'd give them a kind of knowing look and say, "Well, it was tough, but I'm used to foul-weather flying."

My passengers, who could have exposed me, had gone Outside, and I don't think they would have known quite where we were anyhow. So overnight, in just one trip, I acquired the reputation of being one of Alaska's best rough-weather pilots. I never did come clean. I decided to cash in on the reputation, for whatever it was worth, and keep the story my own little secret.

Several years later Gillam and I were both bested as foul-weather flyers by an "outlaw" student pilot named Lee Scott Gardener. I was in Aniak and planned to go down the Kuskokwim River to Akiak, but the weather was so lousy I couldn't even see across the river. I heard that Gillam also was holding his flight to Bethel due to bad weather at Kalskag.

While we both waited for conditions to improve, Lee Scott Gardener flew his Cub upriver from Bethel to Aniak. Gillam and I both got quite a chuckle out of that—being outflown by a student pilot. But Gardener did have the advantage of flying a rather slow airplane into the face of a thirty-knot wind out of the northeast. Our flights would have been made downwind with fast aircraft, and a higher ground speed can make quite a difference when trying to scud-run along a river.

Lee Scott Gardener cost the government a lot of gray hair. With only a student certificate, he nonetheless had been hauling passengers. An inspector tried for months to catch him, but at first Gardener managed to elude the chase. Finally they brought Gardener to court in Anchorage with something like thirty-two violations against him.

He was crazy, but like a fox. He insisted on being his own lawyer.

Then he demanded a jury, as well as the text of the United States Constitution. The clerks had to scramble all over the courthouse to find a copy of the Constitution.

For some reason the trial was postponed, so Gardener went back to Aniak. Of course, he wasn't about to quit flying just because the government had said he couldn't fly and had revoked his license. But on one of his flights during this period, he crashed his airplane—really totaled it.

Now fed up with aviation, when summoned back to Anchorage to continue his trial, Gardener proposed: "Would the government be willing to just drop everything and forget it if I agree not to fly anymore?" After a quick consultation among themselves, the government prosecutors agreed to drop all charges in return for Gardener's promise to stop flying.

That was the last I ever heard of Lee Scott Gardener. But he sure slipped through the back door into Alaskan history during his brief but colorful career.

6

The Crackups

I DEPARTED CORDOVA early one Sunday morning, carrying six passengers and their baggage nonstop to Nome. Since the Vega was on skis, I planned to land on a patch of smooth sea ice in front of town. The winter wind had blown away the snow, leaving behind the glare-ice surface.

Both skis were equipped with skags, runners built on the bottom, which tended to hold the aircraft on a straight heading in snow. But on ice the aircraft rode the narrow skags as if on skates, resulting in very little traction to slow the airplane.

Even though I'd made many successful landings on our frozen airstrip, I became unusually apprehensive that particular day. The smooth part of the waterfront ice was quite short, and there wasn't a breath of wind to help slow me down. I extended the landing lights—not that they'd help very much, but at least in theory they might provide a little extra drag. The Vega was a pretty hot-landing airplane, but I squared away and came in just as slowly as possible.

As soon as I touched down, I killed the motor. (Before the introduction of idle cutoff, we had to shut off the motor with a switch.) In general, this isn't a good policy; if the plane begins to ground-loop or if you want to go around again, it's nice to have power available. But I was low on fuel, so I had to land—period. And I wanted to get rid of the thrust that even an idling propeller would provide.

Well, we just didn't seem to slow down at all. My God, how the airplane ate up the smooth ice! Before long we passed into the rougher ice. The right-hand ski stand cracked, and the Vega turned about twenty degrees. Then all hell broke loose as the stand collapsed fully and the axle slammed down on the ice. The plane turned to about ninety degrees, and we continued our sideways slide.

The noise of a wooden airplane disintegrating is a racket that defies description. The Vega's fuselage was strong, but the ragged sea ice was really ripping up the bottom as we crunched along. It seemed like an hour before we finally got stopped. After the cacophony of breaking wood, the cabin was as quiet as a mausoleum. However, the silence didn't last for long. One of my passengers, an old Swede headed for his mine north of Nome, bellowed in broken English, "Let me outta dis goddamn ting!"

Concerned about fire, I leaped out of the top hatch, jumped down to the ice, and ran around to open the cabin door. Other than having the hell scared out of them, the passengers were fine. But the poor old Vega sat on the ice like a wounded bird. A crowd gathered in no time— I think everyone in Nome came down to witness Jefford's folly.

One thing about crackups—pilots involved in them prefer anonymity and are generally reluctant to recount such experiences in any great detail.

The modern pilot, operating from good airports with reliable airplanes, will likely fly his entire lifetime without even denting a propeller. But in the early days, especially in Alaska, it was a different story—more a question of how few you'd have in a year. And as a matter of fact, many operators preferred a pilot who'd been through a crackup or two. As Bob Reeve would say, "It makes them a little more cunning."

Reeve, nicknamed the "Glacier Pilot," was another of the early Alaskan air pioneers. When I met Bob he was operating his air service out of Valdez. We became good friends, and I always paid attention to his sage words.

One day I was in Valdez to meet the boat and pick up a group of miners headed for Nome. Harold Gillam was also in town, planning to shuttle some passengers to Fairbanks. Gillam was still loading his people when I was ready to leave.

I looked over the takeoff situation and was having a great deal of difficulty coming to a decision. The wind was blowing downhill on the sloping runway at about ten miles per hour. And, due to the fairly warm temperature, the runway's snow surface was extremely sticky.

Should I take off uphill, making the most of the wind's lift? Or should I go downhill, building up as much speed as possible to overcome the sticky snow? I collared Reeve and asked for his opinion. "Bob, I'm in a dilemma here, whether to take off into the wind or downhill. How would you handle it?"

"Son," he said, "let me give you some good words of advice. Always go into the wind. Then, if you do crack up, you won't be going so fast."

True enough, I thought, even though I knew there were some times when it was necessary to go both downhill and downwind. In this instance I followed Bob's advice, taxiing out and gunning the Vega up the strip. I used every inch of the runway and was actually into some brush before staggering into the air. Circling, I saw that Gillam was ready to go.

I'm not sure whether or not he was influenced by my marginal take-off, but he decided to try it the other way, taxiing up the slope for a downhill run. He accelerated very slowly at first, then gradually built up speed and finally lifted off. But not soon enough. He couldn't quite clear the high-tension wires at the end of the strip. The Pilgrim seemed to hesitate for an instant, looking as if it was going to plunge into Valdez Harbor. Then it regained momentum and continued to fly.

Gillam's encounter with the power line had broken a restraining cable on the front of one ski, turning the ski upside down. I flew as close to him as I dared and tried to signal the problem. He nodded, seeming to understand, but then simply climbed for altitude and headed north to Fairbanks.

I really couldn't do any good, so instead of slowing down to pace him, I decided to run ahead to Fairbanks and alert them to his problem. After landing in Fairbanks, I got hold of Tom Appleton, Gillam's maintenance chief and office manager, and told him what had happened. Appleton called out the city fire truck for the rescue. We knew the bad ski would hang up in the snow, at the very least causing the Pilgrim to ground-loop.

We waited and waited for Gillam to arrive, but he didn't show up. It began getting dark; Gillam was long overdue. We were making plans for a morning search when we heard the drone of the Pilgrim off in the distance. Gillam passed over the field, and I couldn't believe it— his skis looked normal. He landed without any difficulty, and we swarmed around to hear his story.

In the Paxson area Gillam happened upon a glare-ice lake, blown clear of snow by a twenty-five-mile-an-hour wind. With the wind to stabilize his direction and rapidly slow him down, he decided it would be a good place to land, slipping over the ice on top of the ski stand.

Then the resourceful Gillam had his ten passengers pull down the high wing, giving him enough clearance to turn the ski back to its normal position. Rerigging it with some rope he had aboard the plane, Gillam took off and returned to Fairbanks without incident.

Pilgrim Hot Springs was the scene of another of my crackups. It was a very pleasant place located north of the Sawtooth Mountains on the Seward Peninsula. I always thought it would be an ideal site for a nice hotel—a winter sports and skiing resort. The Jesuit mission there was surrounded by fantastic gardens, made possible by the perpetually warm ground. Their entire complex was heated by water from the springs. Even their toilets were filled with warm water, a delight to sit on during the cold winters.

I was headed to the mission to pick up a traveling optometrist who made the rounds of the villages and towns with suitcases full of glasses. The frames were more or less standard, and he carried enough of an assortment of lenses to fit nearly everyone. That way the glasses were available immediately and there was never any waiting. The optometrist usually stayed two or three days in one spot, then moved on to the next settlement. On this round he had finished his work at the mission, and we were notified that he was ready to leave.

On the flight over, I stopped at Teller to pick up Marianne Mish, the sixteen-year-old daughter of the Nome postmaster, and together we flew on to Pilgrim Hot Springs. The airstrip is quite close to the mission, so we waited while Father Cunningham and the optometrist walked out to the airplane. The optometrist, a rather elderly gentleman, was on crutches and had some difficulty getting around. Both of his legs had once been broken in a streetcar accident. Various youngsters from the mission were helping him with his suitcases full of glasses, but his progress to the airplane was rather slow. I was in no particular hurry anyway, so Marianne and I sauntered out to meet him and visit with the Father.

The airstrip at Pilgrim Hot Springs was a little marginal, especially for a Fairchild 24. While the Fairchild was great for landing in tight spots, it was really weak on takeoff performance, and getting back into the air again was often difficult. But my fuel had burned down to where the aircraft was becoming rather light, and since the two of them weren't very heavy, I didn't anticipate too much of a problem.

I used almost all the field getting airborne and then started my climb. On takeoff to the east you pass over some brush, which quickly gives way to small trees, perhaps thirty feet high. Ordinarily we'd have had it made. But the engine, for some unknown reason, began to slow down. I knew we were in trouble unless the engine picked up, but it refused to develop power as I tried desperately to stay above the trees.

Finally the engine stalled completely. We plunged down through the trees, striking the ground at about a forty-five-degree angle. Then, amidst the noise of splitting trees and cracking wings, the plane overturned. Steam poured out of the motor as the exhaust stack hissed against the wet tundra, and the stench of gasoline permeated the cabin.

Marianne had been in the back. Young and agile, she quickly loosened her seat belt and climbed free. However, the old gentleman remained hanging in his seat. Marianne and I attempted to lift him and unlatch his belt, but its mechanism had jammed. Positioning myself under the man as best I could, I handed Marianne my knife and told her to cut the strap.

When we'd all crawled out of the plane, we found that I had a couple of bruises but that they were both unhurt. I was pretty sure Father Cunningham would have heard the crash and started our way, so we stayed near the plane.

The Fairchild was one sick-looking airplane. Although the fuselage had survived almost intact, the spars of both wings were badly broken and the propeller was gone.

After the engine had cooled, eliminating the danger of fire, I climbed inside to retrieve our baggage, the glasses, and the crutches. Then, when some of the boys from the mission arrived, we began picking our way through the woods back to the airport.

At the mission I felt completely at loose ends, greatly chagrined over the crackup, and just wishing there were something I could do. The mission operated a regular radio schedule to Nome, but the next broadcast wouldn't be until the following morning. Impatient, I decided to walk to Nome. Pilgrim Hot Springs was about ten miles from the Kougarok Narrow Gauge Mining Railway, and once I reached the railroad I expected that sooner or later I'd catch a passing speeder back to town.

So I struck out across the tundra. Swarms of flies and mosquitoes began to eat me alive, even though I wore a head net given me by Father Cunningham. Modern insect repellents weren't yet available. Many times I wished I hadn't been so ambitious and had just stayed at the mission—but the walking did serve to keep me occupied.

After reaching the tracks I started out for Nome, about forty miles away. I was getting rather tired, but the walking was much easier on the railbed, and I hoped to see a speeder before long. The skies were clear, and it was light pretty much all night long, so the trip was only a matter of endurance. About one o'clock in the morning, I heard the welcome chugging of a motor, and the long-awaited speeder gave me a lift for the last twenty miles to Nome.

I explained the situation to Hans and my brother, Bill. (At my urging, Bill had moved to Nome in 1938 to be a mechanic for Mirow Air Service.) We decided it would probably be possible to rebuild the aircraft, using facilities available at the mission.

The next day I flew back to Pilgrim Hot Springs in our Sikorsky, picking up Marianne and the optometrist and then returning to Nome.

Bill and a native mechanic named Joe Maloney spent the better part of two months working on the Fairchild. They were given a good place in which to work on the wings, and they also completely rebuilt the engine. I flew the repaired plane back to Nome, where they completed the finish work. By the following summer the Fairchild was back on the line, ready for another season on the Peninsula.

Whenever you cracked up, the CAA required you to fill out a form describing the accident. It delved into your background—date of birth, height, color of hair, number of teeth, and all that garbage. Then it asked where you'd learned to fly, the number of flying hours you had, previous crackups, etc., etc. And then there was the clincher: "general ability as pilot." Now, it's been my experience that no pilot is going to badmouth himself. So whenever I answered the question, I'd always say at least "excellent."

However, pilot Murrell Sasseen, who had a really dry sense of humor, made what I consider the classic response. He'd just had two recent crackups when he piled up again on the golf course in Anchorage. As he was filling out his third form, he came to "general ability as pilot." He pondered awhile, then wrote, "I used to think I was pretty good, but lately I've begun to wonder."

The mission church, now abandoned, at Pilgrim Hot Springs on Alaska's Seward Peninsula north of Nome.

Hans Mirow (right), Jack's first employer in Alaska, with the Mirow Air Service's S-39 Sikorsky amphibian.

Eskimo children and dog team in 1937 with the Travelair, one of six hardworking planes in the Nome-based Mirow Air Service, which served isolated native villages on a more or less regular basis.

Jack, old-time Alaskan flyer Archie Ferguson, and an unusual load for the Gullwing Stinson.

The Bach freighter gathers a crowd of admirers. Jack considered the plane "ugly, awkward, and balky," but he liked its soft landing gear, carrying capacity, and speed.

Above: Supplies from a horse-drawn sledge are packed into the Bach. Left: Mirow mechanic Ray Decker and Jack (in sealskin pants and parka) pause at the cabin door of the Bach.

Like a wounded bird, the Lockheed Vega lies with damaged fuselage and crumpled skis after a rough landing on the sea ice in front of Nome.

Dredging for gold with this well-worn rig, Jack and two partners managed to lose $10,000 during a summer of operation.

Above: On the Bering sea-coast with the Sikorsky during the reindeer roundup.
Left: Jack experiments with one of the early Morse code hand-cranked CW radios, of the type that helped save his life when he crashed in the Darby Mountains.

In 1938, Mirow's Gullwing Stinson (above) replaced the dog team as carrier of U.S. mail to several native villages. Jack went down in this plane during a winter gale while on a mail flight and, after six days on a remote mountainside, was rescued by dog-team mushers.

Solomon, one of Jack's stops on the Mirow Air Service mail route.

Jack (left) prepares for a mail run as pouches bound for remote villages await loading on the Stinson.

Victor Novak, a Mirow mechanic, uses a log to pound loose the sticking skis of the straining Stinson-A Trimotor.

During the reindeer acquisition flights in the bitter weather of
Alaska's tundra, firepots were required to keep the Stinson-A engines
warm through the night. Each evening, the engine oil was drained into
large containers, which were stored indoors overnight. The reindeer
acquisition flights were Jack's last official duty for Mirow; in April,
1940, he signed on with the Civil Aeronautics Authority.

Carrying out repairs on the Stinson-A under difficult conditions.

Part 3

There's More to the Job than Flying

1

The Girls and the Godfather

TOM CLONINGER ran the Nevada Club—a combination restaurant, short order grill, dance hall, and saloon. Open poker playing was popular in the saloon, while upstairs Tom personally supervised a special high stakes game, reserved for Nome's gambling elite.

There was a sinister aspect to Cloninger, something in his demeanor that suggested he was not a good man to cross if you were at all interested in longevity. He was truly a man of mystery. No one knew much about him, and after meeting him nobody felt foolhardy enough to ask questions.

Tom dressed with meticulous care, paying particular attention to his white shirts. He always used two of them every day, appearing in the afternoon having exchanged his morning shirt for a fresh one. His collars were immaculate and stiffly starched; his cuffs, fastened with gold nugget links. And he sported a unique trademark—a dazzling diamond stickpin.

One day, Cloninger sent word for me to come down to the Nevada. Tom never went to see anyone—he sent for people. Being interested in longevity, I lost no time in answering the summons. I hurried over to his gilded, velvet-draped office in the back of the Nevada, where he presided like a Far-North godfather.

Cloninger glanced up from his desk when I walked in. Though he seemed friendly enough, there was always an aura of menace about the man. "Sit down, Jack," he said. "Want a drink?"

"No, thanks." I was curious as hell to know what he had on his mind.

He wasted little time getting to the point. "Things have been kind of dull and slow here at the Nevada this year," he said. "The people are just not coming out at night. I don't like things dull and slow, and I plan to do something about it."

He fingered his diamond stickpin. "I'm gonna pep up this place," he continued, "and I think you're the man to help me. The next time you fly into Fairbanks I'd like you to look up an entertainer. Somebody good. Maybe a guy who can play the accordion and sing. Think you can handle that for me?"

"No problem, Tom," I assured him, relieved that it was such a simple request. "I'll take care of it my next trip in."

"That's fine, Jack. I knew I could count on you."

I was accustomed to performing special services for the people of

Nome. You had to do a bit extra to be a good bush pilot; skillful flying wasn't enough. Public relations was a big part of the job. You had to realize you were selling yourself, your aircraft, and your company to prospective passengers and shippers. You didn't have to be the greatest pilot in the world to be successful, but you did need a little charisma and a personality that could inspire confidence. The job also demanded versatility and a willingness to do more for people than simply ferry them from place to place. A bush pilot was often called upon to perform favors for his clients.

For example, we operated a schedule to Fairbanks, and one of the pilot's chores was spending almost a day in town shopping. We usually charged a minimum of fifty cents for this service. If a woman wanted yarn, needles, or a spool of thread, she would come down to the office and describe her wishes to the office manager. He, in turn, would pass on her request to the pilot. Many times I'd leave for Fairbanks with a huge list. A lot of the work could be farmed out to the stores after I got to Fairbanks, but the shopping still took the better part of the day.

Never before, however, had I been asked to provide an entertainer. And never by someone like Cloninger, who didn't like anyone making mistakes. "Get somebody good," Cloninger reminded me curtly as I left the office. "Somebody that'll bring in the business."

"I'll sure do my best, Tom," I told him.

It was an odd assignment from a very demanding customer. But I figured I'd be able to find someone for him and thereby also provide a return fare for Mirow Air Service.

My next trip to Fairbanks was with the ski-equipped Lockheed Vega, a trip that took about three hours and fifteen minutes in that magnificent airplane. It was the time of year when days were short. But by leaving Nome at dawn, even though we were running against the sun, we had enough daylight to make it to Fairbanks nonstop.

The usual procedure was to refuel for the return trip immediately upon landing at Fairbanks and then begin the shopping and chores. The next day—and we always laid over one day—was reserved for more shopping and maybe a bit of leisure.

I was undecided about what to do that evening until I bumped into my good friend, Jack Hermann, now working for Ferguson Airways. He'd just flown to Fairbanks in a Bellanca. "Jack, let's do the town," he said. "As a start, why not join me for dinner at the Club Rendezvous?"

"Sounds good to me," I said. We hailed a cab and rode out to the Club Rendezvous, one of the many night spots that fringed the pioneer Alaskan city. At the club, we had a couple of drinks and then ordered dinner.

We were both feeling great—delighted with our good flying jobs and enjoying the pilot's life in the North. Hermann was one of the happiest guys I've ever known, always a pleasant, interesting companion.

Among the people who gathered at the club were several Pacific Alaska pilots and their wives. Included in the crowd was Joe Crosson and his lovely wife, Lillian.

Jack Hermann loved to dance, and while there was no live music that night at the Club Rendezvous, they had a pretty fair jukebox. Jack danced with every woman in the club. A number called the "Lambeth Walk" was popular at that time, and I can still see Jack stomping through the "Lambeth Walk" in his mukluks. That guy was just good company.

We hung around until about two o'clock, closing time. The Pacific Alaska pilots and their wives had gone home, leaving only a handful of people. The bartender kept drying the glasses, looking bored and wishing he could close the place.

Suddenly a vision of "godfather" Cloninger at the Nevada Club in Nome strayed through my mind and I sat up with a start. "God! I almost forgot!" I said to Jack. "I promised to find somebody to entertain at the Nevada Club. If I don't bring back someone, Cloninger's going to be very unhappy."

Hermann knew Tom Cloninger well. "What are you going to do?" he asked. "I don't know any entertainers."

"I guess I'm in big trouble," I said.

About that time a very pretty brunette peered around from the adjacent booth. "You've got to be kidding, mister!" she said. "Did I hear you say you're looking for an entertainer?"

"You did," I said.

"That's a real coincidence," she said. "I'm a musician, and my partner plays the violin."

Tom had only mentioned hiring one entertainer. But in my expansive mood I said, "You're both hired. I'll fly you to Nome tomorrow."

"Wonderful!" she said. "We'll sure go—and we'll be ready. What time do we leave?"

"Let's try to get away by nine o'clock."

"Fine. Wouldn't you like to hear me play something?" She pointed to the club's piano.

"Great idea!" I said.

"Well, what would you like me to play?" she called over as she walked to the piano.

"How about 'Indian Love Call' by Rudolf Friml," I suggested rather pompously, having studied some piano as a kid and suddenly remembering the number. By throwing in the composer's name, I figured I might leave the impression that I knew something about music.

The girl played "Indian Love Call" beautifully, I thought. However, in my frame of mind, she could have played "Chopsticks" with one finger and it would have sounded beautiful.

"You're hired," I told her. "I'll pick you both up at nine."

After I got the name of the hotel where she was staying, I went back to the booth where Jack was sitting. We both decided we'd had enough for one night and got a cab back to town.

The Alaska Signal Corps used to be open all night, so I went there and sent Cloninger a telegram advising him I'd hired two fine musicians and we'd be arriving in Nome late the next afternoon.

As soon as he got my wire the next morning, Cloninger had the Nome *Nugget* print shop run off a flock of handbills and had them distributed all over town by a bunch of boys. The flyers announced there would be live music at the Nevada the next night with TWO GIRLS DIRECT FROM FAIRBANKS. For good measure, he ran a huge banner across Front Street, proclaiming the arrival of LIVE MUSIC and TWO FAIRBANKS GIRLS at the Nevada.

I awoke the next morning with a head-splitting hangover and serious misgivings about my rashness in hiring two unknown entertainers for a client as unforgiving as Cloninger. If they bombed, my career in Nome might terminate abruptly. Nevertheless, I was committed, so I gathered up the Nome mail from the post office and went over to the hotel to pick up the Nevada's new entertainers.

I walked up the rickety stairs to the second floor and raised my hand to knock, when the sound of sobbing brought my knuckles up short. After a pause, I banged on the door anyway and Marsha—the girl I'd met the night before—opened it.

Her tears were tears of disappointment. I was a bit late and the girls supposed the episode of the night before was just a case of some drunken pilot mouthing off and that there wasn't any job after all. Marsha and her friend, Ginger, were absolutely delighted when I showed up, confirming that the job really did exist.

The Lincoln Cab Company looked out for Mirow's interests when any of us were in town. Old George, the driver, had his big Lincoln parked downstairs. It was a good thing, I thought, after I saw the mountain of equipment the girls proposed to take to Nome.

"This instrument clamps next to the piano keyboard," Marsha explained, showing me what looked like a miniature organ. "It has a range of two octaves. And these are Ginger's violin, clarinet and drums."

In short order, old George packed drums, violin, organ, clarinet, luggage, the girls, and me into the Lincoln and started toward the airport. On the way over, Marsha turned to me, looking pale and frightened. "Neither of us has ever flown before," she confided. "We're both scared to death."

I tried to reassure them—not too successfully.

We stowed all the musical instruments, freight, and accumulated mail in the plane. Then we pulled down a couple of seats for the girls. They were apprehensive about riding in back all by themselves, but the configuration of the Lockheed was such that the pilot sat isolated in the compartment up front, completely shut off from his passengers.

"Don't worry, girls. We'll be in Nome in a little more than three hours—and it won't be a bad flight at all." They didn't seem a bit reassured and were obviously still very frightened.

Ordinarily, such a flight would be routine. But with two terrified passengers aboard I really hoped we'd have fairly smooth flying. It wasn't to be. We took off to the east and made a slow, shallow, climbing turn. Strong southeasterly winds buffeted the plane shortly after take-off, but with a solid layer of clouds at 4,000 feet, there was simply no way I could get to an altitude where I might find smoother air.

It was rough as the devil. The old Lockheed bucked and pitched like a Wyoming bronco, bouncing all over the sky. I was quite concerned about how my passengers were faring. About forty-five minutes out, I noticed the odor of gin wafting my way from the passenger compartment. Looking over my shoulder through the little peephole, I was astounded to see the girls passing a fifth of gin back and forth, gulping it down straight.

One thing about the Lockheed Vega, all odors filter forward into the cockpit. On this occasion, besides the odor of the gin a sour smell soon reached me. Both girls had become deathly sick.

When we landed in Nome, you never saw two more miserable-looking creatures in your life. They were drunk and they were sick. George Bayer, one of Cloninger's aides, was out to meet the plane. He looked over the two girls as they staggered and stumbled out of the plane in great disarray.

"Tom ain't gonna like this." George shook his head disapprovingly. "He ain't gonna like this one bit."

I knew Tom wasn't going to like it, but what the hell was I to do?

Muttering to himself, Bayer loaded up the girls, their instruments, and their luggage, and took off for the Nevada.

I did my chores at the airstrip and then went down to the Mirow office. "Here's a letter Tom Cloninger just sent over," said the office manager, handing me a small white envelope.

Reluctantly, I opened it. "I want to see you right away," said the note, signed "Cloninger." I figured he had a contract out on me for sure.

Worried and despondent, I slipped over to the room I shared with Murrell Sasseen to ponder the situation and devise some way out of the mess I'd gotten myself into. I even considered striking out on foot across the ice to Siberia or holing up in an abandoned sourdough cabin until the heat was off.

Sasseen poured us both a stiff drink. He moved the glass around in his hand, staring into it as he reflected on the matter. "I'm sure as hell glad I'm not in your shoes," he said finally. "That Cloninger's a tough hombre."

"Thanks a lot." Murrell wasn't much help, but like everyone else in Nome, he knew Cloninger and figured I was really in the soup.

The evening wore on. Something had to be done, so I decided I'd sneak down to the Nevada and peek through the back window to sort of get the lay of the land.

I walked down the alley. As I approached the Nevada I could hear music—and by golly, it sounded good. Encouraged, I pressed my face against the window. Through the dense cigar and cigarette smoke I could see two neatly dressed, attractive ladies playing away on a platform amid an assortment of musical instruments. To me they looked like angels. With a little rest, some food, and a bath, the girls had fully recovered from the flight and were putting on an excellent show. In fact, they were really fine musicians.

The Nevada was filled with people, and Tom was behind the cash register smiling, dressed as usual in his impeccable style. It seemed safe to go in the front door.

As I entered the bustling room Tom greeted me like a long-lost brother. I knew I'd lucked out again! "Jack, you old son of a gun, how can I ever thank you for finding these terrific girls for me?"

"No trouble at all, Tom, no trouble at all." I was too relieved to say much of anything else.

The two girls remained in Nome for several years. Ginger showed rare mastery of the violin, clarinet, and drums. In combination with the dulcet tones of Marsha's piano, the result was some of the sweetest music I've ever heard.

They were real troupers. If the audience was a bunch of Scandinavians they'd grind out an assortment of polkas and schottisches. Or if a group was quietly enjoying dinner, they'd come through with soft and mellow dinner music. They were a marvelous pair of performers and a great asset to the city of Nome.

And whenever I went over to the Nevada, Marsha and Ginger would always secretly greet me in their own special way. Within a few minutes they'd begin playing the haunting strains of "Indian Love Call."

2

Gold Fever

THERE'S JUST SOMETHING about gold, something quite apart from its monetary value. Excitement, adventure, allure! Year after year, Nome's old prospectors set out eagerly to seek it. In fact, virtually everyone in Nome with a couple of nickels to spare had at least one fling with gold mining. Even I caught the fever.

It fascinated me to think that you could take money directly out of the earth. You didn't have to outwit anyone or do anything but pick up the money that the good Lord had put there for you.

More than $100 million worth of gold had been extracted from the Nome area diggings since 1900, most of it with flume and bucket dredges. I watched a lot of those dredges in action, huge metal monsters poking their elongated snouts into the gold-bearing gravel, sending down endless chains of buckets to scoop up the soil. The loaded buckets then clanked back into the dredge, where the gravel was washed and agitated down sluices to extract the precious metal.

Where gold was embedded in clay, more sophisticated, complex rotating-screen systems were needed to separate the gold. In other areas where the gold separated more easily, simple draglines or bulldozers could be used to push the gold-bearing gravel into sluice boxes.

Watching all that gold pour out of the creeks into the pockets of individual miners or syndicate coffers finally got the best of me. I simply had to get my hands on some of the tantalizing natural wealth.

One night I met with Clyde Glass, an ex-miner, and Ray Decker. Together we decided that we should get into the mining business. Since Clyde was the only bona fide miner of the group, we thought that the most fitting name for our partnership would be the Glass Dredging Company. The "Dredging" referred to an old, tired dredge we spotted for sale over on Melsing Creek near Council. The purchase price included the rights to work the mining claim on which it sat.

While most of Melsing Creek had already been dredged, we felt that by applying our superior know-how we could go a little farther up the creek and make ourselves rich. We'd often get together for "mining meetings," where we'd toss off a few drinks and discuss plans. Our biggest source of worry was deciding how to spend all the money we were going to make. My own vision ran toward trips abroad in a luxuriously appointed seventy-five-foot sailing yacht.

By pooling our savings and going into debt, we were able to make a down payment on the dredge and mining operation. Mirow agreed to a rather low price for the use of an airplane to haul our gasoline and supplies over to Council. (We found out later that a dredge that burns gasoline instead of diesel fuel is a pretty expensive operation.)

Ray quit his job, and he and Clyde went over to Council at the beginning of the mining season to get the dredge ready. We were as eager as kids to get going and turn on our spigot of riches. Tirelessly we repaired leaks in the dredge hull and overhauled the gasoline engines.

A dredge is a specialized floating ship that creates its own pond as it works its way up a streambed, enlarging the pond forward as it eats up the ground and filling the pond rearward as it dumps the waste-rock tailings. The dredge has two "spuds," vertical metal legs located in the stern. The digging spud is the pivot on which the dredge swings. The walking spud is put down in order to lift and reposition the digging spud. In essence, the two metal spuds "walk" the dredge as it slowly moves forward.

Ours was a flume dredge. The bucket line dumped paydirt at the top of the flume, whereupon it was washed downward through the sluices. The tailings were dumped off an extension arm to keep them far enough away so the boat could swing and float.

I don't know how we finally got this tricky behemoth going, but eventually we did. Then our troubles started.

The dredge was old, and it wasn't a very good dredge even when new. After it had dug a little while, something invariably would go wrong. The old bucket line was an especially weak link and broke at frequent intervals. Whenever I made a trip into the Council area, I'd fly by our mining operation, experiencing a sick feeling every time I saw the bucket line stretched out on the tundra. Clyde and Ray would be out busily welding and repairing it, the rest of the dredge sitting behind them on the pond like a sick dinosaur.

The clincher came when we started running into frozen ground. The old dredge simply couldn't handle it. To make a long, sad story very short—at the end of the season we found ourselves about $10,000 in debt. As far as I was concerned, our business venture had failed. I'd had a bellyful of gold mining. So, at our annual "stockholders meeting," I insisted I wanted out of the enterprise. I promised to pay my share of our deficit—about $3,500—but otherwise I was out.

But some people, once the lure of gold gets into their veins, will keep at it all their lives. Ray and Clyde were still hopelessly hooked, painting rainbows that the next year would be far better. But when they mined again the following year, they wound up in even worse shape than after that first disastrous season.

In reality, $20 worth of gold is no more valuable than $20 worth of anything else, but I guess I had to lose my shirt in the mining venture before finding that out.

3
The Reindeer Study

COMMERCIAL REINDEER HERDING had flourished briefly along the shores of the Bering Sea, but during the thirties the industry fell upon hard times.

The herds were descended from Siberian reindeer brought to Alaska by the federal government at the turn of the century. The original idea had been to provide a better livelihood for the Eskimos, replacing meat and hides taken from dwindling wild caribou herds with a more certain supply from the domesticated reindeer.

As the reindeer multiplied, the government arranged for individual Eskimos to acquire ownership of their own small subsistence herds. Later, white owners also obtained private herds of reindeer, with the goal of establishing a profitable business in meat and hides.

The transplanted reindeer prospered, increasing in number to perhaps a million head when the herds were at their peak. White-owned reindeer ranches also expanded, extending all along the western coast of Alaska, from Port Heiden in the south to Point Barrow in the north.

Just as in a cattle operation, roundups were held to castrate a certain percentage of the young bulls. Then professional herders cared for the reindeer, keeping wolves at bay while the herds matured. Corrals and slaughterhouses were built to process the meat, which was packed and shipped to southern markets. The steers made excellent table fare.

The Lomen Northwest Livestock Corporation was the largest of the reindeer operations, having spreads on Nunivak Island, along the western coast, and as far north as Kotzebue. But by the thirties, times had changed. Some native owners felt threatened by encroachments from the commercial herds, and their protests were carried to Congress. In addition, the economics of bringing the meat to market were unprofitable. The Lomen brothers desperately wanted out of the venture and ceased all processing, other than small kills for local consumption.

In the fall of 1937 Carl Lomen began to spend much of his time in Washington, lobbying in favor of a Congressional bill that would authorize purchase of the reindeer herds from all white owners. The herds were to be owned by the federal government and administered for the natives.

Although I'd never lost much sleep over the issue, I ended up becoming more involved with the project than anyone else not directly engaged in the Reindeer Service. I personally did all the flying for the various Congressional committees that came to Alaska to visit the villages and gather first-hand data on the reindeer acquisition. (Exhaustive studies were required before the government was ready to act on the proposal.)

Mirow Air Service was chosen for these flights because we had the only active amphibian on the Seward Peninsula, our S-39 Sikorsky. Mirow always assigned me to the flying, probably because the flights were lengthy and I'd usually be gone a week at a time, or longer.

I recall one of those Congressional junkets particularly well. In the summer of 1938 I was introduced to a reindeer study group consisting of Dr. Wilson, a professor of biology from the University of Virginia; Senator Reed, a newspaper publisher from Grand Junction, Colorado; Ray Dame, a photographer from the Department of the Interior; and Sid Rood, the local reindeer agent of the Interior Department's Reindeer Service.

I flew the group to Nunivak Island, where the Lomen brothers had one of their installations. (Musk ox were later transplanted successfully to the island, but at that time it was used exclusively for reindeer.) We reconnoitered the herds and made several aerial photographs until it began to rain.

Five days of the foggiest, rainiest weather I've ever experienced kept us grounded at Nunivak. When the weather finally cleared, I found to my disgust that both of the Sikorsky's magnetos had soaked up so much water they wouldn't fire. I had to remove them and haul them into the local trading post. After four hours in front of the stove, the magnetos were dry enough to be replaced, and we were back in business.

Working our way down south as far as Togiak and Naknek, we visited many of the villages and conferred with the native chiefs, discussing reindeer and their significance to the native economy. On the trip back, the group wanted to stop at Hooper Bay, a village without an airstrip. The bay was large, and I expected no problems as I eased the Sikorsky into the water. But when we settled off the step, I realized we were in trouble as the plane came to an abnormally fast halt. I'd landed in about sixteen inches of water on the barely covered mud flats. There we were, completely stuck.

Checking through a set of tide tables we kept in the plane, I found that the tide was only halfway in and still rising. Fortunately, in an hour or so we would be floated off the mud by the incoming tide. The day was nice and balmy, so there really wasn't too much to be worried about.

As we waited, a lone native paddled out to the plane in his kayak. Rood, no doubt trying to impress the committee, spoke to him in the Eskimo language. The native looked very confused, so Sid continued with a little more of his Eskimo. The native seemed only to get more and more bewildered with each additional word. Finally, shaking his head, the native said in perfect English, "I just can't figure out what you're trying to say!"

That must rank as one of Sid's most embarrassing moments. But in his defense I should point out that there are literally dozens of native dialects in Alaska. When I first arrived in Nome, I considered learning to speak Eskimo. But the native dialects were so numerous that each village seemed to have its own. In fact, residents of one village might have difficulty conversing with residents of another. So I gave it up as a bad job. Sid's Eskimo was probably all right; he was just using the wrong kind.

Shortly afterward, the rising tide floated us off the mud. Although I was dragging bottom a little, the native knew the channel through the bay, and with his help we made it into town.

Hooper Bay was the most primitive native village I'd ever encountered. The people lived in sod-wall dugouts roofed with driftwood. Many Hooper Bay old-timers couldn't speak English and had to depend on the younger people to translate, using the English they'd learned in the Bureau of Indian Affairs school.

When the day's work was finished, we decided to fly directly from Hooper Bay to Nome. The accommodations had generally been lousy, and after ten days in the bush without a bath or a square meal, all of us had a severe case of get-home-itis.

By the time we were ready to go, our nice weather had disappeared.

A deck of stratus clouds had moved in off the sea from the west, and the ceiling had descended to less than 400 feet. But there was unrestricted visibility under the low ceiling, and there was nothing but flat land and water along our course. In spite of some gnawing doubts, I left Hooper Bay for Nome.

The CAA had nothing more than a branch office in Alaska, and getting weather reports was a do-it-as-best-you-can sort of affair. A number of amateur radio operators helped, as did operators of the Bureau of Indian Affairs radio network and the Army Signal Corps. If the signals were in, you could get a fair idea of what the weather was like, at least along the coast.

The Sikorsky, with its slow cruising speed of less than 100 miles an hour, was a good plane for the kind of flying we were doing—low ceilings and uncertain weather. Conditions grew worse as we traveled northward. Rain squalls and clinging mists became frequent. By the time we reached the mouth of the Yukon, visibility had dwindled to less than a mile, and the ceiling was down to about 100 feet.

I'd been navigating on a general compass course, hoping to continue in this fashion past the Yukon Delta and across the open water into Nome. I figured I could cross Norton Sound by dead reckoning. Then, when I reached the southern coast of the Seward Peninsula, I'd recognize the terrain and know whether to turn east or west to reach Nome.

But the weather had deteriorated to the point that it would have been sticking our necks out to proceed. I could have set down on some lake or slough along the mouth of the Yukon and waited for improved weather, but that would have been pretty darned miserable. The Sikorsky was without heat, and we were already half frozen.

There was no point in trying to return to Hooper Bay; the weather would be just as bad behind us as it was ahead. So, when I reached the mouth of the Yukon, I decided to fly upriver in hope of spotting a village where we could spend the night. We were in no great danger, because we always had the option of landing in the river. But again, that would have meant tying up and waiting it out, cramped, hungry, and cold—a miserable prospect at best.

Nevertheless, I was just about to close the throttle and land on that lonely stretch of the Yukon, resigned to spending an uncomfortable night with some damned unhappy passengers, when I came around a bend in the river and saw the *Coot.* The *Coot* was the thirty-five-foot Bureau of Fisheries boat skippered by Cal Townsend, a friend of mine who patrolled salmon fishing activity along the Yukon.

Cal's job was to estimate native fish harvests and enforce fishing regulations, as well as look out for poachers and insure a proper escapement of salmon. Most of his time was spent near the mouth of the Yukon, although occasionally he'd travel upriver to the upper villages. In the fall, he dry-docked the *Coot* at Nenana.

Seeing the *Coot* dead ahead of us in the river was like spotting an old friend. I glided down, settling the Sikorsky gently into the water. Cal watched us land and guessed our problem was bad weather, so he hove to.

The Sikorsky was probably as hard an airplane to maneuver on water as you could find. It had no water rudder, and its regular rudder required a lot of speed to be effective. I finally just shut down and let Cal, a very good boatman, come to us. After we made the transfer from the Sikorsky to the *Coot,* Cal anchored and let the airplane trail out behind the boat in the Yukon's current; it held steady at the end of a long line.

There had been no cabin heat in the Sikorsky, and even though temperatures were well above freezing we had all gotten thoroughly chilled. What a contrast to be piped aboard Cal's cozy, roomy patrol boat! The boat had spare bunks, and I always found it a real privilege to be a guest of Cal's.

One of the first things he did was bring out a gallon of Ten High whiskey. I'm not trying to endorse any particular brand of booze—but I've never had liquor taste better in my life.

Cal's lovely wife was the first mate and cook—the two of them were the entire crew.

Mrs. Townsend prepared a delicious meal of freshly caught king salmon. After dinner, most of us were so worn out that we crawled off to the bunks for some sleep. But Cal and Senator Reed stayed up all night, keeping company with that dwindling gallon of Ten High and solving all the world's ills. They discussed boating on the Yukon, running a newspaper in Grand Junction, philosophy in general, and God knows what else. When I awoke the next morning at six, the two were still sitting at the galley table rapping away as spiritedly as the night before, thoroughly enjoying each other's company. I've never seen two strangers develop such a complete rapport and solid friendship in so short a time.

That morning the weather was much improved. After we pulled the Sikorsky up to the boat and got aboard, I started the engine and taxied across the water a while to warm up. Then we were off the river and on our way back to Nome.

In the days that followed, we continued the junket north from Nome all the way to Barrow, stopping at practically all the villages and reindeer corrals, talking to herders and chiefs. Eventually we made our way back to Nome, completing the trip for this committee.

That winter, Congress passed the Reindeer Acquisition Act, which appropriated about $800,000 for the purchase of white-owned reindeer. Carl Lomen's mission as a lobbyist to Washington was finally—and successfully—completed.

4

Progress in the Cockpit

THE FALL OF 1938 was an exciting time for Mirow Air Service. We began installing radio gear in our aircraft.

Our first radio was a home-built two-watt CW (continuous wave) transmitter, which we put in the Gullwing Stinson. Later that winter, when I crashed in the Darby Mountains near Golovin, the radio signal I was able to send helped save my life. Prior to the use of radio, no one knew you were in trouble unless you'd been missing for four or five days. Now, in response to a radio SOS, a search would begin immediately.

Those early radios wouldn't broadcast voice, so pilots had to learn Morse code. If you walked into any airline office, you would usually find a buzzer and two guys working hard at the key. I had an additional motive for learning code. With Hans Mirow's approval, I filed a job application with Pacific Alaska Airways, Pan American's Alaskan subsidiary. One of their requirements was that every pilot be able to transmit code at thirteen words per minute.

I practiced diligently until I became reasonably proficient. On one flight I maintained continuous contact with the company all the way to Fairbanks—a big thing for us. Practically all of my code sending was done in aircraft. As a result, I found I could work better with the key on a pedestal or in some other awkward and uncomfortable position than I could at a table with everything in order.

In addition to installing radio gear, Pacific Alaska established a network of radio bases all along their routes. They used code for many years and generally carried a radio operator on their larger ships. Star Airlines, an Anchorage-based bush service, was even farther ahead of us with their Lear T-30, a radio with two frequencies and voice capability.

During the next year nearly all Alaskan aircraft acquired radios of one sort or another. Most of the airlines and bush services used the same frequencies, the so-called green chain. Pacific Alaska continued with code long after everyone else had switched to voice transmission and had their own special set of frequencies, the red chain. But regardless of equipment type or frequency selection, the advent of radio was a tremendous aviation stride for the North.

Cockpit instrumentation was advancing concurrently with the development of radio during this transition period in Alaskan aviation, although proper navigational aids for routine instrument flight were still in the future. When I first arrived in Alaska I did not have an instrument rating; at that time the rating was not issued on commercial licenses. However, I did have a letter of authority from the government stating that I had passed what is now known as the Air Traffic Regulations instrument check.

Of course, while flying the weather in Oklahoma City, I had become quite experienced with instrument flying. To remain proficient, I would deliberately pull up into fairly high overcasts where I could not see the ground, then cruise along under instrument conditions for ten minutes or so. Periodically I'd ease back down to be sure of my position, then return to the clouds and instrument flying.

It was excellent practice and saved my hide a number of times when I had been scud-running through low-lying clouds or feeling my way through miles of fog. Though I'd lose all reference to the ground, I could easily manage a 180-degree blind climbing turn in order to get out of the soup or through it.

Most of the early instrument flyers I knew were associated with the weather flights. While I was in Nome, Harold Gillam was making weather flights in Fairbanks. He kept his position pinpointed by having an assistant at the hangar listen for his engine and tell him his direction from the airport.

Weather flyers were a close-knit fraternity. Larry Flahart was another Alaskan pilot who had formerly flown the weather. Larry was at Salt Lake the year I was flying at Oklahoma City. While we hadn't known each other outside Alaska, when we met here we often discussed the trials and tribulations of flying the weather.

Then there was Mac Emerson, the head of the Weather Bureau in Alaska for many, many years. Mac didn't pilot an airplane, but he was one of the original kite flyers from South Dakota. We spent many pleasant hours reminiscing over a martini—Mac flying his kites and I making the same type of observations in my aircraft.

5

Crash on the Darby Mountains

WHEN I LEFT NOME in the Gullwing Stinson that morning of November 29, 1938, I had no idea of the ordeal to come. Airborne over the Seward Peninsula, I could see a strong surface wind raging in the distance, blowing thick sheets of snow across the low ridge of mountains between Golovin and Elim.

That winter I had been flying twice-monthly mail runs from Nome to Solomon, Golovin, Elim, Koyuk, Shaktoolik, and Unalakleet. In former years the mail had been delivered to these small villages by dog team, but aviation was coming of age in Alaska, and Mirow had underbid the dog-team mushers for the mail contracts.

An odd thing about those mail trips—it seemed the Stinson's load never decreased after a stop. The mail and cargo I dropped off were usually balanced by an equal amount of mail and freight that had to be packed aboard and taken back to Nome. I'd start the day at nearly gross weight and remain heavily loaded for the entire flight.

On this day I made my first stop at the little gold mining settlement of Solomon, nothing more, really, than a roadhouse and store. Then I flew on to Golovin, a tiny, remote native village located seventy miles east of Nome on Norton Sound. After making a ski landing on the frozen bay in front of town, I gathered up the Golovin mail and delivered it to the postmaster, who handed me the outgoing mail in trade.

Departing Golovin for Elim, I gained altitude over Golovin Bay and circled back to cross the Darby Mountains. As Alaskan mountains go they are quite small; usually I'd scoot across them at 1,500 to 2,000 feet. But this day I noticed a fierce east wind whipping layers of snow across the foothills, so I continued the climb to 3,500 feet, as high as I could go and stay below the overcast.

As I neared the crest, the wind appeared to be far more wicked. The mountains were surfaced in streaming whiteness, covered with a 200-foot-thick blanket of blowing snow. Yet I felt I had plenty of altitude as I started over the ridge; I was even high enough to see some open water in the Elim area.

I was soon to have my first encounter with a hazardous phenomenon pilots now know as the standing wave—a very severe downdraft caused by high-velocity winds sweeping the crests of mountains and creating a roll on the leeward side. My first inkling of danger came when the aircraft began to settle, even though I was applying full throttle and had flattened out the prop.

Hindsight shows that would have been the time to turn and get the hell out of there. But I was sure the sinking would stop, so I kept heading into the mountains. The Stinson began to drop at an alarming rate. In a few seconds the downdraft had pulled the plane below the level of the peaks. Belatedly, I realized I was in deep trouble. Even then, I think there might have been enough time to attempt turning back. Had I elected to risk a turn, I might possibly have gotten away with it. But in the few instants I had to consider the alternatives, I decided my best chance lay in continuing my efforts to clear the mountain.

Moments later, I found myself down in the blowing snow, engulfed by the ground drift. I knew I'd had it after being sucked into the swirling snow. There was no hope. I wasn't particularly frightened—just numb.

Rocks passed by indistinctly, shadows in the whiteness, just before I touched the mountainside. The crash was so mild I wasn't sure whether or not I was actually on the ground. In the confusion of air turbulence and blinding snow, I believed I might still be flying. I kept the engine running full-bore, but the shadows stopped passing by. After a minute or so, I realized I couldn't possibly still be flying in the ground drift. Even so, I eased back gingerly on the throttle, just in case.

Miraculously, the aircraft had come to a halt upright, resting on one ski, the left wing in the rocks. That wing tip and the left ski were gone, but my propeller was undamaged. The trailing antenna, with its attached weight, had been out; and even it remained unbroken.

Because of the extremely strong head wind, my forward speed at the time of impact must have been very slow. In essence, I'd made what amounted to a rapid vertical descent onto this godforsaken mountain. My watch showed noon. Outside, a howling gale swept heavy curtains of snow past the cockpit windows. Nothing was visible but glaring whiteness and blowing snow in the brief subarctic daylight.

From time to time I felt the airplane shudder, then move slightly. The wind seemed to be doing its damnedest to blow me off the mountain. I wanted to leave the aircraft but found I couldn't open the door against the pressure exerted by the savage wind. I was effectively sealed inside the plane on this nameless Alaskan peak.

The Stinson was finally steadied against the gusts by the swirling snow, which drifted over the good ski and packed it in solidly. Then drifts gradually formed along the Stinson's belly, further anchoring it to the mountain and eliminating the danger of its sliding backward over the cliffs.

I made several futile attempts to contact Mirow by radio. The plane's very low-power Morse code CW transmitter had been home-built for us by an Army Signal Corps operator living in Nome. Although aircraft radios weren't yet in general use, some of the bush operators had begun to consider them, and Hans Mirow and I had installed this jerry-rigged device for what might be termed an experimental trial.

However, although I worked the key with deliberate precision, I couldn't reach anybody. After a while I decided I'd better save the battery and attempt to contact someone that evening when the signals might be better. The antenna was lying in the snow, and since I was above timberline, there was no possible way to hang it. I just had to hope and pray the signals would transmit from beneath the drifts.

About nine o'clock that night I gave the radio another try. "SOS from KHBWV . . . SOS from KHBWV . . . ." I sent the call repeatedly. Nowadays the N identification number of the aircraft is used for radio transmission, but in those days we were assigned call letters. My call letters, KHBWV, had a certain swing to them as they were sent on CW.

The chances of anyone's hearing my transmission seemed very slim, but I kept trying again and again. I was tuning across the dial when suddenly my call letters came back at me over the receiver. I couldn't believe it!

My distress signal had been picked up by Bob West, radio operator for Pacific Alaska Airways at Nulato, 220 miles east of Nome. Later, he told me that he had happened—for no good reason—to get up and turn on his radio, fiddling with the dial and tuning through the entire band (our frequency was different from Pacific Alaska's), when he heard my SOS. To a CW operator, nothing grabs attention any faster.

As quickly as possible I told him I'd crashed between Golovin and Elim. I said I was uninjured and that the aircraft wasn't too badly damaged. West assured me he'd relay the word to Nome immediately. It was comforting to know someone would soon be out searching.

But I wasn't rescued yet, and who knew how long it would take? When you're waiting for help to come, time drags intolerably. After finally prying open the door and tossing some mail sacks into the snow to make room for myself on the back seat, I fished out my sleeping bag and wriggled into it.

Alone on that bitterly cold mountain, listening to the moaning and shrieking of the arctic wind and watching snow drift up alongside the fuselage, I became increasingly depressed. Even with the radio contact I had made, would it be possible for anyone to find me?

That night was probably the most miserable of my life. The aircraft's interior was completely coated with a layer of frost half an inch thick, converting the cabin into a gloomy deep freeze. Even though I had a

Woods Five-Star down sleeping bag, I was so cramped inside the plane that I slept only in a series of short catnaps. The long, dark hours seemed endless. I welcomed the faint, then brighter, light of day. The wind had slackened, and I was encouraged by the improvement in weather.

When it was light enough to see, I pulled all the mail sacks out of the Stinson and arranged them nearby on the snow, figuring they might make it easier for a search aircraft to spot me. Unfortunately, the airplane I was flying was white with green trim—a color scheme that blended into the snow and probably couldn't be spotted from the air.

In the cargo compartment I found a carpenter's saw and set to work constructing a snow house. The snow on the mountain, packed solid by the high winds, was ideal for the job. Using the carpenter's saw like a knife, I cut the blocks precisely and stacked them carefully. At first I was tempted to make my snow shelter round, but as I fashioned it, I decided a square shape would be good enough for my purposes. I built it meticulously, finding satisfaction in the work.

Near the top I sloped the sides somewhat inward, using a wing cover, which would breathe, for the roof. After I had added an L-shaped entrance tunnel to keep the wind out, my snow house was complete. I crawled in, made myself comfortable, and sat there waiting . . . waiting.

Several times I heard planes flying south of me in the far distance, and I knew the search was on. Even so, it was disconcerting to see them flying so far south. I wondered if I had been significantly off course. I tried the radio again, but no luck—nor were any of my later attempts to make contact successful. The battery no doubt was too weak.

I had emergency rations in a sealed five-gallon can. But in those days before freeze-dried foods, the rations were distinctly unappetizing. There were chocolate bars, which had a tendency to go rancid and make you sick. There were also some sardines and rice in the can. I decided to combine everything into a kind of slumgullion, using a plumber's firepot to heat the mess.

That second day on the mountain I went to bed as soon as it was dark. I found my snow house very comfortable and spent a good night. The next day I cooked more slumgullion. The poor quality of the food killed my appetite for more than one meal a day.

The hardest thing was just passing the time. I opened the mail sacks and took out some periodicals, but was forced to give up my attempt at reading. It was too cold outside, and inside my snow house the light was too poor. Sleeping was my only escape. By the third day I found that I was almost able to hibernate, and I increased my sleeping period to nearly twenty hours a day.

When the weather turned bad and I heard no more search planes, the hope I had kept kindled began to erode. This was the first time I had ever been totally alone, completely isolated from everyone.

A sense of hopelessness crept over me. I tried to give myself pep talks, but logic told me I might not survive. Each passing hour brought me closer to that realization. My mind began to wander, and all sorts of grim thoughts kept cropping up.

New hope stirred at dawn on the fourth day. The skies were clear, searchers had excellent weather, and I thought they'd find me for sure. Several airplanes flew close by; two flew directly overhead.

I carried a 30.06 rifle in the Stinson and had stored it in the snow house. As search planes passed overhead, I'd wave frantically, but it was obvious they hadn't spotted me. A kind of frustrated rage seized me at those times, so much so that I felt an irrational urge to shoot at them as they flew away.

By the end of the fourth day I was totally discouraged, realizing it was possible I might never be found. Not for the first time, I wondered if I should try to walk out.

There are few options open to a pilot who survives a wintertime crash in Alaska's wilderness. As in my situation, you are usually reduced to two grim choices: stay with the plane, hoping searchers will rescue you before you die; or strike out for civilization, gambling you'll find food and shelter before being overcome by exhaustion and the elements. Down through the years of Alaskan aviation history, scores of planes have vanished without a trace. Undoubtedly, among these tragedies have been instances of pilots who survived and had to choose one of these terrible options.

As the days dragged by, I was continually faced with the same dilemma. Walk out? I was sure I wouldn't have a prayer. Ordinarily we carried snowshoes, but for some reason I didn't have them aboard this flight. I could imagine the grueling, sub-zero, snow-swept miles of frozen Alaskan terrain cutting me off from help. How many miles could I conceivably trudge through the drifts in the face of those killing, icy winds? Ten? Twenty maybe? And then . . . ?

The other option seemed better. For one thing, it meant less suffering. Here, I had the shelter of the plane, the snow house, the sleeping bag. My chances of being spotted certainly were far greater than if I attempted to strike out across those bleak, forbidding stretches of mountain, ice, and snow. Then I'd be an indiscernible dot from the air.

Win or lose, I decided to stick with the airplane—to the end, if it came to that.

On the fifth day, it began snowing again. Drifting snow buried the irregular, dark line of mail sacks that might have alerted search pilots to my whereabouts. My hopes dropped to a low ebb, and dark despair settled over me. I ate my daily meal and attempted to sleep through as much of the time as I could.

The sixth day dawned clear and very cold. I crawled out of my igloo and began dusting off the mail sacks, in the fading hope that they might be spotted. Then, incredibly near, I heard one of the most welcome sounds I've ever experienced—an aircraft zooming close overhead.

It was a Ferguson Airways Stinson flown by Jack Hermann. I saw the aircraft turn and climb, then dive toward me. I waved my arms wildly as it swooped overhead.

I wasn't at all sure what was going to happen next. Hermann kept circling, but there wasn't any place to land within miles. From his flight pattern, however, I figured he must have something up his sleeve. I happened to glance across the rugged valley below, where I spotted a dark, thin line moving slowly across the background of whiteness about three miles away. Approaching were two dog teams hitched in tandem, about twenty-one dogs in all.

The yelping teams stretched against the pure white snowfield like a long, narrow freight train. The parka-clad mushers had spotted me and were headed my way. My ordeal was nearly over. Hermann circled overhead until he was convinced the mushers had seen me. Then, after wagging his wings, he turned and headed back toward Nome.

A few minutes later the two native mushers from Golovin reached me. Saved! For me it was an exhilarating meeting on that lonely mountain, and I couldn't thank those two mushers enough.

Later I learned that after Bob West received my SOS at Nulato, he spread the word to Nome. The Mirow office in Nome contacted Golovin, requesting they dispatch a dog team to search for me. Two of Golovin's young reindeer herders had been scouring the hills ever since. They just happened to be in the vicinity when Jack Hermann spotted me; he directed them to the crash site.

After all the seemingly endless hours I'd endured, the rest of the afternoon sped by. The mushers told me that we would spend the night at a cabin they knew of, off the mountain about seven miles away. One of the boys got a pair of skis out of the sled and skied off down the side of the mountain, down a slope that seemed almost vertical. This fantastic skier carried a teakettle and promised he'd have hot tea waiting at the cabin when the other driver and I arrived.

But my ordeal wasn't entirely over—not quite. As we were going down the steep mountain, the lead dog suddenly swerved off the side of a steep bank. The sled overturned, tumbling all our provisions into the deep snow. The twenty-one dogs, members of two rival teams, promptly started the damnedest dog fight I've ever seen.

Somehow the driver finally got the dogs sorted out and restrained. Then we began a search through the snow to retrieve the scattered food and sleeping bags. In the deepening dusk the job took more than an hour, but at last we located everything and proceeded toward the cabin.

It was dark when we reached the small reindeer herder's hut, just a tiny shelter, not more than twelve feet by twelve. But never in my life have I enjoyed greater luxury, not even at the fanciest hotels. The skier had lighted a cozy fire, and the warm glow of a kerosene lantern dispelled the darkness.

While the two young men fed and secured the dogs, I appointed myself cook, broiling reindeer steaks they'd brought with them from Golovin. I felt so starved for human companionship after six days alone that, following our nourishing meal, I couldn't help talking all the time.

I was inexpressibly grateful to those two wonderful Eskimo youths— and so damn glad to get off the mountain and have a bellyful of good food. I was determined I ought to do something for them, but the only thing I had to offer was conversation. So I launched into a long monologue, enlightening the boys about the North American continent, America's great cities, and Lord knows what else.

Being of a polite, taciturn people, the pair let me run off at the mouth without comment. My tedious oration depicted city life in detail, elaborating on metropolitan wonders such as streetcars, buses, and subways in the most elementary terms. "You know," I continued, "some tall buildings in the Lower Forty-eight have elevators. These are big boxes that people get into, and then a cable pulls them way up to the top of the building or lets them down to any level. That way, they don't have to climb any stairs."

One of the boys apparently had taken about as much as he could. "I understand," he said. "You know, Jack, the elevator in Radio City is really fast. It almost takes your breath away."

That shut me up. After a brief recovery, I asked, "Then you fellows have been Outside?"

"Oh, yes," one of them responded. "We've been in every state in the Union."

Come to find out, they'd been on tour for a soft drink known as Cliquot Club Eskimo. To promote it, the youths had toured all over the country with a dog team, appeared on theater stages, and traveled one hell of a lot more than I ever had.

In their own unassuming way, they had handed me one of the worst put-downs I've ever experienced, there in that little reindeer herder's cabin near Golovin. And I certainly deserved it.

The next day we made Golovin. Mirow Air Service sent me a welding outfit and the parts to repair the wing tip, and the Eskimos agreed to take me back to the airplane by dog team.

We were able to jack up the plane, and I welded the landing gear back in place. Though crude, the repair job made the plane flyable. With the help of the two herders, I turned the Stinson to face down slope and was able to get it moving down the steep mountainside, finally getting up enough airspeed to lift off.

In a way, it was ironic. My rescue had depended on the use of a dog team—the very mode of delivery I'd supplanted on the bush mail runs. And the Stinson also owed a debt of gratitude to the dog team, for without them she would have spent her remaining days on the Darby Mountains.

6
Groping Up the Yukon

THE DECADE OF THE THIRTIES marked a transition period for mail delivery to the bush villages. Dog-team drivers began facing sporadic competition from air service operators. By the end of the decade, regular air mail schedules had virtually taken over.

A rather unusual system had been used when aircraft first began carrying the mail, and in my opinion it was a very good one. Any pilot could go to the post office in Fairbanks and pick up all the first class mail destined for Nome. The rate of pay was fifty cents a pound. If a pilot were flying to any of the smaller villages, he could also take their mail and be paid an additional twenty-five cents a pound. The deliveries amounted only to pin money, but every pilot would stop by the post office and make a few bucks that way.

The wheels of progress changed this efficient, informal system. Contracts for the mail were put out each year and were awarded to the lowest bidder. They usually specified a 500-pound payload of mail.

Winters were a slack time for flying, so Mirow bid on a large number of contracts for the small villages—which the post office euphemistically called Star Routes. Mirow entered the low bids, and our aircraft displaced the dogsleds. We began flying the mail.

Our longest route began at St. Michael, then crossed to the Yukon. We made many intermediate stops at small communities up and down the river, finally ending the trip at Fortuna Ledge (now also known as Marshall).

Fall was very late in coming the first year of our contract, and freeze-up was long delayed. There had been some snow, but the rivers were not frozen heavily enough for our ski landings until quite late in the season. The people of the villages were understandably angry and not at all content with mail delivery via aircraft.

And they resented another thing. The dog teams made the trip rather slowly, and the drivers would stay overnight in each village. That enabled the people to read their mail and answer any letters they might have received. We, on the other hand, came wheeling through with about a ten-minute stop.

I sometimes think Hans had an ulterior motive in sending me out on those first mail trips, knowing I might have to deal with some hostile people. Later everyone became accustomed to air delivery of mail, and of course it's now accepted as the regular thing.

Unalakleet was one of the larger villages along the western coast and was more or less centrally located with respect to most of my routes. I based there during the winter months, lodging with Charlie Traeger. Charlie, who owned the local trading post, rented me a bunk in the living area above his store. Charlie always traded fairly and was one of the all-around nicest people I've ever known. He was also an accomplished cook. I spent the winter very pleasantly boarding with him in Unalakleet while flying the mail on our new bush routes.

On Mondays and Thursdays I'd leave Unalakleet on a twice-weekly mail trip to Kaltag and Nulato, two villages along the Yukon River. Flying northeastward toward Kaltag on February 17, 1939, I found myself under a fairly low overcast. It was pretty obvious that another large winter storm would soon be moving into our area. I was carrying the mail in the Gullwing Stinson, the airplane I'd retrieved only three months earlier from the mountains near Golovin.

I flew past Kaltag, planning to stop there on the return flight, and continued my way north to Nulato. By the time I reached the village, it was snowing very heavily. With the worsening weather, I was concerned that I might not be able to make it back to Unalakleet. So I cut my stay rather short and started back downriver to Kaltag.

The weather kept getting worse, and before long, visibility dropped to less than a mile. Fortunately, I knew the area well and had the river to guide me. Once I got to Kaltag I planned to tie up for the day and wait for better weather.

After landing in the snow on the sandbar west of town, I was securing the airplane for the night when Edgar Kalland, one of the village leaders, came running down. "Jack," he panted. "You're going to have to go to Tanana. We've got an injured man in the schoolhouse, and you've got to get him to the hospital."

It was still snowing heavily, and the wind had begun to rise. I couldn't even see across the river. "Edgar, there's just no way—it's impossible to fly. I was lucky to have found my way into town. I'd sure go if I could, but it's just impossible."

I saw Kalland's dark eyes studying me as he remained silent for a time. Then he spoke. "Well, you go tell him the bad news. *You* tell the guy you can't take him."

I accompanied Edgar up to the schoolhouse and stepped inside, glad to be out of the cold and snow. There on a makeshift bed lay Frank Alba, a grizzled old prospector, moaning in agony and ashen with pain. His pelvis had been broken in a freak fall from a dogsled. After his team ran off, Alba crawled several miles through the snow into town. He was in such misery that, after one look at him, I thought, "I've got to go."

"Can you get some fellows to help me top off my tanks with gasoline?" I asked Edgar. "I'll have to follow the river, and I'll need all the fuel the Stinson will hold."

In those days we burned 73 octane in our planes, a pretty versatile fuel that could be used in almost any engine. So nearly every store and trading post stocked at least a little bit of canned gasoline suitable for aircraft. Edgar headed up to the store and returned with the five-gallon gasoline cans packed on a sled. Some of the villagers trudged down to the plane with us and helped fill the tanks. We didn't stop until they overflowed. Then Frank Alba was brought down on a sled.

He suffered horribly while we loaded him into the Stinson. Although we tried to be gentle, we had to double him up a little to get him inside the plane. The pain was so excruciating that Alba finally passed out. We spread out a sleeping bag for padding and propped him in the back seat as comfortably as possible.

"I'll come along with you," Kalland said. "I might be able to help."

I wouldn't have asked him, but I was glad he volunteered. Edgar had been a fireman on the steamer *Nenana* and knew every island, crook, and bend in the river. His navigational expertise might help us keep from becoming lost. In the heavy snow and fog, I was dependent strictly on following the river. There would be no cross-country shortcuts.

We started groping our way up the river, catching a quick glimpse of Ruby as we went by. I kept the Stinson low over the ice, trying to follow the thin line of black spruce on the south bank. The south shore seemed the better choice, since there were hills on the north side of the river between Ruby and Tanana. We struggled to stay with the main channel, trying to avoid being lured up any of the countless sloughs that fork off the river.

The distance from Kaltag to Tanana is over 200 miles in a direct line, but our winding course took us a great deal farther. With each mile I continued to hope the weather might let up, but it seemed only to worsen.

The village of Tanana is located on the north side of the Yukon, just downstream from the confluence of the Yukon and Tanana rivers. In the fog and snow, we managed to miss the town completely—and in following the south bank, we mistakenly went up the Tanana River.

Even Edgar became confused. By the time he had seen enough to be certain of our position, we were at a bend of the Tanana River at least thirty miles beyond our original destination. Rather than turn back we decided to push on to Fairbanks. There, medical facilities were much better than at Tanana, so Frank should be able to receive more specialized treatment. And, having missed the village the first time, we weren't too sure we'd find it on a second go-round.

We continued up the Tanana. Our next big concern was the Alaska Railroad bridge, which crosses the river at the town of Nenana. Darkness was falling, and I was having to fly so low that I was afraid of slamming into the trestle. But I had to keep the Tanana River in sight. Without it, we'd be lost.

If the Nenana power plant were working, we should see lights on the bridge. Or, at the very least, the lights of Nenana itself might give us some warning. Kalland shared my concern; he was calling out the direction of each new bend, telling me what to expect and estimating our distance from Nenana.

I've noticed (and it's probably true for all pilots) that time seems to pass very slowly when you're under stress. I'd think I'd flown an hour, then I'd look at my watch to find that just five minutes had passed. But eventually we saw the hazy glow of some lights as we moved through the snowy murk over the town of Nenana. Thankfully, we found that the bridge was lighted, and we carefully flew above its network of ice-encrusted girders.

The Tanana River makes a ninety-degree bend at Nenana; we followed its curve, heading northeasterly on our last forty or so air miles to Fairbanks.

We'd put every last possible ounce of gasoline into the Stinson's tanks before leaving Kaltag. Even so, the needle of my fuel gauge was now riding just above empty. We'd been flying for so long that there couldn't be much left. At that point I was already feeling so bad that I didn't really care. After nearly four hours of tension, worry, and terrific eyestrain from trying to stay on top of the mostly hidden river, I was suffering from a massive headache. I had gotten to where I just wanted to be finished with this damned flight, no matter how. Running into a sheer rock bluff would have been fine. At least we'd be done.

The Tanana River couldn't take us all the way to Fairbanks. It flows about eight miles south of the city. However, a small tributary, the Chena River, passes directly through the city. The Chena forms a large slough at its mouth on the Tanana. We hoped we could find it in the darkness and snow.

The rotating beacon on the Fairbanks federal building was usually a good marker into the city. On an evening with any kind of visibility, the beacon could be seen for miles. But it was of no help tonight. With our fuel practically down to fumes, we couldn't do much looking. We had to come straight in.

I worked the CW set and was able to establish communication with Gillam Airlines in Fairbanks. I radioed our predicament to Tom Appleton, who was out at their hangar on Weeks Field. He sweated it out with us as we tried to find our way into town.

Appleton rounded up as many people as he could find and had them park their cars along the perimeter of the strip. The headlamps, along with a bunch of flares carefully placed by Clyde Armistead of Alaska Airmotive, illuminated the unlighted field. Tom also stationed some friends around the city at various listening posts—hoping to hear our engine and direct us to town.

After what seemed like hours, Appleton radioed that they'd heard us; we were in audio range of Fairbanks. We were lucky and discovered Chena Slough, following it right through town. About three-quarters of a mile out, I saw the glow of the flares and headlights from the cars at Weeks Field. In moments we were on the ground.

Kalland and I climbed down and helped load Frank Alba into the ambulance Appleton had called.

Out of curiosity, I checked the fuel tanks before going to the hotel for a badly needed rest. Only a few spoonfuls remained, maybe enough for two or three more minutes of flight.

Looking back at this incident (one of my very worst experiences in the air), I believe its length is what sets it apart from the other tense situations I've encountered. Most panic situations resolve themselves in a few minutes. But that night we were in continual difficulty, unable to relax for an instant from the moment we took off until we landed—more than four hours of groping up the Yukon.

7
Guiding the Columbia

THERE SEEMED TO BE no way out for the steamship *Columbia,* caught in the jaws of heavy pack ice near the mouth of the Yukon River in early June, 1939, with nearly 500 men, women, and children aboard.

The *Columbia,* under the command of Captain "Andy" Anderson, had been making her way north to Nome on a supposedly routine trip. Radio reports from the Alaska Signal Corps kept us informed of the ship's progress. Nome's winter-weary population was eagerly awaiting fresh supplies of food and the arrival of friends and relatives.

With the announcement that the *Columbia* had left Dutch Harbor for Nome, escorted by a Coast Guard cutter and an amphibian aircraft, many of us could already see fresh eggs sizzling in the pan and crisp, green lettuce gracing our salad bowls. We were like kids waiting excitedly for Christmas—until the grim news came.

The captain of the *Columbia* radioed that he was encountering heavy concentrations of ice near the mouth of the Yukon. Conditions were so bad that the Coast Guard cutter and the amphibian had been forced to return to Dutch Harbor. The *Columbia* was left to struggle on toward Nome alone.

Twenty-four hours later, we received another message: The *Columbia* was hopelessly jammed in the ice. The captain requested help from Nome, an aerial survey to find him a path out of the ice pack. Our Lockheed Vega was the only aircraft in Nome with enough range to handle the mission. But there was a problem. The Vega was not yet equipped with radio, and communication with the ship would be essential if we were to pilot the *Columbia* out of its icy trap.

One of the operators at the Alaska Signal Corps said he thought he could rig up a two-way radio that would let us talk to the ship. The *Columbia* did not have voice transmission facilities, but he figured we could receive their messages sent in Morse code—and hope that their equipment would handle our voice reply. As the only pilot in Nome proficient at receiving CW, I was given the dubious honor of making the trip.

The makeshift radio, mounted on a breadboard in the back of the Vega, was truly a piece of junk. We cut an antenna to the proper length for our frequency, and loaded in a couple of batteries to power the set. My brother, Bill, volunteered to come along to help with the radio and string out the antenna through the aircraft's door. Then, as prepared as possible under the rushed conditions, we were ready to start our evening reconnaissance flight.

Finding the vessel was our first challenge. We edged around Norton Sound, tracing that large indentation on the Alaskan coast past Unalakleet then back out toward St. Michael and the mouth of the Yukon. The *Columbia* had radioed its position to the Signal Corps, which supplied us with marine charts and helped us lay a course to the stricken ship. Flying out to sea on the compass heading we'd plotted on the chart, we began sending radio messages toward the *Columbia.* Although the range of our jerry-built equipment was limited, we hoped we might get at least fifty-mile reception.

At one point the radio quit working altogether. Bill tinkered with it but finally gave up in exasperation, so I said I'd have a try at fixing it. That meant changing places in flight—a tricky maneuver in the Vega. I pushed myself backwards into the cabin through the little door behind the pilot's seat. Bill squirmed forward through the hole, taking over the controls while I examined the radio. Finally, I found a loose connection, and we were back in operation.

Bill and I changed places again, and once more I began sending calls to the *Columbia.* Suddenly the miserable little set began chattering. The *Columbia* had answered.

Despite the radio contact, we still couldn't see the ship through the dusk and surface fog, although at this time of the year there were nearly twenty-four hours of daylight. "Turn on all your lights," we told the skipper, hoping this would make the ship more visible. After acknowledging our request, the captain advised us that he'd also had the engine room start a lot of smoke billowing up through the stacks.

Whether from good navigation or sheer luck, about an hour later we finally spotted the columns of smoke and the lights twinkling from stem to stern. We zeroed in on the *Columbia,* a pathetic sight trapped in the crushing ice. As we passed over in the Lockheed the captain blew several long blasts on the whistle, and the crowds on deck waved up at us.

The passengers had been going without baths due to the dwindling supply of fresh water. To relieve the food shortage, the crew had been forced to open some of the cargo consigned to Nome. The miners were losing money each day they were stranded at sea. Everyone was becoming nervous, irritable, and apprehensive.

I suppose the arrival of our little airplane over the suffering ship might have seemed to some of them like the dove that appeared on Noah's Ark. At the time, we felt we would do them about as much good.

"It looks pretty hopeless," I told the ship. "There's heavy pack ice for miles. Ice all around as far as we can see. I'll head out toward St. Lawrence Island. The water's deeper there, and a current passing the east side of the island might have opened up a lead not too far from your position."

I'm sure nobody down there was cheering at our assessment of the boat's predicament. Our somber view of the ship's chances didn't change as we headed northwest, passed over St. Lawrence Island, then proceeded on to King Island and back to Nome without seeing a single lead in all that vast distance.

Although the situation seemed hopeless I couldn't very well give up. There were nearly 500 people trapped out there in the ice. I decided to leave early the next morning with full tanks of gas and head directly for the ship. Curt Springer, the Coast Guard representative at Nome, volunteered to take Bill's place and trail the antenna from the door.

Ordinarily, we tried to avoid long flights over water in our single-engine aircraft, but this time it seemed worth the gamble. Going around the coast ate up so much fuel that, after finding the ship, I would have very little time left to scout the ice. I knew that if I failed to reach the ship by the direct approach, I could turn eastward toward land, find the mouth of the Yukon, and then retrace the previous day's course to make a successful rendezvous.

To our amazement, the direct course to the ship put us over ice-free water—miles and miles of it. I established communication with the ship and had to cross only about eight miles of pack ice before we again found the *Columbia.*

"Your only chance of getting out of there is to steer a direct course for Nome," I told the captain as I circled. "We'll stay and try to guide you through the pack ice to the open lead. Then you ought to have smooth sailing all the way to town." There was enough fog that visibility from the boat was practically zero.

"Will do," his answer came back.

Springer positioned a big marine compass on the floor of the plane's cabin, planning to give me headings to relay to the boat. But the mix of marine and aircraft directions quickly caused confusion. To put it mildly, our attempt at steering the *Columbia* out of the ice by this method wasn't going too well.

I finally stopped sending the compass headings and also quit the *starboard* and *port* jazz—in favor of good old *right* and *left*. "Turn left," I'd radio to the helmsman, and we'd watch as the ship dutifully turned to the left until it was pointing the way I wanted. "Stop turn," I'd say, and the turn would end, the great ship beginning to set a straight course.

Very, very slowly the *Columbia* began to move through the pack ice. I know the passage was pretty tough on the boat, because we could see long streaks of paint, barnacles, and rust left behind on the ice as the vessel squeezed its way through. Contact with the ice eventually sprung some plates, causing extreme concern on the bridge as the boat started to leak.

The strain of that tense situation began to tell on the captain. In caustic remarks relayed to us by radio, he questioned our ability to guide the ship from above. Several times I felt like telling him to jam it. I'd much rather have been safely at home than circling precariously far out over the Bering Sea—trying to get his ship out of her miserable mess and, on top of everything else, getting cussed out for it. But even when I wished I'd never become involved, I knew I had to see it through.

I kept the airplane throttled down to where our fuel consumption was at a minimum. After what seemed like ages, but was actually only about five hours, we got the *Columbia* back into open water. "That's it!" I radioed to the boat. "Clear sailing to Nome."

I'll never forget seeing the back end of the boat sink perceptibly as the skipper rang for full speed ahead. She really took off.

We flew back to Nome and passed on the welcome tidings that the *Columbia* should be arriving in less than twenty-four hours. All through the night the Alaska Signal Corps kept close track of the boat's position. As she got nearer, new notices were posted every few minutes at the Alaska Steamship Company bulletin board on Front Street, telling how many miles remained.

It was an ungodly hour of the morning when smoke from the *Columbia* showed on the southern horizon, but even at that hour Nome's streets were thronged with people in a holiday mood. Excitement raced through town. The *Columbia* had been sighted!

After the *Columbia* dropped anchor, I went out on the first lighter to meet Captain Anderson and discuss the adventure with him. Despite our few bad moments earlier, I found him a likeable person and would have enjoyed spending more time with him.

But for us in the aviation business, the arrival of the first boat meant the heat was on. I went back to shore with the first lighter load, knowing that another big airlift out of Nome was about to begin.

I guess I became somewhat of a hero with the townspeople after the *Columbia* episode. Not that they gave a damn about me or the boat—but they were mighty glad to get those fresh provisions.

8

The Evacuation of Jack Devine

ONE DAY I FOUND MYSELF wandering around Nome, bored, passing the time as best I could. I'd been making repeated, routine flights to Fairbanks and Anchorage, and the same runs over and over again to the many native villages scattered across the Seward Peninsula. The same people, the same faces. To some, the life of a bush pilot might appear exciting, but the routine had become quite stale.

By about three o'clock I had made the rounds of all my usual haunts, so I headed over to the office. Even before I finished closing the door, the office manager was out of his chair, gesturing excitedly. "Where the hell have you been, Jefford? We've been looking for you all afternoon!"

"Well," I replied, "I was out visiting. Just came from the marshal's office. What's up?"

"Plenty! Go home and pack your bag. You're headed for Seattle."

He explained that Senator Jack Devine, a member of the Territorial Legislature, had just suffered a series of heart attacks. Doctors at Nome's hospital were convinced his only hope was to get to Seattle for more sophisticated treatment.

I was in my twenties then, with more guts than brains. The proposed flight was a very long one over territory completely unfamiliar to me, but the mission was so urgent I really didn't take time to weigh the risks. I set a world speed record getting packed and out to the airstrip.

We rigged a bed for Devine in the Lockheed Vega. The plan was to proceed with him to Fairbanks, Whitehorse, Prince George, and

Seattle, trying to make the entire trip without a layover.

After we had fueled and everything was ready, Devine was carried out to the Vega, accompanied by his wife, who asked that we stop in Unalakleet to pick up the Senator's old friend, a reindeer manager named Sam Kendricks.

My logbook shows I left Nome June 26, 1939. We made the short stop at Unalakleet to pick up Kendricks, then took off for Fairbanks. Although we arrived around midnight, it was just after the longest day of the year, so there was still plenty of light.

We refueled rapidly. I was anxious about Devine's condition and hated to spend any more time on the ground than necessary. But then we had a rather lengthy delay with United States Customs. During those years the government required everyone to clear Customs before leaving Alaska, and our office had failed to notify them of our planned midnight arrival. As soon as we were able, we were off and running for Whitehorse, Yukon Territory.

I had only a few Canadian maps. Compared to the excellent maps that pilots have today, mine were just patchy things, geological surveys. One might be drawn at a scale of one mile to the inch, the next at thirty miles to the inch.

I didn't anticipate too much of a problem finding Whitehorse, but I expected that navigation would be tougher on the rest of the journey. Using a large map of the entire North American continent, I plotted some lines with a protractor and figured that from Whitehorse to Prince George a heading of about 120 degrees would get me in the ball park.

I also had been briefed by Hans Mirow, who had flown the route from Prince George to Whitehorse by way of Hazelton and Telegraph Creek. That route was farther west than my direct line, but Hans pointed out that the watershed ran pretty much southeast. If you just got on a big river and stayed with it, you would eventually get to Prince George.

We had installed radio equipment, but it was low-power and its frequencies were incompatible with those used in Canada and the continental United States. In essence, our radio proved worthless after leaving Fairbanks.

We made Whitehorse from Fairbanks in three hours and forty-five minutes—not too shabby, even with one of today's propeller aircraft. Since I had been unable to contact Whitehorse by radio, we had another unfortunate delay. I had to find a cab and haul our fuel in five-gallon cans. Though the people at Canadian Customs and Immigration were very cooperative and cleared us in just a few minutes, we lost quite a bit of time refueling and it was well into the morning before we shoved off for Prince George. Mrs. Devine attended to Jack as best she could, but he had lapsed into semiconsciousness and there really wasn't much she could do.

Out of Whitehorse I had one of the better maps and some pretty good checkpoints. Teslin Lake was an unmistakable marker, and once I saw it I was relatively sure my heading would not miss Prince George by too great a margin. My calculations showed I'd only have forty-five minutes of fuel left when I arrived at Prince George, so I couldn't afford to be too far off course.

The engine was running smoothly, the airplane was performing beautifully as usual, and the weather was good. Though I was getting somewhat punchy from lack of sleep, things seemed to be in good shape.

But the gods of fate always have their little surprises in store for pilots. After having passed our point of no return (more than half our fuel was gone and we could not turn back to Whitehorse), ahead on the horizon I could see a huge thunderstorm barring our path. While it's not usual to run into a thunderstorm at noon, this time it happened.

That towering black wall of clouds was a fearsome thing, at least a couple hundred miles across. There was simply no way around it. The closer I got the more ominous it looked. It became pretty obvious that, like it or not, I was going to have to bore through this fully developed thunderstorm—something I had studiously avoided all my life. Everything I'd ever heard about thunderstorms was nothing but bad news.

I scribbled a brief note and handed it back to the passengers: "We've got a thunderstorm ahead. Prepare for a rough ride." That was the understatement of the year.

I wasn't too sure of my position. (As it turned out I was over the Parsnip River, about 125 miles out of Prince George, when I encountered the storm.) It was time to put into practice a bit of advice I'd garnered from airline pilots flying the new DC-3s: the best altitude at which to penetrate a thunderstorm lies about halfway between the ground and the base of the cloud. Lightning began to blaze, dazzling bursts and jagged flashes illuminating the sky in all directions. I'd never seen so much lightning in all my life.

Metal planes have often been hit by lightning; in fact, on several occasions I would later be piloting metal aircraft when they were hit by lightning. In a metal plane there's usually no cause to get too excited. But in the all-wood Vega? I had seen what happens to a tree that has been hit by lightning, and I imagined the Vega would disintegrate into a pinwheel of splinters in exactly the same fashion.

I was still worrying about the lightning when we passed into a wall of rain. We began encountering moderate turbulence, then severe turbulence. As the saying goes, "It was frightening, and I'm fearless." The Lockheed shuddered and danced uncontrollably in the shifting currents. Sudden freefalling sensations alternated with great upward-wrenching thrusts. Next, hailstones began to slam against the plane. The hail driving against the leading edge of the hollow wooden wings sounded not unlike what might be heard inside a kettle drum at full crescendo. The roar was absolutely deafening.

In the midst of this uncertain passage, I became aware of a strong odor of whiskey. A glance through the peephole behind me revealed Sam Kendricks and Mrs. Devine handing a fifth of bourbon back and forth. I've always marveled at the way some passengers will try to smooth the troubled air with alcohol. But I can't say I blamed them. With all the noise, turbulence, lightning, and hail, any sort of tranquilizer would have been most welcome.

Thunderstorms are usually not too wide, and that one probably wasn't. But when you're scared out of your wits, five minutes can seem an eternity. Eventually the sky became lighter and we popped out of the storm. Beyond, all was bright and serene. It was difficult to believe that anything so terrifying had ever happened.

We began to see signs of civilization—a cabin here and there, some dirt roads. In a few minutes we were over a railroad, and it was a simple matter to follow the tracks on to Prince George.

Considering that Mrs. Devine and Sam Kendricks had been without food since leaving Nome the day before, that they'd lost a lot of sleep during the night, and that they'd consumed Lord knows how many swigs of raw whiskey, it was pretty obvious they'd be smashed when we landed.

The airport was a few miles south of town. I circled the city, then set down on the excellent grass strip. A provincial policeman drove up, and I rapidly explained the situation to him. Here we had a man apparently dying and two passengers in their cups. The whole operation aroused a bit of suspicion, but the policeman gave me a ride into town where I made arrangements for fuel and coffee and sandwiches to take back to the airport. Again, the gas was in five-gallon cans. The airplane was almost empty and seemed to take forever to refuel.

We tried to keep Jack Devine as comfortable as possible, but it was very warm and the aircraft was stuffy. Sam opened the window escape hatch to get a little ventilation. After eating, he and Mrs. Devine napped in the passenger seats.

Most of the afternoon was gone before I finally got squared around.

It was obvious that it would be dark by the time I got to Seattle, since the lower latitudes do not share the Far North's twenty-four-hour daylight.

As I paid for the fuel, I thought, "Just one more leg of this flight and I've got it made." I entered the cockpit through the overhead hatch, cranked up the engine, and started to take off.

The plane had barely begun moving when the provincial policeman darted ahead of us in his car, frantically waving at us to stop. I shut down, slid the hatch back, and stood up. "One of your passengers has his feet out the window," the policeman yelled, pointing at the plane. Sure enough, Sam had fallen asleep with his feet dangling out of the escape hatch. I got Sam's feet back inside, the hatch closed, and we were airborne for Seattle.

Two hours after we left Prince George, it started to get dark. However, I was pretty well established on the Fraser River and had a good high ceiling, though it was overcast. Finally the city of Vancouver showed up on my right. To the south I could see a few towns and in the extreme distance, my destination—Seattle.

While we had radio, none of the frequencies were compatible with the equipment at Seattle, where a control tower had just been established. It was my first tower-controlled landing. Circling the airport, I got a green light and went in to land.

Somehow the local press had gotten wind of our arrival, and while we waited for the ambulance, a couple of reporters approached us. To my astonishment, the next day's Seattle papers carried my picture and the story of our flight splashed over the front pages. We had made the trip—about 2,200 miles—in a total of sixteen and one-half hours flying time, twenty-four hours elapsed time. It was not, I felt, a bad performance.

Despite our effort, Jack Devine passed away during the night at Virginia Mason Hospital. Mrs. Devine called me the following morning with the sad news. The funeral had been arranged, and she asked me to be one of the pallbearers.

At the funeral parlor I met the other pallbearers, including an eighty-five-year-old prospector, obviously quite infirm. I remember feeling some misgivings about his ability to carry the load, as it were.

As we bore the casket out of the mortuary, I was in the middle on the right-hand side and the old-timer was on the front end. Just as we started down a small flight of stairs, he fell. For a moment it looked as though we were going to drop the casket, but I was braced for it. The strain was such that the handles bent up against the side of the coffin.

The mortician leaped forward and grabbed hold of the casket for an important instant. Then someone helped the shaken old-timer to his feet. But the thought crossed my mind that Jack Devine was leaving in a style pretty much in keeping with his adventurous trip down from Nome.

9

The Stinson-A Trimotor

THE VEGA WAS DUE for a major engine overhaul, so I stayed in Seattle for nearly a week following Jack Devine's funeral while the shop work was being completed at Northwest Air Service. I had an abundance of time on my hands. Being a member of the Army Air Corps Reserve, I decided to spend most of it with the local squadron. I put in quite a few hours behind the controls of their most recent acquisition, a P-12F pursuit, and grew very fond of the aircraft.

Seattle was a welcome change from Nome. After a pleasant week in the big city, I was preparing for the return flight to Alaska in the newly overhauled Lockheed when I received a lengthy telegram from Hans Mirow. He wanted me to go to Cincinnati and examine an airplane offered for sale by American Airlines, a ten-place Stinson-A Trimotor which they had been using on their regular schedules. It was slated for replacement, as American was upgrading its fleet with the new DC-3s.

Hans said he would forward a cashier's check, and if the Stinson-A looked good, I was to buy it and fly it back to Nome. To me, this was a terrific challenge—a bigger airplane, one with three engines.

By a lucky coincidence, my association with the Reserve squadron enabled me to fly to Ohio's Wright-Patterson Field as a crew member for Major George W. Kinney—later General Kinney of South Pacific fame. From there I caught a bus to Cincinnati and went out to the airport to check out the Stinson-A.

I liked her. She was right out of the fleet and in mint condition. After one of the mechanics ran up the engines for me, I was convinced. On behalf of Mirow Air Service, I accepted NC-15154, the Stinson-A.

An official from American's finance department flew down from Chicago to help expedite the necessary paperwork. The whole transaction took just a short while. Now all I needed was a check ride; then I'd be on my way north.

We went over to American's dispatch office and found that one of the new DC-3s was scheduled to land in about an hour. Its captain, an old Stinson-A expert, would give me whatever dual time I required to safely ferry the airplane to Seattle and then on to Alaska.

The Stinson-A was fueled and made ready for my check flight. As I strolled across American's parking lot, I couldn't help noticing a gorgeous, well-built blonde sitting in a late model convertible. It turned out that she was also waiting for the captain to arrive.

When we met, the captain seemed understandably irritated. He'd flown his day's work and now, instead of going home with this luscious dish, he had to check out some joker—namely me—in the Stinson-A. As we shook hands I got the feeling this was going to be the shortest check ride in history.

He flew once around the pattern and landed. Then he instructed me to do the same. I lucked out and made a fairly good landing. "Try it again," he commented. "If you make the next one that good, you're all set."

Fortunately for the captain and the blonde, I did all right. After a brief farewell, he jumped into his car and roared out of the lot without a backward glance. I was on my own with our new Stinson-A. I topped off the fuel tanks, tossed my gear into the aircraft, and headed west.

The plane sure seemed large to me as I flew high over the Ohio countryside, especially since I had very little multi-engine time. Also, I found the aircraft's fuel management a bit confusing, so I decided to run on the reserve and see how long it would last. What I didn't know was that the reserve was a standpipe in the right main tank; if you ran on the reserve, you were also depleting the main supply.

I kept a concerned eye on the reserve gauge as it went down very, very slowly. Normal procedure was to exhaust the main tank's fuel, then switch to the reserve. What I was doing, instead, was consuming fuel from both the reserve and the main tanks.

Completely unaware of this, I was flying westward, fat, dumb, and happy, thinking I had plenty of fuel. When the reserve tank showed empty, I switched over to the main tank which, to my consternation, also showed empty. It dawned on me, then, what must have happened.

Shenandoah, Iowa, was just ahead, but at that time the town had no airport. I realized I was damn near out of gas and decided to make an emergency landing while enough still remained to drag the plane in. Spotting a wheat field about a half mile long next to an arterial highway, I squared off and set the old girl down in the stubble. An airplane of this size wasn't the usual thing around Shenandoah, and in a short time a number of cars converged on the site, including the sheriff's.

The sheriff, a burly Midwesterner, sniffed around the plane suspiciously for a while, noting, for one thing, that it still bore American Airlines' insignia. Usually, the identifying markings are removed before a commercial aircraft changes hands, but in this case there hadn't been enough time. The sales documents finally convinced him that I hadn't stolen the bird.

I negotiated with a trucker to bring me a couple of barrels of aviation gas from Omaha. Before long I was able to fuel up, take off from the field, and resume my journey to Seattle, arriving there without further difficulties.

While in Seattle, I got a rating in the Stinson-A. Before leaving, I received a wire from the company advising me that I would have eight passengers aboard for the trip back to Alaska. As bosses will, Hans intended to make the trip pay.

10
The Marshal and Miss Alaska

ABOUT A MONTH and a half later, I stopped in at the Mirow office after returning from a flight to Teller. "Ready to go back to Seattle?" a smiling Bill Barber asked.

"Sure," I said. "I never get enough of the city life."

"Hey, I'm serious! The marshal's thinking of flying some prisoners to Seattle, and we've quoted him a price for the Trimotor. That way the group won't have to take the long boat ride, and we figure the trip might actually be cheaper by air."

I became very interested when I realized he wasn't joking. Pilots in Nome considered it quite an honor to be picked for a flight to Seattle.

Within a couple of days, all the plans were set. Ben Mozee, the marshal, had lined up five prisoners for the trip. Three were convicted murderers; the other two were insane. Mozee was eager to try transporting his charges by air, but had one firm stipulation. He insisted we get through Canada in one day. It would be okay to overnight in Fairbanks, but from there we had to make it all the way to Washington's McNeil Island Penitentiary. I could understand his reasoning; he didn't know what in the world he'd do with the prisoners on a layover in Canada.

Then we unexpectedly acquired another passenger, Jack Skane, a patient destined for a brain operation at the Mayo Clinic in Minnesota.

We watched the weather as best we could, and when it looked good, we were all set to go. At the last minute, the Miss Alaska of 1937, Marguerite Lee, asked if she could ride along to Seattle. Marguerite was the daughter of a pioneering Alaskan mining family, the Lees of Nome, who mined down on the Solomon River. We had enough room and the marshal was agreeable, so Marguerite came aboard. That made a rather unique load: Miss Alaska, five convicts, and an invalid.

Victor Novak, one of Mirow's mechanics, served as my copilot. Both of us were sworn in as United States Deputy Marshals. We had so many prisoners aboard that regulations required they be accompanied by deputies, as well as the marshal.

That night the prisoners were lodged in the Fairbanks jail. Marshal Mozee and I agreed to get a very early start the next morning for the long flight to Seattle.

The first stop was Whitehorse, where we had the usual delay in obtaining fuel. Passing through Customs was also a problem, due to having the prisoners. And we'd lost two hours crossing the time zones, so it was quite late in the day before we got started for Prince George, our next refueling stop. I planned to follow the same route I'd taken on my previous Seattle flight.

We settled into the long, slow routine of grinding down through Canada. Taking a break at one point, I opened the companionway door to go back into the cabin. The marshal and Miss Alaska were asleep, as were almost all of the prisoners. I was preparing to return to the cockpit when I noticed our survival rifle, a loaded 30-30, which we always kept strapped over the companionway door. It was in plain sight. Any of the passengers could simply have gotten up, grabbed the gun, and taken over. I took the rifle back with me to the cockpit, although that was probably wasted effort; people hadn't yet thought of hijacking aircraft, and there didn't seem to be any desperados among our group of prisoners. In fact, I think they were glad to be leaving Nome for Washington State.

Eventually we arrived over Prince George. The day was ending, and a large thunderstorm loomed ahead of us. I told Ben that this was the end of the trail for the day. We had to lay over. Well, Mozee was greatly distressed at the thought of having to settle his prisoners at a local hotel.

Shortly after landing, we ran across a British Columbia policeman and explained the situation to him. "No problem. No problem at all," he said. "We've got a big jail and hardly anyone's in it. We can accommodate five more guests with no trouble at all."

The policeman waited while we secured the airplane. Then he helped transfer the prisoners to the jail. The rest of us checked into a hotel and spent a very pleasant evening.

Looking back at this, I suppose nowadays the Canadians would have to wire Ottawa to get approval from the Prime Minister. And we'd probably have to get clearance from the governors of two states and the President, just to make the trip in the first place.

The next day the weather was beautiful, and we flew down the Fraser River canyon and on to Seattle. As on my previous flight, word of our arrival had preceded us, and we were met by a cluster of reporters and photographers. Most of them were there to interview Miss Alaska and snap a few pictures of her. After the photographers were finished, Marguerite was whisked off by friends and relatives. Vic and I, in our official capacity as deputies, accompanied the marshal and his prisoners on to Olympia and then by ferry to McNeil Island Penitentiary.

There's something grim and hostile about a place where they lock people up. McNeil was no exception. The prisoners were given physical examinations, after which the prison officials signed for them. Our part of the business was finished. But I was rather interested in the prison and asked the warden if we could have a brief tour. He was kind enough to oblige and arranged one for us.

We happened to be touring the facility at dinner time, and most of the inmates were eating. Apparently the dining hall is the place where riots and other disturbances usually start, so the prison rules forbade talking during the meal. Nonetheless you could hear a kind of low mumble. I guess the prisoners had learned to talk to one another without lip movement. In the corner of the room was a cagelike affair housing an armed guard, who monitored dinner. As we looked on I heard a man, who apparently could contain himself no longer, yell, "Jack Jefford!"

The man, an Eskimo from Nome, came running over and began shaking my hand. He wanted to know how things were going at home. Pretty soon another guy came over. He was from Kotzebue. These fellows had gotten into trouble and had been sent Outside to prison. The next thing I knew, I had five or six prisoners from Alaska around me. We were shaking hands and talking. I was telling them all the news from the area. Later I was told I'd violated the rules, but the guards didn't know what to do about it, so they just let it go on for a while.

On the way out Marshal Ben Mozee turned to me with a sly grin. "Boy, Jack, I didn't know you were so popular with the underworld!"

11
Missing Pilots

A LOT WOULD HAPPEN in December, 1939.

On Tuesday the nineteenth, I left Nome in the Stinson-A Trimotor bound for Anchorage to pick up the Reindeer Purchase Committee. It had been a year since the Reindeer Acquisition Act had passed Congress, and the committee was now organized and ready to begin actual purchase of the white-owned reindeer on behalf of Alaska's natives.

I had flown past Unalakleet and was continuing southeasterly toward Anchorage when I began running into heavy weather. Deciding to be prudent, I turned back to Unalakleet and contacted Mirow on the Lear T-30. (We had junked our home-built radios and installed the new T-30 commercial model in most of our aircraft.) The T-30 transmitted voice over a fairly good range, yet had code capability for longer distance communication.

"Hans, the weather's awfully grim, so I'm on my way back to Unalakleet. I'll spend the night there and try again in the morning."

"Hold on a minute, Jack. Curly's overdue at St. Michael." Curly Martin was one of our pilots on the Yukon mail run. "He picked up a sick four-year-old boy at Mountain Village, and we just found out he hasn't arrived at St. Michael." Mirow, deeply concerned, continued, "I'd like you to stay in Unalakleet and start searching for Curly as soon as the weather lifts."

No sooner had I signed off than I heard Hans receive a call from another of our pilots. Fred Chambers was in trouble on a trip from Nome to Fairbanks in the Fairchild. He was carrying three passengers: my brother Bill's wife, Magdalene; their sixteen-month-old son, Billy; and Joe Walsh of Nome.

I listened as Chambers told Hans of his serious plight. In the vicinity of Koyuk, he had run into an overcast that was too low to get through by going underneath. Since Fairbanks was reporting clear weather, he had decided to climb above the overcast, figuring he'd be able to descend again on the other side of Nulato.

Then mechanical trouble turned the situation into a real emergency. An oil line to the plane's engine ruptured, and oil began spewing out of the aircraft. "I'm losing a lot of oil . . ." we heard Chambers say. Then he stopped transmitting.

We could visualize Fred's desperate predicament—trapped above an overcast with a plane that couldn't keep flying much longer, with no idea whatsoever of the kind of terrain awaiting him below. We were tense and silent, fearing the worst. But fifteen minutes later Chambers came back on the radio, assuring us everyone was all right.

As luck would have it, he had broken out of the overcast above a little creek and was able to make a safe ski landing on its frozen surface. Then he got out the plane's trailing antenna and hung it on a tree. The aircraft was undamaged, but Fred was not at all sure of his position. He could be anywhere within thousands of square miles of Alaskan wilderness. About all they could do was pray for a speedy rescue.

I waited on weather that night in Unalakleet. By Wednesday morning conditions had improved, allowing me to fly on to St. Michael in an attempt to discover the fate of our other missing pilot, Curly Martin.

After landing at St. Michael I got some good news. Martin and the boy were safe. Curly had encountered head winds of such strength that he had simply run out of fuel and was forced to land his Travelair on a frozen lake ten miles south of town. He had walked in to the village, carrying the injured child wrapped snugly in a sleeping bag.

With Curly located, our attention was focused on Chambers. Curly suggested that we load a couple of cases of gasoline into my Trimotor and fly over to the stranded Travelair, getting it back into operation so we'd have another airplane for the search. We got on the radio to Mirow, and he agreed with our plan.

"As soon as you finish with the Travelair I'd like you and Curly to get back to Unalakleet and stand by to help me search for Chambers," he said. "I'll be leaving right away for Unalakleet, then on to Nulato." Mirow and flight mechanic Pete Bystedt immediately left Nome in the Gullwing Stinson.

Curly and I found the Travelair, filled it with gas, then spent a few hours getting the engine warm enough to start. Finally, both of us took off for Unalakleet. Weather conditions were deteriorating rapidly, and it soon began to snow. At Unalakleet, we learned that Mirow and Bystedt had touched down for refueling about two hours earlier. Then they had left, planning to go through the pass to Kaltag and on to Nulato to begin the search.

Wondering what our next move should be, I cranked the handle on the antiquated telephone at the Unalakleet roadhouse. The line traced the dogsled trail to the villages of Kaltag and Nulato, and I hoped Hans might have left a message for us. Instead, I received the disquieting news that Hans had never arrived at Kaltag, where they were reporting heavy snow and zero visibility. By then it was nearly dark, and there wasn't much we could do that night.

Now six people were missing: Mirow and Bystedt and Chambers and his three passengers.

Chambers had established a time for regular evening radio transmissions, but the signals were often erratic. Conserving his battery, he made only the one brief daily transmission to let us know how he was doing. Although the Chambers group was in no immediate danger, they didn't have much food and couldn't survive for too long in the numbing midwinter cold of Alaska's Interior. But they were doing their best. Chambers and Joe Walsh were competent woodsmen, and they told us they'd set up a pretty good camp.

As Thursday dawned we mapped out our search strategy. Curly, in the Travelair, was to hunt for Hans and Pete by tracing the route they would have taken into Kaltag. I would fly to Nulato and base there to begin a search for both Hans and Chambers.

The search began to attract international attention. An Associated Press story by AP's stringer at Nulato, U.S. Marshal Stanley Nichols, was sent Outside over the wires of the Alaska Communication System and was picked up by newspapers around the globe (Nichols later showed me the clippings).

It was the kind of situation the press liked to build up—the drama of four persons, including a mother and infant child, down in the merciless arctic wilderness, their chances dwindling by the hour as they sent frantic radio appeals for help to searchers who were unable to find them. Then the reports carried the story that two of the rescuers were also lost.

In the Alaskan tradition, pilots from a number of small bush airlines, including Star Airlines and Pacific Alaska Airways, converged on Nulato to join the hunt for the missing planes. Search efforts were frustrated by a continuing series of snowstorms that swept the area. Dog teams had also been out looking for Chambers and Mirow, but the high winds and drifting snow forced even them to turn back.

Chambers's daily radio contacts kept hope alive and emphasized the grim race we were running against time and the relentless Alaskan winter. Sometimes we had trouble picking up Chambers's transmissions directly, but when our reception was poor, Virgil Hansen of Star Airlines in Anchorage could usually receive the signals and relay the messages to us.

Late Thursday night the winds calmed, the snow stopped, and the overcast lifted somewhat. In fact, the moon was visible occasionally through small breaks in the cloud cover. I decided to try a night flight to locate the Chambers party. Night flying wasn't recommended by the bush fraternity—but this was an emergency. It called for unusual action, and I was determined to take it.

I scouted out ten Nulato Indians to act as observers and then began warming the Trimotor. The villagers placed lanterns alongside the airstrip so we'd be able to find our way back after making the flight.

We took off a little after midnight. I flew around the area awhile, letting my eyes become adjusted to the darkness. I figured that, after searching the mountains, I would always be able to make it back to the Yukon River, then follow it either up or down until I got back to Nulato and the flickering lanterns.

I had been flying for nearly an hour and a half without seeing anything when I heard the natives begin jabbering excitedly. One of them was pointing to the ground. "Light!" he yelled. "Light!"

Fred Chambers and Joe Walsh had been tending a small fire for warmth, as well as to help us find them. Our radio was tuned to Fred's frequency. After broadcasting that he could hear our aircraft overhead, Fred was able to guide us precisely to his location by switching on his aircraft lights. We'd located them, finally.

In our preparations for the flight, we had filled a sack with food and lashed a string of flashlights along the outside. Now we turned on the flashlights, and as I made a low pass over the camp, we tossed the lighted sack and some sleeping bags to the excited foursome waiting below. The flashlights, still visible in the snow, made it easy for them to find the drop. Then I circled and followed the little creek on which Chambers had landed down to where it met the Yukon. This pinpointed the location for the trailwise Nulato dog mushers. Two of them announced they'd head for the downed plane with their dog teams that very night. Those stout-hearted chaps reached Fred the next afternoon and brought the group out without incident.

The jubilation surrounding the rescue of Chambers and his three passengers was dampened several days later by news that the wreckage of Hans Mirow's Gullwing Stinson had been found eight miles from Kaltag. Both Mirow and Bystedt had been killed while searching for Chambers and his passengers.

Curly Martin and I each had a sad duty to perform before closing the book on that tragic episode. Curly's task was to return Hans Mirow's body to Nome in the Travelair. Mine was to fly the body of Pete Bystedt to Anchorage.

Flying back to Anchorage on Pete's last journey, I radioed Virgil Hansen of Star Airlines to tell him I was coming. He alerted all of Pete's friends, and when I touched down at Merrill Field, there was quite a crowd gathered there in Pete's memory.

Pete was from Anchorage and had brothers and other relatives there. A young mechanic for Star Airlines, he had decided to work awhile in Nome for Hans and see how things worked out for him in the Bering Sea area. Pete was a very popular fellow, well-liked by everyone. His passing threw a shroud of gloom over the little community's Christmas season.

The same sadness gripped Nome, where Hans Mirow had pioneered in a raw, unforgiving era of Alaskan aviation.

Hans Mirow, in my opinion, ranks high on the roster of early air charter operators—and his Mirow Air Service was one of the finest air taxis in Alaska. The business employed a full-time operations manager, a chief mechanic, and a radio operator, in addition to the pilots. In the early days, that was considered quite elaborate.

Hans maintained a nice fleet of airplanes, built a good hangar, and even provided his own power plant at the airstrip. His company was solvent and always paid its bills; even we pilots were paid on time.

Mirow's dedication and skill as a pilot were known and respected by all. Time and again, as on his last flight, he demonstrated his concern for others through his numerous mercy flights. One example out of many was his flight in a single-engine plane to St. Lawrence Island— more than 200 miles each way over open sea—in terrible weather to bring the village schoolteacher's wife to the Nome hospital. Her appendix had ruptured, and Hans's flight undoubtedly saved her life.

I have always felt that Hans Mirow never fully received the honor and recognition he so richly deserved. He was one of Alaska's finest, most dedicated, and courageous pilots.

12

The Reindeer Acquisition

THE SPRING OF 1940 witnessed the end of my employment with Mirow Air Service and marked the beginning of my career with the federal government. But during those final few months before going to work for the CAA, I had one last mission to fly for Mirow. Before he died, Mirow had contracted to provide air transportation for the Reindeer Acquisition Committee, and I planned to make sure that obligation was fulfilled.

I joined the members of the committee in Anchorage on December 28, 1939. The time I'd spent on the Mirow and Chambers search efforts had delayed our meeting well over a week, and the committee was anxious to get started. We left the very next day, bound for McGrath to begin the purchase of the white-owned reindeer.

When the Reindeer Acquisition Act passed Congress, Secretary of the Interior Harold Ickes realized that the actual purchase might become a little too political. He thought it wise to select someone from a completely unrelated area to take charge of the purchase committee.

Charlie Burdick, the United States Forester at Juneau, was the man chosen for the job. An ex-marine, he was tough but fair, and also a nice guy. Burdick was accompanied by an attorney for the Federal Bureau of Investigation. The attorney, named Kelley, joined the group to monitor the legal aspects of the purchase. The fiscal responsibilities were vested in Leon Coverly. I'd never before seen anything like it. Coverly traveled with a book of U.S. Government checks. When we'd buy the reindeer, Coverly was authorized to write out a check to pay the owner on the spot. The Department of the Interior also sent Ray Dame back to Alaska. He had been on the earlier fact-finding trips, and his mission was still the same: to obtain a running record of the purchase, using both movies and still photography.

In retrospect, I'm amazed at how well Burdick was able to handle the difficult job—counting the roving herds and paying off the owners in appropriate amounts. He managed to keep most of the sellers at least reasonably happy with his settlements.

The size of the reindeer herds was very hard to determine. The animals were scattered over thousands of square miles of difficult terrain. The herds were thick in some places and thinned out by marauding wolves in others. Charlie applied Department of Agriculture formulas for estimating increase in livestock to place a probable upper limit on the size of the herds. And of course we were able to survey them from the air.

In some cases the owners were reluctant to accept Burdick's estimate of their herds. After dickering for a long while, Burdick finally would say, "Okay, if you think you've got that many reindeer, I'll place this aircraft at your disposal and you show them to us."

We'd take off with the owner as passenger and spend hours combing the hills and valleys looking for what were often nonexistent reindeer. Embarrassed owners would sometimes explain, honestly, that the wolf packs were to blame. Large, blood-splotched, carcass-strewn expanses of snowy tundra testified to the wolves' relentless pursuit of these gentle animals. Some herds had fled to barren mountaintops to escape the wolf packs and had died there of slow starvation. Extreme winter weather conditions also took their toll. But the reindeer thrived wherever they had been properly protected by vigilant herders. Their numbers increased, much like livestock in a cattle operation.

When the committee initially contracted for our flying service, they requested that the pilot become a notary public so that he could officially witness and stamp the reindeer purchases. I sent my application to Juneau. In due time—after an expenditure of $6 for a seal—I became a notary public in and for the Territory of Alaska. Once Burdick and the owners reached agreement, I was always called over to witness the close of the deal.

The contract also set down certain requirements for the airplane. Since winter operation was planned, they specified a multi-engine aircraft on skis. We decided to use a Stinson-A Trimotor. Mirow Air Service now owned two of them, including the one I'd purchased from American Airlines. The Stinson-A was a fine airplane. It would carry ten passengers, plus a crew of two, and even had room for a stewardess. It was a regular airliner with an onboard biffy—something really new in those days. There were several other Stinson-As in Alaska. I think Ray Petersen had two of them at Bethel Airways, and Art Woodley used one in Anchorage for Woodley Airways.

We designated NC-16110 as principal aircraft for the committee's work. Our first few flights were made on wheels to villages and towns suitable for wheel operation. In January I flew the Stinson-A to Fairbanks, where the Smith and Greb Company, specialists in ski conversions, installed a special set of shock-absorbing skis, the first ski installation ever on any Stinson-A. Our other Stinson-A, NC-15154, remained on wheels, allowing us the choice of wheel or ski operation. After a day of flight testing NC-16110's new landing system, we were ready once again to continue the reindeer purchases.

We flew the entire western coast of Alaska, from Port Heiden, Dillingham, and Togiak in the south to Kotzebue, Wainwright, and Barrow in the north. Akularak . . . Shaktoolik . . . Shishmaref . . . Kivalina . . . a steady succession of villages, takeoffs, and landings. In the space of four months, we spent 200 hours in the air, visiting and revisiting more than fifty villages on 175 hops, scanning the vast tundra for the sometimes illusory herds.

The unsung hero of the mission was my flight mechanic and copilot, Victor Novak. The Stinson was quite heavy, and our skis would often stick to the snow. We'd try bouncing the tail and apply other body English, but the damn airplane remained riveted to the spot. Then Novak was forced to coax the Stinson in his own, somewhat unorthodox manner.

Braced against the prop blast, Vic would bang away at the bogged-down skis with a log about four feet long and three inches in diameter.

His slamming and pounding would jar loose the skis, enabling the plane to break free and begin moving. But once we got going I couldn't slow down, or else we'd get stuck all over again.

So, as the plane began picking up speed, poor Vic would chase after us in the snow, tossing the log through the door where eager hands grabbed it (such logs were at a premium in the treeless tundra of western Alaska). Then, with the plane still moving, the other passengers would yank Vic into the cabin. As soon as I heard the door slam I'd ram the throttles fully open. We were usually airborne by the time Vic made his way forward to the cockpit.

Taking care of the Stinson-A on those bitter winter days—when temperatures often dropped to twenty or thirty below, or even lower— was a bothersome chore at best. It required a lot of hard work. Numb with cold, we had to drain the oil out of all three engines before we could even think of bedding down for the night. We kept the oil in closed containers and brought it inside to keep it warm.

Next we had to put on the motor covers. The outboard engines were low enough so that we could use conventional motor covers, which hung all the way to the ground. But the center engine was so high that we were forced to run a stovepipe up to it.

We then lit and nursed along three firepots to keep the engines warm under their covers. Unless we heated all three engines that way, and kept them heated, there was no way we were going to fly the next day. Finally, after the engines were bundled up, we'd put on the wing covers to keep the wings free of frost and snow.

Refueling was another miserable, painstaking task. The Stinson-A burned a lot of gas, nearly thirty-five gallons an hour. Every drop had to be poured out of five-gallon cans and strained through a chamois skin filter.

Tending the airplane was certainly no picnic.

Burdick and his crew purposely picked the southwest coast as the place to begin the acquisitions. Knowing the purchases would take quite some time, they were in no hurry to race north. As winter waned, daylight hours would lengthen and temperatures would rise, making our foray into the Arctic a little more pleasant.

We'd already worked halfway up the coast and had just finished with the herders at Unalakleet. Before heading north, Burdick decided to put back into Nome to catch up on his paperwork, replace supplies, launder clothes, and more or less regroup. He said I could have a couple of days off while they tended to their affairs, so I was eagerly anticipating a day or two of relaxation in town. But it was not to be.

As soon as we landed in Nome I was met by one of our mechanics. His expression told me something was wrong, even before he spoke. "Jack, Sasseen's down in the Trimotor over at Savoonga. He radioed for help just a couple of hours ago."

"How could he get there on wheels?" I asked. The Stinson I was flying was ski-equipped, but Sasseen had to have taken NC-15154. It had no skis, and I knew that Savoonga, a small village on the north coast of St. Lawrence Island, had no suitable landing field for wheels.

"Well, the natives said they had staked out a good strip and told us it was okay for wheels, so Sass went on over." As it turned out, the strip was covered with about eighteen inches of snow. Sasseen rolled along for a hundred feet or so before the wheels sank down through the crust. Then he nosed over, denting the cowling and bending all three propellers.

The mechanic and I walked back to the office and continued to discuss the problem. Our only hope of retrieving the Trimotor was to fly three new props over to Savoonga. And the Reindeer Committee's Trimotor was our only source of propellers. If we pulled them off that airplane and took them to Savoonga in the ski-equipped Vega, we could bring home our downed Stinson-A Trimotor. Otherwise, Sasseen and the airplane would have to remain there the rest of the winter.

I described the situation to Burdick, feeling I should get his approval. After all, dismantling the airplane might be considered by some to be grounds for breach of contract. Burdick graciously agreed to our plans and said that the committee's few days in Nome should allow us plenty of time to complete the mission.

I packed the Vega with my cargo of propellers and set out for Savoonga, navigating by dead reckoning southwestward toward St. Lawrence Island. The large island began looming up on the horizon after I'd been flying about forty minutes. Everything was going fine, though I experienced the usual jitters about possible engine failure on a long journey over water in a single-engine plane. The 175 miles across the Bering Sea to Savoonga seemed like a long way. After finding the village, I spotted the crippled Trimotor and landed nearby.

Murrell Sasseen was more than glad to see me. Savoonga wasn't a place you'd pick to be stranded for the winter. He had already pulled off the bent props and straightened the cowling, so it was not too much of a job to install the replacement props I'd brought over. But we still had to do something about an airstrip.

Our only hope was to make some sort of deal with the natives, though we had nothing to pay them with. I sent Sasseen back to Nome in the Vega and then called upon the village leaders. I've learned that the Eskimos are a very sharp people. If you tell them your problem and leave them alone, they can usually solve it for you. But if you jump in and start ordering them around, your mission will most likely fall apart.

When I'd seen Sasseen take off in the Vega, I'd worried for an instant about my judgment. If the natives couldn't (or wouldn't) take care of the snow, then I'd be the one stranded in Savoonga. I told them I needed about 1,200 feet of snow shoveled before I could take off. The strip didn't have to be too wide, as long as it was reasonably straight.

The entire village—men, women, and children—turned out. I wish I had a movie of the operation; it was incredible that hand labor could do so much so fast. Their method was to pile the snow on walrus hides, drag the hides to one side, and dump off the snow. Then they'd start shoveling again. Their teamwork on the snow removal was a joy to behold.

The strip wasn't completely finished by evening, so I had to stay the night. The following morning I began heating the Trimotor's engines while the natives finished the runway. The hand-cleared strip was beautiful, and the airplane ran perfectly. Even the weather cooperated to make my flight back to Nome uneventful. I rejoined Burdick and the committee, and we continued north for the rest of our purchase work.

While making the reindeer flights, I was also awaiting the offer of a new job. Life in Nome among the honey buckets sometimes left a little to be desired. Having decided I was ready to move on to greener pastures, I had filed applications for two promising positions.

Through my good friend Joe Crosson, I applied for a job with Pacific Alaska Airways, the Alaska branch of Pan American. Joe told me the airline was planning a new run from Fairbanks to Whitehorse and on down through the interior of Canada to Seattle. In those days nobody expected that any kind of an airway could be established along the Gulf of Alaska. The state-of-the-art equipment was thought to be insufficient to establish proper facilities. Although I would later help develop these airways, at the time the interior of Canada, with its better weather and terrain, seemed to be the logical route.

Some of Pacific Alaska's pilots would be moving up to Lodestars to fly the new schedules, and the airline would require replacement pilots to handle the old runs: Fairbanks to Nome and Fairbanks down the Kuskokwim to Bethel. The prospect of working for Pacific Alaska seemed particularly attractive because their aging Pilgrim aircraft carried only one pilot. I figured that, after a week or two learning the Pan Am routine, I'd be checked out as captain on these runs. From there

I could gradually work my way up the ladder. It was quite unusual to step into captain's shoes when just starting out with an airline.

Not wanting to put all my eggs in one basket, however, I also applied to the CAA, since the federal agency was beginning to expand in Alaska. They were looking for a new patrol pilot.

Their first patrol pilot, Steve Davis, had taken their only plane on a flight from Anchorage to Cordova in February of 1940. Davis was unfamiliar with the country, and instead of going up Turnagain Arm to Portage Pass, he must have just drawn a line and started up one of the draws in back of Anchorage to cross the Chugach Range. Steve crashed about twenty miles from town. Fortunately it happened during a spell of mild weather, and searchers found him quickly. He was in pretty bad shape with a broken back and would be hospitalized for at least six months, which left the CAA in quite a bind. They were just starting and already had lost their only pilot and airplane.

Washington was very perturbed over the accident. Officials there sent word to Marshall C. Hoppin, Superintendent of Airways, to hire a local Alaskan pilot—someone who knew the country and had experience with northern operating conditions. The pilot chosen would be sent Outside to learn the fine art of flight checking. This job looked like quite a plum to all the pilots in Alaska, me included. While I had an iron in the fire with Pacific Alaska, I felt it wouldn't hurt to have a second application in the works.

As it turned out, the two front-runners for the CAA job were my good friend Al Horning and I. Though Al had a better academic background than I did, I had the equivalent of an instrument rating. Al and I would pass on the street and good-naturedly rib each other about our chances.

"Who do you think will really get it, Al?"

"I hate to tell you this, Jack, but I've been playing a little politics," Al said. "Tony Dimond's a friend of mine, and I've got him working on it for me." Anthony J. Dimond was Alaska's delegate to Congress.

"Al," I replied, "I'm not one to just sit idly by the road. With all my reindeer flying, I've gotten in pretty solid with the Department of the Interior, and my friends there have got Secretary Ickes promoting for me. So I'm not without my own political clout!"

I'm sure none of it made any difference for either of us, but we worried each other as best we could.

At the time that both my feelers were out, I was in Point Barrow with the Reindeer Committee. We were staying with Stanley Morgan, the Alaska Communication System telegrapher, using a frozen lake in back of Morgan's quarters for our ski-plane operation. (Stanley had worked around the clock transmitting messages at the time Will Rogers and Wiley Post were killed near Barrow and had helped prepare their bodies for shipment home.)

One day Morgan handed me a telegram that had been forwarded to Barrow from Nome. It was from the CAA, offering me the position as patrol pilot, starting immediately. I wired back my acceptance, on the condition that I be allowed to finish the reindeer flights. I felt I had a moral obligation to finish them first. The CAA agreed to my request.

Ironically, when we got back to Nome, a telegram from Joe Crosson was waiting, offering me the Pacific Alaska job. It had been sent earlier than the one from the CAA, but since the CAA telegram was a government message, it had been forwarded to me at Barrow. I had accepted the CAA position unaware that Pacific Alaska was also offering me a job.

I often wonder how differently things might have turned out if I'd been in Nome rather than Point Barrow when those two messages arrived. I know I would have accepted the Pacific Alaska job. It was offered first, and I had made up my mind that I would take whichever job offer came through.

Winter was nearly over before I finished flying for the Reindeer Acquisition Committee—my last official duty for Mirow Air Service. Then I was free to go to work for the CAA.

Part 4

Patrol Pilot

1

Signed on with the CAA

APRIL 28, 1940, I signed all the necessary papers and accepted my identification card, thereby formally joining the fledgling Alaskan operation of the Civil Aeronautics Authority, forerunner of the Federal Aviation Administration (FAA). For my valued services as Airways Flight Inspector I was to receive the munificent sum of $3,600 per annum, beginning a career with the CAA/FAA that would span thirty-two years and over 20,000 flying hours.

The Alaska Railroad, our sister agency in the Department of Commerce, had made some space available for CAA headquarters in their buildings down at the Ship Creek rail yard in Anchorage. The Airways Section, headed by Superintendent Marshall C. Hoppin, occupied a drab and windowless trackside warehouse. The gloom was partially dispelled by a few overhead industrial light fixtures, providing barely enough illumination for me to survey my new office.

I was informed that the battered wooden desk sitting askew in one corner was all mine. Then I was solemnly issued a rifle, a pistol, and a new briefcase containing a book of government travel requests and a supply of Form C-60s, which allowed me to make purchases in the name of the United States government.

The only aircraft the agency owned was an old Army surplus 0-38, which had been fitted with floats at Sand Point Naval Air Station in Seattle. My predecessor, Steve Davis, had spent a considerable part of the summer of 1939 ferrying it up to Anchorage in short, slow hops along the southeast seacoast. A two-place, open-cockpit observation airplane, the 0-38 was totally unsuited for our purposes and had been mothballed for the winter.

Realizing the inadequacy of the 0-38, the CAA brass in Washington had supplanted it with a modern aircraft, a Fleetwing stainless steel amphibian powered by a Jacobs engine. That airplane was well suited for flight checking and logistical support, but Steve had wrecked it in his disastrous crash near Anchorage earlier in the year.

With no plane to fly, I was a horseman without a horse, just marking time at the office while waiting for something to happen. I'd often go over to another building to visit with Al Hulen, Chief of Communications. He had a window in his office. We were both railroad aficionados and enjoyed watching the trains, especially on a maneuver known as the flying switch. The procedure is now outlawed, but back then a car could be unhooked from the train and shunted at high speed across the various tracks.

After a couple weeks of enforced idleness, I was given the welcome assignment of reporting to Seattle. CAA headquarters in Washington, D.C., had sent us a telegram saying they had just purchased an ideal airplane for the Alaskan operation: an S-38 Sikorsky. And they had hired a top-notch flight mechanic named Radky. He and the plane would be waiting for me in Seattle.

I welcomed the news. Watching the trains switch had become a little boring.

Al Hulen was also headed Outside on a trip to Washington, D.C., so the two of us boarded the Alaska Railroad destined for the port of Seward. In those early days, if someone was leaving the region, it was standard practice for everyone from the Superintendent of Airways on down to the last clerk to come over, put you on the train, and wave goodbye.

Hulen and I enjoyed the send-off, both of us looking forward to a very pleasant journey. The train ferried us to Seward, where we eagerly boarded the *SS Alaska*. By coincidence, when the boat made its stop in Juneau, we found that Joe Crosson and his wife, Lillian, had signed aboard as passengers. Their presence made the trip south even more enjoyable.

After arriving in Seattle I checked in with the Seventh Region Airways Office and was given some startling news. Prior to being delivered to the CAA, the S-38 Sikorsky had crashed into New York Harbor. The accident had killed all aboard, including Radky, our new flight mechanic. I was told to stand by in Seattle and work with Cecil Braddick, their veteran Airways Flight Inspector. From him I could learn the ropes of flight checking the low frequency ranges and fan markers, which were about the only air navigational aids available at that time.

Under Braddick's tutelage I helped check a few of the local radio ranges, including Everett, Ellensburg, and Ephrata. Since the Army Air Corps Reserve squadron allowed me to train with their aircraft when I was in town, I arranged for Braddick and me to do most of our range checking in military airplanes: BT-9-Cs, the Boeing P-12-F Pursuit, and the BC-1-A (now known as the AT-6).

After spending the month of May in Seattle, I was told to report to CAA headquarters in Washington, D.C., where I would at last be assigned an airplane.

The first official I met in Washington was Chris Lample. I was greatly impressed by the man; he seemed anything but a stereotypic bureaucrat. Tough, hard-working, and dedicated, Lample ultimately became

Chief of the Federal Airways Division. Over the years he would prove to be the greatest friend the Alaska Region ever had when it came down to getting things done for us. Although he hadn't yet visited Alaska, he was very interested in the Territory's development and was obviously pushing hard to start the ball rolling.

With the war clouds over Europe, everyone felt it would be only a matter of time before the United States would be involved in fighting against Germany and Japan. Congress appropriated huge sums of money to develop airways and airports throughout Alaska, evidently figuring we would most likely be the first line of defense. The CAA was charged with some of the DLAND (Development of Landing Areas for National Defense) construction. The military also shouldered part of the load.

Lample talked with me at great length. He was especially interested in hearing my recommendations, as a pilot, as to where to build the intermediate airfields. The small city fields at Nome, Fairbanks, and Anchorage were already scheduled to be upgraded into major airports. I left Washington with a growing respect for Chris Lample and a better understanding of the CAA's important mission in Alaska.

My next stop was Hagerstown, Maryland, where I took possession of NC-99, our new Fairchild 24. The Fairchild was powered by a 145-horse Warner engine and cruised at less than a hundred knots. While the airplane was no great ball of fire, at least it had wings and was something we could fly.

Bucking headwinds, I spent four days piloting the aircraft from Hagerstown to Seattle. Having been gone for quite some time, I was looking forward to the trip back home. The days would now be nice and warm, and when you live in Alaska, you hate to miss much of the summer. But upon my arrival in Seattle I was informed of another change in plan.

Al Horning, my good friend who had also been an applicant for my job, had just been hired as our second patrol pilot. He was on his way down to pick up the Fairchild. I was to take the plane to the Sand Point Naval Air Station, where it would be equipped with floats for its journey up the Inside Passage to Alaska, with Al as pilot.

During the next week I worked with the sailors at the naval base to install the floats. Then Al shoved off for Anchorage with my mount, leaving me stuck in Seattle awaiting further orders from CAA headquarters. They were angling to get the Alaska Region another plane.

I passed the time by flying in the Reserve squadron. The first week in July, I received word from Washington that a Cessna T-50, NC-34, would be delivered to me in Seattle. Within a couple of days, I was finally heading north at the controls of the shiny new Cessna, serial number 1003. (Serial numbers started at 1001. Since the first two planes had been prototypes, our T-50 was the first off the line to go to a customer.) The CAA was updating its fleet from the old Stinson Reliants and had ordered fourteen of the wooden aircraft for the various regions.

The Cessna had two Jacobs engines and trued out at 180 miles per hour. Though it was a fine airplane and exceptionally fast, it was rather frail. I developed the habit of carrying a pocketful of oversize PK screws so that after each flight I could replace those that had worked loose. The T-50 was later modified by the military and developed into a twin-engine trainer dubbed the "Bobcat." It was a lot heavier than our aircraft, fitted with a much stronger landing gear and structurally beefed up.

Upon my return to Alaska, I was immediately put to work flight checking the new radio ranges. Anchorage was first, commissioned July 21, 1940, followed by Fairbanks on August 8, and Nome on October 12. By autumn we'd established three fully commissioned radio ranges in our expanding system.

Our modest fleet of airplanes was also expanding. The agency acquired a Bellanca Skyrocket, NC-5, from the Tennessee Valley Authority. Al Horning went out to pick it up. The Bellanca was fitted for floats and skis and was repainted in CAA colors of orange and black. Then Washington came through with a second Cessna T-50. Horning returned to the States and flew back in NC-12, increasing our stable of active planes to a total of four: the Fairchild 24, the Bellanca Skyrocket, and the two Cessna T-50s.

In addition to our other duties, Horning and I often used the sleek, fast Cessnas to transport Territorial Governor Ernest Gruening on various flights around Alaska. We flew the T-50s by Instrument Flight Rules to demonstrate to the flying public that we had full confidence in our radio ranges. Our Cessnas were considered to be packed with electronics; actually, all we had was one six-channel Lear transmitter and two receivers. VHF radios had not yet been developed.

What the public might not have known was that we were having a great deal of difficulty with ice. The Cessnas had no deicing equipment, so as soon as we began picking up ice we were in trouble. It all added up to the fact that even though we were able to fly on instruments, we still had to watch the weather carefully and pick our flights with an eye to avoiding icing conditions.

2

General Buckner

AL HORNING AND I were kept very busy supporting the airways program, flying engineers on surveys for proposed airfields, and supplying materials to locations already under construction.

The military also was gearing up for its part of the work. They established Ladd Field, an Air Corps base at Fairbanks, while at the same time construction was proceeding feverishly on the military installations near Anchorage, Fort Richardson and Elmendorf Air Field. There was also a facility on Annette Island in southeast Alaska, and plans were in the works to build new bases along the Aleutians.

Colonel Dale V. Gaffney was in charge of the Air Corps at Ladd Field. Seeking the best advice he could get on preparing troops to defend Alaska under arctic and subarctic conditions, Colonel Gaffney commissioned Vilhjalmur Stefansson, internationally known explorer and author, to write a manual covering cold-weather military operations. No better choice could have been made. Stefansson, born in Iceland, had explored the Arctic coast very extensively. He knew how to live off the country in the most severe conditions.

Somehow, Stefansson heard that I had survived for several days after being forced down in the mountains near Golovin. He sent word from Fairbanks that he would like to talk to me. On my first opportunity I looked him up and found him to be fascinating. While I would have enjoyed hearing more about his explorations, he was more interested in hearing how I survived as well as I did high above timberline, exposed to bitterly cold winds.

I explained about my crude snow shelter, and he seemed particularly interested in the fact that while awaiting rescue I often drifted into what might be called self-induced hibernation, spending about twenty hours at a time sleeping, and eating only one tiny meal a day.

"I'd get up about ten o'clock, air out the sleeping bag, and move around slowly for a little bit. Then I'd cook and eat my one meal," I told Stefansson. "By two o'clock I'd be back in the sleeping bag again, and before long I'd be fast asleep."

"I've heard others talk of the same thing," he said. He then told me a story of survival that I considered far more remarkable than mine.

"An Eskimo woman had been fishing for tomcod," Stefansson began. "A sudden, violent blizzard came up and prevented her from getting back to her village. Rather than wander around aimlessly, as most people might have been inclined to do, the woman huddled motionless on an ice cake with her back to the wind. She sat there for more than twenty-four hours until help came."

I could have spent weeks with Stefansson absorbing his Arctic lore; his experiences seemed to be endless. But I could stay in Fairbanks only a short while.

The Air Corps was just a part of the overall Alaska command of Army General Simon Bolivar Buckner, Jr. Tough, crusty, and full of fiery determination to bolster Alaska's defenses, Buckner arrived in Anchorage in the summer of 1940. He was charged with building the territory into a military bastion, starting out pretty much from scratch. More than any other individual, Buckner was responsible for organizing and toughening Alaska prior to our entry into the war.

When I first met him, he had just been promoted to brigadier general; in fact, he didn't yet have his stars. Elmendorf's major east-west runway and associated buildings were still under construction, so General Buckner headquartered in an old homestead cabin. There was just enough room for the general's desk and a couple of chairs. His two springer spaniels stationed themselves at either end of his desk like a set of bookends—the most well-behaved dogs I've ever seen.

General Buckner and Colonel Gaffney maintained good rapport with the government agencies and the civilians in Alaska, and especially with us in the CAA. Of course, they were vitally interested in the network of radio ranges and airfields we were constructing throughout the Territory. It seemed everyone was just part of one happy family, working toward the goal of enabling Alaska to defend herself.

The Air Corps, at that time, had a very limited fleet of aircraft, consisting of O-19 and O-38 open-cockpit observation planes. Later they acquired a B-18, which enabled them to get around a bit. Even so, they stuck pretty much to nonstop flights between Anchorage, Fairbanks, and Nome. There were no other good airports.

That fall General Buckner asked the CAA to furnish an aircraft and pilot to take him to the western part of Alaska. He especially wanted to get a look at St. Lawrence Island to determine how it could be defended. Then he wanted to go on to Barrow and other points in the Arctic.

I was tapped as pilot for this expedition in one of the CAA's long-range Cessna T-50s. (In addition to the regular wing tanks, we put a third tank in the plane's baggage compartment to further stretch its range.)

We flew first to Bethel, via Bristol Bay. There we refueled and set out for St. Lawrence Island. The island, lying only forty miles from Siberia, is about eighty-eight miles long and about twenty miles wide. After skirting its perimeter we turned eastward, crossing the Bering

Sea to Nome, where we planned to stay overnight.

Ed Snyder, our Flight Service Station (FSS) chief, had been in the service at one time. He was apparently rather nervous and flustered at being visited by a general. As Ed was conducting the general on a tour through the FSS, they passed the little room where the coffee percolator was kept. A number of employees had congregated there, and Ed paused to introduce the general to them.

"I'd like you all to meet Sergeant Buckner . . . I mean *General* Buckner!" Ed's face turned crimson at this faux pas. The general, however, was a nice guy and a good sport. He took no note of the blunder and shook hands all around. But I don't think poor Ed has ever forgotten— or lived down—that embarrassing episode.

Leaving Nome early the next morning, we skirted Cape Prince of Wales, the westernmost tip of the Seward Peninsula, and crossed over historic Tin City, once the greatest tin-producing district on the continent. Buckner intently observed the shoreline. Following the coast past Shishmaref and up to Kotzebue, we noticed a number of walrus carcasses on the beach. I presumed that natives somewhere along the coast had shot these walrus but then had been unable to retrieve them. Now the carcasses had been washed ashore.

At Kotzebue, I sent a message to Barrow requesting that the ACS (Alaska Communication System) station there stand by on 3105 and 6210, the frequencies on which I'd be calling Barrow as soon as I left Kotzebue.

I wanted to keep a close check on Barrow's weather, which tends to be capricious, since vast fields of pack ice always linger just offshore. Alaska's northernmost community is especially subject to onsets of sudden drifting fog.

After we'd refueled at Kotzebue, the general asked me to take him past Point Hope and Cape Lisburne so he could continue to study the coastline from a defense standpoint. That added another hour en route to Barrow.

Once we got going I began calling Barrow, using the CW key in the Cessna, since the station had no voice facilities. About the time we passed over Cape Lisburne, I established communications with Sergeant Stanley Morgan, the ACS chief at Barrow.

It was a very pleasant run from Cape Lisburne up the coast to Barrow, with many interesting things to see along the beach. As we were approaching Wainwright, Stanley inquired by radio, "Who's your passenger and what's his mission?"

"General Simon Bolivar Buckner," I replied on the CW.

There was a long pause. It soon became obvious that Stanley, who had never been visited at Barrow by anyone with a higher rank than major, was so nervous he was having trouble sending.

"We will be staying all night and need billeting," I radioed.

"No problem," came the answer.

Since there was no airport in Barrow, we had to land on a short, soft little strip. It wouldn't have been too bad for the Bellanca, with its big tires, but wasn't the greatest for the Cessna T-50. However, we got in all right and Stanley was there to meet us, obviously in awe of the exalted personage I'd brought in.

Stanley and his wife proved to be excellent hosts and the general put them instantly at ease. We stayed with the Morgans overnight. The next day we returned to Anchorage via Fairbanks.

In 1941 one of the office buildings on the base was completed, and General Buckner invited many of the Anchorage townspeople out for a New Year's party. I accompanied our CAA director, Marshall C. Hoppin.

To help ring in the New Year and toast the town's leaders, the general's orderlies had prepared a potion called artilleryman's punch. I watched a couple of GIs as they mixed in gallon after gallon of everclear alcohol. The punch tasted delicious, but I was understandably cautious about drinking much of it. The old-time Alaskans, most of whom were Scotch drinkers, jokingly referred to the concoction as "lemonade." They guzzled it down with nearly disastrous results. How some of them ever made it home is beyond me.

I kept an eye on my boss and saw that he was into some pretty heavy going, so I steered us both back to town. Had I not been there to haul him home, he might never have found his way back from Fort Richardson that night.

The news of General Buckner's tragic death several years later at a forward observation post, while in command of the assault forces on Okinawa, saddened me deeply. Like General George Patton, Buckner was a real character. He was also a man to whom Alaska owes much.

3

The DLAND at West Ruby

DURING THE TENSE WINTER of 1940–41, our entry into the war seemed more and more inevitable. The United States had already begun mustering its resources to support the Allies, and the CAA received word that Alaska would be involved in implementing the lend-lease program to Russia.

A stream of desperately needed military airplanes, including P-39 fighters, B-25 bombers, and C-47 cargo planes, were to be ferried up through Canada and Alaska. The Russians would then take the aircraft over the Seward Peninsula, across the Bering Sea to Siberia, and farther westward into battle.

The Canadians and the Americans cooperated to build the chain of staging and intermediate airports needed to facilitate the transfer. Military plans called for construction of one of these airfields at a point midway between Fairbanks and Nome. The field had to have a runway at least 5,000 feet long and, in view of Alaska's uncertain weather, needed to be equipped for instrument approach. In those days an instrument approach consisted of a four-course low-frequency range in line with the airport. Optimum performance was provided by placing the range towers exactly two miles from the end of the airport runway.

Since the CAA already had a radio range at Ruby, a town along the Yukon River about halfway between Fairbanks and Nome, money was appropriated to expand the facility into a full-fledged DLAND airfield. But, in truth, the short strip at Ruby was totally inadequate. Situated on a high ridge, there was no way it could have been lengthened to 5,000 feet in order to accommodate fighters and bombers, let alone have room for an instrument approach. And due to its elevation (several hundred feet), the field was often covered with fog when the weather down closer to the river was clear.

The situation at Ruby was just one of the many Alaskan responsibilities of Bill Seeley, Chief of Airways Engineering, a competent, dedicated man who had worked as an airways engineer all over the world. Bill and I ranged across the area for a couple of days in the Cessna T-50, searching for a suitable airport site.

Having flown the area for Mirow Air Service, I knew that the land along the Yukon River was subject to recurring spring floods, although the extent of the flooding varied greatly from year to year. My intention was to locate the airport on reasonably elevated ground, yet not so high as to be often shrouded by fog.

I'd talked extensively with Bill and he seemed to appreciate my recommendations. After hours of aerial reconnaissance, we finally found a site we both liked at a place called Bishop Mountain, near Pilot Mountain, some fifty miles west of Ruby and right along the Yukon. The site was roughly seventy-five feet above the river, so it was protected from flooding. There was adequate room for an instrument approach from the south, and the runway would be more or less in line with the prevailing winds. We agreed we'd found the right place.

The only problem was that the funds had been committed for construction at Ruby. Seeley was a great one for eliminating red tape. He simply renamed our Bishop Mountain site West Ruby and proceeded with the planning. No one in Washington knew the difference, and as long as the place had *Ruby* in its name, the appropriation was secure.

Seeley's work on the Bishop Mountain project received several weeks of my undivided attention. We'd fly as far as Nulato in our Cessna T-50, affectionately known as the "bamboo bomber," and land on a stretch of river ice that Pacific Alaska kept rolled down for wheel operation. Their packed snow strip was familiar to me because I used to stop there and get the mail for the run into Unalakleet. From Nulato we'd charter Jack Hermann of Ferguson Airways to take us over to Bishop Mountain, landing his ski-equipped Stinson on a slough near the proposed site.

Seeley operated a lightweight mountain transit, and I wielded a sharp axe. Assisted by two Nulato Indians, we brushed out some 5,000 feet down the centerline of the proposed runway. Then we cleared another two miles out to the spot where the low-frequency range station would be located.

Seeley thought we'd done enough on our preliminary layout; he planned to have additional engineers come in later to conduct a more detailed survey. To complete the study, he needed to obtain core samples of the ground beneath the centerline in order to determine whether or not the soil was adequate for runway construction. Seeley explained that a regularly spaced set of cores would have to be drilled down to a depth of at least six feet, with soil samples gathered at each one-foot interval.

We obviously were going to need a lot of help with the project. Since I knew many of the Indians in the Nulato area from my days of flying the mail, it seemed that I was the logical choice for organizing an expedition to get the samples. I hired half a dozen young workers from the village and an elderly native, who came along as camp manager and cook. We then began to outfit ourselves with the necessary equipment.

It's almost impossible to dig through solidly frozen ground, so I knew we'd need a boiler to thaw the area around the holes. For many years the Northern Commercial Company had manufactured a lightweight portable gold prospector's boiler that two men could easily carry. The boiler came equipped with one thaw point, steam pressure and water level gauges, and a safety valve. A pan on the top was kept full of snow to obtain meltwater, which was added from time to time with a hand injector whenever the water level dropped. All in all it was an amazingly well-designed little boiler.

I knew of one owned by the Bureau of Indian Affairs in Nenana, so I flew over there and asked to borrow it. When I returned to the crew waiting back at Nulato, the Indians took off for Bishop Mountain with the boiler, a tent, and a mound of provisions lashed onto their dog sleds.

While Seeley stayed in the village to work out his computations and draft technical drawings of the runway, Jack Hermann would fly me over to the survey site, where I'd spend the day with the native crew. In the evening Hermann would return and fly me back to Nulato.

The natives were leery of the boiler, so I appointed myself chief boiler operator. Surprisingly, we found several spots where heavy, moss-like vegetation had insulated the ground from the winter's cold and no thawing was required. But most of the time we had to go through the tortuous process of steaming each test hole. Bringing the boiler up to heat always wasted a couple of hours each morning, so our progress on the cores was rather slow.

One morning, after Hermann had flown me into camp, the weather turned bad. Snow began falling, and when a thick fog rolled in, I prepared to spend the night in camp with the natives. I watched while the Indian cook made up a huge potful of boiled rice and reindeer meat for the evening dinner. Covered with a floating mat of reindeer hair and gray scum, the stew didn't look too appetizing to me. But when you're hungry enough you'll eat almost anything. I took a bowlful, and in fact the meat proved to be delicious.

I thought that, as long as I was going to be there, I might as well keep feeding green wood to the boiler, figuring that with one good stoking in the middle of the night I might be able to keep up steam, giving us a head start in the morning.

The next day the weather was even worse, but I enjoyed spending the time with my Indian friends. I decided to stay with the crew until the entire job was finished.

In a couple of days the weather cleared and Jack Hermann landed his Stinson on the nearby slough. We had a large bunch of samples ready to send back to Seeley for analysis. "Looks like we've got only about three days of work left," I told Hermann. "Since things are going so well, I thought I'd stay here with the boys until we're done." I was getting so accustomed to our primitive living conditions that I felt right at home in the camp.

That night the weather turned cold. Temperatures dropped lower than forty degrees below zero. Even so, the small wood stove in the tent kept all of us warm and cozy. We'd shoot the breeze until we became drowsy, then drift off to sleep.

A little after midnight I got up to check the boiler, intending to keep it going throughout the bitterly cold night. Wriggling out of my sleeping bag, I put on a pair of mukluks and hastily buttoned a heavy parka over my long underwear before braving the walk outside into the chilling air.

When I got to the boiler I was astonished to see that its safety valve had stuck. The pressure indicator was way up into the red, indicating that the tank might explode at any moment. Quickly, I reached down and spun open an emergency valve that permitted immediate dumping of the boiler's contents through a two-inch line.

Steam rocketed out of the pipe, engulfing the camp in great, billowing clouds. The roar of the emptying boiler split the silence of the cold clear night. The malemutes uncurled from their slumber and leaped to their feet, all of them barking and yelping at once. The Indians came rushing out of the tent, wondering what the hell was happening. They were met with a steamy fog so thick you couldn't see your hand in front of your face.

The boiler finally emptied and the fog dissipated, allowing us to see once again. We all enjoyed a good laugh over the incident as we crawled back into our sleeping bags.

After a few more days our mission was completed. Seeley and I packed up the soil samples and engineering data and flew back to Anchorage. Later he recruited a full survey crew, which returned to take cross sections at the site. Shortly afterward a contract for building the Bishop Mountain field and radio range (designated on official records as West Ruby) was awarded to the R. J. Sommers Construction Company.

Winter ebbed, and the mighty Yukon once again shed its seasonal covering of ice. After breakup opened the river to navigation, the Sommers Construction Company encamped at West Ruby and began building the runway.

Our soil samples had indicated a potential problem with permafrost. Before long, Sommers's on-site work confirmed the presence of ice lenses underlying the surface. That discovery meant that two years might be required to complete construction of a usable airport. The ground would have to be stripped and allowed sufficient time to thaw and dry.

The military advised us in no uncertain terms that two years was too long; the airfield *had* to be ready by the end of the summer for use by the lend-lease aircraft. We'd just have to find some other site

—one where thawed ground would permit construction to begin immediately.

Seeley and I pulled out of Anchorage in N-5, the CAA's float-equipped Bellanca. We'd been forced back to the drawing board with very little time left to finish the project. We figured we could find thawed ground almost anywhere along the Yukon if we picked a spot close enough to the shore, so we took a look at the flats near the village of Galena. With no pretense of making a real survey, we just paced out a strip, deciding that if the Army had to have an airport by the end of the summer, then Galena was going to be its location.

The Sommers crew, unaware of the change in plan, was still working full-bore at West Ruby. Seeley and I flew over there and landed in the slough. After finding the Sommers foreman, we told him to shut down the entire operation.

"Well, I'll be a sonovabitch!" he exclaimed. "And I thought this field was supposed to be so damn critical."

"The airport's still got to be built, but you'll have to move your men and equipment—and start all over again. The new site is at Galena."

The foreman shook his head. "And how the hell are we going to get there?"

"By steamboat," I replied. The natives had told me they'd seen the steamer *Nenana* pass by the previous day, heading downriver. Our problems would be solved if I could find the *Nenana* and convince her captain to turn around and go back upstream. The vessel pushed a barge large enough to accommodate all the earth-moving equipment on the trip from Bishop Mountain to Galena, about twenty miles downriver.

I took off in the Bellanca to scout for the steamboat. Skimming not far above the Yukon's waters, I traced the river downstream for miles before spotting the *Nenana* below Kaltag, chugging along with her barge. I dove at the ship a couple of times to get their attention, then landed in the river and began signaling frantically.

The captain finally turned the *Nenana* to head upstream, keeping just enough power to hold steerageway. I taxied up near the barge and shut down the Bellanca's engine. The skipper drifted a boat over to me, and I managed to get into it while holding fast to a line from the Bellanca. Then we trailed the airplane behind the barge while I went up to powwow with the captain.

"The government needs your help in moving the Sommers construction outfit from Bishop Mountain to Galena," I told him. "The military has to get an airfield built there before the end of the summer. And unless we can move the crew in fast, we're not going to make it."

The captain looked me over curiously. I had no documents to corroborate what I was telling him. "I'd better check on this," he said. Using the ship's radio, he made several attempts to reach someone in authority, to no avail. I could see that the captain was doing a little soul searching; he had perishables aboard that were destined for locations downriver.

"Dammit!" he said finally. "I might get fired for this, but if it's going to help the war effort I'll go back and pick up that construction crew." In those days I think individuals exercised far more independent judgment than they do today; then too, the imminence of war modified everyone's philosophy.

"You're making the right decision," I told him. "The CAA will back you all the way."

The captain cast me adrift, and in a few minutes I was airborne. From the cockpit of the Bellanca I could see the *Nenana* moving upriver, headed toward the West Ruby construction site.

The skipper, plying the river at summer's end, would see that his decision had indeed been right. The Sommers crew completed the airport and a hangar in plenty of time. By fall, lend-lease aircraft were using the badly needed refueling stop in their flights toward the Russian front.

However, the Galena airstrip was subject to flooding each spring. Had the West Ruby field been completed, it no doubt would have been a much better facility; but considering the press of war, the Army's decision was probably justified.

After the war, the military thwarted the rampaging springtime Yukon to an extent by building sturdy dikes around the Galena airport. Nevertheless, during one bad Yukon flood, the waters rose to a height of ten feet around the hangar and other airport buildings, prompting some wag to erect a sign: THROUGH THIS HANGAR FLOWED THE BIGGEST DAMN RIVER IN THE WHOLE WORLD.

4

Injured Man Aboard

AS LONG AS I'M AIRBORNE, I usually do all right. It's when I'm on the ground that I tend to get in trouble—the way I did up at Gulkana one day during the busy summer of 1941.

With more and more DLAND airfields entering the development

phase, Bill Seeley discovered he needed to tour the jobs continuously, inspecting the progress and seeing what he could do to get the work moving even faster. Most of the actual construction had been farmed out under contract to companies such as Lytle and Green, Sommers Construction Company, Morrison-Knudson Company, and others. The CAA had assigned a resident engineer and small support group to each location to supervise the day-to-day work. They, in turn, were under the direction of Bill Seeley, the engineer in charge of all facilities. My job—and it had developed into a more or less permanent assignment—was to fly Bill around on his periodic visits to the construction sites. We had a regular circuit, beginning with Cordova, then north to Gulkana, Northway, Big Delta, and Galena, and finally back home via Bethel and King Salmon.

In the Gulkana area we were still occupied with the process of site selection. The tiny community of Gakona had a small airstrip adequate for the Cessna, so we made the settlement our temporary base of operation. Ward Gay, head of the survey crew, met Seeley and me at the strip with a pickup truck. While Seeley went off to confer with some engineers, Ward offered to drive me in the pickup to a spot north of town that looked promising for the DLAND facility. We crawled along at less than ten miles an hour, following an old trail overgrown with tall grass.

We had just started across a small wooden bridge spanning a little creek when the front end broke through the rotted planks, jolting the truck to an immediate stop. Ward came through unhurt because he was braced against the steering wheel, but I crashed into the windshield and split my scalp. Gingerly, I put my hand up to my forehead. When I pulled my hand back, it looked just as though I'd stuck it into a bucket of red paint.

"Oh, my God!" Ward gasped after taking one look at me. From his expression I knew the cut had to be pretty serious. "Stay right here, Jack! I'm going to get help," he said. Then Ward took off, running down the road.

I sat there awhile, and the bleeding gradually slowed. I didn't feel too bad, except that my right eye was swollen shut. While sitting in the pickup, I heard the sound of a large truck somewhere off in the distance; shortly, I faintly heard another truck passing by. I realized I must be near the Richardson Highway, which connects Valdez and Fairbanks.

"To hell with this waiting," I thought. I started walking slowly toward the gravel highway and eventually reached it. I was on the roadside for only a few minutes when a big semi headed for Valdez happened along. I flagged down the driver, who gave me a ride back to Gakona.

Bill Seeley was still afield with his engineers. I figured I should get medical attention as soon as possible, so I decided to fly back to Anchorage and see a doctor. I left a note explaining where I'd gone and saying that I'd have Al Horning come to pick up Seeley the next morning.

As I approached Sheep Mountain Pass in the Cessna T-50, I had to climb above 11,000 feet, trying to get around a huge thunderstorm that barred my path. The damn cut opened up again and began to bleed profusely; I immediately lost all interest in fighting my way on to Anchorage. But the weather seemed pretty good to the south, toward Cordova. I headed the plane over in that direction.

Flying toward the coast over the spectacular Chugach Mountains, I began trying to contact Cordova on the radio, finally reaching the CAA range station there. "I've got an injured man aboard," I told the operator. "Can you get a doctor to meet the plane?"

"Roger, NC-34," the station replied. "We'll have a doctor standing by."

The flight dragged on. I could see through only one eye, and it also had begun to swell. Fortunately the weather remained good. Eventually I landed at Cordova, where my plane was met by several people, including the local doctor and Merle "Mudhole" Smith, founder of Cordova Airlines. When I climbed out of the plane, even the doctor seemed somewhat shocked. Mudhole Smith exclaimed, "Hell, Jack, we didn't know *you* were the injured man!"

The doctor immediately took me to the community hospital. The next thing I knew, I was stretched out on the operating table. I asked for a mirror to see how I looked, then understood why everyone was so taken aback at my appearance. My head seemed to have been chopped with a cleaver. The enormous swelling of one eye and puffiness around the other distorted my features beyond recognition. I certainly seemed to be in doggone tough shape. When the nurse finished cleaning me up a little, the doctor started in with the needle and thread. Thirteen stitches later, he finished patching my scalp. I was then assigned to a room.

After lying in bed quite a while, I realized I was hungry. I got up, put on my clothes, and went down to the local bar and grill, where I ordered up a meal and a before-dinner martini. It seemed to me that I certainly deserved a drink after all I'd been through that day. The bartender didn't seem to pay much attention to my appearance as he poured the martini; all kinds of beat-up fishermen and construction workers patronized the place, and some of them looked in even worse shape than I did.

I sat back to enjoy the martini and was savoring my first sip, when who should walk in but the doctor. "Jefford, this is no way for a patient to act! You should be back at the hospital," he said, rather indignantly.

"But I was just famished," I explained, sheepishly.

He sort of relaxed, then smiled. "Okay, Jefford. I'll stay here until you finish your dinner. Then I'll drive you back."

In less than an hour, we returned to the hospital. After escorting me all the way to my bed, the doctor brought over the night nurse. I've never had a worse dressing down from anyone. She was after me like an old mother hen. "I've never heard of such a thing," she snapped, "leaving the hospital right after an operation! When you're in the hospital, you're in the hospital, and you're supposed to remain here until you're properly dismissed. You've got to promise you'll stay in this room for the rest of the night!"

By the next morning the swelling had gone down considerably, and I felt well enough to fly. I cranked up the airplane, met Seeley in Gakona, and we continued on our circuit of the developing DLAND airfields.

5

War

IT WAS THE EVENING of December 6, 1941. I had flown CAA Director/ Regional Manager Marshall Hoppin to Juneau for a meeting with Territorial Governor Ernest Gruening. Juneau was also home base for U.S. Forester Charlie Burdick. When Burdick found out I was in town, he threw a cocktail party for me, celebrating the friendship we had developed during the reindeer acquisition flights.

Martinis flowed freely. As guest of honor I consumed quite a succession of them, becoming pretty well stoned. At some point late in the evening, the Burdicks "closed the bar" and put me to bed on the daveno in their living room. It snowed six or seven inches that night as I slept soundly upon the couch. When I awoke on the morning of December 7, I was greeted by a soft, clean, pure blanket of whiteness that covered the town and surrounding hills.

I'd gotten some coffee and was trying to recall the murky events of the night before when I heard a newspaper boy out on the street shouting, "Extra! Extra! Read all about it! Japanese bomb Pearl Harbor!"

The news was electrifying, unbelievable. I dashed out and bought the paper, a single-page extra edition of the Juneau *Empire.* I devoured the meager details of the sneak attack and immediately switched on the radio. Those early, breathless bulletins describing the sudden descent of war on the United States seemed incredible.

My first thought was to telephone Marshall Hoppin. "We'd better get right back to Anchorage," he decided. "I'll meet you at the airport in fifteen minutes." All across the Territory the home guard was mobilizing, and everyone was quite edgy.

Normal procedure after taking off from Juneau was to intercept the Ralston Island radio range west of Juneau, pick up a southwesterly course toward Cape Spencer, intercept the Yakutat radio range, then fly to Anchorage via Hinchinbrook Island.

Anchorage was reporting good weather. However, ceilings along the way were low, so I decided to see if I could get on top. Climbing on the southwesterly course, we had barely broken out on top of the overcast when the Juneau range abruptly went off the air. At first I suspected a power failure. We managed to tune in the Yakutat range, but after a minute or so, it too went off the air.

What had happened was that range operators throughout Alaska had received a panic directive to shut down all radio navigational aids on the basis that Japanese aircraft might use them to home in on Alaskan cities. For a week or two, pandemonium reigned. The ranges were repeatedly and arbitrarily shut down, then brought back on line.

We found ourselves above the overcast with no radio ranges to guide us. Fortunately, 15,300-foot Mount Fairweather and 18,000-foot Mount St. Elias were jutting above the clouds in all their majesty. Using those tall peaks as markers, I was able to navigate my way up the coast, landing without incident in Anchorage.

Alaska was quickly placed on wartime footing. All private flying came to a halt. Small aircraft near the coast were ordered dismantled, and any airplane along the lines of a transport was seized and pressed into military service. There was, as yet, no Air Force—military flying was being done by Army Air Corps pilots.

As second lieutenants in the Army Air Corps Reserve, both Al Horning and I were ordered to report to Elmendorf Field for flight physicals and induction into the military service. We were good friends of the air officer, Colonel Davis, who was eager to have us aboard because of our so-called Alaskan expertise. Both of us were gung-ho and all fired up to join the action. Seeing the B-17s touch down at Elmendorf made us impatient to begin flying those huge, sophisticated, highpowered aircraft.

We gave little thought to the fact that our induction into the Air Corps would completely wipe out the CAA's Alaska flight staff. The agency was in quite a jam and was understandably concerned. Even before our induction, Al and I had been unable to keep abreast of the workload, sometimes flying our Cessna T-50s seven days a week.

The CAA, by means of a frantic appeal to the War Department, managed to get thirty-day deferments for Horning and me. We received this news with mixed emotions. At the CAA's urging, the Air Corps even tried to get us to resign our commissions.

Horning, indignant, composed a masterful telegram in which he refused. His wire said No! so eloquently and was such a beautiful piece of prose that I asked his permission to copy it word for word and send it along under my name. Our telegrams advised the Air Corps that we were unequivocally committed to the service for the duration. Under no circumstances would we consider resigning.

The CAA, however, persuaded the military to give us six-month deferments, which the Army kept renewing throughout the course of the war. As a result, both Horning and I wound up fighting the entire war in the CAA—although a time or two we did get pretty damn close to the actual fighting down in the Aleutians at Kiska and Attu.

6

The Queen Mary

THE CAA ACQUIRED a new airplane in the spring of 1942, a large twelve-place amphibian manufactured by the Douglas Aircraft Company. Although it was tradenamed the Dolphin, when our Deputy Director Walt Plett first saw N-26, he facetiously dubbed it the "Queen Mary"—a nickname that stuck for as long as we owned the airplane. The CAA purchased it from Bill Boeing of the Boeing Aircraft Company. He'd had the seaplane accompany his yacht on trips along the Inside Passage, ready for him to use as a classy way of commuting to his favorite British Columbia fishing spots.

The Dolphin was well suited to our exploration work; it was good on wheels as well as in the water. The airplane had wooden wings and a very strong aluminum hull and was powered by two Pratt and Whitney S1D1 engines. The Dolphin did have a couple of drawbacks: its draft was pretty deep, and its airspeed was rather slow. Fuel management was also somewhat of a problem. The aircraft had six tanks, but only two were active; the others had to be dumped into the main tanks when fuel ran low. If you didn't understand the arrangement, it was possible to run out of fuel while actually having plenty in reserve. With its black fuselage and orange-trimmed wings, N-26 was kind of a sinister-looking old bird; but except for the slow airspeed, we enjoyed flying her.

Al Horning was our water expert; in fact, he was widely recognized as one of the best float pilots in Alaska. Al did most of the flying involving the *Queen Mary,* but on one occasion, when he happened to be off on a mission to Washington, I was tapped to take the Dolphin and a crew of surveyors over to Middleton Island out in the Gulf of Alaska. I was to assist them with their work, and when the survey for the radio range was completed, we were to return to Anchorage. It all sounded quite simple.

Matt Parvin, the number-two man in our hangar and an excellent mechanic, came along to act as copilot and swamper. Together we helped the engineers, George Karabelnikoff, Frank Yurg, and George McKean, load up the plane. After the camping gear, rifles, transits, and other survey equipment had been piled into the cabin, we cranked up and headed for the island. The weather was just beautiful, and I congratulated myself on getting such an easy assignment. Flying was so much better than working.

Middleton is a small piece of land located approximately 100 miles south of Cordova. I approached from the west across the much larger Montague Island, then navigated by dead reckoning out over the Gulf. Finding Middleton wouldn't be too much of a problem with such good visibility.

As we neared the island we saw, to our great surprise, that a large freighter had gone aground on the rocks near the west beach. Two Navy ships of the destroyer class, as well as a few smaller boats, were lying offshore near the wreckage. We later found out that the merchant had veered off course and had run aground two days earlier during a severe storm. The Navy vessels were there to assist in the salvage operation.

We hadn't heard anything about the accident and were totally unprepared for the sight of the crippled merchant. But the situation seemed to be well in hand, so we didn't let it concern us any further as we circled on in for a landing.

Although the storm had passed and the weather was good, the Gulf of Alaska was still very rough. Waves were over eight feet high. I made several passes, trying to find a place calm enough to set down the airplane. We eyed a small reef jutting out to the northwest; the waters behind it appeared to be a little smoother and somewhat protected from the open sea. I told everyone to fasten his seatbelt and we'd give it a try.

The strong wind helped slow our landing speed. As we settled onto the top of a large swell, I chopped the engines. Once we were down, waves began breaking over the Dolphin's nose and wings. One particularly large wave slapped into the left engine and killed it. I wished I'd had enough sense not to land, but there was no getting back into the air now. The water was so rough that several members of the expedition became seasick as we lurched through the heavy rollers, trying to make our way into shore.

Fortunately, there was a little cove on the north end, very small, but sheltered so that the waves were not so rough. After what seemed like ages of wallowing through the water, we finally entered the cove. I thought our troubles were over. I planned to taxi onto the shore, and we'd be safely out of the surf.

I extended the landing gear and ran up against the beach several times, but its slope was too abrupt and the sand too soft. We couldn't pull up on shore. After a short conference, we decided to drop anchor and go ashore in our inflatable rubber dinghy.

Our situation wasn't the greatest. With the airplane anchored like that, she was completely at the mercy of the elements. If another bad storm were to blow up, we'd just lose old N-26—and I'd probably be writing memos the rest of my life explaining how it had happened.

We ferried our equipment ashore in the rubber life raft and began to set up camp. Everyone shared my concern about the *Queen Mary,* and all of us hoped to get away from the island as soon as possible.

While the surveyors prepared their equipment, Matt and I set about erecting the tent. Suddenly, Matt gasped and dropped the canvas. I turned around and was astounded to see a squad of nervous Marines with cocked rifles pointed directly at us. Just one little squeeze would have spelled the end. "Put your hands in the air!" shouted a Marine sergeant.

I was so scared I could hardly talk, thinking, "I'm awfully young to die."

"Wait!" yelled George Karabelnikoff, "we're just here to do a survey!" The soldiers seemed shocked to hear him speaking English. While his men kept everyone covered, the sergeant ordered us to come over one at a time for interrogation.

I began pulling out identification and explaining myself, but the CAA meant absolutely nothing to him; and he saw the black-fuselaged *Queen Mary* as something directly out of Tokyo. A copy of our work order finally convinced him we were legitimate. Although the letter didn't actually mean very much, and certainly wasn't official, he saw that our mission to Middleton Island was fully outlined on the paper just as we had been describing it. He and his men went back to their ship, leaving us alone with our work.

Still shaking, the boys began their preliminary survey. I appointed myself cook and started preparing a nice lunch (not to be bragging, but I'm not half-bad as a camp cook). When the meal was ready, I stuck my head out of the tent and yelled, "Food's ready!"

The men came running down to the nice, level place where we were camped. By this time our anxiety over the episode with the soldiers had diminished, and our appetites were back. Inside the tent, away from the bugs, we relaxed for the first time on this miserable day.

As I was serving the food, I heard an unfamiliar sound. Suddenly we noticed water pouring in under the tent. It vanished, but pretty soon more water flooded the floor. We ran outside to discover that we'd pitched our tent below the high-tide line. Waves were lapping against the canvas. After bolting down the food, we grabbed all our equipment, struck the tent, and moved everything to higher ground.

When the dishes were done, I helped the surveyors handle the chain. We finished the survey that afternoon, but the water was still far too rough for takeoff, so I reluctantly said we'd just have to stay on Middleton overnight. Hopefully, we could leave the island the next morning.

When we crawled out of our sleeping bags the next day, wonder of all wonders, the skies were still clear. The wind had died down, and so had the waves. While the water was still rough, it was nothing like the day before. I thought we might go ahead and chance a takeoff.

We broke camp and, after repeated trips with the dinghy, got the plane loaded. Rounding the reef, we headed in a southwesterly direction through the ocean. Timing the crests of the seas, I thought, "It's now or never!"

I poured the coal to her and began moving into the waves. The main problem was keeping the bow high. We finally got up on the step, banging into the waves furiously as we picked up speed. Sometimes I wonder how those amphibians manage to hang together. Eventually we bounced into the sky—a joyous feeling, especially since the airplane was still intact. I immediately made a deal with myself: no more of this real rough water.

Before going back to town, we had a second chore to perform. We had been asked to look at another island, Bald Head Chris, which the CAA was considering as a possible location between Cordova and Anchorage for an observation post or, at the very least, a marker beacon.

Forty-five minutes after leaving Middleton, we were over Bald Head Chris, located in the sheltered waters of Prince William Sound. There were several derelict buildings below us, remnants of an abandoned fox farm. The sea was as smooth as a mill pond. What a relief to have a gentle landing.

I nosed into the beach, and we began unloading the survey equipment. That was a mistake; I should have turned the airplane around first. The tide was going out, and before we realized what was happening, the water was gone and we were lying there aground. Now we were forced to stay until the tide returned to float us off. All of the crew were experienced troopers and accepted our plight gracefully, deciding to finish the survey and make the best of things during the period before the next high tide.

It was a brilliant, beautiful day. With all the work done, George Karabelnikoff and I decided to take the rubber dinghy out into the bay and go fishing. We each grabbed an aluminum paddle and rowed offshore about a quarter mile. We weren't catching any fish, but the weather was lovely—no wind, the water glassy smooth. It was great to be alive.

We lounged in the raft, relaxed and peaceful. Suddenly a whale surfaced right beside us. I've never seen a creature so large in all my life. It broke water, leaping halfway out of the calm ocean, then dove back down. Not being a naturalist, I can't say what species it was— but it was a monster. The whale's backwash almost tipped us over. One brush of its huge tail would have been all that was needed to eliminate George K. and Jack Jefford.

Ordinarily, a rubber life raft of the sort we had is difficult to paddle. The two occupants usually move along slowly and awkwardly, finding it difficult to maintain directional control. Well, the guys on the beach swore we looked like a cartoon as we scrambled back to shore, paddling so fast that the dinghy appeared to be airborne.

The tide returned right on schedule, and we had enough light left to take off for Merrill Field. I was glad to get out of the plane in Anchorage, feeling more than content to let Al Horning continue in his unofficial reign as chief pilot of the *Queen Mary*.

7

Horning's Ordeal

IN THE MIDST of making another of our round-robin visits to the DLAND construction sites, Seeley and I had to overnight at Bethel. Problems had developed in the construction of the Bethel airfield, and Seeley was involved in extensive consultations that lasted throughout most of the rainy night.

In the morning the weather was beautiful, and Seeley was ready to leave for King Salmon. We arrived a little before noon, after a highly enjoyable flight. Seeley immediately walked off to check the progress of the King Salmon project, the building of a second runway. I sauntered over to the Flight Service Station to visit with the crew on watch and have a place to loaf. After the usual greetings one of the guys said, "Say, Jack, did you know Al Horning's due here in a few minutes?"

That rather surprised me. "Are you sure?"

"Yeah, he's headed in from Cold Bay. He radioed he was going to stop for gas and grab a bite to eat."

I knew that Horning and flight mechanic Ray Decker had headed out to Cold Bay three days earlier, just before Seeley and I had left on our trip. The resident engineer on the Cold Bay project had died suddenly, and Horning's mission was to transport the body back to town. Horning had taken the Dolphin, since the runway was still in the survey stage, and the only way in was by seaplane or boat. But it was just a one-day flight; Al must have run into some kind of trouble.

He was only about ten minutes out, so I took the station's battered pickup and drove down to the parking apron to say hello and give him a ride to the mess hall. I saw the aircraft approaching from the south. Horning didn't bother to follow any traffic pattern; he just came straight in and landed. As he pulled up I grew a little concerned; Al seemed to be frowning. Of everyone I knew, Al had the best attitude toward life. He always acted delighted to be alive, and he always wore a smile.

After the engine was shut down I walked back to the rear hatch to greet Al and Ray. When they opened the door, I was bowled over by the incredibly repulsive stench emanating from the cabin. I became so sickened that I began retching right there beside the airplane. A foul smell will get me every time.

Al and Ray lost no time jumping out of the aircraft. Horning had always been the type of guy you just didn't shake. He never got very excited about anything. There was a certain air of assurance about the man that seemed to say "Everything's under control."

But not this day. For the first time I saw him lose his cool. He was carrying a pyrene fire extinguisher, which he placed near the door. I didn't have to ask why. I knew. Many of the early fire extinguishers were filled with pyrene, a volatile substance that was extremely stinky in its own right. He was no doubt spraying the interior of the plane to help counteract the deathly smell.

As Horning filled me in on his trip, I realized they'd been having quite a time. The engineer had been dead for several days before the message came through to Anchorage and Horning was dispatched. It was summertime, and with no proper embalming facilities, the body had already begun to get a little ripe. To make matters worse, after starting for Anchorage Al had run into severe weather between Cold Bay and Port Heiden and had landed on a small lake to wait it out.

For two days they had sat there, waiting for the storm to pass. There was no food except for the rations that were packed with the emergency gear. And, as I've said before, those foods were so bad you had to be on your last legs before you'd bother to open them. Horning and Decker had also been without much sleep, just sitting in their seats and catching what little catnaps they could.

All of us walked away from the airplane to put some distance between us and the horrible stench. Personally, I didn't see how they could carry on with it.

Horning had just two things on his mind. First he wanted to get some food. Then his tunnel vision was focused on getting that grisly load into Anchorage as fast as possible. This was one adventure in which I was happy to be only an observer. After their hurried meal, I drove Al and Ray back to the Dolphin. In these circumstances, it looked much like a black and orange buzzard parked there next to the runway. Horning grabbed the strategically placed fire extinguisher and began spraying the corpse with the pyrene fluid, also dousing the interior of the aircraft to get plenty of evaporated pyrene to mask the smell of putrefaction. Both men grimaced as they boarded the aircraft for the final three hours in to Anchorage.

But, as with so many other situations we encountered in the flying business, especially in the early days, they just had to see it through, distasteful as it may have been.

I stayed in King Salmon with Seeley most of the afternoon. Later I checked with the FSS and found that Horning had arrived home with no further complications. His ordeal was over.

8
The Boeing 247

HORNING AND I were run ragged during the summer of 1942. Commissioning radio ranges, range checking, aerial surveys, personnel transport, and other special missions had to be sandwiched in among our ever-present routine freight runs. Although both of us were going out every day on lengthy supply flights to our burgeoning network of airfields and range stations, we still couldn't keep up with the demand.

Dan Victor, a former employee of Star Airlines, came aboard as our third patrol pilot; but even hiring Dan was only a partial solution. With the agency's construction program in full swing, none of our aircraft could carry enough of a load to get the job done. Some of the cargo could be flown in by bush operators, but they weren't properly equipped for the task either; the largest commercial freighter in the Territory was an old Ford Trimotor. So we'd gotten up on our soapbox, convincing the brass that we needed an aircraft of sufficient size to handle all of the freight destined for the agency's many far-flung installations.

In Washington, Chris Lample joined our search for a larger, better performing aircraft we could use as a freighter in the airways construction program. Chris located a Boeing 247, owned by the Celanese Corporation of New York, and negotiated a purchase price of $42,000. Knowing that the Air Corps was confiscating private aircraft left and right, Chris was afraid they might soon get their hands on the Boeing. We felt our need was far greater than the Army's. So in late August, Lample sent a frantic wire, telling me to come to Washington as fast as possible to pick up a purchase order, then hasten to New York, claim the plane, and hustle it back to Alaska.

I was on the next boat south. After reporting to Washington, I immediately proceeded to New York. Art Jenks and Randy Mulherin, CAA flight inspectors for the Eastern Region, met me at the airport and drove me downtown on a short tour of the city—my first sight of that great metropolis. I stayed in a downtown hotel that night, awed by wartime Manhattan's vast expanse of blacked-out buildings.

The next morning I presented myself at the headquarters of the Celanese Corporation. I showed the purchase order to a lower-echelon executive, who ushered me into the sedate, decorous office of the company president.

After the customary greetings we moved on to business. "Here's the purchase order for the Boeing 247," I said, handing him the authorization. "I'll be flying it back to Alaska for the CAA."

The president stalled a bit, looking over the purchase order without much expression. Then he sent for his chief corporate attorney. Obviously, the president wasn't about to turn loose the company's aircraft solely on the strength of the document I'd given him.

The attorney was just what you'd expect. A stately gentleman, he scrutinized the purchase order carefully, including all the fine print.

Finally, after pointedly looking my way, he vouchsafed his ruling, "Well, if you can't trust the United States government, who can you trust?" He picked up the telephone, called the airport, and authorized release of the airplane.

I'd never ridden in a Boeing 247, much less flown one. However, Randy Mulherin had once served as copilot in this type of aircraft, and he offered to fly with me as far west as Pittsburgh. After an hour and a half of flying under his tutelage, I was confident I could figure out all the knobs and dials. Even so, I hoped I might find someone at Pittsburgh to accompany me the rest of the way north.

After landing in Pittsburgh, we decided I was sufficiently competent to take the plane on to Alaska, so Randy caught the next flight back to New York. I was left all by myself in what I considered to be a giant Boeing 247, and I began thinking about finding a crew. The chap who was refueling the airplane, Harry Lumen, seemed to be a nice, personable young fellow, so I asked, "How'd you like a job copiloting this airplane to Alaska?"

"You've got to be kidding," he replied.

"Not at all," I assured him. "If you want it, the job's yours right now." (In those days we had a lot of latitude.)

The youth stared at me in sheer disbelief for a few moments, but as the prospect of an adventurous new job and a trip to the Far North began to dawn on him, he became obviously delighted. "I'll need a half hour to tell my mother and get my things together!" he said.

"Sure, I'll do better than that," I told him. "Take two hours."

In great excitement he called his mother, dashed home to pick up his gear, then returned promptly to the airport.

Harry Lumen and I brought NC-18 on to Alaska, where Walt Plett tagged it with the unofficial name "King Arthur." Harry decided to stick around and remained with the agency for several years, working at our Anchorage hangar.

I did make one mistake when I picked up *King Arthur*. It had been owned originally by United Airlines, who traded it to Capitol Airlines. After Capitol obtained their DC-3s, the Boeing was sold to the Celanese Corporation. Upon taking delivery of the aircraft in New York, I was asked what I wanted to do about its logbooks.

"Well, just send them to the CAA in Anchorage by Railway Express," I said casually. What I didn't know was that the logbooks documented every flight made with the aircraft in its 20,000 hours with United, Capitol, and Celanese.

Three months later more than a ton of paper, including every flight ticket ever issued on the aircraft, arrived in Anchorage. What made it worse was that I'd specified *express,* and the freight bill was over $500—a large sum of money in 1942. Nearly all that paperwork was completely useless to the CAA and had to be thrown away. Needless to say, my face was pretty red over the incident.

In my book, the Boeing 247 was the forerunner of all the modern airliners. While there were other comfortable planes, such as the twin-engine Curtiss Condor, some of the Fords, and others, the Boeing was the first with retractable landing gear, deicer boots on the wings, and alcohol for the propellers. In fact, the Boeing was one of the best airplanes in icing conditions that I've ever flown. It had the capability for really tough instrument flying.

The 247 made the respectable speed of 140 knots or so, and would haul a lot of cargo—2,800 pounds or more. Its only drawback was the small fuel supply. The aircraft had been designed as a short-range transport and would hold only four hours of fuel. It seemed as though we were always stopping for gas in the Boeing, but we found the plane invaluable during the early days for transporting men, equipment, and supplies to airports under construction in the DLAND program.

Its excellent foul-weather characteristics also made the Boeing invaluable for the business of selling instrument flying in Alaska. We were busy installing the required facilities all over the state, including the southeastern panhandle, which stretches toward the U.S. mainland. Everyone eagerly awaited the day when we would have reliable airline transportation to Seattle and points east. The military was still ferrying most of their warplanes up through the Interior, but even they were interested in the coastal route.

We had established a radio range on Ralston Island near Juneau. One course pointed up Lynn Canal; another led the way across the low terrain to Cape Spencer, allowing traffic to get out over the Gulf of Alaska. The southwest course of the Juneau range intersected the southeast course of the Yakutat range; a pilot, therefore, could proceed northwest on instruments from Juneau to Yakutat and on up the coast to Cordova, Hinchinbrook Island, and Anchorage (Cape Yakataga had not yet been constructed). Flying south from Juneau we could go as far as Ketchikan, where the military had established a facility on nearby Annette Island.

We had good luck flying the southeast coast of Alaska and made the interesting discovery that, if we stayed out to sea a ways, the tops of the overcast were generally quite low. The flow of weather across the onshore mountains had a tendency to lift the cloud cover, but if you were out to sea a considerable distance, you sometimes topped the stuff as low as 7,000 or 8,000 feet. We continued to plug for a facility on Middleton Island so we could easily keep the flyway partly out to sea.

Up until this time everyone felt that the IFR (Instrument Flight Rules) airway from Alaska to the States would have to go down through Canada. But as we began flying the coast as far as Ketchikan with some degree of regularity, we felt that with the addition of a couple of coastal facilities in Canada we would have no problem going all the way to Seattle.

We had several planning sessions with the military, and they agreed with us; so we set up a meeting with the Canadians at Vancouver, British Columbia. Chris Lample came up to do the negotiating. I flew him and the rest of the CAA party IFR down the coast all the way from Anchorage to Vancouver. We were on top of the overcast from Ketchikan south, making use of a couple of marine beacons along the way. Our flight was more or less an attempt to prove it could be done safely.

We spent a couple of days in Vancouver, meeting with officials of the Royal Canadian Air Force and describing our plans for and feelings about a coastal airway. They agreed to put in range stations at Masset, on the north side of Graham Island, at Port Hardy, and at Comox. Our Sitka facility was still in the preliminary stage of construction, so we put in a fan marker between Sitka and Masset on Forrester Island— just a fix, nothing more. When the stations were completed, we finally had established the long-awaited all-weather coastal route between Alaska and the continental United States.

9

A Tale of Two Cessnas

THE TWO TWIN-ENGINE Cessna T-50s had started out being identical. But destiny gave them strikingly different fates.

The T-50 that bore the number NC-34 held an ominous secret encased within its weather-beaten wings. Its successor, NC-118, was brand-new, shiny, and spick-and-span throughout, reflecting the care and fastidiousness of the pilot who usually flew her. Although she seemed destined for happy flying in Alaska's skies, the story of NC-118 unfolded far differently than anyone would have expected.

The strange tale of two Cessnas began one winter evening in January, 1942, at the Anchorage Elks Club, the social center of the bustling community.

It was after midnight, and revelry at the Elks was reaching its height. I'd been hoisting a few while enjoying the camaraderie of friends, swapping stories, and having a roaring good time. Then a figure at the doorway caught my eye. Heading toward me was Gene Berato, of the Merrill Field Communications Station. At first I didn't notice how pale and shaken Gene looked, but when he approached, I realized something was definitely wrong. "Hey, Gene . . . let me buy you a drink!" I called to him, trying to figure out what the trouble was.

"No thanks, Jack. Look, I've got to talk to you. Alone." Gene's voice and his unusual nervousness were quite sobering.

"Sure, Gene," I said. "Let's go outside."

Trembling, he hesitated, as if he didn't know how to explain the problem. "My God, Jack!" he finally blurted out. "I backed into your plane with my car as I was going off watch at midnight. What am I going to do?"

We used to park agency aircraft at Merrill Field beside the old FSS building, which in those days was nothing more than an oversized cabin. "Aw, you probably didn't hurt it too bad" was all I could think to say.

"No, I really tore it up!" he said in great agitation. "I went way into the wing and smashed the stabilizer, too."

Gene had good reason to be agitated. Backing into one of Uncle Sam's airplanes was about the biggest no-no there was. Suddenly I became as sober as Gene. I had to find out how much damage Gene's car had done to NC-34. Then I had to figure out what to do about it.

"Well, there's not very much we can do tonight, but let's go out to Merrill and have a look," I said.

Bad? The damage was awful!

Poor Gene was fit to be tied. He could see his career vanishing and was envisioning the federal investigation that would ensue—the possible fines, the probable dismissal. A guy that was going to be hung at sunrise couldn't have looked sadder.

I was playing the beam of my flashlight over the ripped wing when I saw something that caught me up short. "Hey, Gene, get a look at this!" I said, focusing the light inside the jagged hole in the wing.

"What is it?" inquired Gene anxiously.

"Look at all that moisture damage in there. See those rotted wing spars? This damn plane could have fallen apart on my next trip. For all I know, you might well have saved my life!"

Gene was speechless.

NC-34 was one of the first airplanes we'd brought to the Territory. It had spent quite a bit of time in southeast Alaska and had traveled down the Chain as far as Cold Bay. Both those areas are notorious for drenching rains, and they'd sure taken a heavy toll on the Cessna. To compound the problem, the aircraft had been sent out of the factory with the drains still closed on the bottom of the wing. With no other ventilation for the moisture, the interior of the wing had become extremely damp.

Since the airplane was constructed almost totally of wood, the trapped water produced disastrous effects. The factory varnish and preservative treatments had been insufficient to prevent widespread rot. Wing-spar laminations were separating; the whole wing and stabilizer were literally disintegrating. The water damage was so extensive that several gussets had fallen off the wing ribs and were lying loose on the fabric.

I turned to Gene. "Go home and get a good night's sleep. I doubt if the CAA will give you a commendation for this, but you shouldn't get much of a reprimand, either."

Relief flooded Gene's face. "Thanks, Jack. " As he walked away, the guy looked as though he'd been given a new lease on life.

Early the next morning I was at the hangar helping the mechanics carve open the other wing. Its interior was just as bad as the one Gene had accidentally exposed. Seriously rotted. An air crash waiting to happen.

We patched and reinforced NC-34 as best we could. Then I ferried it back to the Cessna plant at Wichita under reduced airspeed.

In Wichita I picked up NC-118, a new, nearly identical T-50, which permanently replaced NC-34.

In those days we had an unwritten policy of assigning each pilot his own airplane. Unless one of us was sick or out of town, we considered each plane pretty much the exclusive property of a single pilot. Dan Victor, our newly hired pilot, took command of NC-118. The plane was new, bright, and immaculate—a perfect fit for Dan.

Although born in Turkey, Dan was of Greek descent. He had a pronounced accent, which was hard to identify with any particular nationality—it seemed to be a blend of several. Dan was always interesting and a real nice guy to be around.

Dan was one of the few bush pilots I've ever known who always dressed impeccably. If Horning or I had been flying much, we usually looked pretty raunchy. But Dan could be out in the bush for weeks, under miserable conditions, yet return with a sharp crease in his trousers—looking as though he'd stepped out of the pages of *Esquire.* He would always pitch in and load freight with the rest of us, and no matter how disheveled we managed to get, he always stayed neat and orderly. Being a sort of slop-pot myself, I always envied him his well-groomed appearance.

Dan was as fastidious with NC-118 as he was with himself, taking delight in keeping his aircraft in top condition. He lost no time in painting a small *U.S.* up on its nose, and he always saw to it that the interior and exterior were spotless. He couldn't do enough, it seemed, to keep NC-118 looking sharp.

The morning of November 19, 1942, Dan was scheduled to fly to Moses Point with a radio technician, Noble Bass, and a heavy duty mechanic, Henry Weir. Though a routine flight, it was Dan's first trip to Moses Point. I drove him to Merrill Field from the CAA's downtown office. (By then we had moved from the railroad yards to nicer quarters in the new Federal Building.)

"How long will it take me to fly to Moses Point?" he asked as we headed down Fifth Avenue.

"It should run you about two and a half hours," I replied.

I stood beside him as he filed his flight plan, then watched as he walked over to his gleaming NC-118 and got aboard. After he taxied out and took off, I headed back downtown, not thinking anything more about it. But late that evening the FSS called me at home.

"Dan Victor hasn't arrived at Moses Point," the CAA operator informed me. "In his last radio contact with Galena, he told them he was crossing the Yukon just below Kaltag. We've already notified the Director."

I called Al Horning immediately, and Al and I prepared to start searching at daylight the next morning.

This search, I figured, should prove easier than most of them. For one thing, we were looking for a competent pilot, who certainly would have kept on course. Second, the area in which he vanished had been narrowed down considerably; the radio report had him crossing the Yukon. The distance from there to his destination was less than a hundred miles.

One thing troubled me greatly. Weather was apparently not a factor in Dan's disappearance. We'd heard from another pilot who'd been flying in the area at pretty much the same time as Dan that, except for broken clouds at about 4,000 feet, flying weather had been excellent. Then what had happened?

Horning took his twin Cessna, and I had the Boeing with about ten people aboard as observers. The more eyes you can get on a search plane, the better your chances of success. A couple of other airplanes, piloted by Anchorage flyers, also joined the search.

In those days everyone searched on his own without any real organization. Pilots would start by retracing the flight path of the missing aircraft, then begin branching out. The longer the search, the farther out they would branch. Nowadays, with a well-equipped Rescue Coordination Center and the Civil Air Patrol conducting the search, pilots are assigned specific sections of a grid pattern. That's certainly the scientific way to do it. But back then everyone just searched the best way they knew.

We were well into the third day of the search for Dan without the slightest clue. Even though Norton Sound was frozen over, we began to wonder whether it was possible for him to have gone down into one of the open leads and then been covered up by the drifting ice.

We were very discouraged. The hour was late, and everyone was dog tired and about ready to give up. But for some reason I had to give it another try. "Let's go back one more time to where he crossed the Yukon," I said. "Then let's fly a direct course to Moses Point before we call it a day."

We were crossing the Nulato Hills on a course to Moses Point when just ahead, near the top of a mountain, I noticed a black spot that seemed somehow out of place. I zeroed in on it as we flew over, then circled back across again. I realized with deep sadness and sickening certainty that we'd found the wreckage of NC-118.

I called Al Horning on the radio and asked him to join us. Al and I made pass after pass over the wreckage while holding radio consultations. We were sure of one thing—there were no survivors. NC-118 had burned. The only recognizable part of the plane was its door. The impact had hurled it about a hundred yards from the rest of the wreckage.

The next morning we attended a conference in the regional office. Clarence Rhode of the Fish and Wildlife Service had a Fairchild 24 on skis, and he volunteered his services. Rhode was quite familiar with the terrain. He was fairly sure he could land on a ridge above the crash site and then climb down to the wreckage. He and Gene Gull, a CAA inspector, took off the next day.

Meanwhile, Matt Parvin dropped his work in the aircraft maintenance shop and flew with me to a windswept, frozen lake about three miles from Shaktoolik. There we arranged for a dog team to take Matt up to the wreckage and retrieve the bodies. Then I went on to Moses Point, where I kept checking on the progress of both parties.

Rhode stayed with the group in his Fairchild until the investigation was finished. Matt and Gene sifted through the wreckage as best they could, looking for clues that might help explain the accident. But the T-50 had been almost totally consumed by the fire, destroying most of the evidence. About the only thing they could say for sure was that the aircraft had gone down in an inverted attitude (determined from the serial numbers on the engines and the position of the remnants of red and green colored glass from the wingtips).

After receiving word in Moses Point by bush radio that the party had returned to the frozen lake, I flew over to pick up Matt. Together we placed the bodies of Dan and his two passengers aboard the plane and began our flight back to Anchorage. It was a sad time for all of us in the CAA.

Dan Victor was a pilot whose passion in life was order and neatness. The disorder, disarray, and sheer destruction of that awful crash on the snowy, lonely mountain struck me as being totally unlike everything Dan stood for. The wreckage in which he died bore not the faintest resemblance to the trim little ship that had taken off from Anchorage just five days before. This was fate working, I knew, but I couldn't help wondering why it had to be.

It was certainly a cruel fate that snuffed out the life of Dan Victor in the well-maintained aircraft he loved and was so proud of—NC-118.

And conversely, it was a more charitable fate that brought the back end of an automobile crashing into the weather-battered hulk of NC-34 to reveal dangerous structural defects that might have brought destruction to other lives, perhaps even mine.

(Tragically, Clarence Rhode vanished in 1958 while on a flight over the Brooks Range in a Grumman Goose. With him were his son, Jack, and a fellow game agent, Stan Frederickson. All lost their lives in the crash. The wreckage remained undiscovered for over twenty years, finally coming to light in August of 1979.)

Mount St. Elias in southeastern Alaska, by which Jack
navigated after the radio ranges were shut down following Japan's
attack on Pearl Harbor.

190

With Jack's help during the winter of 1940–41, the military chose this site for a DLAND airfield at Galena, along the Yukon River. Although subject to spring floods, the field was ready in the fall of 1941 to facilitate the ferrying of lend-lease planes to Russia.

Jack (left) and crew examine a portable prospector's boiler, which was used to thaw the ground so soil samples could be taken in their search for a suitable DLAND site.

Crewmen refuel the CAA's float-equipped Bellanca, employed to scout out the location of the wartime airfield.

Above: *King Chris* (NC-14), the workhorse DC-3 in which Jack flew wartime patrol over the Aleutians. Left: Jack at the helm of *King Chris*.

The Boeing 80-A was big enough to transport these CAA
pickup truck bodies.

Jack (center) with a pile of freight aboard *King Chris,* flanked by other
CAA staff, among them Walt Plett (second from right).

The DC-3 at Kotzebue station, where Jack put to sea to try to persuade the captain of the *Waipio* to take his ship to Point Barrow.

Jack autographs the cast of an injured child he flew to an Anchorage hospital on a mercy flight.

Above: An improvised plank runway enabled the DC-3 to take off from a soft field at Gambell, with a burn victim aboard.
Right: Snow-covered runway at the Air Force field at Kotzebue.

In 1945, the CAA acquired this surplus military Lockheed Hudson, NR-254, which was fast but didn't have much carrying capacity.

This all-weather Norseman, third of its kind to be acquired by the CAA's Alaskan Region, was equipped for wheels, skis, and floats.

Part 5

King Chris

1
King Chris

EARLY IN WORLD WAR II, the Japanese invaded the Aleutian Chain and captured the islands of Attu and Kiska. There, solidly entrenched in the bleak, fog-shrouded area where violent storms are born, Hirohito's forces became a dagger in Alaska's side.

As part of a total plan to dislodge the Japanese and secure the area from further invasion, the CAA, under Navy supervision, was asked to expand its operation to include the Aleutian Islands. Since we'd be working in conjunction with the Navy, we were issued sailors' uniforms emblazoned with an insignia patch bearing the title "Technician." We also received identification cards stating that we were traveling with the Navy as belligerent civilians—whatever that meant—and should be recognized as such.

The agency was ill-equipped to fly the Aleutians. We began beating the drum for a bigger aircraft, at least a DC-3, because we would need the eight-hour range. Then too, with the completion of additional radio sites, we had more and more people depending on us for commissary runs and other supply trips. The Boeing 247 had already become inadequate to fully service our present system, let alone an expansion to the far-flung western reaches of the Aleutians.

Chris Lample championed our cause in Washington. One day, out of a clear blue sky, we got a telegram from Lample directing us to meet a couple of Air Carrier Inspectors in Spokane, where we were to take delivery of a DC-3, NC-14. It was to be ours in Alaska for use with the airways program.

The aircraft had been purchased brand-new a few years earlier by the Civil Aeronautics Board (CAB) at a price of $119,000. (Nowadays, inflation's toll has made a small, single-engine Beechcraft Bonanza with navigational aids cost close to that.) To my knowledge, NC-14 was the only DC-3 ever purchased new by either the CAB or the CAA. While it was not quite as doggy as some of the corporate aircraft I'd later see, at the time it seemed awfully plush, having been specially fitted to meet the CAB's specifications. Communications were provided by a ten-channel Bendix transmitter and two receivers. Each of the plane's fourteen very comfortable seats came equipped with an individual headphone and radio jack so that passengers could either listen or transmit over the aircraft's radio while reclining in their chairs. The Sperry Corporation had installed the first dual Automatic Direction Finder; everything in the cockpit was the very latest.

As it turned out, the CAB didn't use the aircraft enough and the board was having some Congressional heat put on it, so it transferred the plane to the CAA Air Carrier Division. The CAA based the plane in Houston, Texas, and used it for training and proficiency flight tests. Lample decided we needed the airplane far worse than the inspectors did, so he put enough pressure on the CAA administrators to have the aircraft transferred to Alaska.

Chris also tried to make a deal with the military. What we really needed was a C-47, the military version of the DC-3, which had a wide cargo door. We hoped to trade, since they could use our DC-3 for personnel transport. But it proved impossible to make the swap.

Fuzz Rogers, one of our hangar mechanics, who also happened to have a private pilot's license, accompanied me south on my trip to pick up the DC-3. Since the region was always too busy to spare more than one captain at a time, on this sort of mission we were forced to grab anybody who was willing to act as copilot. (Fuzz later obtained his commercial license and became one of our regular crew.)

The Air Carrier Inspectors took us around the field at Spokane for three approaches with the DC-3. Then they departed for Houston, leaving Fuzz and me at the controls of NC-14 for the journey back to Alaska. To our consternation, we found that they'd left us no manual, not even a scrap of paper we could use for reference on how to run the damn thing. We made it over to Seattle all right, where I had some friends with United Airlines. They graciously supplied us with one of their own DC-3 manuals, and for many years to come, we continued to use the United Airlines manual of operations.

In Seattle we met Marshall Hoppin, our Regional Administrator. He had made his way down from Alaska on a military flight and was standing by to ride back with us in NC-14.

The anticipated arrival of the DC-3 was quite a big event for the CAA. In those days it seemed very large and modern and was the first DC-3 based in the Territory. There were few planes around that even came close in size.

The whole Region, and many of the townspeople, planned to come out and witness the first landing at Merrill Field. Walt Plett was especially excited. He'd already named the plane "King Chris" in honor of Chris Lample, who'd managed to get it for us. Plett cajoled Lorene Harrison, head of the local USO and director of the Community Chorus, to take a group of people to the studio of KFQD radio station and cut a recording of "God Save the King." Then he borrowed a swallowtail coat, a stovepipe hat, and a gold-headed cane for the festivities.

On my approach to Anchorage, I grew somewhat apprehensive

about the length of Merrill Field. The strip was much shorter than it is now, and I didn't have too many hours under my belt in the DC-3. As I circled the airport, I saw that quite a crowd was gathered below. Agency employees had checked on our flight plan and hour of departure from Whitehorse, Canada, so they'd had plenty of time to assemble at the field.

Landing without incident, I taxied up and shut down the engines. Then the electronics people started blaring "God Save the King" over the PA system while others rolled out a set of steps. Plett came aboard and made me put on the swallowtail coat and stovepipe hat before he'd let me off the plane. And just as I was going out the door, he handed me the gold-headed cane. As sure as Plett was the court jester, I must have been the King's fool!

2

Wartime Flight to Attu

THE ARRIVAL OF *King Chris* enabled the CAA to begin its work in the Aleutians. We built airports as far as Cold Bay and established an airway programmed to extend all the way to the embattled island of Attu, a flight of more than 1,800 miles from Anchorage. A second airway was also developed. It began at Umnak, then skirted along the south side of the Aleutians to Kodiak.

In addition to the usual four-course low-frequency navigational ranges, the CAA was called upon to provide point-to-point communication links that could monitor airway traffic and flight plans and also be used to broadcast weather sequences, notices to airmen, and the like. To handle the job, we had to install high-frequency transmitters, termed TLCs, at strategic sites along the Chain. These radios keyed two frequencies simultaneously, one sometimes being a harmonic of the other. With their power supply, the TLCs weighed about 6,000 pounds, and it was all we could do to haul one complete in the DC-3.

After all the plans for the communication network and the airways were finalized at regional headquarters, we decided to make a reconnaissance flight down the Aleutian Chain as far as Attu to inspect the sites where we'd be installing the equipment. Regional Manager Hoppin and four of our engineers were aboard, as well as Captain Babcock of the Military Communications Service at Elmendorf.

Anchorage, a city that was expanding feverishly under the impetus of war, passed beneath the wings of NC-14 as we headed southwest on the first leg of our wartime mission. Following an uneventful day's flight, we overnighted at Adak. There we were joined by two Navy captains, who were later to become admirals, for the next day's flight to Attu.

At that time, the Army and Navy were engaged in a joint operation to retake Attu from the Japanese. The attack began on May 11, 1943. Enemy positions on the island underwent heavy bombardment by the battleships *Pennsylvania, Idaho,* and *Nevada.* The principal assault force landed on Attu's Massacre Bay beach (so named because a group of Aleuts had been slaughtered there by Russians in the late eighteenth century). Our forces secured the beach before midnight and extended command posts more than a mile inland. Though several weeks had passed since the first assault, the fighting was still under way when we made our flight. Even so, we were told we could land safely on the recently captured airstrip, which had been constructed by the Japanese at Massacre Bay.

Fortunately, an overcast—a stratus deck at about 5,000 feet—shrouded the whole area along our flight path and helped hide us from enemy fighters. We knew the Japanese had several Zeros operating out of Kiska, and we felt our unescorted DC-3 with its big orange tail was pretty much a sitting duck.

Radar hadn't yet come into general use, so I had to ease down out of the clouds every twenty minutes or so and take a look-see before climbing back into the clouds again. Although our greatest concern was to avoid being dry-gulched by one of the Zeros, we were also half afraid of our own fighters. Announcements supposedly had been tacked on all the U.S. airbase bulletin boards, notifying everyone that our civilian aircraft would be in the area. Nonetheless, we worried that some trigger-happy military pilot might shoot first and ask questions later.

Three main islands lie west of Kiska: Shemya, a low, flat island; Attu, crowned by a few high mountains; and Agattu, smaller than Attu but pretty much the same shape. After running along in the clouds, navigating strictly by dead reckoning, I eased down out of the overcast. Way up ahead I saw an island that I immediately assumed to be Attu.

As we approached from the southeast, we expected to see the battleship *New Mexico* pounding away at Japanese positions from the harbor on the south side. But we saw nothing. The islands all look alike to me, so I called for Navy Captain Zeusler, a former Coast Guard skipper, who had previously patrolled these waters.

"Recognize that island?" I asked, pointing out the rocky landscape below.

He studied it intently for quite some time. "You know, I'm familiar with this area by boat, but from the air everything looks a hell of a lot different. I'm just not sure."

After spending about forty-five minutes circling the island in an attempt to find something, I was executing a wide turn when I spotted another large island northwest of us. "That could be Attu," I said. "Let's head over there."

Sure enough, when we arrived over the irregularly shaped, mountainous island we found plenty of activity. The harbor was full of boats. The battleship *New Mexico* and a few cruisers were shelling Japanese emplacements on the hills.

We planned to land on the airstrip at Massacre Bay, but a surface fog had rolled in, completely obscuring the runway. I made several approaches, trying to find the airstrip through the fog, but finally I was forced to give up.

"There's just no use trying to get in there," I said. "We'd better head back to Ugly-Ugly." Ugly-Ugly was the code name for Amchitka.

Because we'd been sure we could get in to Massacre Bay, we had made no effort to conserve fuel. Now our fuel supply was more than half gone. We started back toward Amchitka and immediately applied fuel-saving techniques, slowing to an economical cruise.

When we'd gotten pretty close, we called Ugly-Ugly, expecting the station to give us the weather in code. But they must have thought our situation was enough of an emergency to warrant transmission in the clear: conditions were zero-zero; Amchitka was completely socked in with fog. Our only remaining option was to try a return all the way to Adak. However, we knew the situation was very marginal insofar as our fuel supply was concerned.

It was now late in the evening. As the daylight waned, I became increasingly worried about the possibility of fog at Adak. Whenever the weather in the Aleutians is decent, ground fog starts to form as air temperatures cool in the early evening. As we watched the fog forming on the water, our concern about the Japs on Kiska vanished. The fog and our dwindling fuel supply were far greater hazards on this flight over the North Pacific's icy waters. I wondered if we had much of a chance of making it back to Adak.

When a pilot finds himself in a real bind, he tries to think up some alternative, a plan of action in case worse comes to worst. I decided that if we ran out of fuel, I'd aim for the nearest of the small islands in the Adak vicinity and attempt to belly it in on one of the hogbacks or on the side of a hill.

Amchitka had given us the weather for Adak, and while it was reportedly good, the message included a dark section saying fog in all quadrants. All we needed was for fog to bury the airport. Everyone on board knew the pickle we were in, so we all sweated it out together.

Fortunately, our luck held. We skimmed over the flotilla of Liberty ships in Adak harbor, catching glimpses of the vast Quonset hut villages rimmed by antiaircraft emplacements guarding the Navy's PBY base. Then, thankfully, we were down.

3

A Night at North Shore, Umnak

THE ALEUTIAN ISLANDS, which separate the Bering Sea from the warmer waters of the North Pacific, are a breeding ground for weather as severe as you'll find anywhere in the world. The Chain's usually foul climate has been the butt of many a jest: "If the weather's so bad that you can't see your copilot, don't go"; "The wind was blowing so hard that a bear gave birth to the same cub three times"; or, "If you don't like the weather, just wait a minute—it'll soon change."

But there's really nothing very funny about the rapidly forming fogs or the storms that regularly rake the dismal, treeless islands. Fuzz Rogers and I got into one such storm while heading down the Chain with a TLC transmitter destined for Amchitka.

We'd already passed over the island of Umnak. The next station along the way was located at Atka. As we proceeded west on this leg of the trip, the winds aloft increased until our ground speed was only sixty miles an hour. After a little while, we realized that we'd put ourselves into a kind of box. We didn't have enough fuel at this slow ground speed to make it on to Atka, and the weather was deteriorating rapidly. Umnak was about the only place we still had sufficient fuel to reach. So we swung *King Chris* around and began to backtrack.

With the wind at our tail, we returned to Umnak in short order. The Army radio operator at Umnak told us the base was experiencing extremely high surface winds, which were forecast to attain velocities of more than 100 miles per hour later in the day. Our exchange with the operator was complicated by the necessity of having to handle all the weather information in code, then decipher it. He recommended we land on what was known as the North Shore airport. (The North Shore was an alternate strip that had been built upon old lava flows. A group of Canadians were based there, manning a squadron of P-40 fighters.) The winds were not quite so high there as at the Army base, and the wind direction was more favorable.

We continued our descent toward the cheerless, gale-lashed island. Although its treeless emptiness was punctuated by hangars, Quonset huts, revetments, a mess hall, and the usual support buildings, you'd be hard-pressed to find a more barren, lonely place to wait out the war. When we told the Canadians we were coming in, they reported that their winds were gusting above fifty miles per hour. After we'd landed and taxied off the runway, we were given the same information we had already received from the Army base—expect winds of higher than 100 miles per hour later that evening.

We taxied to the parking area and headed *King Chris* into the wind. Then we manned shovels, digging holes into which we positioned the aircraft's wheels. The holes served as chocks and also put the DC-3 into a somewhat flatter position, which helped decrease the lift exerted by the wind. Next we scrounged up a few sandbags and put them on the wings to act as spoilers and to provide some additional weight.

In the face of the mounting wind, our position still seemed rather precarious. Finally we hammered in some deadmen, heavy stakes from which we lashed stout ropes to the DC-3's wings, anchoring the plane to the ground.

"Damn gale's getting stronger all right," Fuzz shouted against the wind's rising wail. "Must be hitting better'n eighty now!"

We found it almost impossible to move against the force of the accelerating wind. Bending low into the gusts, we were able to make some headway, although we frequently lost our footing. Fine lava particles assaulted our faces and attacked our eyes. Very gritty and abrasive, the wind-whipped lava sand was also blowing into the aircraft's engines.

"Can you imagine the beating those poor Canadians must be taking?" I shouted to Fuzz. "They've been getting it here day after day for weeks."

As we struggled toward camp, we passed a row of wind-scoured P-40s. Their cockpit floors were covered with a carpet of lava sand that had sifted in on the winds.

That night we ate at the Canadian mess. Fuzz and I exchanged glances as a soldier plopped an unappetizing mound of greenish re-constituted eggs on our plates. Then we were served up gray slices of Spam. For those of you who have never been exposed to the dehy-drated foods and canned goods put out during the war, it would be difficult to explain how bad they tasted. The butter was an ersatz mixture reminiscent of axle grease. You had to be damned hungry to eat the dried eggs—as well as the other two staples, hardtack and Spam. The Spam manufactured during the war was worlds apart from the product on market shelves today. I'm convinced something has since been done to make it more palatable, but the stuff dispensed then was virtually inedible.

For some reason Fuzz and I decided to use our sleeping bags and stay inside the airplane that night. I'm not sure why. If our DC-3 was going to blow away, there wasn't a whole lot we could do about it. But the quarters the Canadians had to offer us didn't seem that much better, so we elected to stay with *King Chris.*

With some difficulty we struggled back out to the airplane. Once aboard, we arranged our sleeping bags up front in the aisle, between the heaps of radio gear and cargo packed on either side of us. The slant of the floor was a real problem. Inside of an hour we'd slide all the way back to the DC-3's tail as the aircraft rocked and pitched in the incessant wind.

That night the wind got up above 120 miles per hour, according to the weather station's official records. Needless to say, we weren't able to get much sleep on the inclined floor of the wind-shaken airplane. The hell of it was, the weather wasn't any better the next morning, and breakfast was even worse than the evening meal had been—an un-savory menu comprised exclusively of powdered eggs, Spam, and hardtack.

"Another day of this food and I'm getting out of here regardless of the wind!" I told Fuzz.

"I'm with you," came his reply.

Fortunately, that afternoon, after hours spent over dog-eared mag-azines in the dayroom, we noticed with satisfaction that the weather was improving. "Guess we're on the backside of that storm front now," I remarked.

"Looks like it," said Fuzz. "Maybe we can get going soon." And several hours later we did. Good weather greeted us all the way to Amchitka.

A week later I flew back to the Aleutians with another load of radio gear. There was a nice big high-pressure zone sitting out over the

Chain; but, as I said, whenever there's clear weather on the islands, then fog usually becomes a problem. I'd heard that Bob Reeve had gotten trapped in the fog and had had to make an emergency landing on the beach east of Cold Bay. He'd been flying his old Boeing 80-A on a trip to transport a group of GIs.

Rather than fly direct, we began following the beach at low altitude. Sure enough, we found Reeve's aircraft nosed over in the water near the beach and a camp set up on shore. The day of the rescue helicopter had not yet dawned; an amphibian PBY went over and hauled everyone to Cold Bay.

A while later I saw Reeve in Cold Bay and had a chance to talk with him. The accident must have been harrowing for everybody but the laconic Bob. "It's just one of those situations you learn to expect down here in the Aleutians," the tall, serious veteran of the Alaskan skies said calmly.

"The weather was fine all the way down, but at the last minute fog rolled into Cold Bay, covering up the main airport as well as the satellite field. I had to find someplace to let down, so I headed back to Port Heiden, even though I knew we didn't have enough fuel to get that far. Finally the fuel got so critical that my only option was to take to the beach. I got slowed down pretty well on the landing roll, but the beach was too narrow. The right wheel hit the surf and we groundlooped out into the ocean."

The aircraft was a total loss, but no one was severely injured, which speaks very well for Bob's dexterity and judgment as pilot.

The Boeing 80-As were great airplanes and would haul a hell of a load. They did a lot of fine work in Alaska, but they were very, very slow and had a pretty short range.

I once had occasion to fly one of Bob's old mounts, an 80-A belonging to the Morrison-Knudson Construction Company. Getting out of the DC-3 and flying the 80-A from Anchorage to Iliamna, Skwentna, and back to Merrill Field was an experience. As I recall, it seemed a pretty damn miserable airplane, extremely heavy on the controls. But, as they say, it gets you there and it gets you back, and the plane chalked up a very impressive safety record operating here in Alaska.

4

The Waipio *Inveiglement*

I'VE PLAYED A FEW hands of poker in my life, but never had I gambled for such high stakes—a shipload of wartime cargo, badly needed in the little Arctic village of Point Barrow. And this time I held no cards. The game depended strictly on sheer bluff and careful strategy.

My opponent was a tough, determined Scandinavian sea captain whose hackles had risen over the constant harassment he was getting from Alaska's military and civilian brass. Everybody from the Governor on down had pleaded with the captain, urging him to attempt a second try through the ice to Barrow. But Captain "Hollywood" Hansen, understandably concerned about the danger, stubbornly refused to proceed.

His voyage to Point Barrow had begun during the tail end of the mercilessly short northern shipping season. Aboard his ship, the *Waipio,* were three complete houses that the CAA was committed to construct for the Weather Bureau at Barrow, thousands of gallons of aviation fuel for the military, and the winter's supply of fuel oil and other provisions for the Point Barrow villagers.

As he traveled north in the *Waipio* the skipper encountered increasing amounts of ice. At Cape Lisburne the ice became so thick that Captain Hansen abandoned his effort to reach Point Barrow. It was late fall and the shipping season was nearly over. Captain Hansen was taking no chances.

He radioed back that because of heavy ice formations in the shipping lanes, he was returning to Kotzebue. He planned to unload his Kotzebue cargo, then head back to Seattle as soon as he could get out of the waters of Kotzebue Sound.

At CAA headquarters in Anchorage, there was mutual wringing of hands when word arrived of Captain Hansen's refusal. I was called to the office of Acting Regional Manager Walt Plett, where a fretful conference was in progress. Dejected brass from the Army and Navy, along with a worried representative from the Governor's office, were commiserating with Plett.

Walt briefed me on the urgent situation, the others contributing little to the discussion. Then, in a rather affectionate way, Plett said, "Jack, there's one thing you're loaded with—and that's bullshit. If anyone can possibly talk that captain into at least making another try for

Barrow, it's gotta be you. I want you to drop whatever you're doing and fly out to Kotzebue. Advise the hangar this mission is of the utmost importance. See if you can convince Hansen he has to try again. You'll have the full cooperation of all branches of the service."

Plett's speech was echoed by the military officers, although they didn't have much to offer at the time. The mission intrigued me. I'd be pitting myself against that crusty sea captain toward the goal of getting the cargo through.

"Better get going," Plett said. "Time's about run out on us."

"For a trip like that I could take the Bellanca," I replied.

"No," Plett countered. "We're pulling out all the stops. Get a crew and take the DC-3. If we've got some cargo ready for that area, go ahead and take it, but not if it's going to cause any delay. I want you there as fast as possible."

As I left Plett's office in the Federal Building in downtown Anchorage, my sense of self-importance began to inflate. My head swelled to such enormous size it's a wonder I ever got it through the door of the airplane.

Me! Trusted with this top-level wartime mission! And on top of it all, being told that only I could accomplish it! Hastily, I tossed some stuff into a suitcase and phoned the hangar to get the DC-3 ready.

"What's going on, Jack?" one of the mechanics asked. The word was out that something big was up. In Alaska, nothing traveled so fast as the word-of-mouth "mukluk telegraph."

"Sorry, I can't tell you right now," I said, rather mysteriously. While I suppose I could have told everyone what was cooking, I wanted to enjoy my moment of glory and felt like playing the cloak-and-dagger game to the hilt. The hangar had some freight for Nome, so I told them we'd be stopping there on a flight to Kotzebue. They loaded the freight, and we were all set to go.

In Nome we were met by Norm Potosky, who offered to drive us into town for a quick bite to eat. He and his lovely wife, Romayne, were one of the many husband-and-wife communicator teams employed by the CAA during that era. Norm's brilliant mind and warm personality would later propel him to the agency's top rungs.

Norm was also curious, and he could sense that something unusual was afloat. "What's up?" he asked as we drove into Nome. "What's going on in Kotzebue, anyhow? Something to do with the *Waipio*?"

"Can't tell you now, Norm."

"Okay," he said. "But if it's something like that, I'd like to be in on it. Mind if I go along?"

Norm was always good company. And sharp. Maybe he'd come up with something that would help shake Captain Hansen's resolve to head south. "Norm, if you can leave the station for a couple of days, I'd be glad to have you along."

"Let's swing by my place. I'll be packed in half a minute."

After we had eaten, I was eager to push onward. Reflecting on the importance of the mission, I wondered how I was going to make out with Captain Hansen. What type of approach should I use to try to talk him into going on to Barrow? The CAA had sent telegrams. The Governor had sent telegrams. The military had sent telegrams. By now the captain was getting pretty well burned up with people trying to tell him how to run his ship. I knew that convincing him to move on to Barrow was not going to be an easy task. However, old Jack was ready to have a go at it.

We approached Kotzebue from the south, over Eschscholtz Bay. As we neared the village of about 500, we could see the *Waipio* riding at anchor in the shallow sound, perhaps fifteen miles out to sea. Archie Ferguson's barges were busily lightering the *Waipio*'s cargo to shore. I gave the ship a wide berth, thinking that flying directly over the *Waipio* in a DC-3 might further rile the captain.

Kotzebue was a helter-skelter cluster of Eskimo huts situated on the tip of a long, flat, narrow peninsula jutting out into Kotzebue Sound. From the look of the sizeable heaps of cargo on the beach, it wouldn't be long before the *Waipio* would begin steaming south to Seattle.

Deflation of my insufferable ego set in the moment we arrived. All of a sudden I had the feeling I was playing high stakes poker with just a twenty-dollar bill in my wallet. My confidence vanished totally, suddenly replaced by a wrenching uncertainty. Everybody had pinned their hopes on me to win the battle of wits with that salty character, and now I realized he would probably send me packing ignominiously.

By this time Norm had been completely briefed about our problem. For once he had no simple strategy to offer—nor any moral support. "I've heard that guy's a tough old bird, Jack. What makes you think you can sway him? He's the kind who just might gobble up meddling government employees for breakfast."

"Thanks for your help," I said. Norm just grinned.

After parking the airplane at Kotzebue's airport, I was met by Tex Noey, a tall, voluble CAA communicator who later went on to Anchorage and became a local radio and television celebrity.

Before I finished saying hello, Noey began talking about Captain Hansen. "Jack, word's out the old skipper isn't going to Point Barrow under any circumstances—no matter what you or I or the CAA do or say. Why don't you just tell them back in Anchorage that he refused to see you, then relax and join me for a drink?"

"Can't do that, Tex," I said. "We'll have time for drinks later. What I need right now is a boat. I have to get out there to the *Waipio*—fast— before the captain takes a notion to pull up anchor."

"I tell you, Jack, everybody and his brother have already pleaded with the guy, and it's hopeless. Furthermore, he refuses to talk to anyone. He's busy unloading and can't wait to get back to Seattle."

It was true. The *Waipio* was nearly finished unloading its cargo, and time for the critical decision was at hand. If the captain wasn't soon persuaded to go to Point Barrow, he'd be pulling out—probably the next day—for Seattle. Now, more than ever, I felt the pressure was on me to deliver.

"He's going to talk to *me*, Tex—and just as damn fast as I can get out there. Do you have anything I could use to get to the ship?"

"Well, I've got a fold-boat, but it's really not a boat—more like a collapsible canvas canoe. Sure as hell wasn't made for any open sea."

"Sounds good enough to me," I said. "Do you mind if I borrow it?"

Tex scratched his head dubiously. "Jack, it must be fifteen miles out to the *Waipio*—you can hardly see it! And even if you do make it out there, the captain might not let you aboard."

Then he thought awhile. "If you're fool enough to go out there in my boat, I guess I'm willing to come along and help you paddle."

"Thanks, Tex. Let's go!" We went over to Tex's quarters, got his fold- boat, and shoved it into the surf. Both of us hopped in and started to paddle.

That was probably one of the stupidest moves I've ever made. I knew how rough the waters were in the shallow sea surrounding Kotzebue, and I should have realized the obvious limitations of Tex's boat. But I seemed to have abandoned good sense. All I had on my mind was reaching the ship and getting the captain to change his mind.

After some paddling, we got into a brisk tidal current that flowed outward toward the ship. In a little while we found ourselves quite a way from shore.

Bill Hanson, my copilot in the DC-3, was using far better judgment than I. He saw us out there in pretty rough water, so he and Norm Potosky began searching for another boat. They thought they'd come out and, if nothing else, escort us on to the ship. But, whenever you need something in a hurry, it seems to take just that much longer to find. Bill and Norm had a hard time locating anything and finally went knocking at the door of the hospital. The hospital did have a motor-boat, but it required refueling; and the staff insisted on locating their own skipper. Eventually Bill and Norm were able to start out on their own voyage to the *Waipio*.

In the meantime, Tex and I had run into some pretty heavy going for our small, flimsy boat. Waves kept getting larger and larger, but there was definitely no turning back. The swift tidal current was sweeping us out to sea faster than we could paddle, so we would never have made it back to shore. We looked for the lighters, but none were in sight; one was unloading in Kotzebue and the other was loading at the *Waipio*.

We became awfully damn tired of paddling, but that was the only way we could keep the boat from swamping. Salt spray lashed our faces, drenching us to the skin, and several inches of seawater accumulated in the bottom of the boat. A few times we were nearly awash as particularly large waves rushed past. We rode a series of green hills and valleys, each upswing revealing the outlines of the *Waipio* in the distance.

"We can't take many more of these waves!" Tex warned apprehensively. He was scared. So was I.

"We'll make it!" I yelled back, only half believing it.

While the ship appeared larger and larger, the sea kept getting rougher and rougher. I happened to glance backward and saw another boat on the horizon heading our way. It turned out to be Bill Hanson in the hospital boat. We took some comfort in knowing that another boat would be coming close enough for us to hail.

Tex and I continued to paddle for dear life—and we actually reached the *Waipio*. We were only about a hundred yards from the ship when Bill and the rescue party pulled alongside us. Although we climbed aboard their motor boat, in all fairness to ourselves we'd had it made anyway.

All I could think of now was Hollywood Hansen, although he was nowhere to be seen on the deck of the *Waipio*. The jutting gray barrel of the four-inch cannon on the bow was our only welcome.

Protocol and formality did not appear to be much of a consideration on the freighter. So, wet as rats, Tex Noey and I clambered aboard the ship, followed by Hanson, Potosky, and the motorboat skipper.

Making my way along the deck, I felt ill at ease, definitely the intruder. What a screwball mission! Our grand entrance into the captain's cabin startled the heavy-set, middle-aged man napping on his bunk.

"Yes?" The skipper's blue eyes pierced into mine and I could see only raw hostility. What a poker game!

"I'm Jack Jefford with the CAA," I said. Then I introduced the others. The guy was already burned up from all the previous interference, and we received a pretty small hello.

"What in hell are you doing here anyhow?"

"Well . . ."

"Look, damn it—I've about had it with you bastards." Hansen leaped to his feet and you could see the mercury rising swiftly in his thermometer. Right near—then past—the boiling point. "I don't recall inviting any of you buggers aboard, but I know damn well what you're here for! And before I kick your asses off this boat, I'll tell you one more time!"

He began striding back and forth in front of us, working off a monumental rage. "I've had wires from the Governor of the Territory of Alaska, from the goddamn commanding general, and from everyone else—all asking me to take the *Waipio* to Barrow.

"I was up at Lisburne just a couple of days ago. I saw that goddamn ice for myself. Any of you know how ice like that can crush a ship like a friggin' eggshell?

"So I'm not going! Do you hear? What friggin' good would the Governor or the Army or the Navy or the CAA do me if I got caught in that ice and smashed up the *Waipio*? All you bastards would slink away, saying, 'Too bad—too bad the *Waipio* didn't make it.'

"So go back and tell your Governor and your brass and the CAA that I'm the goddamn captain of this ship! I'm *not going* to Point Barrow. *Not going!* Got it? That's final!"

As I say, I've played a few hands of poker in my life, and whether or not you approve of gambling, poker teaches you at least one thing— know what the other guy is thinking. If you win at all, you fast become a student of human nature. I realized this was one time to keep my big trap shut while the skipper sounded off.

The captain paced a few times more, then plunked himself down into a chair at his table and proceeded to glare at us. I sensed he might be cooling a bit, now that he'd let off steam. As if talking to nobody in particular, he said in a lower voice, "It's not even safe to be here in Kotzebue Sound, let alone farther north. As soon as they get the freight off, I'm getting the hell out of here for Seattle."

Any aces I held had to be shown right now. "I understand what you're saying, Captain Hansen," I told him. "I know how you feel. I'm sort of a captain myself—a flying captain with a lot smaller ship, of course. And I agree with you—too damn many people trying to tell captains how to run things. When something happens, some accident, it isn't those people held accountable, it's the captain."

I could see his anger simmer down. He was looking at me attentively, perhaps even with faint appreciation. "You're right—the goddamn captain's always held accountable," he said.

"Captain Hansen, Mr. Plett, the Acting Manager of the CAA, assigned me to bring a government airplane to Kotzebue and place it at your disposal."

"What in hell would a sea captain want with an airplane?" he asked. I could see the mercury beginning to climb again.

"Well, Mr. Plett figured that if you wanted to get a closer look at the ice that had you cut off, we'd put our airplane at your disposal for that purpose. And if it looked okay to you, you might give it another try. And if you did that, every damn Alaskan would appreciate the skipper who made it to Barrow in the face of the worst conditions."

"Barrow!" I saw the captain's face darken and knew I'd said the wrong thing. "Damn it, don't you guys understand plain English? For the last time, I'm not going to Barrow and that's final!"

"Okay, Captain," I conceded. "You're not going to Barrow. But the offer still holds to take off with us, just to get a good look at this part of the country from the air."

I saw a flicker of interest. If only I could get him on that airplane with me! Earlier, I had checked with the Weather Bureau and found that there had been several days with an offshore wind. This should have forced the ice in the shipping lanes seaward, and in all probability the coast would appear wide open from the air—fully navigable all the way from Kotzebue to Barrow.

"Let me get this straight," the captain asked. "The CAA sent you to Kotzebue to place one of their airplanes at my disposal?"

"That's right, sir," I answered quickly. "It's a big airplane—a DC-3— the same kind the airlines use."

"A DC-3," he mused. "Sent here to Kotzebue for me to ride in. Hmmmh."

There seemed to be a little chink in his armor of hostility, so I pressed the advantage. "Our DC-3 is solely for you to use in any way you like, Captain Hansen. You'll get a good bird's-eye view of the whole area." I was careful to say "area" instead of the forbidden words "Point Barrow." By now I knew the very mention of the village was inflammatory, like waving a red flag in a bull's face.

When the captain asked, "You fellows care for a cup of coffee?" I was sure we'd scored. He took us down to the galley and handed steaming mugs all around. Taking a sip of coffee, he turned back to me. "Maybe I will go up with you in the morning and have a look. I've never had the chance to fly much before."

Hansen seemed almost civil. He called out to the steward, "Bring us some brandy and ice cream!" The captain poured a good slug of the brandy into a glass, then filled it with vanilla ice cream and mixed them well. The result was a horrible-looking mess.

"Here, try this," he said, handing the concoction to me. To a bourbon-and-water man it didn't appear at all appetizing. Nevertheless, I took a sip—and it was delicious. The second one tasted even better. After the third, an atmosphere of good-fellowship had set in. The captain became downright friendly.

Sitting at the table belting down the ice-cream brandies with us was a young Navy ensign, the head of the five-man crew assigned to operate the big cannon mounted on the bow.

During the war, the Navy was authorized to clear a spot and mount a gun platform on some of the freighters. The ships traveled without convoy, and even though they were operating in the coastal waters of the United States, they still had to pass through the Aleutian Islands, where there was the danger of enemy warships and submarines. The theory behind the gun must have been to provide freighters with at least half a chance to go down fighting.

After finishing his third ice-cream brandy, the ensign came over to where I was sitting. "Mr. Jefford, can I go along with you on your flight up north? I've been cooped up on this ship for so long that I'd sure like to get off her for a little while."

By then, with the brandies starting to act, I was feeling a bit magnanimous. Moreover, I thoroughly understood the sailor's need for a change of scene. "On one condition," I told him. "If you'll let me shoot that cannon on the bow—just once!"

I could see military orders and regulations parading through the ensign's mind, but despite the obvious misgivings, he was willing to let me have my shot. "Okay, it's a deal."

Captain Hansen bid us a friendly farewell, promising to come ashore in a small boat the next morning at 9:30 for the reconnaissance flight up the coast.

The ensign and I made our way forward to the bow. The cannon was covered with a canvas, which he set about unfastening. When I finally got a good close look at the gun, I began to wonder if I'd done the right thing in asking to fire it. The barrel must have been thirty feet long. A hell of a formidable weapon, it was quite intimidating in its own deadly, powerful way. But after consuming three brandies with ice cream, I wasn't afraid of anything.

"This particular piece of artillery is the largest using a brass-cased shell," the ensign explained. He pointed to a shell about five feet long. It looked exactly like a rifle cartridge, except for its enormous size.

"Our live ammunition is greased and stored in this weatherproof bin. We've got different kinds of projectiles—some are antiaircraft, which explode in the air, others are armor-piercing, and some detonate on contact. We also have a few with fuses you can set to explode the shell at any given time."

The ensign carefully handled a heavy shell from the ammunition cabinet. The breech opened like a safe door. We slid the cartridge home, closed the door, and locked it.

"Sit right here," said the ensign, pointing to the cannon's left seat. As I edged into the seat, I marveled at the intricacy of the weapon's electrical firing controls, located behind a little door at the side of the gun. Two people were needed to aim it, with the operator on the right providing adjustments for windage. My side had the wheel used to adjust elevation, the optical system to sight on the enemy, and a swivel pistol grip in which the trigger was mounted.

"What do you want to shoot at?" asked the ensign.

I looked out across the horizon. "How about Archie Ferguson's scow?" It was on its way back to Kotzebue with another load of freight from the *Waipio*. After some deliberation, I was persuaded to shoot in the other direction.

"Why don't you try that floating oil drum over there instead?" suggested the ensign. "It's about 600 yards, a hell of a target."

"Okay," I said. "Here goes!" I watched the oil drum bob along in the crosshairs, moving the gun barrel up and down to follow it while the ensign manipulated the horizontal control. Then I squeezed the trigger, and all hell broke loose.

A long streak of bright orange flame erupted, accompanied by a deafening roar and a thick, acrid cloud of gunsmoke. Even though the gun was mounted on a special carriage, you could hear stuff falling all over the boat as it shook from the recoil. The gun barrel was still moving backward as the noise faded away.

Norm Potosky happened to be coming toward us on the top of a ladder at the precise instant of the blast. Later, Potosky told me it had been one of the most startling experiences of his life. "It caught me completely by surprise on that ladder. I wasn't expecting the blast, the noise, the flame and smoke—then all that iron rushing back toward me during the recoil."

I wish I could say I hit the oil drum, but as the ensign explained tactfully, "You didn't have the gun aimed quite right." Anyhow, I'd fired the damn thing. The ensign swung open the breech and the spent shell emerged, red-hot and sizzling in the light, misty rain. When the casing finally cooled, he gave it to me as a memento of my day as gunner.

The next morning Captain Hansen showed up as promised, along with the Navy ensign. After a quick greeting, we took off for Cape Lisburne. We traced the coast to the Cape, then continued on to Point Hope. As far as the eye could see, there was clear water—no ice at all. The coast was still blessed with a nice east wind, which had blown the ice far from shore. Even so, I kept the aircraft fairly low; I didn't want Captain Hansen to see any ice in the distance if I could help it.

We proceeded all the way to Barrow. Beyond Barrow, to the north, we saw a little ice. But you always see ice north of Barrow. The captain was quite impressed, and I know the trip was an eye-opener for him. He rode in one of the front seats, asking numerous questions and taking a keen interest in the plane and its operation.

Midway on our trip back he tapped me on the shoulder. "Can you get in touch with Kotzebue?" he asked.

"Yeah," I said. "I'm sure we can."

"Well, tell the *Waipio* to get up steam. We'll head for Barrow as soon as I can get back on board the ship."

I couldn't believe my ears. But I lost no time getting in touch with the CAA station at Kotzebue. "Tell the *Waipio* to get up steam; Captain Hansen's taking the ship to Barrow the minute he gets back."

By the time we neared Kotzebue we could see billows of dark smoke spewing upward from the *Waipio*'s stack, so we knew our message had gotten through.

Although we'd been flying all day, it would still have been possible to head back to Anchorage. But I was reluctant to leave Kotzebue until fully convinced the captain was actually headed for Barrow. So we stayed in Kotzebue that night. The next morning we flew up the coast toward Barrow.

Near Point Hope we spotted the *Waipio* plowing steadily northward. We circled low and wagged our wings, then headed back for home— Captain Hansen saluting our departure with a long blast from the *Waipio*'s whistle.

5

Shungnak Snafu

RUBE GOLDBERG'S old comics, depicting complicated goofball inventions devised to perform otherwise simple tasks, always used to fascinate me. For instance, if Goldberg were to design an apparatus for opening a door, he might start with a carrot dangling on a string. A passing rabbit would eat the carrot, an act that would tip the scales of a balance so that a precariously perched glass of water would fall into a potted plant, causing the plant to grow, etc., and on through a ridiculously orchestrated chain of improbable events—ultimately resulting in an open door.

My delight with Goldberg's inventions wasn't limited strictly to theory. In my own way, I often put them into practice. Like the day I took the radiator to Shungnak.

The Shungnak station was a remote radio facility on the Kobuk River. The communicators at Shungnak, a husband-and-wife team, kept the station running seven days a week, copying vital weather reports off the CW circuits and relaying them to pilots flying through the area.

The station depended on two Superior diesel engines for electrical power. One of them was being torn down for an overhaul when the mechanic discovered its radiator was completely shot. That put Shungnak in quite a bind. If the second engine were to fail, the facility would go off the air. So the mechanic radioed Anchorage, outlining the problem and requesting that another radiator be sent to them as quickly as possible.

His message was passed along to the director, Walt Plett, who arranged for a replacement radiator, then called for me. "The radiator's a weak point on those diesels," Plett said, "and this is the last one we've got. I want you to fly it up to Kotzebue, then get one of the local bush pilots on skis and take it over to Shungnak. There's no telling how long the station's second engine will hold out, so let's get it up there as soon as we can."

Being the Goldberg type, I was mulling over the situation while getting ready for the flight, when I came up with an inspiration. "Why not drop the radiator to Shungnak Station by parachute?" I suggested over the telephone to Plett. "That way we'll save a day or two in getting it there."

"Jack, I think I'd rather deliver it in the conventional way. This is the last one we have, and I want it to get there in good shape."

"Look, Walt," I persisted. "This radiator doesn't weigh any more than the average man, and it's well-packed inside a crate. We've got a parachute right here in the hangar and I've had lots of experience with air drops. It'll be an easy thing to put it down near the station." Though Plett still didn't seem to share my enthusiasm, he agreed to my plan.

After measuring the radiator, we decided we could most easily make the drop if we removed NC-14's baggage door. A static cord would deploy the parachute once the radiator had been tossed out the door opening. We spent quite some time rigging the system. Then we fired up the DC-3 and headed for Shungnak. I smugly sent the station a message saying we were delivering the radiator directly to their door, via parachute.

All the way to Shungnak I sat basking in the glow of my own self-importance, thinking how damn smart I'd been. The CAA was incredibly fortunate to have a guy of such brilliance working for them!

As we neared the station I got the communicators on the radio so they'd be expecting us. Then I circled the village and lined up for the drop. To show them just how great I was, I decided to place the radiator on the river directly in front of their doorstep.

At precisely the right instant I rocked the wings. That was the prearranged signal for the rest of the crew in the back of the plane to pitch out the radiator. Right on schedule, I heard them yell, "There it goes!" so I banked the plane on one wing to witness the spectacle of the blossoming parachute and the pinpoint delivery of the radiator.

Well, it didn't work out quite that way. The plunging radiator neatly snapped the static line before the parachute could open. It went down just like a bullet. Even so, if the radiator had fallen into a deep snowdrift it might possibly have been salvaged. But my aim was perfect—the radiator crashed on a windblown patch of ice at the edge of the Kobuk River, right in front of the station door.

When it hit, I saw pieces of crate and metal fly for a hundred yards in all directions, showering the area with shrapnel. The radiator was completely demolished.

A somewhat chastened Goldberg—me—could do nothing but turn around and head back to Anchorage. So far that day I had cost the CAA one hard-to-get radiator and a round-trip flight to Shungnak.

News of my fiasco preceded me to town. The station radioed that Jefford had dropped the radiator, the parachute had failed to open, and they still needed a radiator.

Plett had several hours to cool off before I got back to Anchorage. In the meantime, he managed to scrounge up another radiator by cannibalizing the engine used in the school for training mechanics. It was absolutely the last radiator in the Region.

Later that day when I called in to report, Plett said, "Now, will you take this radiator to Kotzebue—and goddamn just this once do it *my way?*"

6

Torture Flight to Seattle

OVER THE YEARS, man has developed the torture of his fellow man into a science. The Chinese were experts at it; they devised a cage in which a person could neither stretch out nor stand. And you've all heard of the Chinese water torture. In medieval days, inventive minds produced the thumbscrew, the rack and wheel, and the iron maiden, just to name a few. But in modern times I believe the ultimate torture was the seating arrangement of the C-47, the military version of the DC-3.

Seated on steel benches backed by some scratchy netting, passengers faced each other across the center aisle. The only concession to the body was a meager indentation for a person's derriere. I often thought the military designed the seats that way deliberately; after sitting in such discomfort for a few hours, a commando would relish jumping out of the plane, killing indiscriminately in response to the suffering he'd endured.

Our DC-3, originally ordered by the Civil Aeronautics Board, came equipped with fourteen very plush seats. Those large chairs were truly beautiful. But after we acquired NC-14, the first thing we did was throw all of them away. The CAA wanted compact, high-density seating.

To accomplish this, we built seats that would make those in the C-47 seem almost comfortable. Ours were narrower, with no dish for the derriere, and had no back at all. They were undoubtedly the most uncomfortable benches ever constructed. They were so bad that most passengers, as soon as we were airborne and gave the word, would unfasten their safety belts and stand for the rest of the trip rather than sit on those miserable seats.

I've gone into such great detail to serve as a prelude for a story about some families who flew with me to Seattle during the war. Whenever suffering is mentioned, I still think of that trip.

Periodically we had to fly to Seattle. Wives and children of CAA employees were allowed to go along to visit relatives and get a break from the wartime life in Alaska. Even though they were on their own getting back, there were always many people wanting to ride out with us.

Our departures were generally scheduled for 9:00 in the morning. With the two-hour time difference between Anchorage and Seattle, as well as two refueling stops with their associated delays, we'd always drag into Seattle very late at night. I decided this situation needed improvement, so I passed the word that this time we were leaving at 5:00 in the morning, wheels up.

On the appointed day the weather, though not too good, was flyable. Bill Hanson was making the trip with me, and as we filed our IFR flight plan, the families, mostly women with small children and babies, began showing up at the airport. When we finished helping them aboard— about thirty-five in all—the DC-3 was packed.

Everything was going according to schedule. In the predawn darkness our maintenance people on the taxiway used flashlights to signal our start. We revved up the engines. In a matter of seconds we'd be under way.

All at once one of the mechanics began waving his arms frantically for us to stop. We shut down and I opened the cockpit window. "What's the problem?"

"You've got an oil cooler leaking on the left engine," he called back.

Not that I doubted his word, but I had to go take a look. Sure enough, oil was dripping out of the left engine. "How long'll it be?" I asked him.

"With any luck we oughta be able to change it in about an hour and a half," came his reply.

I climbed back aboard and gave the passengers the news. Some of the children were fussing a little, but otherwise the group was orderly as they all piled into the office and waiting room. The mechanics pulled the airplane into the hangar and methodically started changing the oil cooler.

As is always the case, the mechanics had underestimated the time they'd need by more than an hour, so that we wound up taking off at our usual hour of nine o'clock. The only difference was that we'd all been up since 3:30 or 4:00, and we were worn out even before departure.

There was a frontal system on the coast, with associated turbulence. While we had high enough ceilings for good approaches at Yakutat and Annette Island, our refueling stops, we were bucking strong head winds. And since the front was parallel to the coast, we never passed through it—we just had to rock along in the weather. Even before we'd gotten to altitude and cruised out of Anchorage, I could hear the kids crying and getting sick. By the time we reached Yakutat, two and a half hours later, we had a pretty bedraggled set of passengers. And the trip had just barely begun.

After refueling, it took a while to get everybody rounded up and back aboard, but at last we were on our way again. We received some encouraging weather reports on the radio: the front didn't extend all the way to Seattle, and the skies there were clear. However, fog was forecast for the coastal areas, including Boeing Field. (Seattle-Tacoma Airport had not yet been built.)

For more than three hours, we bucked head winds on our way to Annette Island. On the ground again at last, those poor women and their youngsters were really in tough shape. Walking down the aisle to see about filing a flight plan and getting the plane gassed up, I felt like the Lord High Executioner. The passengers had taken quite a beating from the ceaseless turbulence. Some of the mothers were trying to get a little sleep, just sitting there on the benches. Many of the babies and young children were still crying.

The honeybucket was filled to the brim with the unmentionable and unimaginable, so we had it dumped. After what seemed like an interminable delay at Annette, we took off on the last leg of our journey, not only with fatigued passengers but with a tired crew as well. We still had about four and a half hours to go before reaching Seattle, but at least we were past the halfway point. By now, with the two-hour time change, the day was just about shot and it was getting dark.

At that time we had a good high-frequency radio. Extending the trailing antenna, we established communications with Seattle shortly after leaving Annette Island and got the bad news that Boeing Field was socked in. There was nothing to do but grind on down. If we had to, we could fly over the Cascades to an alternate airport in eastern Washington. However, many of our passengers had friends and relatives waiting for them in Seattle; and with the war in progress, accommodations and transportation were tough to come by.

After passing Port Hardy, about two hours from Seattle, we finally left the bad weather behind and could see some lights on the ground. At least we were out of Alaska. We then got the welcome word that

Payne Field at Everett, Washington, was open. (Everett is located just a few miles north of Seattle.) Landing there would at least enable our passengers to get to their destinations by bus. By now it was about two o'clock in the morning.

I've read about the Black Hole of Calcutta, and as we flew through the night, the interior of old NC-14 could have passed for an American facsimile of that infamous dungeon, complete with the wailing of tortured souls. Everyone had been sick and the fetid odors were penetrating through to the cockpit. But we'd suffered this long; we could make it another two hours.

Then we heard that fog was drifting onto Payne Field and it would shortly be closed. While I was tempted to increase power in order to get there a little quicker, I wasn't about to get sucked into that trap. Maintaining our present speed, we had sufficient fuel to get us over the mountains. So we left the controls as they were and just kept grinding away. Time got to moving so slowly I thought my watch must have stopped. When it seemed as though thirty minutes had passed, I'd look at my watch again to find that only five minutes had gone by.

After a while we got the crushing news that Payne Field was zero-zero. The coastal fog system was very extensive, and both Portland and Olympia were also down. Bill and I decided to overfly Seattle and then go across the mountains to eastern Washington, which was wide open.

We were, therefore, at a fairly high altitude as we approached Everett's Payne Field. To my surprise I could see about a third of the runway lights. While the fog was very dense and resembled a moving white wall, we thought we could get down on the part of the runway that was still clear.

I called the tower and was given clearance to land on the north-south runway, at pilot's discretion. ("Pilot's discretion" means that if anything bad happens, it's the pilot's neck.) We extended the gear and started down. At first sight, about four or five lights had been visible on either side of the strip, but now the number had been reduced to only two. Coming in low over the north end, we dropped onto the runway and braked hard. We aimed her down the centerline and were pretty well slowed down when we rolled into the thick wall of fog.

I'd never seen anything like it. This was not the thin, shallow fog we get in Alaska but an almost tangible whiteness. We braked the airplane to a halt and shut off the landing lights, which were making visibility worse than with no lights at all. The fog was so dense we could barely see the boundary lights abeam us about a hundred feet away.

We called the tower to let them know we had landed safely and were shutting down and to advise that we'd check with them periodically. Operating off batteries, we had to limit our use of the radios and cabin lights.

The steady hum of the engines had apparently been acting as a pacifier, because once they were turned off, all the kids woke up and began raising holy hell. Not that I blamed them. The cabin was dark and the seats uncomfortable. It was getting cold, since the heater in the DC-3 worked properly only in flight. And the kids were very, very tired.

I turned to Bill Hanson; the glance we exchanged summed up our feelings. I told him I'd strike out on foot to see if I could get a car to evacuate the passengers. I didn't tell him I'd had about as much of NC-14 as I could tolerate before jumping ship.

I groped my way toward the murky glow of the only boundary marker in sight. I couldn't make out the next one, but by feeling along the edge of the runway with my feet I was able to make my way forward until I found it. I'd walked past three or four boundary lights when I heard an idling auto engine. I homed in on the sound and found a "Follow Me" jeep parked just off the runway.

My sudden appearance out of the thick fog startled the two men seated in the jeep. After I explained who I was, the driver, a GI assigned to Payne Field, told me how they happened to be there. "We came out to take a runway observation, and the damn fog just rolled in over us. Hop aboard—we've got the heater on."

The other guy turned out to be with U.S. Customs. "I'm supposed to meet your flight," he said. "I've been standing by waiting for you to come in." For some strange reason, all passengers out of Alaska during the war had to get clearance from Customs and Immigration.

Sitting there in the warm jeep, shooting the breeze, I began having terrible twinges of conscience. I had abandoned my passengers and felt that Bill Hanson would never forgive me.

Dawn was breaking, and the driver thought he might be able to work his way over to Operations when it got lighter. Then maybe he could lead a bus back out to pick up my passengers. Reluctantly, I started back to the airplane. It was easy to find; the clamor from the cabin was audible long before I saw the ship, although by this time most of the children had dropped off to sleep from sheer exhaustion.

After half an hour's wait, the fog began to thin. With the arrival of daylight, we could see the edge of the runway, so I called the tower and asked if I could taxi the airplane. We got the same old conditional permission, "Taxi at pilot's discretion."

After studying our chart of Payne Field, Bill and I fired up the engines and started taxiing in. As we approached the terminal, the fog lifted even more and the building's outline emerged. Within a few minutes we had pulled up to the terminal for the final shutdown. Our horrible trip was at last ended.

We started untying baggage for Customs to inspect. "These are all dependents of CAA employees in Alaska. I've got a manifest for all this stuff," I told the inspector I'd met in the jeep.

"Just get up and go," he said. Of all our flights to Seattle that was the fastest clearance we ever had, a favor for which I am eternally indebted to that Customs official. In a matter of a couple of hours, all our people were united with their waiting families, although some had to travel by bus to hotels in downtown Seattle.

Reflecting back on that journey, I believe those mothers deserve some kind of medal for enduring that miserable trip. There is no comparison between those old flights—at least nine and a half hours, with two long stops if we had any load at all (and just a jug of water as far as any amenities for the passengers went)—and today's luxurious three-hour jet service to Seattle. Now you're plied with food and drink and can relax in warmth and comfort. No hard steel benches, either— in fact, your padded armchair will recline if you want to sleep.

We've certainly come a long way.

7

Summer Landing

BILL CLAYTON and I were approaching Nome on a routine freight trip in the DC-3 when the Nome tower called us with a very nonroutine request. "NC-14, would you consider making an emergency trip to Gambell?"

Bill and I looked at each other. Gambell? In the summertime? There was no place to land at that St. Lawrence Island village. In the winter we were able to go in on the frozen surface of a nearby lake, but Gambell had no year-round airstrip. Even our small CAA station there had to be supplied by boat or amphibian aircraft during the summer months.

"I've walked along the Bering Sea near town, and the rocks on that beach are just like marbles," I told Bill, and he nodded in agreement. "I'd take a pretty dim view of any beach landing. The only possibility might be a spot behind the village. There's some dirt back where they store the boats. It may be just trash and stuff from the village, but it has sort of stabilized the rocks to where there's at least a little vegetation growing between them." However, no one had ever attempted to land there.

I radioed Nome that we weren't too keen on going to Gambell. "What's the nature of the emergency?"

"NC-14, there's a little girl who's been severely burned. We have an Air Force doctor standing by to help if someone will fly him in." This is something I've found to be true of all Air Force doctors. Every one I knew would hop aboard anything and risk his own life if there was any chance to save someone else's.

Bill and I did some soul-searching for a few moments. In view of the emergency, we decided it was worth a try. We'd unload all our cargo and go very light on fuel. "Roger, Nome tower, we'll make that trip."

When we taxied up at Nome, the doctor was waiting for us, and some CAA personnel were standing by to help us quickly unload our freight. The trip to Gambell took about an hour and fifteen minutes in the DC-3. A light north wind was blowing, which we took into consideration for our approach. We planned our landing so as to stop just as close to the village as possible, where the ground had been packed down somewhat more firmly.

When we first touched down, she seemed to be rolling along nicely. Then, all at once, we began slowing down and settling into the pebbles. We came to an abrupt stop, unable even to taxi.

While the doctor was treating the little girl, we got some hawsers and the village tractor to see if we could pull the airplane to firmer ground. The tractor just couldn't hack it, but the villagers turned out to help. There must have been 200 people tugging on the rope, and they pulled both the tractor and the plane all the way to the village. It's just amazing how much power you've got on a long rope if you get enough people!

To our disappointment, we were still sinking in too deeply to take off. Fortunately, the little CAA station had some two-by-twelve boards. We got the airplane squared away so that we'd be able to run about fifty feet on the planks and then, hopefully, keep going. We were headed downwind, but the breeze was light enough that I figured it wouldn't matter.

As soon as the doctor and his patient were aboard, we fired up and accelerated down the planks, gathering just enough speed to keep us rolling over the treacherous cobbles. Soon we were airborne and on our way back to Nome.

But even though the landing at Gambell was successful, the rescue was not. Sadly, the little girl died shortly after we got her to Nome.

8

CAA Christmas

"JACK, I'LL STAY UP all night to fix this radio if you'll wait over till morning for me."

I'd just flown to St. Lawrence Island with one of our radio repairmen in December of the first year after the Gambell station had opened. The technician took one look at the job and realized he couldn't possibly finish it that day. That's when he made his anxious appeal. There was no way to reach the island in winter except by air, and he'd have had to stay Lord knows how long once I'd left. So, rather than abandon the guy, I agreed to stay until morning.

I left the communications station with the watch operator, who offered to put me up for the night. The relentless wind tried to find its way into our parkas as we followed the trail beaten through the drifted snow to his home. A huge drift covered one side of his house clear up to the roof.

"Come in and see my Christmas tree," said my host proudly.

I'm sure I must have looked startled—there are no trees on St. Lawrence Island. A few little willow bushes, but no trees. Nome and Kotzebue are the same way. When I worked for Mirow Air Service, we used to fly in holiday trees that had been cut along the banks of the Yukon. Some of them were little more than branches, but nearly everyone had a tree. In Kotzebue the trees were usually brought in by dog team. But how had this guy gotten a tree, living as he did over 150 miles from the mainland?

We stepped into the house and I saw the "tree." The watch operator had drilled holes in a broomstick and inserted little twigs for branches. Then he had cut up a bunch of discarded tin cans, turned the shiny side out, and attached them as leaves.

All my life my family has had a tree for the holidays. To me, Christmas just isn't Christmas without a tree. That operator was a kindred spirit, his homemade tree so crude and pathetic it almost brought tears to my eyes.

The sight of that forlorn tree kept bugging me all the way home. It just so happened that the next day I had a flight to Cape Yakataga and Juneau, located down in southeastern Alaska's heavily timbered rain forest. I told the Cape Yakataga crew, a real nice bunch, how bleak it was up north without a Christmas tree and described the efforts of our Gambell operator to make his own.

One of the men spoke up. "Look, Jack, if you can get them there, we'll get the trees." True to their word, as I was returning from Juneau, I received the message that Cape Yakataga had a load of trees for me. When I landed I found that the whole station had turned out to cut the trees. They were beautiful—thick, symmetric, deep-green jack pines.

We wound up back in Anchorage with a DC-3 chock full of Christmas trees. We stored them alongside the hangar, where they kept quite well in the chill December air. Then, whenever we had a trip to one of the treeless stations, we'd add a bunch of trees to the regular load. Just before Christmas we squeezed in a trip to Gambell, where our cargo produced quite a sensation. Many of the Eskimos there had never before seen a Christmas tree.

Thus it was that we established the Santa Claus tradition of providing our personnel at the outlying stations with Christmas trees, a tradition that is still followed today.

The week before Christmas, 1944, we were quite busy. On our special flights to the remote stations, we carried turkeys and all the trimmings, in addition to the holiday trees. There was a definite feeling of family among the stations, particularly in those early days when everyone was so dependent on Anchorage for support. These feelings reached their height just before Christmas, as we visited the various CAA sites on our Santa Claus runs.

I spent the night of December 23 in Nome after a flight to Gambell. The following day we made Yuletide stops at Unalakleet and Galena on the return flight to Anchorage. We straggled in, tired but happy in anticipation of the holidays. The other flight crews and the hangar personnel were just as eager to call it a day as we were. The Region had a policy to keep an aircraft fueled and a crew on standby, but it was late—and Christmas Eve—and we just didn't bother.

Bob Jackson, head of the Air Transportation Unit, had invited me to his house for dinner. Mabel Jackson met us at the door with a "Merry

Christmas!" and a martini. The delicious aroma of roasting turkey filled the air. Mabel installed us in easy chairs before a crackling fire, then whisked off to the kitchen to check the gravy.

I was settled down, enjoying my second martini and admiring the Jacksons' charmingly decorated tree, when the phone rang. Bob answered it. "Jack? Sure, I'll put him on."

"Oh no! I hope that's not the station," I groaned.

It was the station. "Jack, one of our operators at Farewell is pretty sick—he's having convulsions," the Anchorage operator told me. "They want to get him in to the hospital right away."

"Okay, I'll see what I can do," I responded, my vision of turkey and dressing and mashed potatoes and pumpkin pie rapidly fading away. I knew the chances of finding some other pilot to make the trip were pretty slim. "You can tell Farewell we'll have a DC-3 out there just as fast as we can."

When the station hung up, I tried to find another pilot to go to Farewell. After several phone calls without results, I reconciled myself to the fact that I would have to go and made my apologies to my disappointed hosts.

"Oh Jack, that's a shame! I'll fix some coffee and make you a couple of sandwiches."

"Thanks, Mabel," I said. "Since I'm going to be flying, I'd better put out the fire from those martinis." I turned back to the phone to search for a copilot, finally locating Bill Hanson at a party.

"We're having one hell of a good time here, Jack," he said when I explained the situation. "It'll be hard to tear myself away . . . but I'll meet you at the airport in fifteen minutes."

Now I had a copilot. Relieved, I gulped down the coffee Mabel brought me and started nibbling on a sandwich while I made another call. On an emergency trip like this, someone with medical training was essential. I immediately thought of Edna Thompson, one of the greatest persons I've ever known.

Edna worked in the fabric department of our aircraft maintenance section, but she was also a registered nurse and could always be counted upon for help when she was needed. I don't think my sister would be with us today if it hadn't been for Edna, who spent a critical night with her when she came down with German measles during pregnancy. I had some real qualms about taking away Edna's Christmas Eve, but this was one of those times when she was desperately needed.

"It's an emergency, Edna," I said when I reached her. Like Bill Hanson, she also was attending a holiday party. "We've got to fly in a sick operator from Farewell. He's having convulsions, and the station manager thinks he's in pretty bad shape."

There wasn't the slightest hesitation on Edna's part. "I'll leave right away and meet you at Merrill Field."

"Thanks, Edna. I'm awfully sorry to call you on Christmas Eve."

"Jack, I can't think of a better time to help out."

I'd barely replaced the receiver when the phone rang. The caller was A. V. Carroll, head of the Communications System. "Jack, I understand you're organizing a trip to Farewell to evacuate one of our operators?"

"Yeah, we're all set. I'm heading out to the airport right now."

"Well, I'd like to go along. You might need some help."

"Okay, thanks! I'll meet you at the field."

Bob volunteered to come along and see us off. Outside it was reasonably warm for that time of year, with a light snow falling. Through the gently drifting flakes we could see the multicolored Christmas tree lights shining in the window of the cozy Jackson home. What a strange Christmas Eve this was turning out to be! Just how strange, I didn't yet have an inkling.

Once at the field, Bob and I got the fuel truck started and were fueling *King Chris* when Bill Hanson arrived. I'll never forget the clothes he was wearing. The best way I can describe his outfit is to say it looked like a cross between a tuxedo and a zoot suit. A wide, silken black belt was strapped across his chest and came up under his armpits. The zipper on his fly must have been a full eighteen inches long. His black, flared pants were held up by a pair of delicate, tiny suspenders. I had to suppress a laugh—Bill was big enough and tough enough that you didn't kid him about his clothes, however unusual they might be.

Edna arrived a short time later. No more suitably clad for our mission than Bill, she walked up to the plane looking like the Angel of Mercy in her long white dress, with a bag of medical supplies on her arm. Not far behind her was A. V. Carroll, and we were all set to go.

The field was dark and quiet. No other traffic was in evidence as we taxied to the runway and took off. The weather at Farewell was about the same as at Anchorage—a 2,000-foot ceiling with two or three miles visibility. This meant crossing the Alaska Range on instruments; Farewell lay just to the west of those rugged mountains.

After about an hour we overheaded the station and got the Z-marker—this was long before the omnidirectional ranges—and began our instrument approach. We had just made our procedure turn and started back inbound on the final approach when the range suddenly went off the air.

We immediately executed a 180-degree turn and headed for McGrath, keeping one receiver tuned to Farewell. In about eight minutes Farewell came back on the air. "NC-14, this is Farewell. How do you read me?"

"Farewell, NC-14. We read you loud and clear. What happened?"

"We had a power failure. We're on standby equipment now and should be okay for your approach."

Once again, we reversed course. Within minutes we landed at Farewell and taxied up to the parking area. Back in the cabin I opened the door and fitted our steel boarding ladder into its notches. Bill and I jumped down and turned to help Edna—in her elaborate, flowing white formal—onto the ground. Carroll was descending just behind her when his foot slipped through the metal rungs. He fell, breaking his leg. I was close enough to see that the break was severe; part of his leg was far out of line with the rest of it.

"Get the stretcher," Edna called out calmly. Bill and I quickly got out the stretcher, a part of the DC-3's emergency gear. We placed Carroll on it and carried him into the station, where the operator on duty stared at us in astonishment—Bill and Edna in their formal dress and Carroll with a broken leg. We got Carroll onto a cot where Edna could examine the leg and splint the fracture.

As if that weren't enough, one of the operators came running in with more bad news. The station mechanic had just gotten two of his fingers cut off! The mechanic had known we were on our descent when the range went dead and had visions of our crashing blindly into the mountains. In a panic to get the standby power going, he rushed to the generator building and started the spare engine with the aid of his flashlight. After it caught hold, he reached up to advance the throttle to the running position and in his haste, accidentally put his hand into the path of the engine fan.

This rescue mission was definitely getting out of control. Now we had one of the rescuers with a broken leg and the station mechanic bleeding profusely with two of his fingers chopped off. After Edna finally got the bleeding stopped and bandaged his hand, the mechanic lapsed into a state of shock. In addition, Edna had to take care of the man with the convulsions. Ironically, he was getting over his problem.

"Jack, let's load everybody up and get them back to Anchorage," Bill suggested. That sounded like an excellent plan to me, but the mechanic refused to leave unless he had someone to cover for him.

"We're on standby power as it is. They need a mechanic here in case something else happens," he insisted.

After some palaver we decided that while Edna was patching everyone up for the trip to Anchorage, we'd make a run to McGrath and borrow a mechanic from that station.

Well, Christmas Eve is not the best time to borrow anything or anybody. The CAA and the whole town of McGrath were celebrating. With the aid of the station manager, we finally found a mechanic, but he was bombed right out of his skull.

"Do you want to take him in that condition?" the station manager asked.

"Why not?" I replied. "They can sober him up at Farewell." Accordingly, we loaded the hapless mechanic aboard and flew back to Farewell.

Eventually we got all our patients—the operator with convulsions, the mechanic with the severed fingers, and the communications chief with the broken leg—settled aboard *King Chris* as comfortably as possible, with Edna looking after them. At 4:30 Christmas morning, we taxied up to the Flight Service Station at Merrill Field. Carroll was loaded into the back of the waiting ambulance; the sick operator felt well enough to ride in the front seat. The mechanic climbed in my car, and we followed the ambulance to Providence Hospital.

As a Christmas Eve, the night hadn't been just strange. It was downright bizarre!

9

They Come and They Go

WE FLEW QUITE A VARIETY of airplanes at the end of the war.

In late 1944 the Alaskan Region was assigned two brand-new Navy AT-7 bomber trainers. The AT-7 was one version of the commercially produced twin-engine Beechcraft 18. We returned our Cessna T-50s to Oklahoma City and picked up the new aircraft, Navy 51145 and Navy 51146. But they proved to be quite a disappointment to us. With their glass noses, the airplanes weren't suited for packing much freight, so we used them mostly for flight checking. In 1945 we arranged to return the two AT-7s in exchange for two new C-45s, Navy 90578 and Navy

90579. They were also variants of the Beech 18, but were built in a better configuration for our purposes.

The Region was growing. The Flight Inspection Division moved from the downtown Federal Building to temporary quarters at Merrill Field. We found it much handier for us pilots to be located right next to our planes.

The time spent down in the Aleutians had really wreaked havoc on *King Chris*. Except for a little orange trim, the DC-3 had never been painted. Constant exposure to salt water and abrasive winds had caused corrosion to set in on the fuselage and wings; we felt as though we were watching an old friend who was sick with a terminal disease.

The Boeing had also become pretty weary, having logged over 30,000 hours. During the summer of 1945 we ferried it out to the boneyard in Arkansas. Pilot Jim Hurst picked up a surplus military Lockheed Hudson, NR-254. It was fast but wouldn't haul anything.

In 1946 we obtained our second DC-3, NC-214, a surplus military C-47. Then in 1947 we acquired a third DC-3, NC-62. We hadn't had it long when Jim Hurst cracked it up on a night landing at Moses Point. He was experiencing heavy icing when the deicing equipment on one wing failed. Due to the greater lift on the ice-free wing, he hit the runway off balance on one wheel. In an attempt to go around again, he poured on the power—a good try, but as it turned out, it only made things worse. NC-62 wheeled off the runway, smashed through some antennas, and landed on a truck. No one aboard was scratched, but the plane was demolished and had to be replaced with yet another DC-3, NC-5.

We were also assigned a Norseman on floats. A single-engine, high-wing airplane made in Canada, NC-407 had formerly belonged to the Weather Bureau. Another addition was a third Beechcraft C-45, NC-90. It came equipped with a custom long-range fuel tank installed in the nose. Pilot Charlie Wayer usually flew NC-5, and Jim Pfeffer handled NC-90. When the Navy asked for the return of their two Beechcraft, leaving us just the one C-45, we were then assigned another civilian Beechcraft, NC-389.

The first plane I ever flew for the Region, NC-99—the original Fairchild 24—met its doom in 1947. Pilot Fuzz Rogers, who'd been promoted up from the hangar, was returning from a mercy flight to Iliamna where he'd picked up an injured man. Fuzz encountered strong head winds en route and ran out of fuel at Point MacKenzie near Anchorage. He had to set her down in the trees. After we recovered the wreck, we realized she'd met her end.

Another early plane, our Bellanca on floats, was lost at sea. Fuzz

Rogers had left Seward on a flight to Cordova but had had to turn back on account of weather. By then it was dark, preventing him from landing in some sheltered cove. At last he spotted a light and landed beside a Coast Guard ship. They took him aboard and trailed the Bellanca on a line, but during the night the aircraft sank.

The Civil Aeronautics Board transferred a second Norseman to us in late 1947. It was given the Fairchild 24's old number, NC-99. In 1949 we received a third Norseman, equipped for wheels, skis, and floats.

The corrosion on NC-14, *King Chris,* finally became so bad that it had to be junked. We felt we'd lost an old friend, even though the number was assigned to another DC-3 sent up to be NC-14's replacement.

In 1950 the agency set up a nationwide overhaul base at Oklahoma City, and the DC-3s began losing their identity. In fact, we'd often take one down and bring a different one back.

Our airways navigational equipment was also being upgraded. In the early fifties the omni-directional range VOR (very-high-frequency omnirange) was considered as a replacement for the old low-frequency range. Although it was essentially line of sight, the VOR had many good things going for it. Being VHF, it was free from snow and other precipitation static, and instead of four courses there were 360, as well as two indicators. With the VOR you just couldn't get lost.

The agency began installing them Outside and also sent one up here for us. We were to put it in at Anchorage and see how the VOR would operate in Alaska. We searched for a site, finally locating one in a swamp just north of Lake Hood. The site was rather poor, and we used it only for training purposes. Although the range was never made part of the common system, we ran many, many checks with it and had a program of demonstrating the VOR to commercial airline pilots.

We also experimented with the new DME (distance measuring equipment). Jim Pfeffer made many practice flights, but we were all a little concerned about the accuracy. Jim would be out only thirty miles or so, yet his readings would be in error. So we sent a dirty dispatch to Washington, documenting our results and ridiculing the system. We had no more than sent it before we realized our mistake. The return message justifiably castigated us all: "How stupid can you guys be? All distances are measured in *nautical* miles!" And of course the DME has proven to be very accurate. Although the original system was incompatible with the military TACAN (tactical air navigation), both the DME and VOR were later combined into one facility, the VORTAC, as we know it today.

In 1951 the Alaskan Region took possession of three Grumman Goose aircraft, N-101, N-102, and N-103 (plus a fourth one flown up to Yakutat to be cannibalized for parts). The agency had tough luck with its Grummans.

One day Fuzz Rogers left Katalla bound for Cape Yakataga, carrying the CAA doctor and his wife (a nurse), plus a communicator returning to Yakataga. The ceilings were pretty low. They were running across Bering Glacier when an engine went out. The Goose wouldn't hack it on one engine, and they were already flying low. N-103 went in on the terminal moraine of Bering Glacier. Fortunately the wreck was found the morning after the accident happened, and the Air Force was able to airlift in some paramedics. Fuzz survived, but the doctor, after lingering in a coma, ultimately died. His wife and the communicator had both perished in the crash.

Our Air Carrier Inspectors were using N-101 when they somehow managed to sink it near Sitka. And the last Grumman Goose was lost by pilot Bill Hanson on a trip to Tamgas Lake on Annette Island. The plane ground-looped on landing and sank, although there were no injuries. And that was the end of our Grummans.

Part 6

Gold Medalist

1

Hinchinbrook Beach Landing

AFTER THE WAR, at least a dozen nonscheduled airlines purchased surplus DC-3s and C-46s and began operating up the coast from Seattle to Anchorage. Their flights were made possible as a result of the establishment of the CAA's excellent (for those days) low-frequency coastal airway.

After leaving Seattle, the first range station was Patricia Bay at Victoria, British Columbia. The next major range station was located at Comox, then Port Hardy, Sandspit (formerly at Masset), and on to Annette Island, Sitka, Yakutat, Hinchinbrook Island, and finally Anchorage. There were additional navigational fixes and marker beacons, but those range stations were the key centers of the system. They broadcast the radio beams that made up the airway, thus providing the all-weather guidance needed by the pilots flying the route under Instrument Flight Rules.

In comparison to most stateside airways, our facilities were taxed to the very limit. Specifications listed the operating range of a station to be about seventy-five miles in both directions, but many of our sites were a great deal farther apart than 150 miles. Our airway therefore resembled a very long-linked chain stretching between Anchorage and Seattle, with each station vital to the integrity of the system.

Radio range stations were designed from a safety standpoint to be redundant. Each was equipped with two separate transmitters hooked into a coupling unit; if one of the transmitters were to fail, the operator could simply switch to the other. Each station also had two power plants, arranged so that if one engine quit running, the other would automatically take over the load. The consensus in the agency was that our stations should never fail.

But as in any chain, the system was only as strong as its weakest link. And one day that weak link proved to be our station at Hinchinbrook. I learned about the problem early that morning when I was summoned to the office of Regional Director Walt Plett. "Get down here as fast as you can, Jack," he said. "We've got hell to pay!"

In those days Anchorage's Fifth Avenue was just a gravel road. Even so, I sped from Merrill Field to the downtown Federal Building in less than ten minutes. From the sound of Plett's voice I knew something big and bad had happened.

When I walked into the office I was amazed at the size of the congregation assembled there. It included our plant and maintenance people, as well as electronic technicians and some engineers. But even more unusual was the presence of Clayton Schule, chief of Northwest Airlines' Alaskan operations. Northwest had just recently inaugurated regular nonstop airline service to Alaska using the new DC-4s. Although their flight from Seattle took over seven hours, after what we had been used to with the nonscheds, we thought the service was terrific.

Plett motioned to me from across the room. "Jack, I'll give it to you fast—the range at Hinchinbrook went dead."

Hinchinbrook is an island a little way out from Cordova in Prince William Sound. The radio range transmitter there was controlled from the flight service station at Cordova's Mile 13 airport via a UHF communications hookup. The radio site itself was manned only by a maintenance technician and occasional visiting mechanics.

Plett continued the briefing, a tone of urgency in his voice. "Art Lappi was down there doing a routine overhaul on the main diesel when the spare engine powering the transmitter blew up. He'd already torn down the first engine into about a thousand pieces, and some of its parts are in pretty tough shape. Art figures it'll be at least a couple of days before he finishes putting it together again."

The problem was that there was no airstrip at Hinchinbrook. We could fly a new engine to Cordova, but then it would have to be taken to the dock, loaded on a ship, and barged to the island—probably a two-day operation just getting it to the station. With Hinchinbrook off the air, Seattle-Anchorage traffic could get no farther north than Yakutat. And of course the southbound airway between Anchorage and Cordova was also closed to all IFR travel.

I knew we couldn't allow the airway to remain closed for several days while we shipped down an engine or while we waited for Lappi to complete his overhaul. Schule's impatience testified to that, and I was sure the other airline operators felt the same way.

"Would it be possible for you to land on the beach at Hinchinbrook?" Plett asked. "Provided you can, we could then off-load the engine right there at the range and hook it up temporarily to the transmitter, getting the station back on the air in a matter of hours."

Well, the DC-3 wasn't exactly a bush plane, but then I was certainly no beginner when it came to landing on Alaskan beaches. The one thing I'd discovered about them was that no two are alike. Some are like pavement; others can be very soft or sticky. But the shore at Hinchinbrook was in a class all by itself. The beach gravel appeared solid enough to land on, but I knew it was subject to a peculiar percolating effect. If you stood in one spot and wiggled your feet at all, you'd soon sink in above your boot tops—even though it was a snap to walk along the beach if you just kept moving. A few weeks earlier, some of the maintenance people had gotten themselves into deep trouble by taking a CAA pickup out along the Hinchinbrook beach. They'd stopped for awhile, and when they tried to move again, they found they were stuck. The returning tide rose over the truck, leaving the vehicle a total loss.

Although I wasn't much worried about the actual landing, I was concerned that we might begin sinking as soon as we came to a stop, especially considering the vibrations of the engines. Then too, even though the situation was an emergency, it was no life-or-death thing. If I were to get away with the landing, why fine—old Jefford would have really done the job. But if I nosed over or became stuck and had to watch the tide wash over the wings, well then everyone would be saying, "Look what that stupid Jefford did. Like a fool, he tried to land on the beach at Hinchinbrook and lost a DC-3."

"I'll tell you what I'll do, Walt," I said after some thought. "Wire Lappi to pick a spot on the beach where the surface is as hard as he can find. Then ask him to lay down two four-by-eight sheets of three-quarter-inch plywood, separated by the spacing of the DC-3's landing gear. We'll measure the distance at the hangar so you'll be able to pass it on to him. Then I'll be willing to give it a try. And if I figure I can't make it, I'll just go on over to Cordova."

Even while we were talking, discussing how we might get the engine to Hinchinbrook, agency crews were preparing the substitute engine for the trip. I've found that large bureaucracies like the CAA are usually quite ponderous and slow-moving. But this was just one of a number of instances which convinced me that, once an agency makes up its mind, it's possible for everyone to get into high gear and move with almost incredible speed to get the job done.

Within an hour I was airborne to Hinchinbrook. The new engine I carried was actually designed to be used as a light plant, so it was somewhat smaller than our regular engines. But it was powerful enough to operate the range and give Lappi enough time to finish his overhaul of the other two diesels.

The weather was good enough for us to sneak through Portage Pass flying Visual Flight Rules. While the weather remained overcast in the Prince William Sound area, the ceilings were up high enough so that finding Hinchinbrook was no problem. As we approached the range station, I spotted the two sheets of plywood Art Lappi had carefully set out for us. And our timing was good—the tide was out.

Whenever I've been undecided about a questionable landing, I've usually taken just one good look and made up my mind whether or not I was going to try it. Other pilots might circle and drag the area again and again. While I don't mean to bad-mouth that procedure, my own philosophy was to look things over just once. I always felt the longer I'd circle, the more uncertain I'd become—and as they say, no use prolonging the agony.

So I took just the one pass, circled, extended the gear, and brought the DC-3 down to the beach. The surface felt solid as a paved runway. We kept her moving right along and managed to stay up nicely as we taxied onto the plywood.

A piece of cake!

Art Lappi was standing by with a small Caterpillar tractor to unload the engine. We waited as he dragged it up to the station and temporarily hooked it to the transmitter. In less than an hour the facility was back on the air and Anchorage-Seattle traffic was able to move once again.

Since the tide had turned and would soon be flooding the beach, we had to beat a hasty retreat to Anchorage. Our takeoff also went well, just as smoothly as the landing. But my concern about the beach had been justified. We'd noticed, while unloading the engine, that our feet would become stuck if we worked them very much in one spot. I think the whole secret of our success in the Hinchinbrook Beach operation was stopping on those strategically placed sheets of plywood.

2

Tragedy at Port Heiden

THE FLIGHT SECTION was unusually quiet on January 2, 1948. The holidays had just passed, and many of our people were still out on vacation.

After finishing up a little office work, I dropped by the Weather Bureau to chat with some old friends. Out of habit, I took a look at the weather maps. They showed a large storm moving up the Chain into the Naknek-King Salmon area. Seeing the reports, I considered myself lucky we didn't have any trips scheduled down that way.

I guess I should have knocked on wood. Late that evening, while I was relaxing at home, Walt Plett called me on the telephone. "Jack," he said, "we've got an emergency at Port Heiden. Something quite bizarre." I listened while Plett unfolded the story.

Port Heiden is located 150 miles southwest of King Salmon, roughly halfway down the north coast of the Alaska Peninsula before that arm of land breaks into the Aleutian Chain. The airfield and radio site at Port Heiden had been built by the armed forces. It had been turned over to the CAA after the war's end.

Because of its military heritage, Port Heiden was one of our most austere stations; most people considered duty there very unpleasant. Although the CAA customarily built comfortable family housing and support facilities near each Flight Service Station, the accommodations at Port Heiden were far more basic—just the old Army barracks and a utilitarian mess hall, both located about a mile away from the station. There was no provision for female employees or families. With the exception of the cook and his wife, who lived at the mess hall, the Region assigned only single, male operators to Port Heiden.

Our personnel manned the station twenty-four hours a day, changing watch at midnight, 8:00 a.m., and 4:00 p.m. On January first, watch change had been more difficult than usual. The snowstorm I'd see mapped at the Weather Bureau in Anchorage the following day was, in fact, a howling blizzard as experienced by the crew at Port Heiden. The station was forced to start up its surplus military snow jeep for transportation to and from the FSS building.

A rather poor forerunner of the modern-day snowmobile, the snow jeep was a much heavier, four-cylinder, tracked vehicle developed by the Army. It had a windshield and a canvas top to help ward off the elements, but no sort of interior heat. Although it would haul three or four people, the snow jeep couldn't move around nearly so well as our present-day snow machines.

Even with the use of the snow jeep, the day-watch operators failed to make the 8:00 a.m. watch change. They made three separate attempts, but visibility was so bad in the storm's blowing snow that the operators couldn't get their bearings, and after a few feet, lost the trail. They were forced to return to camp each time.

The communicator on duty, Richard Mills, worked his regular midnight to 8:00 a.m. shift. Then, when no relief arrived, he continued working right through the day shift.

The snowstorm continued unabated throughout the early afternoon. Shortly before 2:00 p.m., a different pair of men left the mess hall and climbed into the snow jeep for a try at reaching the FSS. Leslie Brooks, the station's electronic technician and repairman, was acknowledged to be the crewman most familiar with the area, so he volunteered to drive the swing-shift operator, George Gillingham, through the blizzard to assume his watch at the FSS building.

Richard Mills was more than glad to see the vehicle arrive through the storm. After quickly briefing his relief, Mills hopped aboard the snow jeep with Brooks for the trip back to the mess hall and barracks. But their return journey didn't prove to be that easy.

While crossing the runway in the blizzard, the pair lost all reference to the trail. Before long, Brooks and Mills were hopelessly lost out on the tundra. Winds measured by the station were hitting fifty to seventy miles per hour. Visibility was fifty feet maximum, often dropping down to ten or fifteen feet. Had they stopped immediately and carefully retraced their tracks, the evening might have turned out differently. Instead, they continued trying to find their way, wandering around in confusion until the snow jeep became trapped in a small valley between two large drifts. More than three-quarters of the snow jeep's fuel had already been consumed in their aimless travel, grinding along dead slow in first gear. Rather than continue struggling to free the snow jeep, and possibly run out of gas, Mills and Brooks decided to stop and wait for better visibility.

So there they were, profoundly lost at night in the blizzard. The below-zero temperatures coupled with the high winds produced a deadly wind-chill factor. Brooks was fully dressed for the weather, since he had expected to be out in the storm for quite some time while making his round trip. Mills, however, was only lightly clothed, having anticipated only a short ride from the station back to the mess hall.

Brooks did the best he could for the shivering Mills. Together they dug a cavity into one of the drifts near the snow jeep, then crawled in to protect themselves as much as possible from the killing winds.

Drifting snow soon covered Brooks's body in a foot-thick insulating blanket. Mills, however, was continually kicking his feet in an effort to keep them from freezing and often became uncovered. He'd wrapped a towel around his head and face in lieu of a hat, but he had great difficulty keeping it in position, since he didn't have any gloves and his hands were freezing. Several times during the night, Mills called out to Brooks for assistance. Brooks would help rearrange Mills's protective face towel and shovel snow back onto his uncovered body. In the process Brooks's own mittens became ice-crusted and snow-filled.

The morning of January 2 dawned with no abatement of the storm. The wind was still howling, and temperatures were lower than the day before. Mills and Brooks attempted to start the jeep, but it was so cold-soaked that the engine wouldn't turn. Now desperate, they decided to strike out on foot.

They walked perhaps 200 feet, with Mills falling every ten or fifteen feet due to his frozen feet. Brooks couldn't carry Mills because he weighed over 200 pounds, so they retraced their own tracks back to the jeep.

"Is this the end?" asked Mills.

"No—I'll push on by myself and get some help. It shouldn't take any longer than two or three hours. Just try and hold on until I get back." Brooks buried Mills in the drift and struggled off alone to find help.

For the rest of the day, he plodded ceaselessly across the frozen tundra in a desperate search for camp. After hours of travel back and forth along the ridges, often finding he'd gone in circles, Brooks finally stumbled across a drifted road where he found a suspended control line. Knowing the wire would take him somewhere, he followed it carefully.

Darkness fell as Brooks continued limping along the road. He was now stopping frequently for rest, his feet and hands partially frozen. The wind gradually died, allowing Brooks to catch a glimpse of the radio tower lights. Eventually he found himself at the low-frequency range station, in line with the runway and about two and one-half miles from the airfield.

There was a three-foot drift blocking the entrance. After four attempts, Brooks managed to break the door and crawl through on his hands and knees. Luckily, there was an interphone at the radio shack. He gave it a long ring, contacting both the watch station and the mess hall.

"We need help." Brooks explained the situation, telling rescuers not to waste time coming to him but, instead, to begin an immediate search for Mills. He described, as best he could, where he thought he had left the snow jeep.

The station's other vehicles, a heavy truck and a light pickup, were both blocked in the garage by heavy snowdrifts; there was no way to get at them without extensive digging. Besides, the roads were pretty much impassable. So, two of the men at the barracks bundled themselves in cold-weather gear, gathered up some food and spare clothes, and hiked down to the radio site to see what they could do for the badly frostbitten Brooks. A larger rescue party set out to find Mills. On three separate sorties they failed to find any trace of the jeep, although they did find drifted sections of Brooks's circuitous trail. Twice they questioned Brooks for further information, but he'd already told them all he knew. Meanwhile, the watch operator radioed Anchorage and explained the situation.

I received Plett's call about 10:30 that night. "Jack, we need you to take a doctor down there and organize an aerial search. The storm's apparently breaking. The front's moving east, and there ought to be clearing weather behind it. The only trouble is, the wind knocked out power to the runway lights, so the strip is dark."

"I know that field pretty well," I told him. "If it's cleared up enough, I can probably get down all right without the lights. Did they say anything about the runway surface?"

"They didn't mention it, but there are bound to be drifts."

That didn't sound good, but since the guy's life was at stake, the least we could do was go down and give it a try.

As soon as I hung up the receiver, I began organizing the flight. But no matter how fast you try to put together an expedition like this, it all takes time. The first thing I had to do was get a doctor out of bed. The Region did not yet have its own medical staff, so I called Dr. Coffin of the Sogn-Coffin Clinic. He agreed to meet us at the airport. I couldn't get in touch with any of the regular crew during this holiday period, but I finally did manage to get hold of flight mechanic Bill Clayton. He was tapped for copilot. Assistant Regional Director Al Hulen came along, as did four men of our maintenance section. And I also called upon my brother, Bill, now living in Anchorage, to round out the crew and provide a little extra manpower.

The storm had since moved up our way. The weather in the Anchorage vicinity was pretty raunchy, but west of Homer we began running out of the stuff. By the time we arrived at King Salmon, a full moon was shining down on the frozen Alaska landscape from a completely clear night sky.

We landed at King Salmon to take aboard that station's snow jeep for the rescue operation at Port Heiden. The machine had been readied, and all the King Salmon personnel were on hand to help us load it into the DC-3. But there was a delay. Although the vehicle fit through the door, we couldn't get it to make the turn into the cabin. So we were forced to spend precious time removing one of the tracks.

After looking at the drifts around King Salmon, I could see we were going to have problems over at Port Heiden. As a precaution, we securely strapped down the snow machine way back in the tail, keeping our center of gravity as far aft as possible. That way we lessened the chance of nosing over in a drift.

The flight from King Salmon to Port Heiden takes only an hour; their low-frequency range was still in operation, so we easily homed in on the station. But, except for the glow of lights from the mess hall, everything was dark.

We circled in an effort to find the indistinct, snow-covered runway below us. Port Heiden's wretched collection of converted military buildings, illuminated by the harsh winter moonlight, was our only point of reference. Blowing snow had covered the single southeast-northwest runway with heavy drifts, and the runway's edge was indiscernible against the rest of the snowblown tundra.

Without any outline of the airstrip to go by, I was having a difficult time deciding where to set down. Then too, the drifts looked pretty damn deep. It was just one of those miserable decisions you often have to make.

On the fifth pass I felt we were pretty well aligned with the runway, so I decided to try it. We hit the first drift and the DC-3's tail came up as we started to nose into the snow. I blasted on power, bringing up the nose. Then we hit another drift. Again the tail lifted, and again I poured on power. After plowing through drift after drift in this fashion, we came at last to a halt.

The landing had been so hairy I didn't even attempt to taxi. I turned to Clayton and said, "As far as I'm concerned this is the end of the road!" He nodded in agreement.

The outside air temperature was down below zero. We didn't know what would happen next, so we diluted the engines. This procedure involves injecting a small amount of gasoline into the engine oil, thinning it to facilitate a cold-weather start.

Fortunately, we had enough people aboard so that we could manhandle the snow jeep out of the aircraft. We put the track back on the vehicle and tied on an akio, or large sled, to trail behind. Four of us crammed into the cab, and the rest piled onto the akio for the trip to the mess hall.

Even though it was well past 3:00 a.m., everyone at the station was up and anxiously awaiting our arrival. Over mugs of hot coffee, we planned our strategy. Unfortunately, there wasn't much we could do for Mills until daylight, but we all hoped an aerial search at dawn would pinpoint the lost vehicle.

Meanwhile, Dr. Coffin and a couple of station employees drove the new snow machine down to the range station to pick up Brooks. The doctor treated Brooks for frostbite, bandaging his hands and feet, and pronounced him to be in pretty fair condition.

We spent an uncomfortable few hours sitting around the mess hall, waiting impatiently for daylight. Though we tried to get some rest, slumped in chairs or stretched out on the mess tables, we were too keyed up to get much sleep. All of us were thinking of Mills out there in the cold and wondering: Is he still alive? Can we get to him in time?

After numerous trips to the window, looking for any trace of dawn, we finally noticed the first faint blush of light. That was the signal for Bill Clayton and me to hike to the airplane, about two miles away. The DC-3 had been sitting on the runway for many hours, and we knew it would take quite a bit of warmup to get it operational. As soon as we could see well enough, we planned to take off.

As we trudged toward the plane in the bitter cold, I couldn't help thinking of Mills. More than sixteen hours had passed since Brooks had left him to get help. Mills's chances certainly didn't look good, but we all nourished the hope that somehow he might have been able to pull through.

We were impatient to get started in the gray daylight. We discovered that the drifts on the east edge of the runway were less pronounced, so we thought we'd be able to use that part of the runway without too much trouble. By the time we got the DC-3 fully warmed, there was enough light to give us the visibility we needed for the search. We taxied to the eastern portion of the runway and were able to take off without any problem.

We began circling the camp area. Within just a few minutes, Clayton and I spotted the snow jeep about a mile northwest of the station. We buzzed it several times at low altitude, just to be sure.

"That's it," I said. "But I don't see any sign of life down there. Do you, Bill?"

"Nothing, Jack. Nothing at all."

"Well, we'll buzz it a few more times to alert the rescue party."

A few minutes later the rescuers caught our signal and headed out from the mess hall. We circled overhead, watching as the party reached the bogged-down snow jeep and the thick drift in which Mills had burrowed while Brooks went for help. After poking around for awhile, three members of the rescue party moved away from the marooned snow machine and headed toward the camp area.

"Now what are they doing?" Clayton wondered. "It looks like they're tracking something."

"Mills might have left the snowdrift and struck out on foot for camp," I suggested.

"Yeah," Clayton agreed, "that would explain the tracking."

As closely as we could reconstruct it later, that was exactly what had happened. Mills was still alive after the worst of the storm had passed. Crawling out of the snow shelter, he saw the tantalizing lights of camp about a mile away. Although his arms and legs were probably frozen, he began struggling through the drifts, fighting his way inch by inch toward the beckoning lights.

He had been able to crawl over halfway to camp before succumbing to hypothermia and exhaustion. When they found him, his body was stretched forward toward camp, his head cradled in his arms, his heavy red beard icy and blown full of snow. Dr. Coffin estimated Mills had died only four or five hours before we'd located the body—the torso was still slightly warm.

We landed and regrouped with the rescue party at the mess hall. Brooks saw Mills's motionless form in the back end of the snow jeep and noticed that the others made no effort to bring it inside.

"Was he alive?" Brooks asked Dr. Coffin.

"No—and perhaps for the best. If he'd lived he'd have lost both arms and legs and been in extreme pain from his frozen throat and chest for the rest of his days."

Since the increasing cold was likely to cause problems starting the DC-3, and another storm was forecast to move into the area, I told the station we had to leave as soon as possible. At Dr. Coffin's suggestion, Brooks was brought along for further frostbite treatment at the hospital in Anchorage. We placed Mills's body in the back end of the plane where it would be cold, lying there pretty much as he was found.

3
Fuel Oil Blues

REGARDLESS OF WHAT you might hear, the Alaskan Region of the CAA pioneered the air freighting of bulk fuel oil.

In the early days the diesel supply for the remote stations had to be hauled very laboriously in fifty-five-gallon steel drums. I finally became fed up with that inefficient method after one of our fuel hauls to Skwentna. It seemed foolish to transport all that oil over there in those small barrels and waste considerable time hand-pumping it into bulk tanks at the station, when the installation of a bulk tank in the airplane would make the job so much easier. It would also eliminate the problem of disposing of all the empty drums.

At first we experimented with surplus military tanks, but they really weren't suitable, so we custom-designed a 1,000-gallon tank and had it manufactured to our specifications. The new tank distributed the load evenly over the floor and was anchored in a special rack so that we could adjust its position, depending on our weight and balance calculations for the flight.

We rigged a system of pipes and unions that projected through the DC-3's belly. Upon landing we'd just taxi up to the fuel storage area and hook rubber hoses to the belly pipes. Within twenty-five minutes the small engine we carried could pump our maximum load of 1,000 gallons of fuel oil into the station's bulk tanks.

The piping arrangement also served as an emergency dump valve. If we were to have an in-flight crisis, it would be only a matter of opening some valves to get rid of the oil. The full 1,000 gallons would drain in less than ten minutes.

We routinely hauled oil from Anchorage to Skwentna and Iliamna, from McGrath to Farewell, and from Yakutat to Cape Yakataga. The trip from Yakutat to Yakataga took about an hour in a DC-3. Ordinarily we'd send down a crew with an airplane, and they'd make four or five trips a day until they had completed hauling the whole year's supply of fuel. Fishing was good in Yakataga and there was often a lot of spare time, so it wasn't very hard to get volunteers for this assignment.

However, one year during the scheduled Yakataga oil haul, the agency found itself down to just two airplanes for the entire Region, a DC-3 and one of our much smaller Beeches. Our other two DC-3s were out in Oklahoma City for overhaul. We hated to tie up our one remaining freighter for too long a time, so someone devised a plan to operate the Yakataga oil haul twenty-four hours a day, trying to make the seventy-two required trips in a week or less. Although that's a considerable amount of flying, at the end of the week the DC-3 would be free to cover the rest of the Region.

I held a little pilot's meeting, and all of us agreed we could handle it. We planned to leave Sunday afternoon and start the nonstop fuel runs bright and early Monday morning. I headed home to pack my bags and fishing gear.

We left Anchorage with light hearts, halfway looking forward to the upcoming adventure of operating twenty-four hours a day. Our group consisted of three captains, two copilots, and two mechanics from the hangar. The captains were Jim Hurst, one of CAA's top pilots; Jim Pfeffer, who had flown the hump in a C-46 during the war; and myself. Morgan Davies and Fuzz Rogers were the copilots. Although they were actually captains in their own right, they'd been flying the Beechcrafts and weren't current as captains in a DC-3.

The mechanics were along to service the airplane, planning to conduct what is known as a progressive hundred-hour inspection. The schedule we set for ourselves on these flights meant that we would be logging roughly 150 hours of air time, with only short breaks in the flying to load and unload the plane. That would put us over the time limit before which we were due for a mandatory hundred-hour inspection. So the mechanics were going to perform the checks as we went along and not tie up the plane for a formal hundred-hour inspection. While this was certainly nothing like a full-blown, regulation, in-the-hangar inspection, at least it was enough to keep us legal.

The mechanics were also going to supervise the DC-3's refueling; we would carry only a minimum amount of gasoline due to our heavy loads of diesel oil. We didn't want to rely on the gas gauges at such low readings, so the mechanics would measure our gasoline levels with calibrated dip sticks before every flight.

As Monday morning dawned, we were all set to start. Three of us, two pilots and a mechanic, headed over to the airport for the first flight. The other four stayed behind in the apartment assigned to us by the Yakutat station manager.

Morgan Davies was wondering how we'd divide the work so that all of us would get an equal share of the miserable shifts. Of course the two mechanics had no choice but to organize their work into two twelve-hour watches. But it wasn't quite that simple for us pilots.

If we'd had six pilots, we could have split up into three groups of two men each, and each group would have been responsible for an eight-hour stint. But we were shy one pilot, so we realized that the five of us were going to have to work staggered shifts of somewhat longer duration than eight hours. At first that didn't seem too much of a problem, but we were never able to get really organized. As the days passed, we pilots gradually lost track of time and gave up any pretense of assuming definite shifts. We'd just work until we got tired, be it night or day, and wait for relief from someone back at the apartment.

Unfortunately, life at the apartment wasn't a bed of roses either. A large family lived above us, and the children were active and noisy. Between the irregular shifts and the constant commotion at the apartment, none of us were getting much sleep.

After four days of inadequate rest, we all succumbed to cabin fever. Although I'd often flown with every one of those guys—and they were my respected friends—as I became more and more tired following several days of less and less sleep, their slightest actions began to aggravate me, their mannerisms grew bothersome, even the way they combed their hair became annoying.

At least we could see the light at the end of the tunnel on the sixth day, although by then we were hardly speaking to one another and nothing seemed to be going right. The following morning I arrived at the airport to begin yet another shift. As it happened, this one last flight was all we needed to finish up the oil haul.

The weather had turned really stinking. Turbulence was so bad that the top of the 1,000-gallon tank had been split, although Jim Hurst, captain on the previous flight, hadn't realized it. He did growl at me in passing that the weather was a little turbulent (the understatement of the year), then took off for the apartment house.

I was filling the tank for the final trip to Yakataga when I noticed oil pouring from the top. I had the mechanic jump in and hold his arm on the crack until we were airborne. Once I had the tail up and the aircraft level, I hoped the leak would stop. With just minimal maintenance during the last 150 hours of operation, the DC-3 was already dirty and ratty, and now the airplane was soggy with fuel oil. The smelly diesel gathered in the belly and was running out the tail wheel. But in spite of the DC-3's grimy condition, the little sweetheart's engines kept running without a whimper.

I brought the load in to Cape Yakataga, pumped the oil into the bulk tanks, then worked my way back to Yakutat. Finally, our fuel haul was over. Strangely enough, all of us became fast friends again as we loaded our gear on board for the trip home to Anchorage. Looking back, I can now see that we had operated under too great a physical stress, and each of us had nearly reached his breaking point.

I still believe it's an amazing record, and I've never heard of anyone else having operated an airplane around the clock for seven days. But we had been able to do it, and we wound up in Anchorage happy and still good friends, despite several bad moments in Yakutat.

However, I'll always remember Jim Hurst as he muttered under his breath, "What's old Jefford trying to do, prove something?"

All I know is that flying around the clock wasn't my idea!

4

The Rescue of Cliff Uzzell

JOHNNY FREELAND and Bill Hanson were with me in the DC-3 on December 11, 1950, flying a routine cargo trip from Anchorage to Cape Yakataga, Yakutat, and Juneau. As we passed over the Cordova station on the return flight, we received an urgent message. I was told to contact the Regional Director immediately upon landing at Anchorage. As it turned out, I could hardly have missed him. Even though it was quite late in the evening, he and most of the hangar personnel were anxiously awaiting me at the airport. This was the story:

Cliff Uzzell, our CAA station manager at Iliamna, had held his private pilot's license for only a short time when he decided to buy a new Piper Clipper. He and the local school teacher, Forrest Jones, had been flying that morning when they ran into a fog condition and crashed the Piper near Nondalton. Both Uzzell and Jones were severely injured.

The nearest airfield was at Iliamna, where the weather was now reported to be poor, with moderate snow and restricted visibility. Earlier in the day, under somewhat better weather conditions, the Tenth Rescue Squadron had dispatched a military doctor, Captain Roy Patterson, to Iliamna in one of their C-54s. The doctor was then ferried by dog team to Nondalton, where he provided emergency treatment for the two men.

Jones, who was less seriously injured, had been sent back to Iliamna in the dogsled and was already at the hospital in Anchorage. Uzzell, however, had suffered multiple fractures, which prohibited any travel by dogsled. Captain Patterson had radioed back that Uzzell was in very bad condition and needed immediate evacuation. An airlift was his only hope.

The military had sent a rescue helicopter from Elmendorf Air Force Base, but it had iced up and been forced down near the entrance to Lake Clark Pass. A ski-equipped C-47, the counterpart to our civilian DC-3, had departed on a mercy mission from Eielson Air Force Base in Fairbanks, but it too had run into such heavy icing that it was forced to return.

The Director turned to Johnny, Bill, and me. "I don't suppose there is a damn thing you guys can do over there, but we thought it might boost the station's morale to have our own aircraft standing by at Iliamna. And maybe you can figure out some way to help once you're there."

We refueled in short order and were on our way. En route we encountered moderate icing at 6,000 feet, the minimum instrument altitude over the mountains to Iliamna. Iliamna's weather was indeed lousy—a 500-foot ceiling, snow, and less than a mile visibility. Even though it was past midnight when we landed, all of the Iliamna CAA personnel were at the Flight Service Station.

It was a tough situation. One of our people was badly hurt, but even though the little native village of Nondalton was only thirty miles away on the shore of Lake Clark, there seemed to be nothing we could do to help him. All of us were concerned; yet everyone felt completely useless.

We kept in constant contact with Nondalton via Iliamna's high-frequency bush radio, and I was able to talk with the young military doctor who was taking care of Uzzell.

"What's his condition now?" I asked.

"Very serious," Patterson replied. "There just isn't much I can do for him here. If he isn't flown out soon, I doubt if he'll survive."

After listening to the doctor's report, I realized that Uzzell wasn't likely to make it through the night. There had to be something we could do. In the back of my mind, I began toying with the idea of making a wheel landing on the frozen surface of Lake Clark. There would be plenty of room, but the ice was probably blanketed with too deep a layer of snow.

"Is Oren Hudson anywhere around?" I asked. Oren was a bush pilot working out of Nondalton.

"He's standing here with us," said Captain Patterson. "I'll put him right on."

"How's your weather at Nondalton, Oren?"

"Not so hot. Ceiling's about 500 with maybe a mile visibility, if you stretch it."

"Oren, do you think there'd be any chance we could get away with a wheel landing on the lake ice in front of the village using our DC-3?"

There was a long pause. "Jack, I'd hate to give you a recommendation on a thing like that." Oren was familiar with the performance of the DC-3, having flown them for TWA before coming to Alaska. But he was understandably reluctant to venture an opinion, one way or the other, on what would undoubtedly be an exceedingly risky operation.

I keyed the microphone, "How deep is the snow on the lake?"

"About fourteen or fifteen inches, and it's still coming down," Oren answered.

I signed off without having made any firm decision. Conditions didn't sound very promising, but Bill and Johnny and I kicked around the idea and discussed its possibilities. We borrowed a pickup truck from the Iliamna station and drove it out to the cross runway, which was never plowed in winter. Thinking that the unplowed runway's snow cover should be similar to what we'd find at Nondalton, we experimented by running the truck across it. The snow was light and fluffy, offering almost no resistance.

At worst, we might get stuck at Nondalton and not be able to take off. But, by putting as much weight as possible in the aircraft's tail and using quite a bit of power at touchdown, we all felt we could safely make the landing on the lake without nosing over.

We called back to Nondalton on the radio. "We've decided to give it a try," I told Oren, "but I think we'll need some kind of lights on the lake. Can you organize everyone to put out all the lanterns they can find and mark out an area on the ice for us to land?"

We knew the only electric power in the village was at the schoolhouse, but we hoped they could find enough gas lanterns so they could get a strip of ice lighted for us.

"We'll set out all the lanterns we can get, Jack. Good luck!"

As soon as we left the Iliamna airport, we found ourselves flying mostly on instruments, even though we were trying to stay low enough so that we wouldn't lose sight of the ground. The situation was very sticky for a few minutes, until we devised a workable system. I began flying the airplane strictly by instruments, while both Johnny and Bill endeavored to keep track of the ground below. Their vertical visibility, what there was of it, turned out to be only patchy and intermittent.

The north course of Iliamna's low-frequency radio range ran to the south shore of Lake Clark, a long, slender body of water occupying the bottom of a precipitous mountain gorge known as Lake Clark Pass. When traveling between the Alaska Peninsula and Anchorage, small planes must fly through this treacherous valley, hidden deep in a glacier-laden area, studded with craggy peaks that also border both sides of the eastern part of the lake.

We worked out a timing arrangement to keep us from smashing into the towering peaks near the pass. We'd fly a given number of minutes on the north leg heading into the mountains. If we couldn't spot the lights on the ice at Nondalton, we'd circle back to Iliamna.

On the first attempt, we flew until we were out of time and then circled back. We agreed to try it once again and maybe go a minute or two longer. Even with their limited visibility, Johnny and Bill could still see occasional trees, and we figured we would be safe until we came to the edge of the lake.

The plane moved along the north course on the second run as we lengthened our pass by a couple of minutes. Finally, I could wait no longer and was forced to begin the turn. "Lights!" Johnny and Bill yelled simultaneously. "We see the lights!"

Sure enough, the natives at Nondalton had marked us a runway, and the illumination of their gasoline lanterns reflecting on the snow was excellent. I aimed the aircraft at the rectangle of lights and came in for the landing.

If anything, the snow was deeper at Nondalton than at Iliamna. In addition, there was a crusty layer underlying the new snowfall. I literally had to fight the controls to keep the plane from nosing over, decelerating faster than on any other landing I'd ever experienced. I kept practically full power on and held back tightly on the wheel; it was touch and go for a few tense moments.

But eventually we settled to a stop in the heavy snow. I tried to taxi and found, to my relief, that we were able to move. I figured, then, that there was a pretty good chance we'd be able to get back off the lake.

In just a few minutes they brought Uzzell down to the plane in a sled and got him aboard, along with Captain Patterson.

We used a little bit of flap to lift out of the snow and begin our takeoff run. Drawing all the power we dared, it seemed as though we could get up to only about twenty-five miles an hour, then the DC-3 stubbornly refused to go any faster. Repeatedly we'd turn and try to head back in the same tracks. As long as we kept in the tracks we'd begin to accelerate and think we were going to make it, but then we'd get out of the tracks and slow down. It must have been quite a sight from the village—the big DC-3 roaring up and down the lake between the gas lanterns.

I don't know how many attempts we made, but finally we must have done something right because we were airborne. When our knees stopped shaking, we called Iliamna and filed IFR into Anchorage. We were on our way.

A few minutes later Captain Patterson came up to the cockpit. He was very worried about Cliff and was especially concerned about the altitude to which we were climbing.

"We're going to have to get above 6,000 feet, at least until we pass Mount St. Augustine," I told him. "Then maybe we can drop a bit lower. But we'll have to stay at 6,000 for at least thirty minutes before we can descend."

We had just leveled off when the doctor returned to the cockpit. "Is there any way we can get a little water and heat it? I've got to mix some powdered plasma and inject it right away." Apparently, Cliff's veins were starting to collapse from loss of blood, and a transfusion was urgently required.

Fortunately, we had a jug of water and an electric hot cup we used to make coffee. We questioned its sterility, but we did what we had to in the emergency. Bill got the water up to body temperature, mixed the plasma thoroughly, then aided the doctor in giving Cliff the intravenous injection.

When we got to Anchorage, an ambulance was waiting at the airport to rush Cliff to the hospital. Our rescue mission was finished.

I went to see Cliff a few days later, as soon as he was able to receive visitors. Both his legs were in traction, and his spirits were rather low. "I guess I'm in for a long, long stay here in the hospital, Jack. The orthopedic surgeon said I couldn't go home unless I had a special bed capable of providing the necessary traction for my legs."

"Look, Cliff, we'll see what we can do," I promised.

Johnny Freeland and I sketched out an arrangement of pipes that could be erected over Cliff's bed to provide the required traction. We planned to get the lengths of pipe cut and threaded; then we intended to assemble them with Ts and Ls. One of the mechanics at the hangar offered to weld on a couple of pulleys, and a bucket of sand could be used for the weight. Even though it was homemade, we were sure it would work.

We went down to Alaska Plumbing and Heating to order the material. After we had finished giving the manager of the shop the dimensions for all the pipe we needed, he looked at us rather quizzically. "Do you mind telling me what in the hell you fellows plan to do with all that pipe and all those Ts and Ls?"

"Cliff Uzzell, one of our CAA people, was in a plane crash and now he's over at Providence Hospital in traction. The doctor told him he could leave the hospital if he had a bed with traction on it—so we designed one that ought to work."

"Glad you told me," he said. "I'll get the whole crew working on it immediately. They'll have the pipe cut and threaded in a jiffy." In a short while our order was ready.

"What will that be?" I asked.

"Not a cent. Just consider it AP&H's contribution."

I always thought it was a very nice gesture, and the bed worked out fine. Despite the fact that both legs had been broken in several places and the surgeons had had to rebuild an ankle, Uzzell was later able to walk without a limp.

The story of the mercy flight for Cliff Uzzell has a sequel. Years later, I was at a farewell dinner for Bernt Balchen, who had been the commanding officer of the Tenth Rescue Squadron. At many such functions they rounded up the old bush pilots, myself included, to roast the departees with vignettes and stories and in the process lay a little honor upon them in appreciation of their Alaska accomplishments.

After we got down to the serious drinking and began our dinner, I noticed there was a full colonel in dress uniform across the table. He studied me awhile before finally saying, "You probably don't remember me, but I'm the doctor who flew with you when you brought Cliff Uzzell in from Nondalton."

The trip came back to me. The colonel had been a captain then, fresh out of medical school, and I remembered how impressed I was with his competence and courage.

"That was some trip, Colonel," I said.

"It sure was! Jack, that's one mission I'll never forget."

I recalled our difficulties in finding the lantern-lit lake, our harrowing landing, and our nerve-wracking takeoff. I'll never forget it, either.

5

Juneau Backfire

JOHNNY FREELAND and I were ready to head home. We'd been gone several days, flight checking the southeast Alaska airways with stops at Yakataga, Yakutat, Annette Island, and Juneau.

Johnny was a small chap, born of parents who were missionaries in South America. He had been twelve years old before he learned to speak English. Freeland was one of those people who seldom walked— he always ran. Even when he rested, he did it in a hurry. On this trip in the DC-3, he was serving as my flight mechanic and copilot. Johnny was especially good for going down the airway IFR. He was just like an autopilot; our heading wouldn't vary by more than a degree.

The day was waning, but the weather was reasonable and we were eager to get home, so we filed nonstop from Juneau to Anchorage. "November one four, you are cleared for takeoff," the tower informed us. We gunned the engines, building speed as we rolled down the runway. Just as we were ready to rotate, the left engine began backfiring.

Juneau's runway was quite long, so we were able to abort our takeoff. We pulled off onto the taxiway and ran up the engines several times, but the backfiring continued. Neither of us felt much like beginning an inspection so late in the evening, so we taxied back to the parking area and resigned ourselves to spending the night in Juneau. After putting on the control locks and completing the various other chores necessary to bed down the airplane, we grabbed our suitcases and went over to the Baranof Hotel.

We spent a pleasant night, and checked out the next morning. "See you next trip," I called across the lobby to the desk clerk as we left. We didn't anticipate much of a problem fixing the engine, as the backfiring seemed rather minor, and we expected to be able to leave for Anchorage in the afternoon. Since the FSS had loaned us a car the night before, we stopped there first before walking over to examine our plane.

We opened up the engine and checked the compression on each cylinder; everything seemed to be normal. A visual inspection revealed nothing amiss, so we decided to run up the engine once again to be sure we really had a problem. That miserable backfiring was still with us.

We finally concluded that the trouble must lie in the carburetor. After trying various adjustments, all to no avail, we went ahead and fiddled around with other parts of the engine in an effort to analyze the intermittent miss. As the day rapidly slipped away, we became less sure of our carburetor diagnosis. Maybe the problem was an intake valve with insufficient clearance. We debated whether or not to check the tolerances; the Pratt and Whitney 1830 power plant had fourteen cylinders, and just getting the cowling off is a hell of a job.

While Johnny and I continued to think about it, we heard from the station that another of our DC-3s was due to arrive in town. Jim Hurst was captain, and with him was Bill Clayton, a fine mechanic. We thought we'd just take a break until Bill had a chance to look at the engine. It turned out that Jim was in quite a hurry; however, he had a third person aboard who could serve as his copilot, so he suggested, "Bill, why don't you just stay here in Juneau until the engine's fixed, then ride back with Johnny and Jack?"

That sounded like an excellent idea to us; we definitely were in need of some new blood to help us get a handle on the problem. Accordingly, Jim Hurst departed for Anchorage, and Bill Clayton stayed with us. We walked over to the airplane and Bill cocked his trained ear to the obnoxious miss.

"It's a bad carburetor, guys. No question."

Now Johnny and I had been messing around with the engine until we were absolutely sick of it, and Clayton seemed superbly confident of his diagnosis, so okay—we accepted it. We telephoned our Anchorage hangar and asked them to ship us the new carburetor via Pacific Northern Airlines.

The next morning we began removing the bad carburetor. For those of you who have never had the pleasure of removing a carburetor from an 1830, I might say that it's a difficult job, even under the best of conditions with all the proper tools. In the wind, rain, and snow of the Juneau airport, the work was miserable. After a while I let Johnny and Bill proceed with the carburetor exchange while I turned my talents to carpentry, erecting a crude shelter above the aircraft's wing. When the new carburetor arrived that afternoon, we were ready to install it and had about half the work done before the end of the day.

That night we checked into the Baranof Hotel for the third time. By now the hotel personnel began looking upon us with amusement. Each morning we'd check out with a loud "Goodbye"—and each night we'd stumble back in, wet and greasy.

We were sure, damn sure, that the next day we'd have the carburetor on and be able to get out of Juneau. "This is it—see you next trip," we once again told the smiling desk clerk as we left on our last journey to the airport.

We finished installing the carburetor, then tested the engine. Instead of hearing a steady purr, we were shocked to find the 1830 was still backfiring. We just couldn't believe it! We had been so confident of the repair that we'd even rather stupidly replaced all the cowling before running up the engine. Now we were forced back to the drawing board. We tried this and that, but it was as though the engine hated us. Nothing we did seemed to help.

The day came to a close, and we'd still gotten nowhere. We grabbed our bags disgustedly and returned once again to the Baranof. The FSS proved how little was their faith that we would ever leave by assigning us a government car indefinitely.

Our only change in routine that evening was to stop at the liquor store and buy a bottle of booze. Up in the room we poured ourselves a drink and I opened the informal proceedings, saying in exasperation, "What in hell could be wrong with that engine?"

I was losing face, along with Johnny and Bill. I held an Airframe and Engine Mechanic's license and had been immersed in the flying business all my life. I thought I knew an 1830 from one end to the other. Now I was starting to wonder.

We began talking and drinking. Perhaps the liquor loosened our tongues, because we hashed and rehashed our problem late into the night. But we came to no real conclusion. Finally I said, "Look, Pan American's flying DC-3s in here. Let's go over and ask one of their mechanics for some help. This must be some freak problem we have—something none of us has ever run across before. Just maybe the Pan Am mechanic will have the answer."

Sleep was nearly impossible for me that night. I couldn't get the engine off my mind. In the morning we drove out to the airport and stopped at the Pan Am office. Their mechanic was an expert on the 1830. After listening to it he announced, "It's the carburetor."

We all smiled. "Well, that's what we thought," Johnny told him, "so we replaced it. That's a new carburetor and it hasn't helped a bit."

He listened a while longer, then said, "Let's have lunch. We'll talk about it some more while we're eating." Late in the afternoon we were no better off. The Pan Am mechanic hadn't been very much help; we three were still baffled. When any of us had an idea, no matter how screwy, we'd go ahead and try it. But we'd already tried about everything.

That evening we once again headed back to the Baranof. Time was marching on, day after day, and Anchorage kept sending us dispatches that only rubbed salt into the wound: REQUEST YOU ADVISE YOUR APPROXIMATE ARRIVAL IN ANCHORAGE.

Hell, we didn't know when we were going to arrive in Anchorage—we hadn't yet made any progress at all! By now the people at the hotel were fully aware of our travails, and their little jokes were also beginning to pall on us. We checked out the next day, altering our parting words, "Hold the room, we'll probably be back."

Out at the airport, we were still at a loss about what to do and had no firm plan of action. We began another half-hearted examination, covering old ground. The incessant rain kept pouring down. I'd finally had it. "Look, we're not getting anywhere! We're fighting to fix this thing under this rough shelter and we're not doing any good; let's throw in the towel. We'll just phone Anchorage and tell them we can't fix it."

Johnny and Bill reluctantly agreed. Maybe that was the best thing to do. We telephoned Anchorage. In response to our plight, they said, "We'll send someone down." Now, that was a little annoying. How was anyone else in the hangar going to accomplish any more than we had? But we'd given up on it, so the decision was up to them. We went back to the hotel, went through the checking-in exercises, enjoyed a drink or two, and called it a night.

Bright and early the next morning, we were back at the airport. The station told us that a flight plan had been filed on one of the Beeches. Morgan Davies was pilot, and his passenger was Matt Parvin, head of aircraft maintenance at our hangar. They'd gotten an early start and were due to arrive in about an hour and a half. We weren't in the mood to bother any more with the 1830. We'd done everything we could, so we decided to sit and wait for Matt.

Now Matt was an excellent mechanic, but he had one little quirk I always found amusing. He believed almost religiously in a product called Pyroil. It was a very thin, highly refined lubricant, much like sewing-machine oil. There were quite a number of nearly identical substances; Marvel Mystery Oil was the trade name of a similar product marketed for use in automobile engines. They all acted mainly as top-cylinder lubricants. Just as some people believe that a liberal dose of castor oil can cure almost any human ill, Matt believed that Pyroil would cure nearly any ailment an engine might have.

The Beechcraft landed, and as they taxied up I said facetiously, "You know, I bet old Matt comes down here with a can of Pyroil." Sure enough, when they began unloading the gear, there wasn't just a can; there were five gallons of the stuff! I could hardly keep a straight face—here Matt was planning to fix it with Pyroil.

After a pretty curt "Hello," we took Matt over to where the plane was parked. Matt's paraphernalia consisted of his five gallons of Pyroil and a special oilcan with a spout about two feet long—the kind once used by railroad engineers to oil their locomotives. We didn't question a thing he was doing. We'd called for help and here it was.

Matt got out a small can and measured a quart of Pyroil into each gas tank. Then he filled his oilcan and climbed up a stepladder to get on the wing behind the sick engine.

"Now start it up," he yelled.

"Don't you want to hear the backfiring before you do anything?" I asked.

"I don't need to," said Matt.

Rather sullenly I climbed aboard, thinking, "Well, he'll sure hear something," as I brought up the engine. It began backfiring loudly.

Matt lifted his oilcan so he could squirt the Pyroil into the induction system where the air enters the engine. It worked just like magic! After the third stroke of oil, with a faint trail of blue smoke pouring from the exhaust, the engine cleared up and began running perfectly. Matt slid off the wing and said, "Well, we can go home now."

We finished some last-minute chores as we prepared to leave. Frankly, we were glad to be getting out of Juneau so quickly, even though the whole thing had been pretty embarrassing.

In retrospect I can see what happened: the engine had some sticky intake valves and the lubrication freed them. Matt, as on many other occasions, had known just the right thing to do. After that, I never again laughed at his Pyroil.

6

The Black Cat's Path

AFTER SEVERAL YEARS under our civilian supervision, the Port Heiden facility was declared nonessential, and the CAA was directed to close it as part of an economy move. I was given the task of shutting down the station and transporting its twenty-one-member staff back to Anchorage for reassignment.

I arrived early that day in a DC-3. I watched while all the vehicles were stored in the garage, while the windows were boarded as a precaution against bears, and while other preparations were made for the abandonment of Port Heiden. In the process, I made the discovery that closing a station was nearly as hard as getting one started. The final closure activities dragged on until late afternoon. I was anxious to get away before dark, because the generators had been shut off and sealed in the shed. There would be no runway lights if we remained after nightfall.

I kept pushing the personnel to get the station locked up before darkness. Even though they were hurrying, things kept cropping up that had to be done. However, we finally got everyone out to the airstrip and loaded their baggage aboard. It seemed that the CAA had at last accomplished the abandonment of Port Heiden. We closed the aircraft door, got the passengers seated, and removed the plane's control locks. Then we started one engine.

The cook's wife had been holding their little black cat. When the engine roared to life, the cat became frightened. It leaped out of her arms and jumped across the seats. I saw a black streak shooting through the companionway as the cat dashed forward and darted up behind the instrument panel, losing itself in the spaghetti-like maze of wires, chains, cables, and controls that runs the entire aircraft.

I shut down the engine. It was no-go until we got that cat out of there. I opened a side window and hung out of the airplane, beating my fist against the plane's nose, hoping to frighten the cat back out. But it just climbed higher out of reach, emitting an occasional meow.

There are about a thousand screws in the nose of a DC-3 and to remove them is a job of several hours under controlled conditions in a warm hangar, let alone on a cold, dark, rainswept runway. The only way we were going to get that cat out of there was for it to come down of its own accord.

Some of the bachelor personnel, who probably weren't very fond of the cat in the first place, began growling about being held up. After weeks at the remote station, they were looking forward to a night on the town in Anchorage. "Leave the little bastard in there and fly on to Anchorage," yelled one of the more impatient men.

"Can't do that—too risky," I replied. "We don't move until the cat's out."

There was more grumbling throughout the ranks of the passengers; morale had fallen rather low. And I was concerned too; it was getting dark, and we were on an unlighted strip. A little black cat had brought the CAA at Port Heiden to a screaming halt.

Of course, we could have unloaded everyone from the plane, reopened the station, and spent the night there. But that would have required several hours of work, undoing all our previous effort, so that idea was far down on our list of alternatives.

No further sounds were heard from the cat. Apparently it had settled down to nest within the dark jungle of cables behind the instrument panel. I wondered if the little devil was prepared to outwait us all. Finally we decided that everyone should vacate the cabin and walk over to the hangar several hundred yards away, leaving the cat alone with her owner. We hoped the cook's wife might then be able to coax her pet out of the cockpit.

So we deplaned. It was miserably chilly and windy, as Port Heiden always is. We gathered in a cluster at the hangar, killing time by swapping stories and telling a few jokes. There wasn't a damn thing else to do. As we talked, paced around, and shivered in the chill air, the late evening gave way to total darkness. Finally we heard the cook's wife calling, "I got her! She came out!" We all dashed toward the plane. The lady stood in the doorway holding her now peaceable cat.

This time I securely closed the door to the companionway before starting the engines. With the aid of the landing lights, we were able to get airborne, heading off toward Anchorage.

The cook later told us the cat purred most of the way back to town. I guess that perverse animal must have been celebrating her feline victory over the intricacy of man's flying machines.

7
Taylor Weather

THE CAA WAS OVERHAULED in the late fifties, and the resultant structure was renamed the Federal Aviation Agency, later changed to Federal Aviation Administration. In the process of reorganization, a new policy was established whereby the deputy director of each region would be an officer selected from the Air Force.

They were usually brigadier generals, or were promoted to brigadier general shortly after joining the FAA. Two of the Alaskan Region's most popular deputy directors were General Bill Comstock and General Ralph "Zach" Taylor.

Both men had been fighter pilots, both were still active flyers, and both were fun to fly with. When General Comstock retired, many FAA employees attended his retirement dinner—he was just as well liked in our agency as he was in the Air Force.

The same thing was true of General Taylor, another colorful, interesting person. A World War II ace, he had downed nine enemy airplanes while flying a P-38 in the North African campaign. He was certainly no stranger to aircraft; in fact, he was an excellent all-around pilot.

Zach called my office one day and asked me to arrange a flight for the following afternoon. He had to go to Juneau, meet with the Governor, and make a speech. So I set it up with Dick Pastro and myself as crew; we always enjoyed trips with the General.

Flying weather was awfully grim the following day; a very intense storm was sitting over the Gulf of Alaska. Cordova reported marginal conditions, and Yakutat was even below minimums. High surface wind, turbulence and high winds aloft, low ceilings, icing conditions—the reports listed them all.

However, Juneau was reported well above minimums and seemed pretty far east of the weather, so we expected no problem getting into Juneau once we had passed through the Gulf of Alaska storm. Since we were carrying only 1,500 pounds of freight in the DC-3, we were able to depart Anchorage with full fuel tanks. At that time we felt that a DC-3 with full tanks could fly through anything.

The trip was uneventful until we passed over Whittier, a fan marker on the old low-frequency range. Eastbound toward the Gulf, we were then allowed to descend below 10,000 feet. General Taylor was flying the aircraft, and Dick was copilot. Having nothing better to do, I sat in the jump seat and computed our speed.

We had been experiencing a little turbulence and were picking up some ice. Even though the deicer boots on the wings were handling it without any trouble, we descended to 6,000, looking for more comfortable flying.

Once we reached Cordova I performed another calculation. Our ground speed from Whittier to Cordova worked out to only ninety nautical miles per hour. Since Juneau was still 470 nautical miles away, we were in for a long, slow trip.

Daylight was already ebbing on that short winter's afternoon as we passed the radio station at Hinchinbrook. The air had become quite turbulent. No matter what your altitude, you always think you'll find something a little smoother if you change elevation. We went up and down a few times, finding each new layer worse than the one we'd just left.

There was no other air traffic, none at all. Everyone else must have had better sense and stayed home.

I had a feeling we were traveling even slower than before. Sure enough, after passing the Katalla fix, fifty nautical miles farther along the air route, I computed our ground speed to be seventy nautical miles per hour. At this slow a ground speed, we didn't have sufficient fuel to reach Juneau or our legal alternate, Whitehorse, Canada.

I told Zach the bad news, that we'd better give up on Juneau. All of us agreed to get the hell back to Anchorage. We called the Air Traffic Control Center and received the necessary clearance. Anything we wanted to do was fine with them—no other aircraft were in the sky. Of course, westbound toward the mountains a different set of IFR rules applies. You have to be flying at a minimum of 10,000 feet before you cross the Cordova station.

So we ascended to 10,000. All at once we began getting ice like I'd never seen before. Our DC-3 had special wingtanks in which we carried twenty gallons of deicing alcohol, designed to be sprayed on the propellers. We also carried five gallons in the cabin, to be used for the windshield. Then too, the mechanical deicing boots were still flexing on the wings. But none of our equipment really had a chance. The ice came on so fast, it immediately domed out over the windshield. The wings became heavily laden, and we heard funny grinding noises as chunks flew off the props and struck the fuselage. I couldn't believe any plane would ice up so fast.

Zach was getting a little uncomfortable in the left-hand seat. He turned to me and said something I'd later remember with a smile,

"Jack, we've just run out of Taylor weather! You take the controls."
Well, I was pretty sure we'd run out of Jefford weather, too. But at least
I was current in the DC-3 and had been flying it a lot, so we switched
seats.

The front windshield was completely domed over with ice, so I asked
Dick and Zach to open the side windows, hoping for a little visibility.
But they were also iced to the point where they were hopelessly stuck.

Our airspeed was slowing, even though we'd brought the engines
up to METO (Maximum Except Takeoff) power. As it got worse I told
Dick to alert Air Traffic Control that we'd have to be coming down.
Finally I was forced to begin sacrificing altitude at an alarming rate
just to keep the DC-3 from stalling. We were literally falling out of the
sky, pulling METO power and fighting to save altitude every foot of
the way. I announced that we'd have to go in to Cordova, although that
was actually rather obvious; we had no hope of making it anywhere
else.

The Center immediately cleared us to Cordova and okayed us to
their frequency. The station gave us a rather grim weather report: a
600-foot ceiling, two-mile visibility, and nil braking action—Cordova's
runway was a sheet of glare ice. But there was one redeeming feature.
The high surface winds were east at twenty-eight knots, aligned perfectly with the runway, so that we shouldn't need to use the brakes.

We were down to 6,000 when we crossed Hinchinbrook range, still
drawing METO power. Cordova had a little loop range that intersected
the east leg of the Hinchinbrook range at a fix called Egg Island. From
Egg Island you went directly to the Cordova range, located east of the
airport.

We were halfway to Cordova. Our airspeed was very low, and we
were still losing altitude under METO power when suddenly the airplane took off climbing and regained proper airspeed. Apparently we
had descended into a warm stratum of air and the ice had sloughed
off the wings. We couldn't see the wing surfaces, but we knew they had
to have cleared; we were back to normal cruise, and the airplane was
performing beautifully.

Now all we needed was to be able to see enough of the ground to
land. Zach and Dick kept hammering and banging on the side windows.
Finally they jarred them both open. It was awfully drafty in the cabin,
but at least we had some sideways visibility.

We were at the minimum altitude for instrument approach when
Zach unexpectedly saw the light from Cordova's rotating beacon. However, we were in a bad position to turn in toward the airport; we'd be
streaking downwind toward the mountains if we tried to keep the

beacon in sight from the side window. But at the same time we hated to abandon our visual reference to proceed on a blind approach, and there was a chance we might not find the light again.

We made our decision, accepting the left downwind turn and keeping the airport in sight. We had a few uneasy moments as we went through patches of crud and temporarily lost the light, but eventually we made our turn to final approach. While we had no forward visibility, at least we did have the side windows.

An odd thing, but my first airplane, the Robin, also had had poor forward visibility. This landing, gauging our position from the side, actually wasn't much different from those early landings.

There was absolutely no braking, just as the station had said, but the wind stopped us and we taxied cautiously to the side of the strip. FAA station mechanic "Skip" Skipper, a former pilot and flight mechanic, came down to meet us. We walked around to the nose, switched on a flashlight, and couldn't believe what we saw. More than a foot of ice covered the nose and the windshield. We'd no doubt had the same thing all over the wings until the warm air allowed the ice to break away.

Skip took us home for the night. He poured each of us a stiff drink, and his wife fixed us some steaks. In the morning we returned to the airplane. The block of ice had partially melted and fallen off the nose, but even then it must have weighed 100 pounds—really quite incredible.

We all thought about it and agreed this story might not be worth the bother of telling. No one would believe us!

8

Fiddling Around in Nome

IN MY THIRTY-TWO YEARS with the agency, I watched while many administrators passed through the Washington, D.C., head office. Generally, I found them to be very nice, competent people. One thing they all would do sooner or later, and rightly so, was visit the Alaskan Region. They'd usually come up on N-1, the FAA flagship. In the early days it was a Lockheed Lodestar, later a Grumman Gulf Stream, and finally a Lockheed Jet Star.

The administrators' inspections were normally leisurely affairs. They'd want to see how we did things up here, get acquainted with our personnel, and tour the bush facilities. The Regional Director would be on hand to meet and greet the Washington brass when they arrived in Anchorage. After a few days in town, we would head out with the DC-3, flying them to as many of the bush stations as their agenda would allow. Barrow and Kotzebue were always musts on the list. But eventually the administrators would have had their fill of the tour, and our group would be ready to return.

I usually saved Nome for the last stop. Our arrival there signified that the administrator's visit was pretty much over. He would soon be headed back to Washington, and our own Regional Director would shortly be back in Anchorage. The crew and I always felt good once we hit Nome; we were ready for a little relaxation. Say what you will about the seemingly innocuous task of flying the "wheels" around, there was always the worry that things might not go well. We'd much rather have been flight checking or hauling freight.

Well, on one of these tours, everything had been going fine and we'd just pulled into Nome. A group of the FAA employees rented the basement of the North Star Hotel for the evening and threw a party for the administrator and the Regional Director. Since this type of gathering gave the wives a rare opportunity to put on their fancy clothes, these parties were always well attended.

The bar was open for cocktails during the extended social hour prior to the meal. I was into my third martini before the call to dinner and ordered yet another during the course of being served. So I was ripe for enjoying the time of good-fellowship that followed the food. A small band was playing up on stage, a group of professional musicians from Outside who'd been engaged for the evening's entertainment. The leader played saxophone; he was accompanied by a drummer, a guitarist, and a man on clarinet.

We'd just applauded the band when the administrator from Washington, who was sitting close by, said, "Jack, I hear you're quite a musician in your own right—a violinist, aren't you?" He'd no doubt learned that from reading a chapter written about me in *The Flying North,* by Jean Potter.

Back during the war, a team from *Fortune* magazine had come to Alaska to do a story about the CAA and the Weather Bureau and the part they played in the Alaskan military operation. Writer Don Stewart and researcher Jean Potter were here for quite a long while working on the story, and they used to travel with us quite a lot.

Jean Potter, a very attractive young woman, was enamored of the lives of many of the bush pilots of the day. She decided to return to Alaska after her assignment was finished and write a series of bush pilot biographies. I was the subject of her last chapter.

In the book I said that I enjoyed playing the violin (implying that I played it rather well) and described a music combo I'd organized in Unalakleet during the time I'd based there hauling the mail. Actually I'm a lousy musician, but I did take some piano lessons as a kid and I can halfway read a sheet of music. Several natives at Unalakleet played guitar, there was a really good piano player, and one fellow fancied himself an expert on the xylophone. We'd often get together and improvise a few tunes—you get rather desperate for something to do in Unalakleet, I'll tell you. In any event, mention was made of it in Jean Potter's book.

The Region was in the habit of giving a copy of *The Flying North* to the administrators from Washington when they arrived in Alaska. They'd usually have a good opportunity to meet some of the more renowned pilots, like Noel Wien and Bob Reeve, who were also in the book. The text served as an interesting introduction to the history of aviation in the Territory, and the administrators seemed to appreciate it.

"Yes," I heard myself answering the administrator somewhat pompously (and I hope it was the martinis talking), "I am a rather good violinist." Then I continued a little more modestly, "If only I had a violin I'd be happy to play something for you," feeling pretty secure in making that statement at our party there in the basement of the North Star Hotel.

Nothing more was said, but about five minutes later I looked up and there was one of the guys from the Nome station bringing in a beautiful, darkly varnished violin. I could have strangled him.

So my hand had been called!

I walked slowly up to the stage and introduced myself to the band. "About the only thing I can play is 'Indian Love Call' in E flat," I told them.

The bandleader, the guy with the sax, said, "I don't believe I've ever heard 'Indian Love Call' on the violin."

"Well, I guess I had to be different." I lowered my voice. "Just between you and me, I'm a pretty poor violinist," I confessed.

"Well, we'll see what happens."

I made a big to-do of tuning, buying a little more time while trying to remember what the first note was. "It starts on B flat, in case anyone gives a damn," the bandleader said to no one in particular. Then he blew a B flat. I found it on the violin and very shakily started out.

The guy began leading me with his sax. Once I'd picked it up a little, he started to fade out. Actually, there were certain parts that I managed to play extremely well. The sax player would back off completely, leaving just the drummer's soft brushwork to accompany me, soloing at the microphone with the violin and putting a beautiful tremolo on the few notes I remembered.

Then I'd get into rough going again. The sax man would come belting in, drowning me out with the saxophone until we'd get to another part where I could play it pretty well. But all good things come to an end. I finally stopped, and, my gosh, I got a good hand from all those people. Of course, they'd been drinking martinis, too.

I bowed and walked back to my table, where the administrator was still applauding. "By golly, Jack, you were really good! Except that the guy with the saxophone kept drowning you out all the time." Little did he know that the bandleader with the saxophone had been saving my life.

One of the earliest of our regional inspections occurred in June of 1946. We received word that administrator T. P. Wright and his party would come to Alaska in the Lodestar N-1. They wanted to tour the entire Region.

We held a round-table planning session during which we described our continuous battle with the elements and told him he was really going to see some bad weather. On June 14 we started our trip by going down the Aleutian Chain. In all my experience I'd never seen anything like it. There weren't any clouds whatsoever and not a breath of wind. We flew all the way to Attu and spent the night. Our return on the fifteenth was the same—still no clouds, fog, or turbulence. We explained that we'd been unusually lucky, but for our flight to Barrow we guaranteed him we would certainly see some instrument flying in problem weather.

On June 17 we left Anchorage for Farewell, McGrath, Bethel, Unalakleet, and Nome. June 18 we continued to Barrow, then back to Anchorage. Other than an occasional high cirrus cloud, the weather was perfect. Of course, by then it was raising hell down in the Aleutians, but the weather was certainly good where we were flying.

On the nineteenth we proceeded to Yakutat, and would you believe it? The weather was beautiful, even in the rain forests of southeastern Alaska.

So the great administrator T. P. Wright left Alaska, no doubt convinced we were full of bull, at least insofar as our descriptions of the extreme weather we had to face.

9

Gold Medalist

WINNING the Department of Commerce Gold Medal was one of the high points of my government career.

For several weeks during the winter of 1956-57, the Airways Flight Inspection office was buzzing in undertones of hushed activity, although no one would explain their furtive actions. Even our faithful secretary, Dorothy Revell, wouldn't tell me a damn thing as she continually checked through old logbooks and made mysterious phone calls.

I was finally let in on the secret. Chris Lample, along with Art Jenks and some of my other friends, had decided that I deserved a medal for my work in Alaska with the CAA. Chris wasn't satisfied to submit my name for any of the lesser honors; he went for the big one—the gold medal, the highest award given by the Department of Commerce.

It often seems that the recipient of a medal is not the one who is actually most deserving of credit. Rather, the honors should really have been bestowed upon the supervisor who has nominated his man for the award. I know it's true in my case. Chris Lample spent many long hours in Washington working to secure the medal for me, and in all sincerity I believe he was far more deserving of it than I.

Well, I received word from Washington that I'd been awarded the gold medal, and they requested I attend the awards ceremony if at all possible. I was already scheduled for a meeting in Washington, and the ceremony dovetailed nicely with my trip. I wired back that I'd be happy to attend.

Nearly a hundred medals were awarded. Many were bronze, a few were silver, and three were gold. I met one of the other gold medal recipients, Don Stewart, also of the CAA, who had made contributions in the scientific and technical world through his work with advanced instrument landing systems.

The ceremony was held in the Department of Commerce auditorium. Sinclair Weeks, Secretary of Commerce, was at the head of the stage. Each individual agency chief, twenty or so, was also in attendance. There were a far larger number of agencies under the Department of Commerce umbrella than I had ever before realized, including the Patent Office and the Coast and Geodetic Survey. Jimmy Pyle, head of our CAA operation, was prominent among the many assembled administrators.

I was quite nervous while sitting in the auditorium. A small symphony orchestra played mood music while the seats filled with people. The music softly came to a close, the master of ceremonies ascended to the lectern, and before I knew it my name was called.

With wobbling knees I walked on stage and was presented with the gold medal and a citation. The medal weighed over an ounce, struck with the Commerce Department Seal on one side and my citation inscribed on the reverse. Although I'd handled quite a bit of gold in my time, nonetheless I was highly awed and impressed. After a final handshake from Secretary Weeks I was allowed to leave the spotlight and return to my chair.

Old Chris Lample was there grinning from ear to ear. I showed him the medal, which read:

THE UNITED STATES DEPARTMENT OF COMMERCE AWARD FOR EXCEPTIONAL SERVICE: Jack T. Jefford is hereby commended for exceptional service.

CITATION: For significant contributions to the development of Alaskan aviation, for resourceful and willing performance of flight transportation services for Alaskan facilities and personnel, often beyond the call of duty and at great personal risk, for over sixteen years.

Above: Hinchinbrook Island, where Jack once landed a DC-3 on a treacherous beach to deliver a badly needed generator and engine. The unit (similar to the one on the opposite page) powered a transmitter broadcasting directional radio beams.

Above: Unloading a snow jeep from NC-214, a DC-3. While driving such a vehicle, two Port Heiden CAA technicians became lost in a howling blizzard. Jack took part in the intensive search for the two men. Left: Fuel oil carried in a 1,000-gallon tank aboard the DC-3 supplied remote CAA stations.

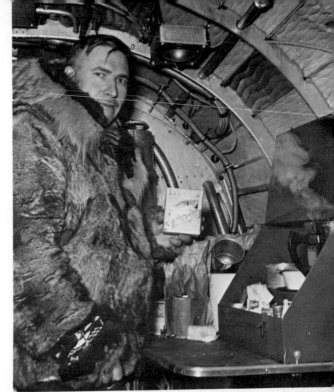

Right: Jack warms water for some soup in the cabin of the DC-3.
Below: Lake Clark Pass. Jack flew blind toward these mountains in darkness and snowstorm seeking an improvised lantern-lit airstrip at Nondalton, where badly injured Cliff Uzzell required immediate evacuation.

Jack at the time he won the Department of Commerce Gold Medal.

Jack (left), Bill Clayton (center), and Johnny Freeland pause at the
Juneau airport while trying to fix a troublesome backfire in the DC-3.
Jack constructed the crude shelter around the engine to shield
them as they worked.

Jack with "Glacier Pilot" Bob Reeve at the nose of N-123.

Above: The onetime barn-stormer takes to the skies in a Sabreliner jet, which he piloted in his final years with the FAA.
Left: Jack with instructor Leo Suter at the Sabreliner jet school.

Jack in the cockpit of the fat, squat N-123, which he thought was "the weirdest-looking airplane I'd ever seen."

N-123, a military Fairchild C-123 freighter, proved to be perfectly suited to the FAA's need for a plane capable of handling massive loads.

Heavy freight could be backed right up to the C-123 and loaded via a rear ramp into the hold of the giant plane.

Inside, the C-123 provided ample space and clearance for bulky loads.

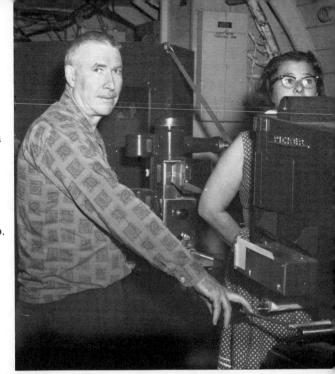

The C-123 even served as a flying TB X-ray screening unit (right), with Jack assisting patients.
Below: Amazingly, trucks and other large vehicles could be driven right into the plane via the rear ramp.

Jack and the two observers he flew along the route of the Iditarod
Sled Dog Race—veteran musher Orville Lake (center) and the
race marshal.

The finish gate of the Iditarod race, which begins in Anchorage and ends
more than 1,000 miles away in Nome.

Part 7

Into the Jet Age

1
N-123

ON A COLD, CLEAR DAY in January of 1957, I was helping unload cargo from the DC-3 after a routine commissary flight to Nome, when the weirdest-looking airplane I'd ever seen landed on the runway and rolled up to the station.

Its high wings supported two massive reciprocating engines and two small wingtip jets. The fuselage was almost rotund, a wide, rounded box set close to the ground. The aircraft also featured a rear ramp door below its elevated tail and a cockpit perched high atop a blunt nose. My overall first impression was one of a squat and stubby, but powerful and utilitarian, airplane that must have been designed strictly for business.

I was intrigued, so I walked over and spoke to the pilots. I found out that the plane was a military Fairchild C-123 freighter that had been brought up from Wright-Patterson Air Force Base on a cold-weather evaluation flight to Alaska. While examining the airplane, I suddenly realized it was perfectly suited to our agency's needs. The Fairchild was capable of hauling huge loads, including large trucks or tractors up to the size of a Caterpillar D-4. (We would later haul many such vehicles.)

Not really thinking for a minute that we could actually get one, I sat down anyway and, with the assistance of my very able secretary, Dorothy Revell, ground out a letter to the Regional Director. I explained that I thought I'd seen the perfect plane for the CAA and went on to extoll the virtues of the C-123.

Now it just so happened that Congress had recently been applying some heat to both the CAA and the Air Force in an effort to make the two agencies patch up their somewhat strained relationship. The government directed them to bear in mind that they each were supported by taxpayers' dollars and therefore should, at the very least, be able to maintain a reasonable degree of interagency cooperation.

Perhaps in response to these winds blowing out of Washington, the local director forwarded my letter on through the chain of command—adding that the idea of acquiring a C-123 sounded good to him. As usual, Chris Lample also went to bat for the Alaskan Region. He convinced the upper level administrators to go through appropriate channels and request a C-123 as a bailment from the Air Force to the CAA. As it turned out, the response of the Air Force was to say, in effect, "Great! Send down a crew and pick one up."

When the message came back from Washington, we just couldn't believe our luck. We were actually scheduled to receive one of the large C-123s! Dick Pastro, Bill Hanson, and I went down to Hagerstown, Maryland, and enrolled in a tech-rep school to learn something about the new airplane. Our C-123, numbered N-123, was still in the process of being manufactured during our four weeks of training. In May of 1957 we completed school and accepted the just-finished N-123. Then we flew it up to Anchorage, where it has been based ever since.

N-123 was the first C-123 in Alaska, except for the one I'd seen on the cold-weather test flight to Nome. Later we received word that an entire squadron of C-123s was to be assigned to Elmendorf Air Force Base in Anchorage. In preparation for the arrival of the aircraft, many of the young Air Force pilots rode with us whenever possible to obtain a little advance flight training.

So the story of N-123 did represent a modest step forward in co-operative relations between the Air Force and the CAA.

2

Trouble in the C-123

FLYING, it has been said, is "hours and hours of boredom interspersed with moments of sheer terror."

There's a grain of truth behind the hyperbole, especially for the commercial pilot. I've had that old saying brought home to me vividly on a number of occasions during my flying career, including several hairy episodes in the workhorse C-123.

One of those times occurred as a result of hauling a large wooden telephone pole. The FAA needed it delivered from Anchorage to Fire Island, a radio site located in Cook Inlet just offshore from Anchorage International Airport. After sizing up the pole, over forty feet long, all of us thought we'd best be pretty scientific about this unusual load. So using a forklift, we picked up the pole at its point of balance and then computed our center of gravity for the flight. The center of gravity turned out to be quite rearward, but within limits.

We went ahead and chained the pole securely onto the floor of the C-123, leaving the ramp door level and the upper door open—a safe configuration in which to fly. But N-123 must have been a weird-looking sight as we taxied down the runway with twenty feet of telephone pole sticking out the tail.

We couldn't rotate very much due to our special load, so we applied a little flap and let the aircraft fly itself off the ground.

Then all hell broke loose!

The part of the pole extending behind the tail began to vibrate wildly. Since we were already fully airborne, we were committed to continue the flight. The oscillations became so severe I couldn't read the instruments on the panel, and as our speed increased, the vibration worsened.

Fortunately we had only a very short distance to travel, about five minutes air time. And luckily we were able to make a straight-in approach to the runway on the south tip of the island (later destroyed in the 1964 earthquake).

Everything ended well, but it was sure a "shaky" five minutes.

Anyone who flies very often will sooner or later encounter some type of emergency. The really bad situation is when more than one emergency occurs on the same flight.

I was on a midwinter commissary trip to Kotzebue. We scheduled the hauls monthly, usually carrying about six tons of supplies nonstop from Anchorage. The weather was excellent; everything was running smoothly. Tim Jackson, the regular engineer on our cargo C-123, had needed time to take care of some personal business in town, so on this trip another pilot, Emitt Soldin, volunteered to go along as flight engineer. Our policy was to rotate the duties en route so that every member of the crew acted as engineer on one leg of the trip, copilot on another leg, and captain on a third. The third member of our crew, Gene Stolz, hadn't been flying regularly in the C-123 but asked to accompany us on this particular journey.

We made the flight to Kotzebue in a little more than three hours, quite a routine trip. Prior to our landing, the station operator at Kotzebue gave us the weather. Although it was clear, the temperature had plunged to thirty-five below zero; a twenty-knot wind was blowing, and with the chill factor added to the already frigid temperature, we wanted to get in and out of Kotzebue as quickly as possible. But we would need to take on some fuel. The FAA operated a small tanker trailer that was a pretty efficient little rig. We let the Kotzebue station personnel know that we'd appreciate all their efforts to keep our time on the ground to a minimum.

We landed, taxied to the parking area, then shut down the engines and began the simultaneous unloading and refueling. I noticed upon leaving the cockpit that the C-123's cylinder head temperatures were dropping at an alarming rate due to the extreme chill factor. We all put our shoulder to the wheel and helped the station personnel offload our freight in a hurry.

Fortunately there wasn't any cargo going back, so in a very short time we were unloaded, refueled, and ready to crank up and make our return flight home. Then the trouble began.

Soldin started up the auxiliary power unit, but for some reason it wasn't giving us any voltage. Checking further, we found that the engine shaft that spins the generator had broken, so of course the unit was doing us no good whatsoever. Because the aircraft depends almost entirely on the generator's output, the battery itself is quite small, just enough to fire up the auxiliary power plant. If conditions are ideal, if the battery is fully charged and the main engines are warm, then it's possible to start one of them on battery power alone.

We tried desperately to get an engine started. With one engine in action, we'd have a generator on line to start the second engine. But we couldn't get either of them going—and as expected, in a few minutes the battery was dead.

We had a further problem. Since we'd planned only a short stay in Kotzebue, we hadn't bothered to dilute the engines. In the dilution process, gasoline is injected into a hopper of engine oil, thinning it and allowing the engine to turn over easily even after prolonged exposure to cold weather. Once the engine starts, the gasoline rapidly boils out of the oil.

We decided, given the undiluted engines and the broken power unit, that we were sunk without help. Our start, if we'd ever get started, was going to be long and difficult. We called Anchorage and relayed our problems. They promised that a new auxiliary power unit and a mechanic would be sent to Kotzebue the next morning in a DC-3. Having done all we could, we decided to give up for the day and checked in to our quarters.

Headquarters was apparently in a hurry to get us home, because quite early the next morning they dispatched the DC-3, flown by Elvin Jackson. A mechanic, Dick Thatcher, came along to help us, and Tim Jackson was also aboard. The crew brought along a replacement auxiliary power unit, as well as motor covers and Herman Nelson heaters so we could get heat to the main engines.

Elvin Jackson stopped in Kotzebue just long enough to unload his passengers and the equipment. He must have figured one FAA airplane down in Kotzebue was enough, because he was out of there and on his way to Anchorage in a matter of minutes.

It was still bitterly cold and windy; thawing the engines was a slow, torturous process. In the meantime we installed a Herman Nelson in the cabin to keep it warm while we replaced the faulty auxiliary power unit with the new one. Along about dusk we got the auxiliary power unit installed, and it functioned fine. Even though the two main engines were not yet very warm, we figured we could probably get them started. Then, with a careful, measured warm-up we'd be back in business.

We were anxious to get back to Anchorage, so we stowed away all the heaters and other paraphernalia and made ready for takeoff. The engines started without difficulty. After idling them for a long time, we slowly increased the rpm. Since each engine held fifty gallons of frozen oil in its oil tank, getting all the oil thawed took a long time.

At first, the fluid part of the oil circulates pretty much exclusively through the small hopper tank. That's why dilution can so effectively thin the oil. Gradually all the frozen oil in the main tank thaws and becomes part of the active system.

After warming the engines to the point where we thought we were safe for takeoff, we taxied out and filed a quick flight plan for home. Tim said that the weather was clear all the way, so we just checked on the current airport conditions in Anchorage. Everything looked fine.

The boredom phase of flying was about to end on this particular trip; the moments of sheer terror were not far off.

Knowing the engines hadn't been diluted and that therefore the oil might still be a bit thick, we decided to go easy on them and not take off at full power. No problem, since Kotzebue's runway was plenty long and we had a light load. Tim Jackson went up to METO power and we more or less let the airplane fly itself off the ground. We were very lucky that we happened, on account of the engines, to do it that way. Our cautious, level takeoff was what probably kept us from becoming accident statistics, because as soon as we became airborne the airplane's elevators froze.

Ask any pilot. Other than having a wing fall off, the next worst thing is losing the use of the plane's elevators. Of the three principal aircraft controls—elevators, rudder, and ailerons—the elevators are the most important.

Fortunately for us, the elevators had locked into a position that allowed for a very slow, steady climb. We found that by using the trim tabs, we could get a limited amount of control. So we eased the C-123 on up to a cruising altitude of 7,000 feet and were able, by judicious shifting of our cargo, to get the plane leveled off. Another thing in our favor was that the air happened to be exceptionally smooth—there wasn't a bump in it. Turbulence at a time like this would have been miserable, perhaps even disastrous.

Gene and I pulled as much as we dared on the elevator control, but we were afraid of using too much force. Some component might snap, causing the control to slip either forward or backward but still remain locked. That would put the aircraft into a dive or climb. So we finally gave up muscling the control.

By now it was dark, and darkness always makes it a little harder to assess situations like this.

The C-123 was so noisy that the only way you could talk to other crew members was through headsets plugged into an interphone circuit. We were all wearing our headsets as we held what amounted to a staff meeting—a strategy conference to try to figure out what the hell had happened and what we might do about it. Everybody except me started poring over the plane's maintenance manuals. I concentrated on keeping the damn plane headed toward Galena.

We put forth—and discarded—several theories about what was wrong with the elevators. We thought there might have been a malfunction in the elaborate, hydraulically operated system designed to lock the elevator controls when the engines are reversed on landing. We couldn't be sure. To explore this theory, Jackson took a flashlight and crawled around the tail section. He came back to tell us that the control locking system was still free and apparently had not been activated.

We were desperately trying to figure out some course of action, some way to solve the problem. At one point we even considered severing the hydraulic line leading to the locking device. But we finally decided that would probably spray the inside of the cabin with hydraulic fluid under pressure and therefore wasn't a very bright idea. Moreover, Tim was pretty sure we were looking at the wrong area as the source of trouble.

Tim Jackson kept dividing his time between being flight engineer and studying the reference manuals along with Gene, Emitt, and Dick, all of whom were absorbed in a frantic search to find a way of unlocking the elevator controls. Tim reached over and poked me on the shoulder, at the same time saying over the interphone, "More bad news, Jack. The left engine's losing a lot of oil." Sure enough, it was.

The C-123's engines are "dry sump"; that is, oil originates in a tank equipped with two pumps, one pressurizing the system and the other, the scavenger pump, gathering the oil and pumping it back to the main oil-supply tank. If for any reason the scavenger pump malfunctions, the engine will continue to run. However, without the oil-gathering process functioning, the engine will begin to throw oil out its breathers, and in a short period of time you lose all your oil.

First, no elevators. Now, a bad engine spurting out oil at a rate that would let it keep running no more than about thirty minutes. "Well," I told Tim, "let's start up the jet."

Mounted on the C-123's wing tips were two 1,000-pound-thrust jet engines. Although the jets can be used for climb, they're normally used for takeoffs if you have a gross load. They also come in handy if you lose an engine in flight; you can start up the jet opposite the engine that's still running and this combination results in a real nice job of flying. Without the jet assist, the C-123 performs rather poorly on a single reciprocating engine.

But when Tim attempted to fire up the jet on the plane's left wing, it refused to start.

"Might be frost on the igniter," I said. "Try again."

"No use, Jack," Tim said after a moment. "It just won't go."

Then, with a sinking feeling, I saw a flicker on the oil pressure gauge monitoring the sick reciprocating engine. I nodded to Gene, who quickly feathered it.

No elevators. No jet power. Just one engine. The situation was getting worse by the minute—a really sticky wicket. We went to METO power on our remaining engine, and it seemed that the trim was still okay. At least we could limp along.

We were nearing Galena, the closest place we could land. We sure didn't want to waste any time getting on the ground. But, as if we needed it, we received still more bad news. The station radioed that Galena was zero-zero—tightly wrapped in dense ice fog.

We exchanged glances. "Looks like either Fairbanks or Nome," I said.

"Nome's closer," said Gene.

"Nome it is," I said, swinging the big plane in a slow arc back to the area from which we'd just come.

Then, as we were wondering what would go wrong next, we got our first break. Tim got the jet started. Bringing the jet on line increased our airspeed and made the plane much easier to fly, especially with the locked elevators.

"We've got a problem here," I told Galena. "We've got one engine out and a locked elevator control. We're diverting to Nome." I also alerted Nome and Kotzebue to our predicament. Passing over Golovin, just sixty miles out of Nome, we began to wonder more and more just how we should handle the plane on this landing without elevators.

The Nome operator—and this was good news for a change—advised that the weather was clear and calm. "We're going to have to make a straight-in approach," we told him. We'd already mutually decided that just past Golovin we'd start a very, very slow descent.

The hard part of this plan was that any change of power would cause the airplane to go up or to go down. We finally became stabilized at reduced power, and with the limited control afforded by the trim tabs, we got her coming down about 300 or 400 feet a minute. Unless there were further complications, we could just fly the plane onto Nome's runway in exactly that fashion.

As it turned out, our rate of descent worked very well. Approaching the Nome airport from the east, we were able to keep our sink rate about what you'd have on a normal descent.

Just as we flew over the boundary marker, I yelled to Tim, "Cut the jet!" Then I pulled back the throttle on the recip engine. The C-123's nose started to drop. We felt the jolt as the gear hit the ground pretty hard. Then a strange thing happened. As soon as we thudded to the ground, the control unlocked.

I saw Alaska Airlines' B-727 getting ready to taxi out on its flight to Anchorage and asked the captain over the radio if he'd mind stalling a bit until we could taxi in and get our gear together.

"We'd like to ride back to Anchorage with you," I told him.

"We'd be glad to have you aboard," the captain replied.

We had just one thing in mind now—that was to get home. We parked the C-123 and were assured by station personnel that they'd tie it down and look after it. Grabbing our stuff, we headed over to the 727 and got aboard. And, after a couple of martinis on the flight back to town, the harrowing situation we'd just been through didn't seem so grim after all.

What had happened to the elevators? Strange to say, that's still a mystery. Our maintenance people couldn't find anything amiss. They phoned the factory, and the experts there were also puzzled as to what could have gone wrong. Mechanics covered the aircraft with a fine-tooth comb but failed to pinpoint the control-locking problem.

The Air National Guard flew a replacement engine to Nome, enabling us to bring the C-123 home. In the following years we never encountered any similar problem, nor have we heard of its happening to anyone else.

Sometimes you can create a panic without even knowing what you've accomplished.

A number of years ago when hijacking (air piracy) first surfaced as an international problem, many security measures were introduced, including methods whereby a pilot could unobtrusively inform controllers that his aircraft was being hijacked. If you were without radio, leaving your flaps down in flight signalled that your aircraft had been commandeered. But by far the most effective signal was the code frequency of your radar transponder. The code frequencies of VFR (Visual Flight Rules) and IFR transmissions were changed periodically, and certain of them were relegated strictly to emergency signals that indicated hijack.

I paid a lot more attention to the program after flying one day to Cold Bay in the C-123. The weather was nice, and the air was smooth as we traveled VFR along Bristol Bay at an altitude of about 4,500 feet.

We were all very relaxed, including Fred Klouda, who was acting as flight engineer. The flight engineer's seat pivots on a hinged device. Everyone had a tendency—and it was a real easy thing to do—of lolling back in the chair and putting his feet up on the radio panel. Somehow Fred inadvertently managed to switch our radar transponder to broadcast on the hijack code.

Before the single-frequency outlets were installed at Port Heiden and Port Moller, VHF communication was rather limited. Unless you were flying very high, you were out of communication much of the way between King Salmon and Cold Bay.

The Air Force site at Port Heiden received our signal first, alerting Anchorage that they were getting a hijack code transmission originating from an aircraft en route from King Salmon to Cold Bay. As we went along a little farther, Port Moller started picking up the signal, and soon all the various stations were calling us on every frequency. But at our low altitude we were not receiving them.

I can't believe the FAA was really too concerned; no hijacker in his right mind would want to take over a C-123. After we'd gotten within radio range of Cold Bay, I called the operator. Very guardedly, the operator asked, "Are you okay?"

"Yes, we're just fine," I replied.

"Well, maybe you should call the Air Force on 126.2," he continued in a flat, measured cadence. The tone of his voice was so strange that we all three looked at one another questioningly. But we accordingly shifted over to 126.2, calling the Air Force at Cold Bay.

Their operator also asked, in a reserved voice, "Are you all right?"

Once again I offered an even stronger assurance, "Of course we're all right!"

Then he said, rather annoyed, "Well, you've been squawking the hijack code for the last hour!" Three heads in the cockpit looked down at the transponder, and sure enough, we were on the hijack code.

It took a long time for us to live that one down.

Then there's the sort of emergency for which everyone is totally prepared.

The C-123 was loaded with the year's supply of lubricating oil needed at Cape Yakataga, as well as five modern electric ranges, which were to be installed in the kitchens of the government houses at the Yakataga station.

We made an intermediate stop at Middleton Island to offload a minor amount of cargo. Then we proceeded on to the Cape. The weather was lovely across the Gulf of Alaska—very light winds aloft, a few scattered and broken clouds—really one of the fun days for flying.

Lee Burns was my copilot and Dick Pastro served as engineer. After reaching Cape Yakataga we circled the field once, then I called for gear down. However, the nose wheel didn't cooperate, becoming stuck when only partially extended. Dick recycled the gear several times. The main gear would deploy and retract perfectly, but the nose gear remained at half mast. It wouldn't come up, nor would it go down.

Dick searched through the onboard library of service manuals and found the one dealing with the landing gear. Although we realized there probably wasn't much we could do in flight, at least we knew the landing gear was readily accessible. The main gear folded up into the fuselage, where there were open ports designed to facilitate a visual check. And the nose wheel could be viewed after removing a couple of inspection plates.

After lifting the coverplates and examining the nose gear, Dick reported back to the cockpit. "Jack, I couldn't see any problem, but it's sure locked tight!"

Dick and Lee and I hashed out the situation over the interphone for a few minutes, finally agreeing that we should jettison all of our load and return to Anchorage. So I banked N-123 and headed back toward town while Dick and Lee began working on a system for safely pitching out the cargo.

But I began to have second thoughts about the electric stoves. They were actually very light, weighing almost nothing in comparison to our heavy load of fifty-five-gallon oil drums. I was thinking maybe we should give them a reprieve. I caught Lee's attention and offered a change of plan. "Let's keep the stoves. I'm all for getting rid of the oil, but will we really gain anything by dropping the stoves?" He and Dick analyzed the stove cartons and also came to the same conclusion— they posed no real threat.

We had advised Yakataga of our problem while we'd been circling and recycling the gear. Now I radioed a final message, telling them our decision to jettison the cargo on our way back to Anchorage. Unbeknownst to us, some of the wives at the station had been listening to our transmissions. A woman's anxious voice came plaintively over the radio. "Will you have to drop our stoves?"

"No," I assured her, "only the oil. We'll lash down the stoves securely before attempting our landing in Anchorage."

The crew and I debated where to dump the oil. I was inclined to drop it on land, thinking the spilled oil might not have as great a chance to be too polluting. But the others were worried that there might be an unsuspecting prospector out in the woods who wouldn't appreciate a stray fifty-five-gallon drum of oil raining down upon his head. So we decided we'd better let it go into the water.

To keep from putting too much of it in one spot—there were over twenty barrels—we went out to sea a little way, opened the ramp, and starting at Cape St. Elias, we began dumping the barrels one by one. We also kept close watch to be sure we weren't passing over the boats of any hapless fishermen. When the barrels first hit the water, they formed a large green bull's-eye, but then the highly refined lubricating oil spread out over the water and dissipated rather quickly.

We soon established communication with both the Anchorage Center and the Flight Service Station. Since it's about an hour-and-fifty-minute flight in the C-123 from Cape Yakataga to Anchorage, the personnel at the regional office had plenty of time to worry themselves into a tizzy.

We were still blessed with lovely weather as we arrived over Anchorage. In fact, you might say we were right in God's pocket. We had plenty of fuel, the airplane was pretty much empty, and each of us had taken time to carefully think through his part in the coming emergency landing. Although everyone was concerned about the partially retracted gear, we felt that the chance of a dangerous crash was quite remote; the risks were very small as far as our lives were concerned. The worst we expected to happen was a badly scratched-up nose.

But whenever you have an accident in a government airplane—especially in an FAA airplane—no matter how small the accident, it is investigated like no other. We wanted to be absolutely sure there could be no reflection on us, the crew. As I've often heard other pilots exaggerate, "It doesn't matter much whether or not you're killed, so long as it isn't 'pilot error.'"

The hangar had set up a radio so that we could talk directly to our maintenance people while circling the airport. They began asking a barrage of questions: Did we recycle the gear? Did we check for obstructions? Did we do this? Did we do that? In each case we answered that we had. The mechanics then asked us to continue circling while they conferred by telephone with the Fairchild factory engineers.

In the meantime, Dick and I decided to go down for a second look at the nose wheel. While peering through the inspection ports, we came up with an interesting idea. It just might be possible to get a chain around the scissors-type extension on the gear and pull the wheel into position, using the cabin's cargo winch.

We began by using our shoelaces to tie a length of chain onto the handle of a broom. I poked the stick through one of the holes, getting it as close as possible to the wheel. Dick put his arm through another of the holes and managed to secure the chain to the scissors. Then we hooked the other end of the chain to our winch cable. I put power to the winch and watched as it tightened up the chain.

We managed to pull the gear down a little farther, but it still refused to lower all the way into its proper position. We locked up the winch, leaving tension in the cable. That way the winch line would be helping to support the nose wheel. Perhaps the gear, even in its bent position, could withstand the shock of landing and not collapse after hitting the runway.

We radioed the hangar and told them what we'd done. They hadn't come up with any new information, so we squared around and began our approach. People from the regional office, including the chiefs, had driven out to witness the landing.

We settled in on our main gear and used almost no brake, holding the nose wheel up as long as we could. Then we gently rotated down onto the nose gear. Sure enough, the chain held. I thought we'd have lost all steering, but even that wasn't a problem; and we were able to taxi up to the hangar despite the bent nose wheel.

I guess our placid arrival was a bit of a disappointment for some of the excited spectators—at least we could have dinged up something for all their trouble. But we'd come through without any damage whatsoever. It was just the same as all our other incidents in N-123. Although the aircraft may have given us a few bad moments, it never let us down!

3
The Flying X-Rays

DURING MY LATER years of service with the FAA, the agency hired its own medical staff and developed a full-scale health program, designed to serve its widespread group of employees located at the various remote sites. I'd always been rather interested in the "bush" style of medicine, dating back to the days when I used to fly the mail up the Yukon, stopping in at the villages served by medical personnel of the Bureau of Indian Affairs.

Mountain Village was a typical outpost. When I was flying the area, the population was under a hundred, but the Bureau of Indian Affairs maintained a nice hospital and school. The hospital was run by Dr. Werble, an interesting, personable young guy, not too long out of medical school.

Whenever I overnighted at Mountain Village, I'd usually wind up spending a large part of my time visiting with the doctor. He appeared delighted to see someone other than the nurses and patients, and we soon became very good friends. One night, while we were sitting around shooting the breeze, he began talking a little shop. "Jack, this isn't a bad little hospital we've got here, but I just wish we could get the damn X-ray to work!"

"Let me take a look at it," I volunteered. "I'm no X-ray technician, but I might be able to figure out something."

I followed him upstairs to the small hospital's operating room. He walked over to turn on the X-ray and spun a dial or two, but nothing happened. It just sat there, cold and dead.

Then, suddenly, it dawned on me that an X-ray machine, due to its transformers, has to be hooked up to alternating current in order to operate. The regular power plant serving the hospital produced direct current.

"Are there any other generators around here?" I asked.

"I think there's a small one in the basement, but we've never used it since I've been here."

Together Dr. Werble and I checked on the spare generator. Sure enough, we found a nice little Kohler AC power plant, and I could see a set of wires going upstairs through the floor. It appeared to me the generator had been installed strictly to power the X-ray.

Since the engine hadn't been used for months, I had to tinker with it quite a while before getting it to run. Then Werble and I rushed upstairs and once again threw the switch. The X-ray immediately came to life.

We mixed up the proper chemicals to develop the film; then the doctor wheeled in a patient, and we placed a cassette under his chest. Werble checked the books to find the correct power setting and exposure time. Then we shot the X-ray.

To our great surprise, the picture turned out good. Of course I felt quite proud, very pleased with myself that I'd been able to pinpoint the problem and get Werble's X-ray back on line.

I wasn't, therefore, totally unacquainted with X-ray equipment when the FAA's medical staff began using it in the field as one of their diagnostic tools. At first they used a reduced-size X-ray that was easily portable. But they soon found that too many things were escaping their attention, so they decided to go for the full-size picture, using the big cassettes. Their large, hospital-type Picker X-ray and all the associated paraphernalia, including a power plant on wheels and a portable darkroom, were so bulky we had to use the C-123 to haul the gear around on our periodic circuits of the stations.

I rather liked the X-ray trips because they gave us flight crews a rare chance to slow down. After we pulled into a station, the personnel would turn out a few at a time as they came off duty and gathered up their families for the medical checkups. So the pace was rather slow and easy, and those of us operating the equipment (I always pitched in) never worked too hard.

The expeditions were organized by the regional flight surgeon, who came along to supervise the health examinations. On one particular trip to Cold Bay, Dr. Jack Hepler was the man in charge.

Now I suppose Hepler must have a "Dorian Gray" portrait of himself stashed away in some dusty attic, with his likeness continually growing older. But the man himself looked like a teenager. I don't mean to cast any aspersions on his professional ability; it was just that his youthful appearance gave the impression that he couldn't possibly have gone all the way through medical school.

Quite a few people began trooping through for the exams, so we were relatively busy. A lot of them were locals who weren't employed by the FAA, but the agency would always take a look at anyone who wanted an exam, regardless. Dr. Hepler started us going on the X-rays and supervised the exams. After a while things settled down and became more or less routine. Then Hepler slipped out to make sure we were set up to go duck and geese shooting later that evening. An avid sportsman, he had managed to schedule our program at Cold Bay to coincide with the hunting season. (The whole area is a paradise for waterfowl enthusiasts.)

In the meantime, we'd experienced a lull in the demand for X-rays, so we shut off the power plant and relaxed for a spell. Tim Jackson was along as flight engineer and Elvin Jackson was copilot. We were all in a cheerful, lighthearted mood, sitting around enjoying the lovely warm day—a highly unusual occurrence for Cold Bay.

A petite, attractive young woman came up to us while we were lounging at the rear of the airplane. "Do you have a doctor here?" she asked.

Elvin, up to his old tricks, answered, "Yes, ma'am. Matter of fact, we're all doctors."

"Well, I've got a nasty infection on my toe, and I was hoping one of you could take a look at it to see if anything needs to be done."

Jackson's bluff had been called, and we expected him to admit he'd only been kidding. Instead, he replied with a straight face, "Well, our toe doctor isn't here right now, but he should be back in a minute or two."

At that instant Dr. Hepler walked up to the airplane, shorn of his white smock and dressed in full hunting regalia, looking like anything but a doctor. Elvin quickly piped up, "Here comes the toe doctor now."

"Him?" She looked incredulous.

"Why, certainly." Elvin immediately strode over and put the finger on Jack. "Dr. Hepler, this young lady's got a problem with her toe."

Dr. Hepler at once became very professional and asked the woman to walk over to the temporary clinic where he would inspect the infection. About an hour later he returned, rather bemused. Apparently the lady had only reluctantly taken off her shoe and stocking; she never did seem fully convinced he was a doctor.

Many of the people were getting X-rayed for the first time in their lives and were often half afraid of the machine, wondering whether or not it would be painful and asking how badly they'd be shocked. I'd reassure the patients, then press them up against the cassette with their hands on their hips and say, "Now, take a deep breath and hold it." While they held their breath I'd walk around the lead shield and make the microsecond exposure, the power plant speeding up for an instant as the electrical load was thrown on it.

I'd placed one guy in front of the cassette, instructed him to hold his breath, and taken the picture. Then I got to talking with some of the crew behind the screen and sort of forgot about the patient. Suddenly remembering him, I walked around front to find the guy turning purple—and still valiantly holding his breath!

4

Sabreliner Jet School

ALTHOUGH THE COMMERCIAL airlines had long since joined the jet age, late into the sixties the FAA was still flying the old and venerable DC-3 for range-checking purposes.

Since the end of World War II the DC-3s had been the mainstay of the federal flight inspection operations. Fully standardized as flight check aircraft in 1950, they were used throughout the growth of the omni-directional ranges and instrument landing systems.

The DC-3s were good airplanes for flight inspection. They had enough room to accommodate the large amount of necessary electronic test equipment and the power plant required to run it, as well as the panel operator and all his monitors. And following the war they were cheap; most of them were surplus military aircraft.

The "gooney bird" served us well, but eventually any aircraft outlives its usefulness. In the sixties, many of our pilots were younger than the DC-3s they were flying. The propeller era had phased out, as far as the air carriers were concerned, so it seemed as though the FAA was still operating in the horse-and-buggy days.

In addition, there were certain features to radio signals (especially of the omni-directional ranges) that were peculiar to extremely high altitudes—conditions we couldn't possibly experience in our low-altitude DC-3s. Occasionally the FAA would use Air Force KC-135s to perform high-altitude checks, but finally Washington headquarters decided it was time for each region to get its own Sabreliner—a small jet aircraft they deemed most suited to agency needs.

The transition from propellers to jets was more of a challenge for some of us older flight check pilots than it had been for the airline pilots. The airlines had gradually worked their way through progressively faster aircraft, up the ladder from the DC-4 to the DC-6 and DC-7. So, when they graduated to the jets, they were already well-schooled in aircraft that traveled faster than 200 knots. However, we were making an abrupt jump from the DC-3s, which ambled along at 100 knots, to the sophisticated, high-performance jets.

In order for the transition to be made in as short a time as possible, the FAA established an excellent jet school for all its old DC-3 pilots. The intensive course was taught in Oklahoma City by top-notch instructors. Word among the pilots was that it would be pretty tough, and if you couldn't cut it, you'd be washed out of the agency. So most of us went to Oklahoma City filled with apprehension and trepidation.

In deference to the creature comforts, a fellow student, Dallas Cope-land, and I rented a nice apartment in downtown Oklahoma City and laid in a good supply of potables. Then we were more or less ready for the six-week course.

Students worked in pairs with an instructor. Half the day was de-voted to flying; the other half was spent in the classroom studying the aircraft and its systems. I was paired with Howard "Mike" Hunt, a guy who was a pleasure to fly with during our training.

Several times during the early instruction, I got so swamped in the material that I thought I'd never sort it out. But I gradually came to realize that although flying a jet aircraft presented you with a number of new problems, it also did away with some of the old ones. For example, an engine failure didn't have the serious consequences that it did on the old reciprocating engines. If a recip were to fail on takeoff, there were many things that had to be done. But in a jet, about all you had to do was check to see if the engine was on fire, then shut off the fuel.

About halfway through the course, I figured I'd probably survive and might even get a jet rating.

Mike and I had an excellent instructor—Leo Suter, one of God's noblemen, who spent five weeks training us. Then we were turned over to another instructor for our Air Transport Rating check.

Almost any pilot becomes somewhat edgy when taking a flight check, laying on the line what he knows and how he functions as a pilot. I'll never forget one critical point of my flight check in the Sa-breliner. We had climbed to about 35,000 feet for some high-altitude exercise and everything was going smoothly. The inspector turned to me and said, "We're going to simulate that the aircraft's on fire. I want you to show me exactly what you'd do in case it was the real thing."

We'd been properly briefed in class on the best way to handle that problem. Normal procedure was to don your oxygen mask, make a steep ninety-degree turn to kill off most of your speed, and deploy the dive flaps (they'd extend at any speed, but made one hell of a racket). Then you should point the aircraft's nose down and get her right up to the red line, diving to a lower altitude as rapidly as possible.

"Okay," I heard the inspector say. "The aircraft's on fire!"

I remembered that the first step was to put on my oxygen mask before carrying out the rest of the maneuver. But when I grabbed the mask and started to slip it on, my glasses flew off and struck the floor. Then by some damn quirk the mask sheared half apart.

I was beginning my steep turn when the inspector said, "Hold it!

Hold it! Why don't you pick up your glasses, get the mask together, and try it again?"

The second time went a lot better, and I finally wound up on the ground with my type rating, despite the difficulty I'd had. I liked flying the Sabreliner and felt really good about passing my check ride.

After we obtained our ratings, we devoted the last week of school to what was called "pilot in command" training, similar to what is more commonly known to student pilots as "cross-country." Word was they'd let us go pretty much anywhere we wanted for our pilot in command flights.

"I'd like to go to Las Vegas," I told Suter, our instructor, who was also in charge of the assignments for this part of the training.

"Well, that's kind of a no-no," he said.

"Why's that?"

"Just because it's Las Vegas, I guess."

The policy seemed to exclude places where you might have a little too much fun. But I wasn't yet ready to give up. "I have a legitimate reason for wanting to go there," I said. "General Zach Taylor's stationed there. He was Deputy Director for the FAA in Alaska, and I'd like to pay him a visit."

"I'll have to check it out," Suter said, with a dubious smile. But he later called me back, after having checked with his higher-ups. In this particular case, they'd agreed it would be all right for me to go to Las Vegas.

So, after phoning Zach Taylor and telling him I was coming, Leo, Mike, and I got aboard the Sabreliner for the "instructional" trip to Las Vegas. As we approached Nellis Air Force Base, just outside of town, it appeared to me we were getting VIP handling from controllers in the military tower. A controller directed us to taxi to the airport terminal, where I was astonished to see a big sign proclaiming: WELCOME TO NELLIS AIR FORCE BASE, JACK JEFFORD.

Although I had caught General Taylor at a very bad moment—he had been conferring with a number of other generals—he took the time to come out and meet us and invited us to drop in at his quarters. "Take my car over, and I'll be along as soon as I can get free," he said.

I was given directions on where to repark the airplane, and after I'd taxied it to the proper spot and gotten out, the airman in charge of the ramp said, "I wonder who the hell that guy Jefford is? Must really be a bigshot!"

"Damned if I know," I said, deadpan. "Never heard of him—but he must be pretty high on the totem pole!"

After a brief visit with the General we checked into a downtown Las Vegas motel. Now that school was officially over and we were about to go home, we could relax a bit, and we began to relax in earnest.

After a few martinis we went out to eat. Then we had a few more martinis and decided to see one of the shows on the strip. General Taylor's influence got us a table close to the stage. As it happened, Milton Berle was the featured performer. I was in such high spirits that every time I'd look at him I'd burst out laughing. I've always thought Berle a very funny man, but that night—in the glow of the martinis and the successfully completed jet course—he was positively hilarious.

After we'd cracked up at several of his one-liners, Berle took notice of us. As, I suppose, any veteran comedian would have done, he then put us to good use. Approaching the end of the stage and pointing a finger at me, he declared, "I'm delighted my cousin was able to get here. At least *somebody's* laughing at my jokes!" And of course, after that—funny or not—we virtually collapsed with laughter. All in all, we enjoyed an excellent time at Berle's show.

Afterward we ended up in the casino, where something uncanny occurred. Although it's never happened to me since, that night I became psychic. I was possessed with a very strong feeling, much more than a hunch—almost a voice—telling me whether or not I would win.

I was playing at a little two-dollar blackjack table. Maybe if I'd been at the richer crap tables I could have come out of there with a bundle. When the "voice" told me to bet, I'd bet fairly heavily. And if the voice urged caution, I'd bet only lightly. I seemed to know just when to stay with the cards I had and when to ask for another.

I got to winning so damn much that the casino changed dealers on me twice. The pit boss even came over to watch me for a while. In one instance, the dealer dealt me two aces and I decided to split them. But the dealer, who seemed fed up with the way I was winning, said, "Too late, too late! You can't split those aces!" However, the pit boss called out, "No, that's okay—let him split those aces if he wants." The annoyed dealer then proceeded to deal me two blackjacks.

It was one grand and glorious evening!

The next morning we had breakfast with General Taylor, then headed back to Oklahoma City. That was the end of my schooling in the Sabreliner, except for an appropriate finishing touch.

When we first began our jet school, we noticed several of the instructors wearing tiny gold sabers on their lapels. I figured they must belong to some special fencing society. But after we got our type ratings, each of us students received a tiny gold saber, courtesy of Remett Warner, a St. Louis Sabreliner dealer, who came up with the idea of giving this appropriate memento to every pilot who received a type rating in the aircraft.

5

McKinley Rescue

AFTER PUTTING IN thirty-two years with the government, I finally retired from the FAA in the summer of 1972, round-tripping the C-123 to Summit station on my last official flight for the agency. The very act of retiring was something of an accomplishment in itself, or so it seemed to me, having spent more than half my life at the controls of agency aircraft.

When I started with the government, my position was classified as a P-3. Within a couple of years I had been promoted through to a P-7 (the equivalent of the present-day GS-14 rating) and made Chief of the Flight Section. I always disliked bothering with administrative details and much preferred to be flying, so I let my secretaries handle the better part of the red tape and paperwork. Dorothy Revell got so good at it that, after looking over a letter she'd prepared for me, I'd swear that I'd written it myself. Throughout the many agency reorganizations, I was tagged with a number of dubious titles. From Chief of the Airways Transportation and Flight Inspection Division my position was relabeled Chief of Operations and Procedures of the Flight Standards Division. Later I was hailed merely as Chief of the Air Support Branch, and eventually I was reclassified as Training and Logistics Control Officer. Actually, my work never changed much, despite all of the variously changing titles. I'd delegate enough of the duties assigned to me so that what I always really did was fly. However, the various official designations did allow me to maintain my GS-14 supervisory rating throughout my career. As an executive I guess I more or less started out at the top and progressively worked my way down to the bottom.

In 1972 the Alaskan Region went through a manpower reduction, and one of our flight staff was due for the axe. Although I still had a few years to go before reaching the mandatory retirement age of sixty-five, I knew that if I volunteered to retire, the least senior pilot wouldn't have to face a layoff. So I bowed out.

Rather than just grow roses, I became involved with a private air service, flying a four-place V-tail Beechcraft Bonanza on charter work throughout the state. I operated from the small town of Wasilla, where I'd built my retirement home on Wasilla Lake.

Our charter service was loosely associated with International Air Transport, an Anchorage-based firm. One day I dropped into the IAT office and found helicopter pilot Jim Sink in animated conversation on the telephone. He pointed to a seat and motioned me to sit down. I could tell from his side of the conversation that the discussion involved some sort of emergency on Mount McKinley.

"I'll give it a try," he advised the other party. Then he turned to me, "Jack, how about taking the Cheyenne and helping me with a rescue on Mount McKinley?"

International Air Transport's Piper Cheyenne was a pressurized light twin with two PT-6 engines, capable of fantastic performance. In fact, I don't believe I've ever flown anything that will get off the ground in less time.

"I'd be glad to help," I told Jim, who quickly filled me in on the details. It seemed that a climber up at the 17,000-foot level was suffering from mountain sickness, a syndrome brought about principally by lack of oxygen. Saving his life required his immediate evacuation down to sea level.

Jim figured that by taking the Gazelle, a French high-performance jet helicopter and stripping it of all possible extra equipment, including the battery, the aircraft might then be light enough so he'd be able to reach 17,000 feet and pick the climber off the peak.

"What would you like me to do?" I asked Jim.

"I want you to go on ahead and spot the climbers so that I don't have to waste time looking for them—I'm going to carry only minimal fuel. Then I'd like you to fly cover for me on the return trip. I won't have any emergency gear along, only a bare radio—and no battery to power it in case I'm forced down."

Before I knew what was happening, I'd checked the fuel in the Cheyenne and departed Anchorage for Mount McKinley. The day was reasonably fair; however, I could see some cloud rings near the top of the mountain. Jim and I had both left at about the same time, but with the superior speed of the Cheyenne, I arrived over McKinley with at least a ten-minute lead.

When I got to the mountain, the situation proved to be pretty sticky. The Cheyenne was being buffeted by considerable turbulence, and clouds were obscuring the area where the climbers were supposed to be. (I'd been given a large-scale map that pinpointed, I hoped, their exact location.) At 17,000 feet the turning radius of any aircraft is much greater than at sea level; I poked my way against the mountain several times before being forced each time to turn away.

I finally spotted the climbers just before Jim was due. They were camped in a little basin on the southeast side of the mountain, with fog and clouds immediately to the south of them. I radioed Jim that I had them in sight, but that the situation looked pretty grim due to the drifting clouds. The climbers waved as I attempted to get closer. Even though I was racking up the Cheyenne in pretty steep turns, it seemed as though my turning radius was huge. But I didn't want to lose sight of the party.

When Jim came through the edge of the clouds, I gave him the climbers' exact location. He spotted them right away and headed into the mountain. It was obviously a one-shot deal; they were in an area that wasn't really very flat, and there were no reference points for a landing. Blowing snow whipped by the downblast from his rotor blades made it impossible for me to see him. I thought, "Oh Lord, he's had it."

However, after what seemed like ages I was relieved to hear him call, "I'm down okay. I'm loading the guy in and I'll be out of here in a minute or two." Jim had done a hell of a job. He later told me that the billowing snow had created a complete whiteout condition; his only estimate of ground position came from faint shadows of the climbers themselves.

Our original plan was to regroup in Talkeetna, a small town located close to the mountain. Jim was carrying just enough fuel to make it that far. Then we'd transfer the sick climber into the Cheyenne for the balance of the trip to Anchorage. As soon as Jim was airborne, I flew ahead to Talkeetna, radioing that we needed a fuel truck. It would be necessary to refuel Jim's helicopter with its engines running, since he had no battery for restarting.

After landing in Talkeetna I checked with the fuel truck driver, then waited at the radio shack for Jim to arrive. Since everything was set up so well for the quick refueling, Jim said, "You know, I think we can get this fellow to the hospital quicker if I just keep him. I'll be able to land directly at the heliport at Providence Hospital."

The jet Gazelle is such a fast helicopter that we agreed it would be the best plan. When the refueling was complete, Jim departed for Anchorage, and once Jim was clear I took off, following the Gazelle on in to town.

It's a funny thing about altitude sickness—while it's dangerously debilitating and potentially fatal, recovery can be quite fast when the patient has proper treatment down at sea level. Jim landed the sick climber at the hospital, where he was discharged in complete health a few days later.

6

Back to Nome on the Iditarod

I CONSIDER the Iditarod Sled Dog Race to be one of the greatest sporting events in the world.

For two weeks or so in early spring, all eyes in Alaska turn toward the group of about thirty mushers who trace the historic Iditarod Trail for more than 1,000 miles between Anchorage and Nome.

Leaving Anchorage, the racecourse passes through the mountains of the Alaska Range via Rainy Pass to McGrath and Ophir. Then the trail branches.

Some years the race has followed a northern loop to Ruby, then down the Yukon River to Kaltag and across to Unalakleet. Lately, racers have taken a southern loop via Iditarod to the Anvik area, then along the Yukon up to Kaltag and over to Unalakleet. From Unalakleet the trail traces around Norton Sound until reaching Nome.

It's amazing to think of the distances a man can travel across the snow, how fast he can move, and how great a load he can carry with the aid of a well-trained dog team. I've always admired sled dog drivers, especially after being involved in so many early rescues where their efforts meant the difference between life or death.

Fred Chambers and his passengers had been picked up in dogsleds driven by the men of Nulato; a dog team had ferried the young Air Force doctor from Iliamna to the badly injured Cliff Uzzell; and I'd still be on the mountain near Golovin had it not been for the two young mushers who rescued me. I'm glad the Iditarod helps keep the sled dog tradition alive.

I became involved with the race myself a few years back, courtesy of my old friend Merle Smith (nicknamed "Mudhole" by Bob Reeve). Smitty and I had been rather close over the years; we'd both come up to Alaska at about the same time. Although he was from Kansas and I was from Nebraska, each of us had experienced the dust bowl and the Depression and had struggled through the early barnstorming days. In fact, when Smitty left for Alaska, he wired me to ask if I'd be interested in his old job flying a Trimotor for the Inman brothers.

Smitty's been very successful. He organized Cordova Airlines and became its president and hasn't yet gotten out of the flying business. He now owns Chitina Airlines and is also involved with Alaska Aeronautical Industries.

Merle telephoned me one day, apparently to no particular purpose. After bringing ourselves up to date on our current activities, we fell to talking about some of the old times. I still recall his horrified expression that day he met me at the Cordova airport after Ward Gay and I had crashed through the bridge in a pickup truck.

Smitty knows me pretty well—well enough to know that, with the proper amount of cajolery, I'll do almost anything. I guess he must have been deliberately maneuvering me into an unsuspected trap. Before long his reminiscences were centered around dog teams. Smitty pointed out that, having lived so long in Nome, I must surely be interested in the Iditarod Trail race. When I agreed, he really perked up.

"Jack," he said, "I've got a special favor to ask of you. The job's right down your alley. You'll meet all your old friends and relive the days when you first came to Alaska. What we need is someone to fly a 180 to transport the race marshal and Orville Lake along the Iditarod."

The 180 he was referring to was a Cessna 180, a small high-wing four-place tail dragger used as a bush plane throughout the state. The race marshal was the man whose job it was to monitor the contest and assure that none of its stringent rules were violated. He arbitrated any disputes and kept track of all the dog teams' positions. Smitty had also mentioned Orville Lake, a well-known old-time musher, whose expertise is put to good use each year as a special radio and television race commentator.

Before I had fully realized what I was doing, I agreed to fly the race. I woke up the next morning with some second thoughts, knowing I had committed myself to about fourteen days away from our own business in order to fly the 180 on the Iditarod Trail. But, as Robert Service said, "A promise made is a debt unpaid." And I had given my word.

The race began that year at a ceremonial starting gate in downtown Anchorage. The dog teams mushed out alongside the Glenn Highway as far as Eagle River. Then the drivers and dogs were picked up by their handlers and taken to Knik, a ghost town located just across Cook Inlet from Anchorage. Knik was the place where the old Iditarod Trail actually began, and from there the teams were off and running on the true start of the race.

During the first day the teams were so close to Anchorage that there wasn't much percentage in observing them from the air. On the second day the race marshal was ready to make use of me, so I went out to Lake Hood and picked up the 180. The Cessna looked to be pretty old and tired. As I walked around inspecting the aircraft, I noticed a full case of oil stowed aft in the baggage compartment, so I asked one of the mechanics why they'd loaded in so much oil.

"Well, it's been using a bit," he replied, which turned out to be more than a minor understatement.

After the first day's flying, I spent the night at my home in Wasilla. The second night all of us stayed in Farewell with some of my friends from the FAA. We talked late into the evening; the story of that Christmas Eve when I'd flown in with Bill Hanson dressed in his zoot suit and Edna Thompson wearing her long white formal still bore the brunt of a few well-intentioned jokes.

In the morning we continued our task of flying back and forth from the head of the pack to the last trailing racer, keeping track of the front-runners as well as the stragglers. That's quite an easy chore at the beginning of the race, but as time goes on, the mushers become strung out, separated by hundreds of miles. When the winner finally arrives in Nome, some of the slowest stragglers have been known to be barely past McGrath.

I found it fascinating to watch the race, especially in my unique capacity as pilot for the race marshal. He was ever vigilant for infractions of the rules, and I was privy to most all of the developments as soon as they happened. We always knew who was in the lead.

Snow machines were opening the trail and marking it so that the drivers wouldn't inadvertently take any wrong turns. Every fifty miles or so, the drivers had to stop in at the various check stations, where veterinarians often spot-checked the dogs to be sure they weren't being pushed beyond their limits.

It's a funny thing, but the dogs seem to enjoy the race more than anyone else. They exhibit a spirit of fierce competition that's really something to see, straining at the traces in eager anticipation of the command to "mush." There's been some adverse reaction to the race by individuals who consider it cruel to the dogs, but that's certainly not the way I saw it. In fact, I flew some members of the local SPCA group along the race route so they could inspect a few of the dogs running the trail. They pronounced the Iditarod a very humane, well-run race.

In my opinion the drivers are the ones to be pitied. They're beset with all sorts of unanticipated problems, and their life is a hard one, even if everything goes routinely. When the team camps, the dogs can begin to rest, but the musher has to pitch his little tent, cook his own food and food for the dogs, and melt drinking water. Each musher has his own pet dog-food formula with which he hopes to bolster the health and stamina of his team. The ingredients run the gamut of meat and fish, salmon roe, vitamins, and other specialties. After the dogs are cared for, the musher can crawl into his sleeping bag for a scant few hours of sleep, then it's back up and on the trail again. Of course they don't just ride the sled; they often run alongside or even push it themselves when helping the dogs through the tough spots. Being a musher requires great stamina and excellent health.

After we'd moved over to McGrath, I began having a series of small problems with the airplane. While I no longer had to drain the oil and warm it by the fire, as we did back in the old days at Clough's Road-house, the constant breakdowns were very aggravating in their own right. If I'd had a choice, I think I might have preferred flying the old Vega. To cap things off, I wound up in a snowdrift after one particular landing. The aircraft was on skis, but the tail gear was just a wheel; the Cessna was not equipped with a tail ski. Somehow the wheel mechanism became cocked to one side during flight and, when I touched down, the locked wheel caused us to slide off the side of the runway. Fortunately there was no damage to the airplane, although my pride took a beating—having to put up with the snickers of my friends in the FAA.

We'd already consumed our first case of oil, so I picked up a second case when we refueled with gasoline. Even though the engine was burning oil like mad, at least the motor continued to run throughout the entire trip.

One morning I checked over the aircraft before departure and found that the stabilizer was in such bad shape we couldn't fly. I contacted Smitty, and he had a new one sent over to me. After getting it installed we were ready to hit the trail again, moving our base of operations to Galena.

I remembered back to when engineer Bill Seeley and I had paced out this strip during the war—and the previous winter's survey of the West Ruby site. I'd sure startled a lot of dogs that night after dumping the over-pressured boiler!

When the front-runners pull into the various small communities along the way, it's always cause for celebration; the whole town usually gets about half-crocked. Galena was no exception. The town was filled with reveling spectators, and the roadhouse was packed. I wound up spending the night sleeping under the stairway of the local store. As the evening wore on, the partying people kept traipsing up and down the stairs. I got almost no sleep that night, tossing and turning on a cot and wishing I'd never managed to become involved in this venture.

From Galena we moved to Unalakleet. I had a room located directly over the town's only jukebox. As usual, everyone was celebrating as the teams came through. Country singer Hoyt Axton performs a song entitled "Bony Fingers." While I'm not badmouthing the song (indeed, it was the hit tune in Unalakleet), after hearing it played continuously all night long, the muffled bass notes penetrating even through my pillow, I doubt if I'll ever be able to listen to that song again without cringing.

I kept thinking back to Charlie Traeger's old trading post and the music we'd played there during those long winters at Unalakleet when I'd been flying the mail.

From Unalakleet the dog trail follows the curve of Norton Sound—directly north to Shaktoolik; Shaktoolik to Koyuk; and then west to Nome. The drivers are really pushing themselves now; they're on the last leg of the trip.

They cross the sea ice on Norton Bay, perhaps ten or fifteen miles offshore. The trail has to be marked with stakes across the windswept ice. It's about as miserable a piece of real estate as you'll ever find. Strong winds are invariably blowing. Just a few miles inland I had spent nearly a week on the mountains after crashing the Stinson in a fight with some similar winds. In talking to the mushers, I discovered that they believe the teams from Nome have a distinct advantage on this part of the trail, being accustomed to facing the howling winds.

We moved our base to Nome for the last part of the race. The city really gets excited when the dogs are approaching. When the first team is about five miles away, a siren begins to wail, alerting everyone that the race has come down to its last few minutes. The mushers always seem to arrive at some ungodly hour of the morning, but the whole town is up for it and the people line both sides of the streets. It reminded me of the old days when we all waited eagerly for the first boat to come over the horizon in spring.

Usually two, but sometimes three of the front-runners are racing neck and neck. Even though the racecourse runs more than a thousand miles, the mushers pace one another carefully and there's often a photo finish. You never know exactly who's going to win the race until the very last minute.

Mudhole Smith and Alaska's first state Governor, his old friend Bill Egan, were on hand to greet the incoming mushers. The official finish line on Main Street in Nome was marked by a large rustic gate—two peeled-tree uprights supporting a massive, elaborately carved and painted burled log crosspiece that announced: END OF IDITAROD DOG RACE.

The crowds lining the street clapped appreciatively as the first driver passed alongside them, and an enthusiastic cheer arose as the team crossed the finish line.

After it was all over, I realized that I'd truly enjoyed the trip and wouldn't have missed it for the world. Forgotten memories of some of my earlier, crazier adventures had flooded back to me. For that alone, the trip was worthwhile.

While I'm not exactly beating the drum to do it again, I guess old Smitty had known what he was doing when he suggested the flight to me. I'd had fun with the Iditarod, after all.

Index